Human–Computer Interaction Series

For further volumes:
http://www.springer.com/series/6033

HCI is a multidisciplinary field focused on human aspects of the development of computer technology. As computer-based technology becomes increasingly pervasive—not just in developed countries, but worldwide—the need to take a human-centered approach in the design and development of this technology becomes ever more important. For roughly 30 years now, researchers and practitioners in computational and behavioral sciences have worked to identify theory and practice that influences the direction of these technologies, and this diverse work makes up the field of human–computer interaction. Broadly speaking it includes the study of what technology might be able to do for people and how people might interact with the technology. The HCI series publishes books that advance the science and technology of developing systems which are both effective and satisfying for people in a wide variety of contexts. Titles focus on theoretical perspectives (such as formal approaches drawn from a variety of behavioral sciences), practical approaches (such as the techniques for effectively integrating user needs in system development), and social issues (such as the determinants of utility, usability and acceptability).

Titles published within the Human–Computer Interaction Series are included in Thomson Reuters' Book Citation Index, The DBLP Computer Science Bibliography and The HCI Bibliography.

Andreas Holzinger · Martina Ziefle
Carsten Röcker
Editors

Pervasive Health

State-of-the-art and Beyond

Springer

Editors
Assoc. Prof. Dr. Andreas Holzinger
Ph.D., M.Sc., M.Ph., BEng, CEng, Dip.Ed., MBCS
Head Research Unit, Human–Computer Interaction for Medicine and Health
IBM Watson Think Group
Institute for Medical Informatics (IMI)
Medical University of Graz (MUG)
Graz
Austria

Prof. Dr. Martina Ziefle
Lehrstuhl für Communication Science
Human–Computer Interaction Center
Geschäftsführende Direktorin
Institut für Sprach- und Kommunikationswissenschaft
RWTH Aachen University
Aachen
Germany

Priv.-Doz. Dr. Dr. Carsten Röcker
Human–Computer Interaction Center
RWTH Aachen University
Aachen
Germany

ISSN 1571-5035
ISBN 978-1-4471-6998-7 ISBN 978-1-4471-6413-5 (eBook)
DOI 10.1007/978-1-4471-6413-5
Springer London Heidelberg New York Dordrecht

Softcover reprint of the hardcover 1st edition 2014

Printed on acid-free paper

Springer is part of Springer Science+Business Media (www.springer.com)

Foreword

Health is off the desktop. As with other computer-mediated personal services and applications, health is moving to mobile devices. And rightly so; supporting health is complex, dynamic, and inherently situated. Pervasive health provides a range of challenges and opportunities for technology, for human-centered informatics, and for social policy.

Pervasive technologies present critical new affordances for managing human health. In many cases, they provide a new key source of support that can make the difference for a person in coping with the external world confidently and autonomously. For example, prosthetic mobile devices can ameliorate sensory disabilities in hearing and seeing in real-time/real-world interactions through speech recognition and smart camera capabilities mediating real-time/real-world interactions.

Many people, in countries with no dietary reason for it, are obese; they are ticking time bombs for a host of serious medical problems. Most of these risks can be eased by making healthy eating choices, situation by situation. Pervasive tools can help people track and confront their own dietary practices, and can provide advice when it is actionable.

Health problems often emerge from a nexus of lifestyle issues, for example, obesity can be exacerbated by sedentary routines and high levels of stress (as well as by hereditary factors). Being more active, coping with stressors, and developing strategies and resources for coping and resilience are long-term lifestyle changes. Achieving change of this sort requires feedback, guidance, and various kinds of support. Pervasive tools can help people monitor and integrate many facets of their daily activity, and can provide feedback and guidance, as well as access to social or even professional support, in the event, when advice is actionable.

Health is not merely the absence of morbidity. The contemporary concept of health is salutogenetic (Antonovsky); it emphasizes strengthening life factors that enhance health and well-being, rather than merely attenuating or eliminating those that cause illness. Pervasive technologies enable a wide range of reciprocal human-to-human interactions and cooperative activities that develop social capital, and thereby enhance well-being. For example, in mobile time banking people can arrange to do favors for one another, or to engage in activities together.

More generally, pervasive health support can allow elderly people and people with disabilities to function more independently through a wider range of life contexts and for a longer period of time. Enabling personal autonomy is more than just cost-effective for society, it enhances human well-being, and helps patients to remain people.

It's great to see Holzinger, Ziefle, and Roecker's "Pervasive Health: State-of-the-art and Beyond" helping to summarize our progress and set sights on further directions.

John M. Carroll

Contents

Contributors

A. Ackaert iMinds—IBCN, Universiteit Gent, Gent, Belgium

Reem Alnanih Department of Computer Science and Software Engineering, Concordia University, Montreal, Canada; Department of Computer Science, King Abdulaziz University, Jeddah, Saudi Arabia

Bert Arnrich Department of Computer Engineering, Bogazici University, Istanbul, Turkey

L. Bleumers iMinds—SMIT, Vrije Universiteit Brussel, Elsene, Belgium

Martin Böcker Böcker und Schneider GbR, Konstanz, Germany

A. J. Bongers Faculty of Design, Architecture and Building, Interactivation Studio, University of Technology, Sydney, Australia

Nicholas Caporusso QIRIS, Via Dieta di Bari 36, Bari, Italy; INTACT Healthcare, Via Dieta di Bari 36, Bari, Italy

Lorenzo T. D'Angelo Institute of Micro Technology and Medical Device Technology (MiMed), TU München, Garching, Germany

Victor Donker Faculty of Design, Architecture and Building, Interactivation Studio, University of Technology, Sydney, Australia; Department of Industrial Design, Eindhoven University of Technology, Eindhoven, The Netherlands

P. Duysburgh iMinds—SMIT, Vrije Universiteit Brussel, Elsene, Belgium

L. Galway Smart Environments Research Group School of Computing and Mathematics, University of Ulster, Newtownabbey BT37 OQB, UK

Erik Grönvall IT University of Copenhagen, Rued Langgaards Vej 7, 2300 Copenhagen S, Denmark

Rebecca Hall Faculty of Design, Architecture and Building, Interactivation Studio, University of Technology, Sydney, Australia

Paul Havinga Electrical, Mathematics and Computer Science, University of Twente, PO Box 217 7500 AE, Enschede, The Netherlands

Andreas Holzinger Institute for Medical Informatics, Medical University Graz, Graz, Austria

A. Jacobs iMinds—SMIT, Vrije Universiteit Brussel, Elsene, Belgium

Seongho Jang Department of Physical Medicine and Rehabilitation, Hanyang University College of Medicine, Wangsimni-ro, Seongdong, Seoul 133-792, Korea

Juan Jiménez Garcia Electrical, Mathematics and Computer Science, University of Twente, PO Box 217 7500 AE, Enschede, The Netherlands

David Keyson Department of Industrial Design Engineering, Delft University of Technology, Postbus 5 2600 AA, Delft, The Netherlands

Jieun Kim Graduate School of Innovation and Technology Management, Hanyang University, Wangsimni-ro, Seongdong, Seoul 133-792, Korea

Joachim F. Kreutzer Institute of Micro Technology and Medical Device Technology (MiMed), TU München, Garching, Germany

Stefan Lie Faculty of Design, Architecture and Building, Interactivation Studio, University of Technology, Sydney, Australia

G. Lightbody Smart Environments Research Group School of Computing and Mathematics, University of Ulster, Newtownabbey BT37 OQB, UK

Tim C. Lueth Institute of Micro Technology and Medical Device Technology (MiMed), TU München, Garching, Germany

Stefan Lundberg KTH Royal Institute of Technology, Alfred Nobels Allé 10, 14152 Huddinge, Sweden

P. McCullagh Smart Environments Research Group School of Computing and Mathematics, University of Ulster, Newtownabbey BT37 OQB, UK

Jakob Neuhaeuser Institute of Micro Technology and Medical Device Technology (MiMed), TU München, Garching, Germany

F. Ongenae iMinds—IBCN, Universiteit Gent, Gent, Belgium

Olga Ormandjieva Department of Computer Science and Software Engineering, Concordia University, Montreal, Canada

Giovanni Perrone QIRIS, Via Dieta di Bari 36, Bari, Italy; INTACT Healthcare, Via Dieta di Bari 36, Bari, Italy

Michelle Pickrell Faculty of Design, Architecture and Building, Interactivation Studio, University of Technology, Sydney, Australia

T. Radhakrishnan Department of Computer Science and Software Engineering, Concordia University, Montreal, Canada

Samuel Reimer Institute of Micro Technology and Medical Device Technology (MiMed), TU München, Garching, Germany

Carsten Röcker Human-Computer Interaction Center, RWTH Aachen University, Aachen, Germany

Natalia Romero Department of Industrial Design Engineering, Delft University of Technology, Postbus 5 2600 AA, Delft, The Netherlands

Hokyoung Ryu Graduate School of Innovation and Technology Management, Hanyang University, Wangsimni-ro, Seongdong, Seoul 133-792, Korea

Matthias Schneider Böcker und Schneider GbR, München, Germany

Kyoungwon Seo Department of Industrial Engineering, Hanyang University, Wangsimni-ro, Seongdong, Seoul 133-792, Korea

Stuart Smith Healthy Eating, Active Living Technology (HEALTHY) Research Centre, University of Tasmania, Launceston, Australia

Elizabeth Stokes Department of Computer Science, Middlesex University, School of Science and Technology, Hendon, London, UK

Michelantonio Trizio QIRIS, Via Dieta di Bari 36, Bari, Italy; INTACT Healthcare, Via Dieta di Bari 36, Bari, Italy

Gerhard Tröster Electronics Laboratory, ETH Zürich, Zürich, Switzerland

Kenneth J. Turner Computing Science and Mathematics, University of Stirling, Stirling FK9 4LA, UK

S. Verstichel iMinds—IBCN, Universiteit Gent, Gent, Belgium

Daniel Waltisberg Electronics Laboratory, ETH Zürich, Zürich, Switzerland

Martina Ziefle Human-Computer Interaction Center, RWTH Aachen University, Aachen, Germany

Chapter 1
From Computer Innovation to Human Integration: Current Trends and Challenges for Pervasive HealthTechnologies

Carsten Röcker, Martina Ziefle and Andreas Holzinger

1.1 Introduction

Identifying and understanding current trends and challenges for pervasive health technologies in the twenty-first century is a challenging endeavor [70, 108, 122]. It requires the careful consideration of two major trends and their interplay. A first line of research addresses emerging technological innovations over time. Technology itself has made substantial progress and has undergone a fundamental change over the last decades in both the medical sector as well as the field of information and communication technology, which brings a variety of new possibilities to provide and deliver medical services [56, 62, 83]. A second line of research addresses differences in the characteristics of target groups and user profiles [11, 109]. Today, users of medical technology show completely different requirements than earlier users of these technologies did. The diversity of users who come into contact with medical and/or information and communication technologies is constantly increasing [11, 69]. Hence, the adequate consideration of personal factors like gender or age as well as aspects of culture and ethnicity are key concepts for human-centered technology development [4, 31, 67].

At the same time, today's information and communication technologies touch a fragile cross-over point between surveillance and control on one side and support and personal benefit on the other [59, 77, 106]. Especially in the context of medical

C. Röcker (✉) · M. Ziefle
Human-Computer Interaction Center, RWTH Aachen University, Aachen, Germany
e-mail: roecker@comm.rwth-aachen.de

M. Ziefle
e-mail: ziefle@comm.rwth-aachen.de

A. Holzinger
Institute for Medical Informatics, Medical University Graz, Graz, Austria
e-mail: andreas.holzinger@medunigraz.at

A. Holzinger et al. (eds.), *Pervasive Health*, Human–Computer Interaction Series,
DOI: 10.1007/978-1-4471-6413-5_1, © Springer-Verlag London 2014

technology, a sensible trade-off between benefits and empowerment of patients on the one hand and barriers and stigma on the other hand needs to be respected.

The potential of pervasive health technologies is connected to a multitude of possible benefits on different scales [83]. They reach from societal benefits on a macro level, in terms of meeting existing shortcomings with regard to the care of elderly and providing universal access to medical technology, up to individual benefits on a micro level, in terms of independent living. However, there are also serious concerns regarding the violation of personal boundaries and comfort zones as well as issues of data security and privacy [60, 85, 112, 119]. As current medical technology is increasingly entering private spheres and literally crosses personal borders in case of invasive technologies, questions of 'control,' 'intimacy,' 'trust,' 'risk,' and 'reliability' are critical aspects to address [5, 76]. Also, societal attitudes towards frail and old people as well as constructive handling of the ageism problem are serious issues which need to be considered [71, 73].

In addition to the negative and stigmatizing attitudes towards older persons in public perceptions of most societies [49, 120], older persons themselves regard a dependency on technology and the resulting perceived loss of autonomy and control as highly negative. This situation requires a profound change in the way the individual aspects are addressed and calls for more holistic concepts of balancing the various requirements that have to be met [52, 93]. Beyond the exclusive focus on the technological potential and feasibility of pervasive health services, the inclusion of human values, different usage contexts, and requirements of user diversity are key aspects for the successful development of pervasive health technologies [6, 121].

In the following, we first concentrate on the description of technical innovations and the way technology has changed over the years. In a second step, social and societal challenges are outlined. Bringing both lines together, the third part of this paper identifies future research challenges.

1.2 Technical Innovations

1.2.1 Intelligent Objects and Smart Environments

Over the past 50 years, we went through different phases of computing (see [94]). The years between 1960 and 1980 were characterized by mainframe computers that were primarily used by big companies, universities, and governmental organizations. With the emergences of smaller and more affordable computers in the 1980s, computing ushered into a new phase. Personal computers found their way into many offices and were used as general-purpose tools for a variety of office activities [79]. The third wave of computing started with the wide-spread availability of mobile devices and increased networking capabilities around the turn of the century. This so-called ubiquitous computing era enabled computing anytime and anywhere [80] (Fig. 1.1).

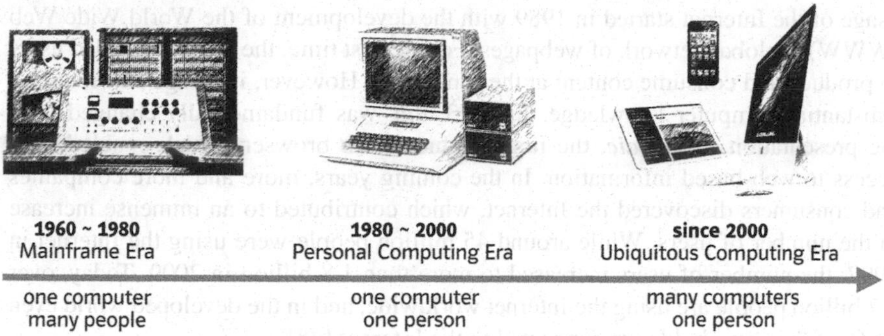

Fig. 1.1 Phases of Computing

During this time, we did not only see a tremendous increase in computing power, we also experienced a shift in the relationship between computers and users [81]. While early computing systems required an entire team of engineers and computer scientists to be operated and were jointly used by many people, this situation changed with the introduction of personal computing systems. This one-to-one relation between users and computers changed again with the emergence of mobile and embedded computers. Today, users interact with a multitude of computational devices throughout the day.

While this situation represents normality for many people, we are currently on our way towards a new era of intelligent, interconnected objects and smart environments in which more and more computers are embedded in our physical environment and unobtrusively support us in different areas of everyday life (see, for example, [35, 53, 84, 100]). In recent years, the term "Internet of Things" (IoT) is increasingly used to describe this vision. Especially in business literature, the original concept of ubiquitous or pervasive computing is often referred to as the Internet of Things. Projections about the growth of the IoT vary considerably. Estimates range from 15 billion [47] to 25 billion [29] interconnected devices in 2015, and from 50 billion [28, 29] to 100 billion [46] in 2020. Nevertheless, there is little doubt that a world of networked devices will be the next big step. Some authors even argue that the "IoT represents the future of computing and communication" ([34], p. 297).

1.2.2 Computing Moves to the Cloud

The Internet is often cited as one of the most influential developments of the last decades. Originally started as a project of the US defense department to enable the efficient usage of scarce computational resources in the late 1960s, the nature of the Internet changed significantly over the following decades [78]. While in the beginning access was restricted to a few research institutions, the wide-spread public usage of the Internet started in 1989 with the development of the World Wide Web (WWW), a global network of webpages. For the first time, the WWW enabled users to produce and consume content at the same time. However, its usage still required substantial computer knowledge. In 1993, this was fundamentally changed with the presentation of *Mosaic*, the first graphical web browser, which enabled easy access to web-based information. In the coming years, more and more companies and consumers discovered the Internet, which contributed to an immense increase in the number of users. While around 45 million people were using the Internet in 1997, the number of users increased to more than 1.8 billion in 2009. Today, over 2.7 billion people are using the Internet worldwide, and in the developed world even 78 % of the households are connected to the Internet [48].

The availability of broadband Internet lines and the introduction of flat-rate fees structures in the last decade contributed to a variety of new web-based services. Today, it is widely accepted that "cloud computing has emerged as a dominant paradigm" [46]. Cloud computing does not only allow distributed computing over a multitude of connected computational devices, it also enables nearly unrestricted access to information for end users. Many cloud services are provided on a pay-per-use basis or are free of charge, reducing the costs for users and thereby lowering the entry barrier. Cloud computing also enables device independence as most services can be accessed via web frontends which means that only a web browser is necessary that can either run on a personal computer, tablet PC or mobile phone. In addition, applications and personal data are usually stored on a third-party server in the Internet which enables a location-independent use of services. Cloud-based services denoted a substantial increase in the number of users over the last years which was fueled by a steep drop in the costs for broadband connections. Worldwide, prices for fixed broadband decreased by 82 % between 2008 and 2012 [48]. At the moment, an end of the cloud computing trend is not foreseeable. Instead, current estimates predict a further increase in cloud computing by 130 % within the next two years [95].

1.2.3 A World of Mobile Services

Besides cloud-based services, mobile computing is often regarded as the most important technological innovation of the last century [46]. With currently 6.8 billion active mobile phone contracts, the number of subscriptions comes close to the world population of 7.1 billion people [48]. In its 2013 report, the International Telecommunication Union ([48], p. 6) announced that "mobile-broadband subscriptions have climbed from 268 million in 2007 to 2.1 billion in 2013" which "reflects an average annual growth rate of 40 %, making mobile broadband the most dynamic ICT market." And this trend is not restricted to mobile phones alone. Recent sales data show that mobile devices replace stationary computers in many areas. In the fourth quarter of 2012—and less than three years after their introduction—global shipment of tablets PC surpassed the shipment of desktop computers and notebooks or the first time [66]. With the widespread diffusion of mobile devices, it is highly likely that the usage of cloud services will further increase.

1.2.4 Collective Intelligence and User-Generated Content

The previous sections illustrated significant achievements in computer science which had a fundamental influence on our everyday life. However, not only technology was refined and advanced. The behavior of users and their attitude towards technology has undergone a significant process of change as well [123]. One of the most important changes of the last years is probably the increased willingness of users to generate web content. User-friendly webpages and new interaction concepts offer easy and intuitive ways of providing feedback and thereby contribute to a continuously increasing database. This independent collaboration in form of personal user feedback does not only increase the informational value of a specific webpage, it also contributes to the Internet as a whole: the more people contribute, the better the result. This effect is often referred to as collective or swarm intelligence. Group processes enable to accumulate knowledge in a way that goes far beyond what an individual would be able to achieve. A good example for such processes is open-source software. The collaboration of many independent programmers leads to sophisticated software, often on a par with commercial products. Open-source programs are written by dozens, sometimes even as many as thousands of individuals. None of these persons would have the ability to write the code on their own, neither from the technical programming skills required nor from the time that would be necessary to complete the code.

User-added value and collective intelligence are the founding principles of many Web 2.0 applications. This 'microwork' principle is the key to the success of most social media websites which would not be able to exist without the multitude of small contributions by a broad user base. Low technical entry barriers and high usability of most of today's websites are the basis for multi-party communication and the direct exchange of experiences and knowledge within communities.

1.2.5 Big Data and Knowledge Discovery

Biomedical sciences are becoming increasingly data intensive and require as well as advance new research strategies. Instead of following the classical research paradigm, i.e., to set the hypothesis first and then gain data from experiments designed to test this hypothesis, it is now the other way around. Consequently, data science is now established as the fourth paradigm in the investigation of nature [36], after theory, empiricism, and computation [14, 20]. Data science is the study of the generalizable extraction of knowledge from data [25]. The masses of unstructured information as well as dealing with large, complex, and often weakly structured data are often cited as mega challenges in biomedicine today [42]. The increasingly large amount of data requires new, efficient, and user-friendly solutions for handling biomedical data. With growing expectations of end-users, traditional approaches to data interpretation often cannot handle the demands. Consequently, new computational and user-centered approaches are vital for coping with this rising flood of data [42].

1.3 Societal Transformation Processes

In contrast to technical systems and devices of past centuries, technology usage is no longer restricted to single technical systems within the working context but increasingly enters all areas of daily life. In addition, more diverse user groups have access to these new technologies. Yet the development of technology still seems to be limited to the requirements and characteristics of young, technology literate males of the middle and upper class in Western societies [64, 89, 101, 116]. It is therefore highly imperative that the development of pervasive health technologies adequately addresses both the specificity and diversity of users. This is not only a matter of considering cognitive and sensory abilities and/or restrictions of target users, but also includes issues of technology acceptance and human values in the context of technology usage which are considerably affected by age and gender as well as culture and ethnicity. These three aspects will be briefly illustrated in the following sections.

1.3.1 Age, Technology Generation, and the Demographic Change

As a consequence to the demographic change [43], more and older adults are confronted with a broad range of technology that they have to understand and use in different situations of everyday life. Up to now, interfaces are often designed without considering the abilities and needs of this user group [64, 89, 116]. Another blind spot of today's system design is user differences in technology education and experience [114]. Although technologies are supposed to be accessible to everyone, a gap between computer literate and less computer experienced users (predominantly older users) emerges. In this context, it should be kept in mind that older users differ considerably with regard to their needs, abilities, and competencies [26, 69, 124]. This aggravates the situation especially for older adults, as the understanding of how technology works is mainly gained through upbringing and socio-cultural factors. Older adults were educated in times when technical devices were far less ubiquitous and complex [115]. In order to address elderly users as a growing consumer group, age-sensitive interface designs are needed [11].

1.3.2 The Impact of Gender

While there is a considerable number of studies addressing gender differences in the interaction with information and communication devices [105], comparably few studies addressed gender differences in the field of acceptance of medical technology [119]. However, especially gender seems to have specific importance for the acceptance of pervasive medical technologies. Research has shown that women report lower levels of computer-related self-efficacy and higher computer anxiety [1, 19, 32] as well as a lower perceived technical confidence when using technical devices [111]. As a consequence, more negative attitudes of women towards technology reduce the probability of active interaction and lead to a generally lower computer-expertise [88]. The lower technology aptitude and/or affection in general could also negatively bias the acceptance of medical technologies. In addition, there are gender-specific body-related attitudes that should be considered. Women have different standards of morality and ethics in comparison to males [58], especially in combination with expected physical harm [30, 55, 68]. This could also have an influence on women's evaluation of pervasive medical technologies and, in turn, modulate the acceptance attitudes. Furthermore, it was found that women have different health-related cognitions, connected to higher vulnerability perceptions towards feelings of physical threat [16, 90]. Additionally, the degree of risk-taking behaviors turned out to be gendered. Men have a higher risk threshold and take higher risks than women [104, 119]. Finally, the acceptance of invasive medical technology is of specific interest, given the gendered nature of the nursing profession which is associated with the traditional female role of caring for and nurturing others [113]. As women have a higher life expectancy, an increasing number of female seniors will be a major target group of pervasive health technology. Consequently, gender should be taken serious as a key factor of technology acceptance in the medical sector.

1.3.3 Ethnicity and Culture

A clear shortcoming of current research in the field of pervasive health is the discussion of interaction between technology, society, and culture. The claim for "universal access" and overcoming of the "digital divide" is related to political systems, socio-economic standards, and legal frameworks. Even today, there is a striking lack of knowledge of how society and culture affect technology acceptance and the underlying reasons for or against technology usage [98, 99]. Comparably few studies have been concerned with the investigation of technology acceptance across national boundaries [3, 10, 86, 96, 102]. It is highly probable that the knowledge about technology acceptance and its underlying framing conditions referring to highly developed western countries do not hold for other cultures and ethnical groups. Cultural beliefs, habits, and values form a cultural mental model [38] and impact the willingness to adopt and use medical pervasive technologies in different ways [23, 54, 61, 98].

Technology is never used in isolation but within a social and cultural context. Social taboos, legal and political constraints as well as ethical, social, and religious traditions and habits differ across cultures. These contextual factors influence how humans interact with technology [116] as well as how they evaluate the usefulness and the need of a technology [4, 21, 72, 82, 112].

Thus, users around the world do differ in perceptions, cognitions, and the individual styles of thinking, cultural assumptions, and values [45]. This especially applies to the developing world and countries with underdeveloped societal and economic standards. But it also applies to those countries that experienced a very fast technological change over the last years, strive for economic welfare, and that are keen on closing the technological gap to highly developed countries [8, 9]. Whether pervasive health technology is accepted in different cultures also depends largely on cultural mindsets of family care, as well as on cultural ageing concepts [109]. Last but not least, the openness to adopt pervasive technology also relies on societal frames and healthcare structures [21], which might imply a different form of social and societal responsibility of others. In addition, the cultural handling of illness and the acceptance of end of life decisions are highly culturally sensitive [15, 57, 91].

1.4 Resulting Research Challenges

The changes illustrated above lead to a variety of new research challenges of technical as well as non-technical nature. Some of the most important ones are addressed in the following sections.

One of the mayor technical research problems refers to the meaningful visualization of the vast amount of medical data that is collected and stored in pervasive health systems. In general, biomedical data models are characterized by significant complexity [2, 40]. This makes manual analysis by end users often impossible. At the same time, experts are able to solve complicated problems almost intuitively [74], often enabling medical doctors to make diagnoses with high precision without being able to describe the exact rules or processes used during their diagnosis, analysis, and problem solving [75]. Consequently, it is a grand challenge to work towards enabling effective human control over powerful machine intelligence by integrating machine learning methods and visual analytics, and thereby supporting human insight and decision making [39]. While *Human-Computer Interaction* (HCI) deals mainly with aspects of human perception, cognition, intelligence, sense-making, and most of all the interaction between human and machine, *Knowledge Discovery and Data Mining* (KDD) deals primarily with aspects of machine intelligence, in particular with the development of algorithms for automatic data mining. Both disciplines have large areas of unexplored and complementary subfields. Consequently, possible solutions to many current problems in data intensive systems may be found at the intersection of HCI and KDD. One very promising approach is to combine HCI and KDD in order to enhance human intelligence with computational intelligence [41] and enable end users to find and recognize previously unknown yet potentially useful and usable information.

Further technical challenges include solutions for unobtrusive and ethically acceptable patient monitoring [107], new forms of patient-centered interaction devices [63] as well as approaches for efficiently integrating such devices into a shared environment [103]. However, current research challenges are not restricted to the technical domain alone, but they also include more general questions and conceptual design decisions like viable solutions for integrating hospital and home care [33, 92], new concepts for independent rehabilitation [18] as well as ways of providing universal access to such solutions [17].

However, when addressing these challenges, it is important to also adapt the resulting systems and applications to the dynamically changing needs of a diverse and culturally biased user population. Against the background of user diversity, there are a number of reasons that the acceptance of medical technology distinctly differs from acceptance patterns of other technologies. First, medical devices are used for critical health conditions and essential usage, instead of only for communication and entertainment purposes as is the case for most modern information and communication technologies [12]. Second, beyond the importance of patient safety, medical technology refers to "taboo related" areas that are associated with disease and illness [65, 111, 119]. Third, medical technology touches serious personal and vital issues. As a consequence, medical monitoring is often perceived as intruding into private spheres and violating individual intimacy, thereby provoking feelings of being permanently controlled [59, 117]. The acceptance of medical technology is a consequence of balancing the envisioned benefits against the perceived concerns in a dynamic process, influenced and shaped by a variety of individual and situational aspects [13]. Consequently, design approaches have to undergo a radical change by taking current societal trends into account [118]. User diversity, in terms of age, gender, social, and cultural factors, has to be systematically integrated into the development process in order to provide human-centered pervasive health technologies that truly meet the diverse requirements of their users. Studies show that older users face difficulties in learning and using new computer applications and have higher demands for usable interface designs [27, 37, 88]. Whenever interfaces are designed with the abilities of older users in mind (meeting the age-related decrease in sensory, motor, and cognitive abilities over the life span), the interaction of older users with technology is considerably improved and even able to match the performance of younger adults. Age-sensitive interaction concepts allow users with different ability levels to successfully interact with new technical applications. Consequently, only the integration of technical, personal, and societal requirements [50] can lead to truly personalized [22, 97], age-sensitive [24], and context-aware designs [7, 51].

1.5 Conclusion

A systematic inclusion of human perspectives into technical development is a crucial challenge for the design of future healthcare applications. Even though the idea of user-centered design has been formulated a long time ago, the development focus of technical products and services is still predominately on technical, economic and legal aspects. Especially in the field of medical services in which technical innovations led to numerous novel applications in the last years, it is of high importance to consider the requirements and the needs of patients—and in particular elderly and frail persons—in early phases of the design process. In this context, user acceptance is a delicate good which can be supported by integrating the intended users into the technical design process.

Only if needs, values, and individual usage habits are included into technology development, humane and human technology designs may result. Higher acceptance can be achieved by a conceptual device design that includes usability aspects and human values from the very beginning. In this way, a medical device can turn into something that patients are proud to wear or to possess, even for persons who have to cope with illness.

Consequently, the huge potential of pervasive health technologies in terms of daily support and medical care of the increasing number of seniors can only be leveraged if current technology design follows the demands raised by the need of incorporating human needs and values into its design development. This includes aspects of user diversity like age, gender, upbringing, culture and technology generation, but it also contains usage requirements arising from different application contexts. As such, addressing the fragile trade-off between the potential benefits of pervasive healthcare applications (ubiquitous support, reachability and universal access) and possible pitfalls (disregard of human values, violation of privacy and security) is of utmost importance.

References

1. Adam, A. (2002). Exploring the gender question in critical information systems. *Journal of Information Technology*, *17*, 59–67.
2. Akil, H., Martone, M. E., & Van Essen, D. C. (2011). Challenges and opportunities in mining neuroscience data. *Science*, *331*(6018), 708–712.
3. Alagöz, F., Calero Valdez, A., Wilkowska, W., Ziefle, M., Dorner, S., & Holzinger, A. (2010). From cloud computing to mobile internet, from user focus to culture and hedonism: The crucible of mobile health care and wellness applications. *IEEE 5th International Conference on Pervasive Computing and Applications*, *1*, 38–45.
4. Alagöz, F., Ziefle, M., Wilkowska, W., Calero Valdez, A. (2011). Openness to accept medical technology—a cultural view. In H. Holzinger, K.-M. Simonic (Eds.), *Human-Computer interaction: Information quality in eHealth* (pp. 151–170) LNCS 7058. Berlin, Heidelberg: Springer.
5. Alhakami, A. S., & Slovic, P. (1994). A psychological-study of the inverse relationship between perceived risk and perceived benefit. *Risk Analysis*, *14*, 1085–1096.

6. Allen, F. W. (1987). Towards a holistic appreciation of risk: The challenges for communicators and policymakers. *Science, Technology and Human Values, 12*, 138–143.
7. Alnaniha, R., Ormandjievaa, O., & Radhakrishnana, T. (2014). A new methodology (CON-INFO) for context-based development of a mobile user interface in healthcare applications. In A. Holzinger, M. Ziefle, & C. Röcker (Eds.), *Pervasive health—state-of-the-art and beyond*. London: Springer.
8. Anandarajan, M., Igbaria, M., & Anakwe, U. (2000). Technology acceptance in the banking industry: A perspective from a less developed country. *Information Technology & People, 13*(4), 298–312.
9. Anandarajan, M., Igbaria, M., & Anakwe, U. (2002). IT acceptance in a less-developed country: A motivational factor perspective. *International Journal of Information Management, 22*(1), 47–65.
10. Arenas-Gaitána, J., Ramírez-Correab, P., & Rondán-Cataluñaa, F. (2011). Cross-cultural analysis of the use and perceptions of web-based learning systems. *Computers and Education, 57*(2), 1762–1774.
11. Arning, K., & Ziefle, M. (2009). Different perspectives on technology acceptance: The role of technology type and age. In A. Holzinger & K. Miesenberger (Eds.), *Human-Computer interaction for eInclusion* (pp. 20–41). Berlin, Heidelberg: Springer.
12. Arning, K., Gaul, S., Ziefle, M. (2010). Same same but different. How service contexts of Mobile technologies shape usage motives and barriers. In G. Leitner, M. Hitz, A. Holzinger (Eds.), *HCI in work and learning, life and leisure. 6th Symposium of the WG HCIandUE of the Austrian Computer Society*.
13. Arning, K., Kowalewski, S., & Ziefle, M. (2013). Health concerns Vs. mobile data needs: Conjoint measurement of preferences for mobile communication network scenarios. *International Journal of Human and Ecological Risk Assessment*. ISSN: 1080–7039. doi:10.1080/10807039.2013.838127
14. Bell, G., Hey, T., & Szalay, A. (2009). Beyond the data deluge. *Science, 323*(5919), 1297–1298.
15. Berger, J. T. (1998). Cultural discrimination in mechanisms for health decisions: A view from New York. *Journal of Clinical Ethics, 9*, 127–131.
16. Billings, A. G., & Moos, R. H. (1981). The role of coping re-sponses and social resources in attenuating the stress of life events. *Journal of Behavioural Medicine, 4*(2), 139–157.
17. Böcker, M., & Schneider, M. (2014). E-Health applications for those in need: Making novel interaction technologies accessible. In A. Holzinger, M. Ziefle, & C. Röcker (Eds.), *Pervasive health—state-of-the-art and beyond*. London: Springer.
18. Bongers, A. J., Smith, S., Donker, V., Pickrell, M., & Hall, R. (2014). Interactive infrastructures—physical rehabilitation modules for pervasive healthcare technology. In A. Holzinger, M. Ziefle, & C. Röcker (Eds.), *Pervasive health—state-of-the-art and beyond*. London: Springer.
19. Busch, T. (1995). Gender differences in self-efficacy and attitudes toward computers. *Journal of Educational Computing Research, 12*, 147–158.
20. Buxton, B., Hayward, V., Pearson, I., Kärkkäinen, L., Greiner, H., Dyson, E., et al. (2008). Big data: The next google. Interview by Duncan Graham-Rowe. *Nature, 455*(7209), 8.
21. Campiniha-Bacote, J. (2002). The process of cultural competence in the delivery of health care services: A model of care. *Journal of Transcultural Nursing, 13*(3), 181–184.
22. Caporusso, N., Trizio, M., & Perrone, G. (2014). Pervasive assistive technology for the deaf-blind—need, emergency and assistance through the sense of touch. In A. Holzinger, M. Ziefle, & C. Röcker (Eds.), *Pervasive health—state-of-the-art and beyond*. London: Springer.
23. Choon, Y.-Y. (2005). Cross-Cultural issues in human-computer interaction. In W. Karwowski (Ed.), *International Encyclopedia of Ergonomics and Human Factors* (Vol. 1, pp. 1063–1069). London: Taylor & Francis.
24. D'Angelo, L. T., Kreutzer, J. F., Neuhaeuser, J., Reimer, S., & Lueth, T. C. (2014). Personal assistive devices for elderlies: Executing activities of daily living despite natural aging-related changes. In A. Holzinger, M. Ziefle, & C. Röcker (Eds.), *Pervasive health—state-of-the-art and beyond*. London: Springer.

25. Dhar, V. (2013). Data science and prediction. *Communication of the ACM, 56*(12), 64–73.
26. Durndell, A., & Zsolt, H. (2002). Computer self-efficacy, computer anxiety, attitudes towards the internet and reported experience with the internet, by gender, in an East European sample. *Computers in Human Behavior, 18*, 521–535.
27. Ellis, D. R., & Allaire, J. C. (1999). Modeling computer interest in older adults: The role of age, education, computer knowledge and computer anxiety. *Human Factors, 41*, 345–364.
28. Ericsson. (2011). *More than 50 Billion connected devices*. Ericsson, Stockholm, Sweden: White Paper.
29. Evans, D. (2011). *The internet of things: How the next evolution of the internet Is changing everything*. Cisco IBSG, San Jose, CA, USA: White Paper.
30. Feingold, A., & Mazella, R. (1998). Gender differences in body image are increasing. *Psychological Science, 9*, 190–195.
31. Gaul, S., & Ziefle, M. (2009). Smart home technologies: Insights into generation-specific acceptance motives. In A. Holzinger & K. Miesenberger (Eds.), *Human-Computer interaction for eInclusion* (pp. 312–332). Berlin, Heidelberg: Springer.
32. Gefen, D., & Straub, D. (1999). Gender differences in the perception and use of e-mail: An extension to the technology acceptance model. *MIS Quarterly, 21*, 389–400.
33. Grönvall, E., & Lundberg, S. (2014). On challenges designing the home as a place for care. In A. Holzinger, M. Ziefle, & C. Röcker (Eds.), *Pervasive health—state-of-the-art and beyond*. London: Springer.
34. Guo, B., Zhang, D., Wang, Z. (2011). Living with internet of things: The emergence of embedded intelligence. *Proceedings of the International Conference on Cyber, Physical, and Social Computing* (*CPSCom*, pp. 297–304). USA: IEEE Press.
35. Heidrich, F., Ziefle, M., Röcker, C., Borchers, J. (2011). Interacting with smart walls: A multi-dimensional analysis of input technologies for augmented environments. *Proceedings of the ACM Augmented Human Conference (AH'11)* (pp. 1–8).
36. Hey, T., Gannon, D., & Pinkelman, J. (2012). The future of data-intensive science. *Computer, 45*(5), 81–82.
37. Himmel, S., Ziefle, M., Lidynia, C., Holzinger, A. (2013). Older users' wish list for technology attributes. A comparison of household and medical technologies. In A. Cuzzocrea, C. Kittl, D.E. Simos, E. Weippl, L. Xu (Eds.), multidisciplinary research and practice for information systems. *IFIP International Cross Domain Conference and Workshop on Availability, Reliability and Security* (pp. 16–27). *CD-ARES 2013, LNCS 8127* Heidelberg: Springer. ISBN: 978-3-642-40510-5.
38. Hofstede, G. (1980). *Cultures consequences*. Beverly Hills, CA: Sage.
39. Holzinger, A. (2011). Interacting with information: Challenges in human-computer interaction and information retrieval (HCI-IR). *Proceedings of the IADIS Multi-Conference on Computer Science and Information Systems (MCCSIS), Interfaces and Human-Computer Interaction* (pp. 13–17). Rome: IADIS.
40. Holzinger, A. (2012a). *Biomedical informatics: Computational sciences meets life sciences*. Norderstedt: BoD.
41. Holzinger, A. (2012). On knowledge discovery and interactive intelligent visualization of biomedical data: Challenges in human-computer interaction and biomedical informatics. In M. Helfert, C. Fancalanci, & J. Filipe (Eds.), *Proceedings of the International Conference on Data Technologies and Applications DATA 2012* (pp. 5–16). Italy: Rome.
42. Holzinger, A. (2013). Human-Computer interaction and knowledge discovery (HCI-KDD): What is the benefit of bringing those two fields to work together? In A. Cuzzocrea, C. K., D. E. Simos, E. Weippl, L. Xu (Eds.), *Multidisciplinary research and practice for information systems, LNCS 8127* (pp. 319–328). Heidelberg: Springer.
43. Holzinger, A., Ziefle, M., & Röcker, C. (2010). Human-computer interaction and usability engineering for elderly (HCI4AGING): Introduction to the special thematic session. In K. Miesenberger, et al. (Eds.), *ICCHP 2010, Part II LNCS 6180* (pp. 556–559). Heidelberg: Springer.

44. Holzinger, A., Stocker, C., Ofner, B., Prohaska, G., Brabenetz, A., & Hofmann-Wellenhof, R. (2013). Combining HCI, natural language processing, and knowledge discovery—Potential of IBM content analytics as an assistive technology in the biomedical domain. In A. Holzinger & G. Pasi (Eds.), *Human-Computer Interaction and Knowledge Discovery in Complex, Unstructured, Big Data, LNCS 7947* (pp. 13–24). Heidelberg: Springer.
45. Inglehart, R., & Klingemann, H. D. (2000). Genes, culture, democracy, and happiness. In E. Diener & E. M. Suh (Eds.), *Culture and subjective well-being* (pp. 165–183). Cambridge: MIT Press.
46. Institute of Electrical and Electronics Engineers, IEEE (2013). Top Trends for 2012. http://www.computer.org/portal/web/membership/13-Top-Trends-for-2013. Accessed 30 July 2013
47. Intel. (2009). *Rise of the Embedded Internet*. USA: Intel Corporation.
48. ITU. (2013). *The world in 2013: ICT facts and figures*. Telecommunication Development Bureau, International Telecommunication Union, Geneva, Switzerland: ICT Data and Statistics Division.
49. Iweins, C., Desmette, D., Yzerbyt, V., Stinglhamber, F. (2013). Ageism at work: The impact of intergenerational contact and organizational multi-age perspective. *European Journal of Work and Organizational Psychology, (ahead-of-print)* (pp. 1–16).
50. Jacobs, A., Duysburgh, P., Ongenae, F., Ackaert, A., Bleumers, L., & Verstichel, S. (2014). The innovation binder approach: A guide towards a social-technical balanced pervasive health system. In A. Holzinger, M. Ziefle, & C. Röcker (Eds.), *Pervasive health—state-of-the-art and beyond*. London: Springer.
51. Jiménez García, J., Romero, N., Keyson, D., & Havinga, P. (2014). An integrated patient-centric approach for situated research on total hip replacement: ESTHER. In A. Holzinger, M. Ziefle, & C. Röcker (Eds.), *Pervasive health—state-of-the-art and beyond*. London: Springer.
52. John, B. (2013). Patterns of ageism in different age groups. *Journal of European Psychology Students*, *4*(1), 16–26.
53. Kasugai, K., Ziefle, M., Röcker, C., Russell, P. (2010). Creating spatio-temporal contiguities between real and virtual rooms in an assistive living environment. In J. Bonner, M. Smyth, S. O' Neill and O. Mival (Eds.), *Proceedings of Create 10 Innovative Interactions* (pp. 62–67). Loughborough: Elms Court.
54. Kedia, B., & Bhagat, R. (1988). Cultural constraints on transfer of technology across nations. *Academy of Management Review*, *13*(4), 471–559.
55. Keogh, E., & Mansoor, L. (2001). Investigating the effects of anxiety, sensitivity and coping on the perception of cold pressor pain in healthy women. *European Journal of Pain*, *5*, 11–22.
56. Kleinberger, T., Becker, M., Ras, E., Holzinger, A., & Müller, P. (2007). Ambient intelligence in assisted living: Enable elderly people to handle future interfaces. *Universal Access in HCI, LNCS 4555*, 103–112.
57. Klessig, J. (1992). Cross-cultural medicine a decade later. The effect of values and culture on life-support decisions. *The Western Journal of Medicine*, *157*, 316–322.
58. Kreie, J., & Cronau, T. P. (1998). How men and women view ethics. *Communications of the Association for Computing Machinery*, *41*(9), 70–76.
59. Lahlou, S. (2008). Identity, social status, and face-keeping in the digital society. *Journal of Social Science Information*, *47*(3), 299–330.
60. Lahlou, S., Langheinrich, M., & Röcker, C. (2005). Privacy and trust issues with invisible computers. *Communications of the Association for Computing Machinery*, *48*(3), 59–60.
61. Leidner, D., & Kayworth, T. (2006). A review of culture in information systems research: Toward a theory of information technology culture conflict. *MIS Quarterly*, *30*, 2.
62. Leonhardt, S. (2006). Personal healthcare devices. In S. Mekherjee, et al. (Eds.), *Malware: Hardware technology drivers of ambient intelligence* (pp. 349–370). Dordrecht: Springer.
63. Lightbody, G., Galway, L., & McCullagh, P. (2014). The brain computer interface: Barriers to becoming pervasive. In A. Holzinger, M. Ziefle, & C. Röcker (Eds.), *Pervasive health—state-of-the-art and beyond*. London: Springer.

64. Maguire, M., & Osman, Z. (2003). Designing for older and inexperienced mobile phone users. In C. Stephanidis (Ed.), *Universal access in HCI: Inclusive design in the information society* (pp. 439–443). Mahwah, NJ: Lawrence Erlbaum.
65. Malinowski, M. (1996). Capitation, advances in medical technology, and the advent of a new Era in medical ethics. *American Journal of Law and Medicine*, *22*, 331–360.
66. Meeker, M., Wu, L. (2013). Internet Trends. http://www.kpcb.com/insights/2013-internet-trends. Accessed: 1 August 2013
67. Meyer, S., & Mollenkopf, H. (2003). Home technology, smart homes, and the aging user. In K. W. Schaie, H.-W. Wahl, H. Mollenkopf, & F. Oswald (Eds.), *Aging independently: Living arrangements and mobility*. New York: Springer.
68. Miller, S. M., Brody, D. S., & Summerton, J. (1988). Styles of coping with threat: Implications for health. *Journal of Personality and Social Psychology*, *54*, 142–148.
69. Mynatt, E. D., & Rogers, W. A. (2001). Developing technology to support the functional independence of older adults. *Ageing International*, *27*, 24–41.
70. Necheles, T. (1982). Standards of medical care: How does an innovative medical procedure become accepted. *The Journal of Law, Medicine and Ethics*, *10*, 15–18.
71. Nelson, T. (Ed.). (2004). *Ageism: Stereotyping and prejudice against older persons*. Cambridge: The MIT Press.
72. Pai, F.-Y., & Huang, K. (2011). Applying the technology acceptance model to the introduction of healthcare information systems. *Technological Forecasting and Social Change*, *78*(4), 650–660.
73. Palmore, E. (2001). The ageism survey first findings. *The Gerontologist*, *41*(5), 572–575.
74. Polanyi, M. (1974). Personal knowledge: Towards a post-critical philosophy. Nature Publishing Group.
75. Popper, K. R. (1996). *Alles Leben ist Problemlösen*. München, Zürich: Piper.
76. Renn, O., & Swaton, E. (1984). Psychological and sociological approaches to study risk perception. *Environment International*, *10*, 557–575.
77. Renn, O., Burns, W. J., Kasperson, J. X., Kasperson, R. E., & Slovic, P. (1992). The social amplification of risk: Theoretical foundations and empirical applications. *Journal of Social Issues*, *48*, 137–160.
78. Röcker, C. (2009a). *Design requirements for future and emerging business technologies: An empirical cross-cultural study analyzing the requirements for ambient intelligence applications in work environments*. Taunusstein: Dr. Driesen.
79. Röcker, C. (2009b). Ambient intelligence in the production and retail sector: Emerging opportunities and potential pitfalls. *Proceedings of the International Conference on Innovation, Management and Technology (ICIMT'09)*, May 27–29, 2009, Tokyo, Japan, 1393–1404.
80. Röcker, C. (2010a). Services and applications for smart office environments—a survey of state-of-the-art usage scenarios. *Proceedings of the International Conference on Computer and Information Technology (ICCIT'10)*, January 27–29, Cape Town, South, Africa, 387–403.
81. Röcker, C. (2010b). Chances and challenges of intelligent technologies in the production and retail sector. *International Journal of Business and Economic Sciences*, *2*(3), 150–161.
82. Röcker, C. (2010c). Information privacy in smart office environments: A cross-cultural study analyzing the willingness of users to share context information. In D. Tanier, O. Gervasi, V. Murgante, E. Pardede, & B. O. Apduhan (Eds.), *Proceedings of the International Conference on Computational Science and Applications (ICCSA'10), March 23–26, Fukuoka, Japan, LNCS* (Vol. 6019, pp. 93–106)., Springer-Verlag Germany: Heidelberg.
83. Röcker, C. (2011). Smart medical services: A discussion of state-of-the-art approaches. In: S. Thatcher (Ed.): *Proceedings of the International IEEE Conference on Machine Learning and Computing (ICMLC'11)*, Vol. 1, 334–338.
84. Röcker, C., & Etter, R. (2007). Social radio—a music-based approach to emotional awareness mediation. *Proceedings of the International Conferences on Intelligent User Interfaces (IUI'07)* (286–289) . New York, USA: ACM Press.
85. Röcker, C., Feith, A. (2009). Revisiting privacy in smart spaces: Social and architectural aspects of privacy in technology-enhanced environments. *Proceedings of the International*

Symposium on Computing, Communication and Control (ISCCC'09), October 9–11, 2009, Singapore, 201–205.
86. Röcker, C., Janse, M., Portolan, N., Streitz, N.A. (2005). User requirements for intelligent home environments: A scenario-driven approach and empirical cross-cultural study. *Proceedings of the International Conference on Smart Objects and Ambient Intelligence (sOc-EUSAI'05)*, October 12–14, Grenoble, France, ACM International Conference Proceeding Series, 121, 111–116.
87. Röcker, C., Ziefle, M., Holzinger, A. (2011). Social inclusion in AAL environments: Home automation and convenience services for elderly users. *Proceedings of the International Conference on Artificial Intelligence (ICAI'11)*, (Vol. 1, pp. 55–59) July 18–20, Las Vegas, NV, USA.
88. Rodger, J. A., & Pendharkar, P. C. (2004). A field study of the impact of gender and user's technical experience on the performance of voice-activated medical tracking application. *International Journal of Human-Computer Studies*, *60*, 529–44.
89. Rogers, Y. (2009). The changing face of human-computer interaction in the age of ubiquitous computing. In A. Holzinger and K. Miesenberger (eds.), *Human-Computer-Interaction and usability for e-Inclusion. LNCS 5889* (pp. 1–19). Berlin: Springer.
90. Schwarzer, R. (1994). Optimism, vulnerability, and self- beliefs as health-related cognitions: A systematic overview. *Psychology & Health*, *9*(3), 161–180.
91. Searight, H., & Gafford, J. (2005). Cultural diversity at the end of life: Issues and guidelines for family physicians. *American Family Physician*, *71*(3), 515–525.
92. Seo, K., Kim, J., Ryu, H., & Jang, S. (2014). RehabMaster: A Pervasive rehabilitation platform for stroke patients and their caregivers. In A. Holzinger, M. Ziefle, & C. Röcker (Eds.), *Pervasive health—state-of-the-art and beyond*. London: Springer.
93. Sharma, R., & Thomas, C. J. (2013). *Ageism: problems and prospects*. New Delhi: Akansha Publishing.
94. Shiode, N. (2004). When space shrinks—digital communities and ubiquitous society: Digitally united? A case study on the penetration of wireless and ubiquitous information technologies in Japan. *Proceedings of the Winter International Symposium on Information and Communication Technologies (WISICT'04)*, 1–6.
95. Smith, R. (2013). 5 Cloud Computing Trends For 2013. http://www.cloudtweaks.com/2013/05/cloud-computing-trends-security/. Accessed 30 July 2013
96. Srite, M., & Karahanna, E. (2006). The role of espoused national cultural values in technology acceptance. *MIS Quarterly*, *30*, 3.
97. Stokes, E. (2014). The ongoing development of a multimedia gaming module to aid speech, language and communication. In A. Holzinger, M. Ziefle, & C. Röcker (Eds.), *Pervasive Health - State-of-the-Art and Beyond*. London: Springer.
98. Straub, D., Keil, M., & Brenner, W. (1997). Testing the technology acceptance model across cultures: A three country study. *Information & Management*, *33*(1), 1–11.
99. Straub, D., Loch, K., & Hill, C. (2002). Transfer of information technology to the Arab world: A test of Cultural influence modeling. In M. Dadashuadeh (Ed.), *Information Technology Management in Developing Countries* (pp. 92–151). Hershey: IRM Press.
100. Streitz, N. A., Magerkurth, C., Prante, T., & Röcker, C. (2005). From information design to experience design: Smart artefacts and the disappearing computer. *ACM Interactions, Special Issue on Ambient Intelligence—New Visions of Human-Computer Interaction*, *12*(4), 21–25.
101. Tedre, M., Sutinen, E., Kähkönen, E., & Kommers, P. (2006). Ethnocomputing: ICT in cultural and social context. *Communications of the ACM*, *49*(1), 126–130.
102. Teo, T., & Su Luan, W. (2008). A cross-cultural examination of the intention to use technology between Singaporean and Malaysian pre-service teachers: an application of the TAM. *Educational Technology and Society*, *11*(4), 265–280.
103. Turner, K. J. (2014). Managing telehealth and telecare. In A. Holzinger, M. Ziefle, & C. Röcker (Eds.), *Pervasive health—state-of-the-art and beyond*. London: Springer.
104. Vaughan, E. (1993). Individual and cultural differences in adaptation to environmental risks. *American Psychologist*, *48*, 673–80.

105. Venkatesh, V., & Morris, M. (2000). Why don't men ever stop to ask for directions? Gender, social influence, and their role in technology acceptance and usage behavior. *MIS Quarterly, 24*, 115–139.
106. Vlek, C., & Stallen, P. (1980). Rational and personal aspects of risk. *Acta Psychologica, 45*, 273–300.
107. Waltisberg, D., Arnrich, B., & Tröster, G. (2014). Sleep quality monitoring with the smart bed. In A. Holzinger, M. Ziefle, & C. Röcker (Eds.), *Pervasive health—state-of-the-art and Beyond*. London: Springer.
108. Webster, A. (2002). Innovative health technologies and the social: Redefining health, medicine and the body. *Current Sociology, 50*, 443–457.
109. Wilkowska, W., Ziefle, M. (2011). User diversity as a challenge for the integration of medical technology into future home environments. In M. Ziefle, C. Röcker (Eds.), *Human-Centred design of eHealth technologies. Concepts, methods and applications* (pp. 95–126). Hershey: IGI Global.
110. Wilkowska, W., & Ziefle, M. (2012). Privacy and data security in e-health: Requirements from users' perspective. *Health Informatics Journal, 18*(3), 191–201.
111. Wilkowska, W., Gaul, S., & Ziefle, M. (2010). A small but significant difference—the role of gender on the acceptance of medical assistive technologies. In G. Leitner, M. Hitz, & A. Holzinger (Eds.), *HCI in work and learning, life and leisure USAB 2010, LNCS 6389* (pp. 82–100). Berlin, Heidelberg: Springer.
112. Wilkowska, W., Alagöz, F., & Ziefle, M. (2012). How age and country of origin impact the readiness to adopt e-Health technologies: An intercultural comparison. Work: A Journal of Prevention. *Assessment and Rehabilitation, 41*, 2072–2080.
113. Wilson, M. (2002). Making nursing visible? Gender, technology and the care plan as script. *Information Technology and People, 15*(2), 139–158.
114. Ziefle, M. (2002). The influence of user expertise and phone complexity on performance, ease of use and learnability of different mobile phones. *Behaviour and Information Technology, 21*(5), 303–311.
115. Ziefle, M., & Bay, S. (2005). How older adults meet complexity: Aging effects on the usability of different mobile phones. *Behaviour and Information Technology, 24*(5), 375–389.
116. Ziefle, M. Jakobs, E.-M. (2010). New challenges in human computer interaction: Strategic directions and interdisciplinary trends. *4th International Conference on Competitive Manufacturing Technologies*, South Africa: University of Stellenbosch, 389–398.
117. Ziefle, M., Röcker, C. (2010). Acceptance of pervasive healthcare systems: A comparison of different implementation concepts. In *Proceedings of the 4th International ICST Conference on Pervasive Computing Technologies for Healthcare* (PervasiveHealth'10), Munich, Germany, March 22–25, CD-ROM.
118. Ziefle, M., & Röcker, C. (2011). *Human-Centered design of e-health technologies: Concepts, methods and applications*. Niagara Falls: IGI Publishing.
119. Ziefle, M., Schaar, A.K. (2011). Gender Differences in Acceptance and Attitudes towards an Invasive Medical Stent. *Electronic Journal of Health Informatics*, 6, 1–18.
120. Ziefle, M., Schaar, A.K. (2014). Technology acceptance by patients: Empowerment and stigma. In J. V. Hoof, G. Demiris, E. Wouters (Eds.), *Handbook of smart homes, health care and well-being*. New York: Springer.
121. Ziefle, M., Röcker, C., Kasugai, K., Klack, L., Jakobs, E.-M., Schmitz-Rode, T., et al. (2009). eHealth—enhancing mobility with aging. In M. Tscheligi, B. de Ruyter, J. Soldatos, A. Meschtscherjakov, C. Buiza, W. Reitberger, N. Streitz, & T. Mirlacher (Eds.), *Roots for the future of ambient intelligence, adjunct Proceedings of the Third European Conference on Ambient Intelligence (Am I'09), November 18–21* (pp. 25–28). Salzburg: Austria.
122. Ziefle, M., Röcker, C., Wilkowska, W., Kasugai, K., Klack, L., Möllering, C., et al. (2011a). A multi-disciplinary approach to ambient assisted living. In C. Röcker & M. Ziefle (Eds.), *E-Health, Assistive technologies and applications for assisted living: Challenges and solutions* (pp. 76–93). Niagara Falls: IGI Publishing.

123. Ziefle, M., Röcker, C., Holzinger A. (2011b). Medical technology in smart homes: Exploring the user's perspective on privacy, intimacy and trust. T*he 3rd IEEE International Workshop on Security Aspects of Process and Services Engineering (SAPSE'11). 35th Annual IEEE Computer Software and Applications Conference*, July 18–22, 2011, Munich, Germany, pp. 410–415, ISBN: 978-1-4577-0980-7 DOI 10.1109/COMPSACW.2011.75.
124. Zimmer, Z., & Chappell, N. L. (1999). Receptivity to new technology among older adults. *Disability and Rehabilitation*, *21*, 222–230.

Chapter 2
On Challenges Designing the Home as a Place for Care

Erik Grönvall and Stefan Lundberg

2.1 Introduction

Demographic trends over the next 15–20 years show an increased percentage of people aged 65+ in western countries. This shift in the composition of the population is expected to put a great deal of pressure on societies' financial resources all over the industrialized world. This demographic change brought about the definition of an 'ageing-in-place' philosophy [1], which resulted in more nursing and personal care moving out of the hospitals and professional care institutions and into private peoples' homes [2, 3]. From time to time this relocation of care can turn private homes into wards or places for rehabilitation and care.

A number of studies have shown that home-based care has been positively perceived from both a patient and societal perspective (e.g. [4]). To sustain home-based care, the care receiver might have to be subject to both technological and human support. Hence, Information Communication Technology (ICT) has for some time now been regarded as an important tool in handling the growing number of older adults without reducing the quality of care. Technological support for home-based healthcare range from simple solutions such as pill boxes, personal social alarms and blood pressure measurement devices to more complicated technologies such as dialysis machines and oxygen flow/breathing apparatuses. Additionally, home care

E. Grönvall (✉)
IT University of Copenhagen, Rued Langgaards Vej 7, 2300 Copenhagen S, Denmark
e-mail: erig@itu.dk

S. Lundberg
KTH Royal Institute of Technology, Alfred Nobels Allé 10, 14152 Huddinge, Sweden
e-mail: slundb@kth.se

A. Holzinger et al. (eds.), *Pervasive Health*, Human–Computer Interaction Series,
DOI: 10.1007/978-1-4471-6413-5_2, © Springer-Verlag London 2014

workers and nurses may visit a home regularly, even many times a day, to support the 'patient at home'. The above mentioned home-based care assistance range from help to get dressed, personal hygiene to more specialist interventions such as providing injections or doing bio-measurements.

Much of the HCI research within home-based healthcare has focused on designing novel technological solutions or on ergonomics and usability concerns related, for example, to how older adults can be supported by technology and how they can handle the introduced technological aids. However, as the authors argue in this chapter, the consequences of implementing pervasive healthcare solutions in private homes may go beyond application specific considerations, such as the selection of the right bio-sensor or the development of a user friendly interface. The authors suggest that, in an extension of medical and usability demands (e.g. to be able to operate a device and interpret an interface), other challenges exists that should be addressed already at design-time. Home-based healthcare may not only be an issue for the patient (and the immediate family) and the day-to-day healthcare provider but may include and affect also the local community, regional, national, and in some cases even global concerns.

This chapter exemplifies non-functional-related aspects of home-based healthcare (i.e. aspects that are not directly related to the medical functionality of a device or how a person can interact with a medical device) and discusses their impact on the individual patients, their care providers and the society at large. The seven challenges discussed in this chapter are: (1) Appropriation, (2) Aspects of control in multi-site healthcare scenarios, (3) Societal concerns, (4) Heterogeneity of care providers, (5) Mobility, (6) Installation and maintenance, and (7) Training and learning. From the authors perspective have these challenges not been satisfactorily considered in most home-based healthcare designs despite the fact that they are indeed important when designing for holistic and sustainable home-based healthcare scenarios.

More specifically, this chapter aims to raise awareness about non-functional aspects of home-based healthcare, which can both inform and challenge large scale implementations of home-based healthcare technology. The focus of this chapter is to provide foremost HCI (Human Computer Interaction) designers, but also patients, healthcare professionals, policy-makers and politicians with an understanding of the issues that would be beneficial to address when designing home-based healthcare solutions. We also propose strategies on how to identify, address and work with the above-mentioned challenges in home-based healthcare design projects.

The rest of this chapter will be outlined as follows: The chapter will start with a description of Sect. 2.3 within home-based care and the Sect. 2.3.2. It is in that section where the above mentioned seven challenges are further described and their impacts on home-based healthcare designs is discussed. This will be followed by an examination of Sect. 2.4. Section 2.5 will then conclude this chapter.

2.2 Glossary

Appropriation How for example technology becomes part of people's everyday lives.

Bio-value A measured biological value, for example SpO2, pulse or body temperature.

Bio-waste Discarded medicines, cytotoxic drugs, infected tissues, solid waste tubes, catheters, intravenous set etc

Care network Constellation of formal and informal care providers.

CSCW Computer supported cooperative work

FCC US federal communication commission

HBHC Hospital-based home care

HCI Human computer interaction

Home-based care Professional care at the patient's home

ICT Information communication technology

Informal care Care provided by a relative, a friend or voluntaries

In-patient A patient in the hospital

IP Internet protocol

Non-clinical settings The patient's home, workplace or vacation resorts

PD Participatory design. Design together with current and future users and other stakeholders.

QoS Quality of service. A measurement of quality (e.g. up-time, mean time between failure (MTBF) and bandwidth).

Self-monitoring Monitoring of bio-values done by a person for his or her own needs.

SIAT Swedish institute of assistive technology

Social alarm A safety alarm system. Usually connected to the telephone system with an alarm-button worn by the user so s/he can call for help if needed.

SCAIP Social care alarm internet protocol (a Swedish standard for how social alarm communicates).

Tele-monitoring A collaborative service where a person at home send bio-values to a care professional.

Tele-care Collective term for diverse healthcare scenarios including a remote partner.

User-centred design Design with a specific (group of) users interests in mind.

VoIP Voice over IP. Voice communication over Internet rather than land-line or GSM telephones.

2.3 State-of-the-Art

Traditionally, there has been much attention on workplace studies and design for work within the HCI and CSCW (Computer Supported Cooperative Work) communities. Some years ago these research domains increased their interest in healthcare and professional healthcare settings. Since then, numerous research projects have investigated work-related activities within professional care settings such as hospitals. Research projects have for example studied handover between shifts [5] and how in-patient care can be supported through novel technologies [6]. These studies have to a large degree focused on designing care worker support, rather than patient support. More recently, attention has also been given to non-professional care settings such as patients' private homes [2, 7–10]. Indeed, as sensor technology becomes smaller, more stable and more economically attractive and infrastructures such as mobile 3G networks becomes ubiquitous available more and more Pervasive health and home-based care scenarios are explored [11]. As a consequence, a growing number of projects put attention on the patient and other non-professional actors at home.

Two growing application-domains for home-based care, both in research and commercial systems, are tele-monitoring of diverse bio-values and video consultations. However, not all tele-care initiatives have been designed with the end-users' needs in focus. For example is it important to consider how the ICT support is implemented in the users home [12]. Already in 2009 Chan et al. [13] pointed out that the technology development of home-care support was dominated by a technology-push rather than a demand-pull approach and a better understanding of human needs would help put attention on use demands rather than what is technologically possible. In recent years there has however been an increased interest in pervasive health applications and the end-users of healthcare technology, from both industry and the CSCW and HCI research communities [10, 14–19].

The interest in home-based healthcare emerges from a number of different reasons. The translocation of care from hospitals to the patients' private homes (i.e. hospital-based home care (HBHC) or home-based care) can enable a more sustainable and economic care solution from a societal perspective [20]. Patients also tend to prefer home-based care compared with being hospitalized [4]. However, the home (in contrast to the hospital) is not designed as a place for care. Indeed, moving healthcare activities, including treatments of severe diseases, to private homes' and other non-clinical settings (e.g. the patient's workplace or vacation resort) not prepared for these care activities challenge on different levels the patients, their care providers and society at large. Still, many home-based healthcare scenarios explored in research consider only the patient and the care provider (and their respective use settings) in isolation. However, these care initiatives are inserted into pre-existing, larger ecologies of actors, service providers, contexts and geographical locations. As exemplified in Fig. 2.1, the implementation of a home-based care regimen may influence (and be influenced by) other actors than the care provider and patient, for example the water and electricity service providers and the society at large. A home-based care scenario (e.g. enabled through the use of a specific technology) may require a number of services such as broadband internet connectivity, electricity or even water. Home-based treatments may also produce waste such as trash and liquids flushed away in the toilet. The handling of such bio-waste may be regulated in different laws and challenge local wastewater treatment plants and waste disposal services that may not be dimensioned to handle bio-waste at a larger scale [21]. Generated bio-waste (especially in non-clinical settings) may therefore affect the environment at large and hence become a national and international issue. Also, novel treatments and affiliated technology require education and training.

The effects and relationships exemplified in Fig. 2.1 may not be directly relevant to consider in any small-scale test or local implementation of a home-based care system. As an HCI researcher it may therefore be hard to identify a link between for example one's research project, national legislations and potential environmental effects a wide-spread use of a system may have. However, neither technology nor design is neutral and it may be fruitful to envision the effects of large-scale deployment of research projects and solutions. There is a risk that we fail to understand the full cost and effects of moving care out of the hospitals and into private homes if we neglect the societal effects of implementing diverse home-based care scenarios. Figure. 2.1 also illustrates the fact that we in our design work normally only consider the most obvious consequences such as education and installation to some degree, but not the environmental impact at all. The 'red' arrows (Initial action arrow + arrow going to Education and Support) represent the traditional focus and the 'blue' arrows (Initial action arrow + the following chain of arrows (Sawyer and Waste etc)) the new, extended focus discussed in this chapter.

We will now look at three scenarios illustrating possible effect-chains as a result from implementing care and treatments in private homes and everyday life.

Example 1: The move of advanced care from the hospital to private homes' is happening without any discussion about legal responsibilities and possible cooperation

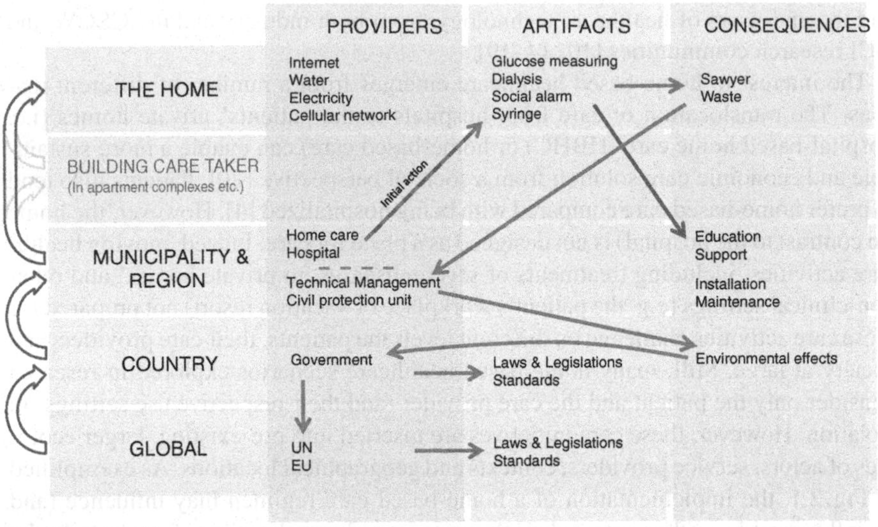

Fig. 2.1 Example effect-chains and active relationships when inserting care in private homes

between the house inhabitant(s), house owner, infrastructure providers and the caregiver. The society should already be warned by the catastrophes with non-function social alarms due to a switch from analog to digital technology in the telephone system. For example in Sweden several lethal accidents have been reported related to a pre-sequel move from landline telephones to IP based communication systems and the social alarm providers today warn anyone from using analog alarms on digital tele-lines [22]. Since the consequences of a possible catastrophe scenario when medical care is moved to private homes have not yet been legally assessed, the responsibilities are unclear. Is the caregiver responsible if a critical function provided as an infrastructure to a household suddenly is lost with severe consequences for the patient, or is it the house owner, or someone else, that bares this responsibility?

Example 2: In a multi-storey building there is normally a caretaker running different maintenance activities, for example to turn off electricity or water for a couple of hours while maintenance work is performed. What information must the building caretaker have regarding ongoing medical care in the apartments and how would the possible sharing of such information interfere with the patients' privacy? One could hypothesize that in diverse breakdown scenarios, the patient should be (pro)-active which requires a resourceful person that can both mentally and physically act on the breakdown at hand. As home-based healthcare aim to treat ill people, it might not always be the case that the patient has such available resources.

Example 3: Another issue is how the caregiver should handle hazardous waste when treating someone in their own home. Examples of hazardous waste could be contaminated rags and bandages with blood and other body liquids, cannulas, medicine etc. Home care providers have special containers for such potentially hazardous materials that they place in a person's home or that they bring with them.

However, if not only professional home-based care increases in the future, but also self-management of one's health or family-provided care increases, there may be less control of correct management of bio waste generated in non-clinical settings such as the home. With increased home-based care, there will also be much more medication remains in the sewage as some of the administered medication's potent components passes through, and leaves the body, together with the urine (at the hospital, this is handled through for example filtering).

To investigate and develop healthcare solutions for sustainable and large-scale home-based deployment we must understand the above mentioned, and similar, issues. When moving healthcare out of the controlled hospital environments and into private homes there are both easily identified and harder to recognize effects, or effect chains, that may emerge. The example challenges discussed in this chapter should be understood and considered when developing healthcare prototypes and products for a future, realistic insertion into peoples' everyday lives. In this chapter the authors argue that in an extension of medical and usability demands (e.g. to be able to operate a specific device and interpret an interface), other challenges exists that should be addressed or at least considered at design-time. These challenges have not yet been satisfactorily taken into account in much homecare HCI research and design. Our chapter proposes that designers and HCI practitioners should be aware of, and reflect upon how these particularities can challenge the value, feasibility and a wider implementation of their homecare designs.

We will now continue this section with related work, followed by an investigation of the identified challenges.

2.3.1 Related Work

A range of projects have examined how to support a patient in the transition from the hospital to the private home [23–26]. Also, a range of healthcare solutions exists to support patients once at home, for example different tele-medicine and monitoring solutions [20, 27, 28]. Much of the previously reported on homecare design work within research have been rather technology-driven [13], demonstrating for example technological requirements and possibilities with tele-care and tele-monitoring [29]. Homecare applications include for example vital signs monitoring (e.g. heart rate, ECG, and SpO2) [30], diabetes [31, 32] and asthma [33]. Mental health problems such as bipolar disorders [34] have also been investigated as possible candidates for home-based care. Pre-existing off-the-self technologies can also enable self-measurements (not necessarily in a tele-monitoring context) in unsupervised settings such as the home [35]. Two examples of such pre-existing self-monitoring technologies are the thermometer and the blood pressure measuring device.

The (re-)configuration of care challenges both the novel places for care and what it means to be a 'doctor' and 'patient' in such places [28, 36]. Challenges previously reported on in home-based care include (but is not limited to) the acceptance of technology in peoples' homes [37], to find a physical place for the technology within the home [17] and how care technologies can be successfully integrated in everyday life [23], without creating unwanted dependencies or foster social isolation [38]. Others have discussed the need to reflect on how the technology actually gets transported to, and installed in, a person's home [39]. Will for example a solution require broadband or other technical installations and can the required technology be carried home and put to use by the patient him/herself or is there a need of some special service person to perform such tasks [39]? As pointed out by Palen and Aaløkke [14] technology for the home must be extra robust and built to sustain activities also during technology breakdowns. Research projects have also investigated the possible negative effects healthcare technology can have once implemented in a private home (i.e. people can be "alienated by the technology" [40] and experience stigmatization [41]).

Lang et al. [2, 42, 43] have investigated safety concerns in homecare and reports that while risks exists in all healthcare settings, private homes lacks the uniformity of institutional care environments. Lang also mentions that homecare is superimposed on peoples' everyday lives. As described in the work of Palen and Aaløkke [14], people develop their own strategies to integrate for example medication administration into their everyday routines. However, people have also expressed a need to retain control over their lives when prescribed with care at home, something that can challenge adherence or a successful treatment or home-based monitoring [44] if not properly designed for.

User Centred Design and Participatory Design (PD) are common design approaches and these methods both have long track-records within HCI research and design [45, 46]. While PD has been used in diverse healthcare projects (e.g. [16, 23, 47, 48]), the use of PD have been challenged in diverse home-based healthcare scenarios [39, 40]. An important question in many HCI projects, and in particularly PD projects, is what stakeholders and interests should be included and safe-guarded in the design process. A natural minimum of stakeholders to be involved in a HCI and Participatory design project are normally the directly involved actors plus the design team. In home-based healthcare projects this usually intend, a part from the design team, some healthcare professionals directly involved in the project and the target patients [39]. Some projects have used mediators [49, 50] speaking on behalf of some specific user-group, rather than involving that particular group directly. The use of mediators may be applied for example when working with user groups that can be challenging to include as equal partners in a design process, for example due to difficulties to express one's needs and wishes or dementia such as Alzheimer. A mediator can for example be a close family member or care provider that talks on the behalf of the care receiver. The idea of mediators could however include other, also non-person entities, which could benefit from being represented in the design process. However, to consider including legal or environmental entities have not been previously reported on, something that could add novel input to home-based healthcare designs.

2.3.2 On Challenges Designing for the Home as a Place for Care

As presented in the Introduction and Related work sections, much previous research has focused on technological challenges and possibilities when designing and implementing different home-based care scenarios, including self-monitoring, rehabilitation and treatment. These previous investigations has primarily been grounded in an engineering perspective (for example investigating how to construct better blood pressure monitoring devices [51]), a HCI perspective (such as designing for home-based stroke rehabilitation [16]) or a medical perspective (such as how to use game-consoles in rehabilitation and their clinical effects [52]).

The relevance of this previous research can be exemplified by projects like ACCENT (Advanced Component Control Enhancing Network Technologies) that allows effective management of a home care system [53]. Nevertheless, designers of home-based care solutions and services may be both challenged and inspired by more directly consider the effects a large-scale deployment of their home-based healthcare designs may have on for example patients, care providers, organizations, laws, legislations and the environment. A goal of this chapter is to help designers of future home-based healthcare systems to understand what roles their designs may take considering a larger context. To do so, this chapter will now present and discuss seven challenges that we argue can influence the design and realization of diverse home-based healthcare services, namely: (1) Appropriation, (2) Aspects of control in multi-site healthcare scenarios, (3) Societal concerns, (4) Heterogeneity of care providers, (5) Mobility, (6) Installation and maintenance, and (7) Training and Learning. The authors are not aware of HCI related research that actively have reported on, and incorporated, the wider set of challenges (exemplified by the challenges mentioned above) that may affect home-based healthcare designs to different degrees.

Another important aspect of implementing assistive support in people's home is how this influences the relation between the care receiver, professional caregivers and possible informal caregivers. Ward-Griffin and MacKeever point out that the relationships between community nurses and family members caring for frail elders are complex, dynamic, and multifaceted [54]. A new device that is supposed to support independent living for someone in need for support might stress the formal caregiver by demands such as settings, checking batteries and other supportive actions not normally a part of the work. Bossen et al. [55] have also identified this need and developed a mobile, collaborative tool for professional and informal care providers. The above-mentioned works shows that it is important to understand how a design may decrease or increase the burden for the caregivers around a care receiver and users of healthcare technology.

In the following sections, we present and explore the above-mentioned seven challenges. We have selected these seven challenges as they represent a cluster of challenges that, at a glance, might not be considered relevant in a HCI research project. One reason that designers may not reflect on these (and other similar) challenges may be that normally research projects are not designed for long-term use, large-scale deployment and commercialization. However, the authors' perspective is that an active reflection and understanding of these challenges could both challenge and inform healthcare designs and provide the means for developing more sustainable home-care solutions in the future.

2.3.2.1 Challenge 1: Appropriation

To become part of people's everyday lives, new technology must be interpreted and ascribed meaning. This is an on-going process called appropriation [56, 57] and it is through a dialogue between the user and a contextualized artifact that appropriation takes place. As healthcare technologies are introduced into peoples' pre-existing routines, homes and everyday lives they become, to different extent, appropriated. To design for appropriation can facilitate an acceptance and everyday use of healthcare technologies. Carrol et al. [58] even distinguish between technology-as-designed and technology-in-use. In home-based healthcare scenarios appropriation may be challenged for example due to how a technology is introduced into a person's everyday life. Indeed, in contrast to traditional consumer products, people normally do not select a specific healthcare technology out of interest or its aesthetical properties but rather out of a specific need identified by a healthcare professional.

Furthermore, when developing healthcare IT one must consider that all homes are different, and so are their inhabitants. After all, the only thing that might connect or be shared among a group of people with a specific diagnose may be their illness. Designers should be aware of how to design for a wide acceptance of a particular healthcare technology and allow for tailoring or other strategies to align healthcare technology to its intended users, their everyday lives and homes. Also, the appropriation process is far from mere physiological as it also involves issues like how a particular healthcare technology can be installed, powered and maintained in a person's home.

User's acceptance and appropriation of any system, including healthcare technologies, are important aspects to understand (especially over time) when evaluating any product or research prototype. As a consequence designer could benefit from understanding how to design, also in research projects, solutions that do not only fit a few lead-users but can be appropriated by a large variety of users in different contexts. As illustrated in the related work section (e.g. [39]), this issue has been previously highlighted but few research projects have actively disseminated work where HCI healthcare research projects' design-decisions have been inspired also by large-scale deployment requirements. In commercial products the large-scale implementation factor naturally is more common, but these products may embed other HCI design limitations that challenge the appropriation process.

Looking at the research field of HCI at large, two related (and during the last years widely researched) topics that affects the appropriation process are aesthetics and the aesthetics of interaction [59, 60]. Aesthetics of interaction explore both the expression of the designed object and the human experience in interacting with that object [34]. However, while these two HCI related domains have been studied

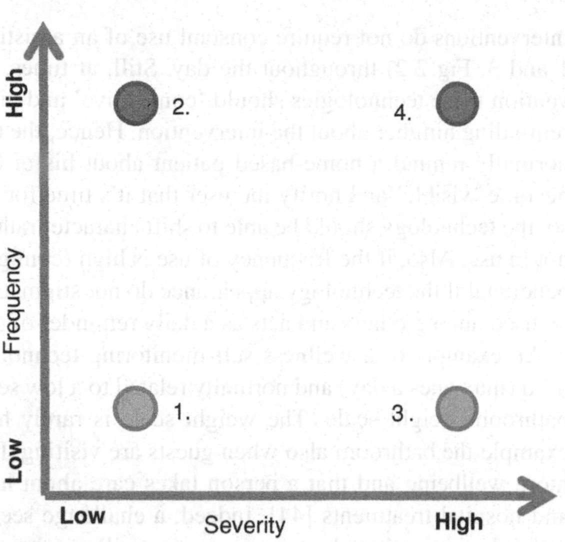

Fig. 2.2 Example configurations of Frequency-Severity relationships in home-based care scenarios

at large, they have not been widely reported on regarding work on home-based healthcare designs.

To further discuss aspects of aesthetics we now present two use-related home-based care and healthcare technology concerns; frequency of use and intervention severity (see Fig. 2.2). The frequency of system use deals with how often a home-based care support system is needed and in use (i.e. low (e.g. once a day or less) or high (continuous support throughout the day)) and the severity of the intervention (i.e. ranging from preventive wellness to direct life-support). We identify four extreme-points where a home-based care scenario can be located in these two interlinked continuums.

To promote the appropriation of both healthcare technologies and prescribed treatments into a person's life, it could be argued that the further a person moves towards the left side (configuration 1 and 2, Fig. 2.2) and especially the lower-left corner (configuration 1, Fig. 2.2) the more important become the non-medical aspects of a home-based care technology. Similarly, in configuration 3 (Fig. 2.2), it's beneficial if the technology can remind the user about the needed intervention. In configuration 4 (Fig. 2.2) a high level of technology acceptances may be found, not out of the technology's aesthetics but out of required use, but there is still a wish to move towards a situation where the technology does not remind the user about one's illness or the hospital. In interviews with tele-monitored heart patients we have identified these aspects of aesthetics as these heart patients tend to accept the technology due to a strong perceived need. However, these heart patients still prefer technology that do not stigmatize them in their daily lives (an example of this could be to use a standard tablet device for hospital communication rather than a special-made tele-monitoring input and communication device) [44]. In a rehabilitation project [61], the project participants had a low acceptance rate inserting care technologies into their everyday lives as they did not perceive their illness to be so severe. Many home-based care interventions do not require constant use of an assistive technology (configuration 1 and 3, Fig. 2.2) throughout the day. Still, at times, when it's time for the intervention these technologies should 'come alive' and give clear cues to the user, and reminding him/her about the intervention. Hence, the technology should maybe not normally remind a home-based patient about his or her illness, but when needed become 'visible' and notify the user that it's time for a treatment. To be able to do so, the technology should be able to shift character rather than be hidden away when not in use. Also, if the frequency of use is high (configuration 2 and 4, Fig. 2.2), it's beneficial if the technology appearance do not stigmatize as the system may have to be used among others and acts as a daily reminder of one's illness.

An example of a wellness self-monitoring technology that is not so frequently used (max ones a day) and normally related to a low severity treatment is a common bathroom weight scale. The weight scale is rarely hidden and left visible in for example the bathroom also when guests are visiting. Indeed, a weight scale signals more wellbeing and that a person takes care about him/herself rather than illness and hospital treatments [44]. Indeed, a challenge seems to be how to design care technologies so they do not communicate illness in peoples' everyday lives as this can hinder the appropriation process. Previous work has discussed (especially in less frequent care technology use scenarios) what role the technology has when not in use (for providing care). If a home-based treatment that requires a purpose-made technology takes 15 min a day to perform, the treatment-specific technology remain 'useless' for the rest of the day (i.e. 23 h and 45 min). Can we design for a secondary usage of healthcare designs and by that lower stigmatization while promoting use? In a previous project, we explored scenarios of such secondary use where the care intervention was in the vicinity of configuration 1 (Fig. 2.2). In the project, a specific rehabilitation tool intended for home use was developed. One design aspect explored in that rehabilitation project was that the rehabilitation tool could act as a reading lamp when not used for the rehabilitation exercises [39]. In that way, the rehabilitation tool had a function also outside of the prescribed care intervention and hence did not 'occupy a lot of space'. As a lamp, the rehabilitation tool could remain visible and hence also be ready for rehabilitation use.

As designers of home-based care we should design for user acceptance, appropriation and everyday use. One popular way to design for user acceptance and motivation (for example in home-based rehabilitation) is to work with serious games and Gamification [62]. Another less discussed strategy could be to design also for non-medical or non-treatment scenarios. This could be especially relevant in care scenarios that do not require care activities to be performed more than ones a day.

2.3.2.2 Challenge 2: Aspects of Control in Multi-site Healthcare Scenarios

In a care situation where the patient is hospitalized, the hospital in a way represents a setting with 'total' control of 'everything'. When a person is admitted to a hospital, the hospital takes over the day-to-day care of that person (a responsibility normally handled by the individual him/herself, or that is shared with actors in the person's Care

Network [63] (e.g. close family members and homecare workers). Indeed, different physical settings can embed different configurations of control. Also, how control is granted, taken, negotiated or given in any particular setting or configuration of people depends on a number of aspects; for example cultural, organizational or authority reasons. While a person is admitted to a hospital, that hospital controls the treatment including exercise, rehabilitation and medication. The hospital also controls what and when a patient eats, when people can visit, and where the patient should be at specific times (for example to make x-rays). In contrast to the hospital setting, one may assume that a person is in full control when at home; both over his/her own time and the home as such. However, this is not always the case. It is not uncommon that even an adult patient at home is subject to control-limiting factors in relation to how prescribed care activities and technologies are inserted into his or her everyday life, for example;

(1) The patient might live with other people such as a spouse and/or children. The lived space and the actual time for conducting treatments might therefore have to be negotiated among the household inhabitants. In households where more than one person undergoes treatments there may also be conflicting needs that have to be taken into consideration. It might for example be that two people in the household should both use the TV during the same morning hours to perform video-consultations with different wards at the hospital.
(2) To support home-based care, treatment-specific equipment and aids may be inserted into the home and hence into a person's everyday life. The need for such particular equipment (special beds, dialysis equipment, rehabilitation tools, pill dispensers, oxygen tubes, hygiene aids, and etc.) directly limits the level of control a person have over his or her own home. For example if a specific bed has to be used to assist the home-care workers in caring for a person at home, the care receiver can no longer choose to use his or her own bed. This in turn may imply that a couple no longer can share bed, or even bedroom. Also, that a person is 'ill' or 'weak' becomes obvious for anyone entering the home by just looking at the bed. Furthermore, at home the patient becomes a citizen with many other roles than being ill [64]. Hence, one has to negotiate (with oneself and possibly others) what role an illness will take in everyday life.
(3) The hospital may impose control outside the hospital, for example in a patient's home and everyday life, through video- and bio-monitoring and remote consultations. Still, the hospital's influence is diminished at home. However, someone (e.g. the patient, a family member, a home care worker) should carry out care activities in the home that otherwise may have been carried out together with a healthcare professional at the hospital. Indeed, healthcare technology in peoples' homes both enables and requires articulation work [65]. The technology inserted into a patient's everyday life introduces a division, and translocation, of labor among two or more actors. As a minimum this translocation includes the hospital and the patient (at home), but may expand to include also homecare workers, family members and friends (i.e. both professional and informal members of a patient's Care network) [55].

As presented in the related work, much research has worked with tele-monitoring and control from the healthcare professionals' perspective. However, as care is pushed out of the hospital, much work and responsibility is moved out of the professional hospital setting and into private peoples' homes and everyday lives. We argue that the citizen and his/her everyday life to a higher degree must be acknowledged in home-based care designs to raise the level of positive outcomes in home-based care. There seem to be a general assumption that 'just' because people may benefit from home-based healthcare technologies (for example since they might not have to visit the hospital as often) they will comply. This assumption may in some care situations be challenged. Also, when people do comply, other challenges may exist. Investigating a remote monitoring project [44] where pregnant women with preeclampsia (i.e. pregnancy poisoning) were tele-monitored from home instead of hospitalized, it became clear that these women performed their daily measurements as scheduled (this was also checked by the hospital midwife as the women's daily values were sent to the hospital). However, some of the women deliberately reported false values at times so the midwife would not have them come to the hospital for a more extensive test (something that could 'ruin the day') for the woman. This was for example done by a woman who had been called to the hospital as a result of her monitoring results. However, once at the hospital it was found out that the values was not alarming or did not need to be corrected in any way [44]. The example of the pregnant women illustrates the complexity of calling for action when not really needed but not knowing exactly if it is. For safety's sake the midwife will always want to call one time too much than missing any critical issue. This can only be solved by information and understanding that the alternative to self-monitoring is regular visits to the hospital and that this includes some visits of unnecessary sort.

A first step to design for the diverse, and possibly distributed, notions of control in home-based healthcare scenarios could simply be to acknowledge that for many people, (also prescribed) healthcare is not the highest life-priority [66] and neither is technology. Working with different projects we have observed that people can have problems integrating treatments and associated technology into their everyday lives and hence there is a risk of less successful treatment outcomes [44].

2.3.2.3 Challenge 3: Societal Concerns

As previously mentioned, a hospital is explicitly designed to be a place for care. To sustain both critical and day-to-day care, the hospital has not only control over the patient, but also over the complete hospital-environment and required infrastructures. For instance may a hospital be equipped with backup electricity to be used in case of a power-failure, water cleaning facilities (e.g. filtering medication remains away from the waste water) and ventilation that do not spread airborne diseases. A hospital also has routines to handle bio- and toxic waste that can be the results of different interventions and treatments. As such, a hospital is built to answer to societal concerns and requirements regarding medical care.

In contrast to the hospital, a private home is seldom built to sustain diverse care scenarios and hence do normally not incorporate strategies to handle care-related societal concerns. Even in the case where a patient is his/her own house owner, the provision of water, (bio- and toxic) waste treatment, and electricity is handled by others (e.g. different service providers such as energy companies). A part from providing a specific service to a household or building complex, such as water or electricity, the interaction between a house owner and a service provider is sparse. If one or many of such services would be turned off (for example due to an invoice not being paid on time) or interrupted due to a system failure there are no backup systems that can guarantee the home-based care (at least for a longer period of time). Wireless and wired communication can also be interrupted due to for example interruptions in the provision of electricity. The effect on care situations that a loss of IP-connectivity can have has been publically discussed concerning emergency calls using Voice over IP (VoIP) to national emergency numbers such as 911/112. Government bodies such as the US Federal Communication Commission (FCC) have even published consumer guides to inform about the effect of VoIP-connectivity and care-critical services. The FCC guide state that VoIP consumers must be informed about the limitations with VoIP regarding emergency calls and that such calls may not work due to for example Internet Quality of Service (QoS) related problems [67]. However, IP connectivity issues and IP QoS and their impact on home-based care have not been brought to public attention at any larger scale.

Today more and more advanced medical care is provided in people's home and can involve both critical waste and complex equipment. The regulations that normally are applied to workplace contexts now have to be implemented in private home-environments. For example may storage space in the home need to be built to keep oxygen tubes or toxic waste in a safe way. According to the Swedish regulation AFS 1998:7 oxygen tubes and spare tubes should be placed close to the entrance, which is also the place where older adults may have their outdoor wheel walker or a chair they can use when they put their shoes on. Cancer treatment with cytostatic in the home is a wonderful development in medical care giving the patient a much better comfort in a complicated treatment and can help reduce some of a stress that can emerge from living with this condition. But the medical waste is dangerous for the care personnel involved in the treatment and for the personnel responsible to handle the waste. It takes careful packaging, sealing and handling of such material. This is applicable both in the home and during the transportation of waste from the home. While we can expect home nurses or other care personnel to follow rules and legislations, unsupervised care interventions done by the patient may result in for example bio-waste that is not satisfactorily handled from a society perspective. In a report from the central hospital in Linköping, Sweden, the risks and challenges that follows with more and more advanced home care of home based patients has been analysed [68]. One important result from the Linköping study is the fact that in the home there is not really any control of vital infrastructure such as water, electricity and communication. The report states that "Staying in a home without electricity or water is not reasonable for any longer times. We believe that a sick person needs to be moved to a secure accommodation within a half to a day" (ibid). The fact is that it is not only medical devices that need electricity; electric wheelchairs, beds and lifts may all need power to operate. So even if the medical device itself is powered by battery this will not necessary mean that the apartment is possible to use as a place for care during for example a power failure.

From both a national and local community perspective there are also other issues to consider. For example do parts of the medication we consume leave the body together with the urine (i.e. excretion). At the hospital medication waste and medication remains in the urine can be extracted through sewage filters, but that is seldom the case in our private homes where the water closet transmits these substances directly to the waste water treatment plant. As a direct consequence, medication remains are nowadays found in both the ground- and surface water [69].

We can expect several conflicts in the future between demands related to storage and handling of medical equipment and our perception of the home. Indeed, the transition of care from the hospital to the home must be done in a way that complies with both legislations and the private sphere.

2.3.2.4 Challenge 4: Heterogeneity of Care Providers

The demographic change has led to a growing prevalence of informal or family-based care [70]. As a consequence of the increasing level of homecare in society, family-based care can be expected to continue to grow. Non-professional care at home have been regarded as a way for society to save money [9] while it also have shown to provide families with a much higher quality of life (ibid). Both formal and informal collaboration normally take place between for example family members of a referred older adult and municipality care workers. However, as stated by Bødker and Grönvall, on neither side of the family-municipality collaboration there is a simple and open relationship; families are complicated as are municipal bureaucracies [8]. Indeed, both possibilities and conflicts may arise as professional and informal care providers enter the care receiver's home with different stances, roles and time rhythms to collaborate around the care of a person [55].

At the hospital or other care institutions there are mainly one group of care providers; professional caregivers (such as physicians, nurses and physiotherapists). At home, these actors are supplemented by home care workers and home care nurses. Furthermore, at home there may also be a mix of both professional and informal care providers. Indeed, a part from the mentioned professional care workers, the home may also embrace informal care providers such as next of kin, close friends and neighbors. All these diverse actors have different relationships and roles in respect to the care receiver. While diverse actors' roles and the internal relationships between members of the care network have previously been discussed [55], it is evident that these actors have different temporal rhythms, stances and relationships to the care receiver and there is a de-facto division of labor between the diverse care actors [63]. For example, a home care worker may visit ten different clients a day and handle both cleaning, care and intimate hygiene while a close relative usually provide simpler household tasks such as shopping and cleaning. A close relative may act out of love or a perceived need to 'pay back' for care received during childhood while the professional care worker perform a paid labor [55, 71]. Potential conflicts do exists between these diverse care providers and their roles [63]. To safeguard one's personal health, care workers often try to retain a professional stance, or distance, to the care receiver and the care receivers family [63]. Family members providing care of a loved one may care for just that one person. They act out of love rather than a professional stance and may hence lack proper care training and insight in the professional care workers routines, laws and possibilities. Similarly, the professional care worker is 'trapped' in a professional role with a tight schedule and the need to care for many people throughout a day. Designers of home-based healthcare should hence acknowledge both professional and informal care providers, their relations and needs in relation to the care receiver.

Another aspect to consider in home-based care designs is that both informal caregivers and the majority of frontline long-term care workers are women [72] and caring for someone (as a professional or informal care provider) is not always an easy burden to carry. Sequeira reports that caregivers of older people with dementia are more vulnerable due to their higher levels of burden, which are associated with higher levels of difficulties and reduced sources of satisfaction [73]. It has also been noted that informal caregivers experiences problems with mental health and social participation [74]. For example can informal caregivers of relatives with dementia experience depressive symptoms [75, 76]. To acknowledge and cater for diverse care providers and their needs could prove important in future healthcare designs. We must not only design to allow diverse care providers to deliver care in terms of using a specific care technology, but we should also consider designing for the care providers' potential need of physiological support.

2.3.2.5 Challenge 5: Mobility

When people are outside of the hospital they do other things than being 'ill'. People go to work, visit friends and travel. For the person undergoing a treatment and society at large, it is important both from an economic and social perspective that the person can return to work as fast as possible. This is mere two reasons why it would be preferred if technology for treatments and cures could sustain care activities outside of the home. Indeed, many illnesses and rehabilitations do not require people 'per se' to remain at home or in another fixed location. If healthcare technologies were developed to allow a person to bring (also parts of) the required healthcare technology to work and diverse leisure activities, a higher freedom could be achieved while lowering stigmatization and isolation for the patient. One could argue that a continuous and active participation in different activities and in the society at large is a democratic perspective that should not be considered irrelevant when designing for non-institutionalized care.

To make care technology transportable is naturally a fundamental aspect to support mobility during treatments. There are many examples of current care solutions, for example within rehabilitation [77, 78] that are rather stationary in their setup.

However, there are other concerns that could be important to consider when designing for the integration of non-clinical treatments in a person's everyday life. A less thought of difficulty that could be handled in the design of healthcare technologies is that different countries have different protocols, standards (e.g. radio bandwidth) and legislations that challenge a 'lawful' roaming of care technologies between different locations. If healthcare technologies were designed to support different national standards and legislations, healthcare technology could more easily be brought along on business trips and vacations.

A current topic is social alarms and their transition from analogue to digital communication protocols. In Sweden the government has given the Swedish Institute of Assistive Technology (SIAT) the assignment to study the future of social alarms. The assignment was to "implement development and information activities to support municipalities in strengthening security in security alarm services in connection with the ongoing technology shift to Internet-based technologies (IP) in the telecommunications sector" [79]. The assignment lead to the development of a Swedish standard for how social alarm communicates called SCAIP, which is an abbreviation of Social Care Alarm Internet Protocol. This protocol will make it possible to select a social alarm system without having to check whether a specific call centre can receive the signals from the alarm terminal or not. With traditional social alarms today this cannot be done. When buying a new social alarm today, one must first know which call centre will receive the alarm, and then buy the proper alarm according to that call centre's specification. Furthermore, if the alarm operator is replaced by a new procurement it may be that the new call centre uses another protocol and consequently, all the alarms must be replaced or modified. Also, a user of social alarms can in most cases not use the alarm outdoors. The municipality social responsibility is limited to the apartment and does not cover an outside stay.

But today users are used to GSM and 3G telephones which can be brought to almost any country with full functionality. Some people also live a very mobile life that takes them both to other parts of the country and abroad. It is a natural step forward, for example within the EU, to allow social alarm users to also use their social alarms anywhere, at least in Europe. This is not blocked by technology at first but by local laws and regulations in diverse countries and practical arrangements how to handle these 'roaming' users of social alarms. But it has not yet promoted an EU standard protocol for social alarms. Still, this is also on the agenda and SIAT has an assignment versus the EU commission to present a standard protocol for social alarms [80].

Since the market for assistive devices is not expanding very fast, many small companies are trying to introduce systems based on proprietary protocols, which in itself will lead to difficulties for users to incorporate more than one system in the home. Accordingly, the only way to develop sustainable products within the field of homecare technologies is to look at the global market and more open standards and protocols.

2.3.2.6 Challenge 6: Installation and Maintenance

A number of HCI research projects have investigated functionality, use and effect of diverse pervasive healthcare solutions targeting private homes (e.g. [19, 55, 61, 81]). However, few HCI design projects have reported on non-functional requirements such as how to install a solution in a private person's home (exceptions include for example: [39, 44]). While focusing on usability concerns like interface design, the HCI research field to a large extent has not reported on usability issues related to the installation and maintenance of home-based healthcare technologies.

The installation of consumer electronics and household appliances is by many people perceived as cumbersome. DVD players, stereos and computers are all examples of technologies that many people find complicated to install and configure. Many home-based healthcare technologies have a similar minimum complexity in setup and installation as these above-mentioned consumer products; they may require Internet connectivity, a connection to the TV or other existing technology and mains power or batteries to function properly.

We argue that it would be beneficial, also from a design research perspective, to extend the research-field of technology acceptance and usability to explicitly include also the installation and maintenance of everyday healthcare technologies. To challenge research-based healthcare designs by including also easy installation and maintenance requirements in the design work could allow researchers to evaluate, from a more holistic perspective and over time, the value of a particular healthcare design.

2.3.2.7 Challenge 7: Training and Learning

Home care technology that exist in private peoples' homes range from simple devices such as blood sugar level (glucose) monitoring devices to systems to sustain for example complicated cancer treatments and blood dialysis. With a more wide-spread use of home-based treatments one cannot expect that either professional or informal care providers can keep up to pace with the technological development and the rather advanced technology that may enter into the home. At the hospital, a given number of people handle a specific kind of technology or perform certain activities (e.g. blood analysis or x-rays). This defined set of people hence work with a technology over time and it is predefined that they will handle a specific type of technology. As care move into private peoples' homes and the main responsibility of a patient, treatment and handling of advanced apparatus is transferred from the hospital to a municipality or general practitioners office, the number of people in need of training increases. When informal care providers, such as family and friends get involved in the day to day care—further people, also without a formal healthcare training, may have to operate advanced healthcare technologies. Economic drawbacks within the healthcare sector can also put less emphasis on dedicated training sessions, favouring situated learning, both for professional and informal care providers. Furthermore does homecare work represent a work domain with a high turn-around number of employees and where many people work extra to finance their studies etc. Short-term or time-limited work situations challenge how structured training for all care workers within a homecare organization can take place. Also new members of a care network, such as a vacation substitute care worker should be able to use and benefit from existing machinery when visiting a particular client. New healthcare designs for non-clinical settings may consider in-activity learning support for both professional and informal actors as a strategy to work-around the above mentioned issues while still provide training and ensure that people can operate assistive care systems distributed throughout a home.

Earlier non-healthcare projects have examined 'sandbox' use of technology, for example in private-municipality communication and collaboration [82]. A sandbox provides a 'safe space' for experimentation within a system-in-use. To be able to experiment with functionality and try out different use scenarios and be able to discover the answer to 'what if'-questions may not only demystify the care technology but also promote learning. How experimentation and learning during use can be done within a healthcare context still has to be investigated, but if possible from a patient safety and legislation perspective, one fruitful strategy could be to allow heterogeneous users with diverse background and formal training to use and interact meaningfully with healthcare technology.

2.4 Open Problems

This chapter has on a high level introduced and discussed a set of challenges that is important to consider and reflect upon when designing the home as a place for care. The presented seven challenges were: (1) Appropriation, (2) Aspects of control in multi-site healthcare scenarios, (3) Societal concerns, (4) Heterogeneity of care providers, (5) Mobility, (6) Installation and maintenance, and (7) Training and Learning. While not being directly related to a system's technological or medical functionality, these challenges should still be seen as aspects relevant to consider for developing future, sustainable home-based healthcare systems and services. One interesting point is how ICT-based care services influences the home environment and can transform it into a care institution [83]. It is therefore important to provide users with systems that support their perceived needs and that empower them [20].

The authors' perspective on Pervasive healthcare development is that it can be beneficial for researchers to know about, consider, and explore a wider set of 'non-functional-related' aspects of home-based care in their design work than currently is being done. The seven challenges discussed in this chapter represent examples of such 'non-functional-related' aspects. As the use of ICT is expected to increase in the future, there are additional aspects which need to be considered as new services are introduced insofar they challenge the traditional beacons of healthcare ethics and values [84, 85].

How we build homes, ranging from apartment buildings to single-family houses, also influence how care can enter into peoples' homes. A building is rarely built to function only for a few years. Rather, it is not uncommon that a building is used for 30–100 years. Therefore, and in combination with people's mobility (we change jobs, move to new locations, etc.) it is not uncommon that a building or apartment has many different people living in it, and at very different stages of their lives. At different levels, a building adapts to its current inhabitants and their needs [86, 87]. However, this adaptation is often limited, based on some technical constraints, existing building materials and the inhabitants' economy. It may however be difficult to foresee needs that may follow from illness or aging. Therefore it could be beneficial if (residential) buildings were designed with care in mind and those emerging needs that may follow from illness and aging (e.g. large door posts to allow a wheelchair to easily move from one room to another). Today it is not uncommon that people move from a house or apartment, where they have lived for many years and where they have their friends nearby, to another living location only because their original living location could not support some emergent needs and requirements as they age. Furthermore, the home as such is also just one node in a larger system of infrastructure- and service-providers such as water and electricity providers and municipalities. Additionally, there are also regional concerns, national laws, regulations and interests to consider.

One thing that has not been included in our discussion on design so far, but still is a most important problem, is how to keep the cost of assistive devices to be implemented in the home at a reasonable level. The total cost of installing much research-based solutions in a home-setting is often far too high and hence will never reach the beneficiaries. This aspect must be included in the design process and the cost effects of different design choices evaluated as a part of the research outcome.

As we design for home-based care, we should also reflect on the methodological stance we apply. Within for example the HCI community there is a long tradition of using different co-design approaches, lead-users and Participatory Design methods when developing novel technology. As this chapter has presented, the diverse set of challenges present when designing for the home as a place for care makes us question who should be part of a cooperative design process and whose interests must be safe-guarded. Instead of limiting the represented partners in the home-based healthcare design process, it might be beneficial to bring in the municipality as a partner, not (only) to have access to municipality home care workers or other care professionals but to understand and design for data-safety (legislations) and environmental laws. Lawyers with specific environmental expertise, city plan offices, architects and infrastructure service providers may represent other relevant design-partners when we design future, sustainable home-based care services. There is also an issue of how we test and evaluate the impact of home-based care services. Within HCI, there has been a move away from lab-testing towards testing 'in the wild' [88]. As a middle ground there are also so called 'living labs' where technologies can be tested in a 'close to real' context. It should be stressed that private homes as a setting for healthcare design is very heterogeneous and so is its inhabitants [44]. While living labs are purposefully built to function as labs, most private homes are not [87]. As a consequence, and to truly understand the large-scale impact of a home-based care design we must favor so called 'in the wild' testing. To understand the impact a specific service or technology have on society, to allow for appropriation and to see how use and behavioral change over time we should also initiate tests and evaluations over longer time periods. We further suggest that care providers, and house and apartment owners make mutual check lists on prerequisites needed to handle risks, logistics, infrastructures and backup systems to minimize failures or the impact of failures. Next step is to understand how different aspects relate to each and every-ones responsibility. All this must be anchored in legislations and laws.

The authors perspective on the issues presented in this chapter is that these issues represent 'the next step' when designing for, and conducting research within, the ever-growing field of home-based healthcare.

2.5 Future Outlook

It is clear that there are many possibilities with care at home and many possibilities for ICT to support such home-based care. However, as presented in this chapter there are numerous challenges in implementing care at home. Some challenges might be, at a first glance, easily overlooked by HCI researchers. Such challenges extend usability and fundamental technological issues like data resolution and data integrity when transferring data between the home and a hospital.

To better understand the challenges presented in this chapter, and to identify other relevant challenges in designing the home as a place for care, much more work and practical experience is needed. As noted in the Open Problems section above, architecture and how future homes will be designed and built represents only one area of future interest. Another example topic that would be relevant to investigate further is cloud-services and patient-integrity as data in theory can be located in different countries that have diverse privacy laws. Also, to investigate trans-national infrastructures to support safe and lawful translocation of patients and their care services is another field that deserves further research attention.

The authors will continue to work with projects examining how to design better home-based healthcare solutions and what impact and consequences healthcare ICT can have on patients, their private homes, care givers and society at large. The authors also like to develop more clear guidelines and strategies for designers to help them to limit the impact of the challenges discussed throughout this chapter. Finally, we see the education of researchers, healthcare professionals, patients, government bodies, policy-makers, politicians and IT developers as an important vehicle for change, and we hope to contribute to this area through further research and dissemination of our work.

Finally we would like to emphasize the novelty we introduce in in this chapter namely the connection between two of the most important societal challenges the world is facing right now: the demographic development and the environment. Here we try to show that they are linked through primarily the care moving from the hospital into the home, which also will be much more common in the future. The environmental consequences must be taken into consideration when designing the home as a place for care.

Acknowledgments The authors would like to thank the reviewers and the editors of this book. We would also like to thank everybody that in different ways have contributed to this book chapter. We also like to thank Morten Kyng and Aarhus University where one of the authors was employed while developing a part of this book chapter.

References

1. Hillcoat-Nalletamby, S., Ogg, J., Renaut, S., & Bonvalet, C. (2010). Ageing populations and housing needs: comparing strategic policy discourses in france and england. *Social Policy and Administration, 44*(7), 808–26. doi:10.1111/j.1467-9515.2010.00745.x.
2. Lang, A. (2010). There's no place like home: research, practice and policy perspectives regarding safety in homecare. *International Journal for Quality in Health Care, 22*(2), 75–7. doi:10.1093/intqhc/mzq007.
3. Rodriguez, M. J., Arredondo, M. T., del Pozo, F., Gomez, E. J., Martinez, A., & Dopico, A. A. (1994, Sept). Home Telecare Management System. In *Computers in Cardiology* (Vols. 25–28, pp. 433–436). doi:10.1109/CIC.1994.470152
4. Gesano, G., Heins, F., & Naldini, A. (2009). *Regional challenges in the perspective of 2020–regional desparities and future challenges*. Roma: ISMERI Europa.
5. Randell, R., Wilson, S., Woodward, P., & Galliers, J. (2010). Beyond handover: supporting awareness for continuous coverage. *Cognition, Technology and Work, 12*(4), 271–83. doi:10.1007/s10111-010-0138-3.
6. Pabllo, C., Soto, R., & Campos, J. (2008). *Mobile medication administration system: Application and architecture*. Paper presented at the Proceedings of the 2008 Euro American Conference on Telematics and Information Systems, Aracaju, Brazil, Sept 10–12.
7. Dalgaard, L. G., Grönvall, E., & Verdezoto, N. (2013). Accounting for medication particularities: Designing for everyday medication management. In *7th International Conference on Pervasive Computing Technologies for Healthcare (PervasiveHealth)*, Venice, 5–8 May 2013.
8. Bødker, S., & Grönvall, E. (2013). Calendars: time coordination and overview in families and beyond. In O. W. Bertelsen, L. Ciolfi, M. A. Grasso, G. A. Papadopoulos (Eds.), *ECSCW 2013: Proceedings of the 13th European Conference on Computer Supported Cooperative Work* (pp. 63–81), 21–25 Sept 2013, Paphos, Cyprus: Springer. doi:10.1007/978-1-4471-5346-7_4
9. Zhang, H. Y., Cocosila, M., & Archer, N. (2010). Factors of adoption of mobile information technology by homecare nurses a technology acceptance model 2 approach. *Cin-Computers Informatics Nursing, 28*(1), 49–56. doi:10.1097/NCN.0b013e3181c0474a.
10. Mamykina, L., Bardram, J. E., Korhonen, I., Mynatt, E., & Pratt, W. (2004). *HCI and homecare: Connecting families and clinicians*. Paper presented at the CHI '04 Extended Abstracts on Human Factors in Computing Systems, Vienna.
11. Ziefle, M., Röcker, C., & Holzinger, A. (2014). Current trends and challenges for pervasive health technologies: From technical innovation to user integration. In M. Ziefle, C. Röcker,& A. Holzinger (Eds.), *Pervasive Health: State-of-the-Art & Beyond* (pp. 1–18). London: Springer.
12. Lundberg, S. (2013). The results from a two-year case study of an information and communication technology support system for family caregivers. *Disability and Rehabilitation: Assistive Technology*. 1–6. doi:10.3109/17483107.2013.814170.
13. Chan, M., Campo, E., Estève, D., & Fourniols, J.-Y. (2009). Smart homes—current features and future perspectives. *Maturitas, 64*(2), 90–7. doi:10.1016/j.maturitas.2009.07.014.
14. Palen, L., & Aaløkke, S. (2006). Of pill boxes and piano benches: Home-made methods for managing medication. In *Proceedings of the 2006 20th Anniversary Conference on Computer Supported Cooperative Work* (p. 88). Banff, Alberta: ACM Press .doi:10.1145/1180875.1180888
15. Kristensen, M., Kyng, M., & Palen, L. (2006). *Participatory design in emergency medical service: Designing for future practice*. Paper presented at the Proceedings of the SIGCHI Conference on Human Factors in Computing Systems (Vol. 11). Montreal, Quebec.

16. Balaam, M., Egglestone, SR., Fitzpatrick, G., Rodden, T., Hughes, A-M., Wilkinson, A., et al. (2011). *Motivating mobility: Designing for lived motivation in stroke rehabilitation*. Paper presented at the Proceedings of the SIGCHI Conference on Human Factors in Computing Systems, Vancouver, BC.
17. Axelrod, L., Fitzpatrick, G., Burridge, J., Mawson, S., Smith, P., Rodden, T., et al. (2009). The reality of homes fit for heroes: design challenges for rehabilitation technology at home. *Journal of Assistive Technologies*, *3*(2), 9. doi:10.1108/17549450200900014.
18. Egglestone, SR., Axelrod, L., Nind, T., Turk, R., Wilkinson, A., & Burridge, J., et al. (2009). A design framework for a home-based stroke rehabilitation system: Identifying the key components. Paper presented at the 3rd International Conference on Pervasive Computing Technologies for Healthcare. PervasiveHealth 2009, London, 1–3 April 2009.
19. Mynatt, E. D., Rowan, J., Craighill, S., & Jacobs, A. (2001). *Digital family portraits: Supporting peace of mind for extended family members*. Paper presented at the Proceedings of the SIGCHI conference on Human factors in computing systems, Seattle, Washington.
20. Milligan, C., Roberts, C., & Mort, M. (2011). Telecare and older people: who cares where? *Social Science & Medicine*, *72*(3), 347–54. doi:10.1016/j.socscimed.2010.08.014.
21. Biswal, S. (2013). Liquid biomedical waste management: An emerging concern for physicians. Muller Journal of Medical Sciences and Research, *4*(2), 99–106. doi:10.4103/0975-9727.118238.
22. Jonsson, O. (2013). Digitala trygghetslarm (Vols. 2012–13326). Swedish Institute of Assistive Technology.
23. Ballegaard, S. A., Hansen, T. R., Kyng, M. (2008). *Healthcare in everyday life: Designing healthcare services for daily life*. Paper presented at the Proceeding of the Twenty-Sixth Annual SIGCHI Conference on Human Factors in Computing Systems, Florence, 5–10 April.
24. Korhonen, I., Parkka, J., & Van Gils, M. (2003). Health monitoring in the home of the future. *Engineering in Medicine and Biology Magazine, IEEE*, *22*(3), 66–73. doi:10.1109/MEMB.2003.1213628.
25. Mort, M., May, C. R., & Williams, T. (2003). Remote doctors and absent patients: acting at a distance in telemedicine? *Science, Technology & Human Values*, *28*(2), 274–95. doi:10.1177/0162243902250907.
26. Grönvall, E., & Kyng, M. (2011). *Beyond Utopia: Reflections on participatory design in home-based healthcare with weak users*. Paper presented at the Proceedings of the 29th Annual European Conference on Cognitive Ergonomics, Rostock.
27. Cartwright, L. (2000). Reach out and heal someone: telemedicine and the globalization of health care. *Health*, *4*(3), 347–7. doi:10.1177/136345930000400306.
28. Andersen, T., Bjørn, P., Kensing, F., & Moll, J. (2011). Designing for collaborative interpretation in telemonitoring: re-introducing patients as diagnostic agents. *International Journal of Medical Informatics*, *80*(8), e112–26. doi:10.1016/j.ijmedinf.2010.09.010.
29. Taylor, A., Aitken, A., Godden, D., & Colligan, J. (2011). *Group pulmonary rehabilitation delivered to the home via the internet: Feasibility and patient perception*. Paper presented at the Proceedings of the SIGCHI Conference on Human Factors in Computing Systems, Vancouver, BC.
30. Steele, R., & Lo, A. (2009). Future personal health records as a foundation for computational health. *Computational Science and Its Applications-ICCSA*, *2009*, 719–33.
31. Owen, T., Buchanan, G., & Thimbleby, H. (2012). *Understanding user requirements in take-home diabetes management technologies*. Paper presented at the Proceedings of the 26th Annual BCS Interaction Specialist Group Conference on People and Computers, Birmingham.
32. Aarhus, R., Ballegaard, S., & Hansen, T. (2009). The eDiary: bridging home and hospital through healthcare technology. In I. Wagner, H. Tellioğlu, E. Balka, C. Simone, L. Ciolfi (Eds.) ECSCW 2009 (pp. 63–83). London: Springer. doi:10.1007/978-1-84882-854-4_4
33. Gupta, S., Chang, P., Anyigbo, N., & Sabharwal, A. (2011). *mobileSpiro: accurate mobile spirometry for self-management of asthma*. Paper presented at the Proceedings of the First ACM Workshop on Mobile Systems, Applications, and Services for Healthcare, Seattle, Washington.

34. Bardram, J. E., Frost, M., Szántó, K., & Marcu, G. (2012). *The MONARCA self-assessment system: A persuasive personal monitoring system for bipolar patients*. Paper presented at the Proceedings of the 2nd ACM SIGHIT International Health Informatics Symposium, Miami, Florida.
35. Arnrich, B., Mayora, O., Bardram, J., & Tröster, G. (2010). Pervasive healthcare: paving the way for a pervasive, user-centered and preventive healthcare model. *Methods of information in medicine, 49*(1), 67–73. doi:10.3414/ME09-02-0044.
36. Mort, M., Finch, T., & May, C. (2009). Making and unmaking telepatients. *Science, Technology & Human Values, 34*(1), 9–33. doi:10.1177/0162243907311274.
37. Grönvall, E., & Kyng, M. (2013). On participatory design of home-based healthcare. *Cognition, Technology & Work, 15*(4), 389–401. doi:10.1007/s10111-012-0226-7.
38. Milligan, C. (2009). *There's no place like home: Place and care in an ageing society*. Farnham: Ashgate Publishing.
39. Grönvall, E., & Kyng, M. (2012). On participatory design of home-based healthcare. In Cognition, Technology & Work (pp. 1–13). doi:10.1007/s10111-012-0226-7
40. Aarhus, R., Grönvall, E., & Kyng, M. (2010). *Challenges in participation: Users and their roles in the development of home-based pervasive healthcare applications*. Paper presented at the 4th International ICST Conference on Pervasive Computing Technologies for Healthcare 2010, Munich, 22–25 March.
41. Mulder, I., Schikhof, Y., Vastenburg, M., Card, A., Dunn, T., Komninos, A., et al. (2009). Designing with care: the future of pervasive healthcare. *Pervasive Computing, IEEE, 8*(4), 85–8. doi:10.1109/mprv.2009.71.
42. Lang, A., Macdonald, M., Storch, J., Elliott, K., Stevenson, L., Lacroix, H., et al. (2009). Home care safety perspectives from clients, family members, caregivers and paid providers. *Healthcare Quarterly, 12*, 97–101.
43. Lang, A., Edwards, N., & Fleiszer, A. (2008). Safety in home care: a broadened perspective of patient safety. *International Journal for Quality in Health Care, 20*(2), 130–5. doi:10.1093/intqhc/mzm068.
44. Grönvall, E., & Verdezoto, N. (2013). Beyond self-monitoring: Understanding non-functional aspects of home-based healthcare technology. In *UbiComp 2013: The 2013 ACM international Joint Conference on Pervasive and Ubiquitous Computing*, Zurich, 8–12 Sept 2013.
45. Bødker, S., Ehn, P., Kammersgaard, J., Kyng, M., & Sundblad, Y. (1987). A utopian experience. In *Proceedings of the 1986 Conference on Computers and Democracy* (pp. 251–278).
46. Kyng, M. (2010). Bridging the gap between politics and techniques: on the next practices of participatory design. *Scandinavian Journal of Information Systems, 22*(1), 49–68.
47. Clemensen, J., Larsen, S. B., Kyng, M., & Kirkevold, M. (2007). Participatory design in health sciences: using cooperative experimental methods in developing health services and computer technology. *Qualitative Health Research, 17*(1), 122–30. doi:10.1177/1049732306293664.
48. Piccini, L., Ciani, O., Grönvall, E., Marti, P., & Andreoni, G. (2008) New monitoring approach for neonatal intensive care unit. In *5th International Workshop on Wearable Micro and Nanosystems for Personalized Health* (p. 6), Valencia, 21–23 May 2008.
49. Lanzi, P., Marti, P., Pozzi, S., & Scrivani, P. (2004). *Users as cultural mediators in interactive system design*. Paper presented at the XII European Conference on Cognitive Ergonomics, York, September.
50. Grönvall, E., Conci, M., Giusti, L., & Leonardi, C. (2010). *The intrinsic fragility of elderly care networks: Five challenges in participatory design practices*. Paper presented at the Therapeutic Strategies - a Challenge for User Involvement in Design—one day workshop at NordiCHI 2010, Reykjavik, 17 Oct 2010.
51. Wagner, S., & Toftegaard, T. S. (2011). Bertelsen OW Increased data quality in home blood pressure monitoring through context awareness. In *5th International Conference on Pervasive Computing Technologies for Healthcare (PervasiveHealth), 2011* (pp 234–237). 23–26 May 2011.
52. Deutsch, J., Borbely, M., Filler, J., Huhn, K., & Guarrera-Bowlby, P. (2008). Use of a low-cost, commercially available gaming console (wii) for rehabilitation of an adolescent with cerebral palsy. *Physical Therapy, 88*(10), 1196–207. doi:10.2522/?ptj.20080062.

53. Turner, K. J. (2014). Managing telehealth and telecare. In *Pervasive Health: State-of-the-Art & Beyond* (pp. 157–180). New York: Springer.
54. Ward-Griffin, C., & McKeever, P. (2000). Relationships between nurses and family caregivers: Partners in care? *Advances in Nursing Science*, *22*(3): 89–103.
55. Bossen, C., Christensen, L. R., Gronvall, E., & Vestergaard, L. S. (2013). Carecoor: augmenting the coordination of cooperative home care work. *International Journal of Medical Informatics*, *82*(5), e189–199. doi:10.1016/j.ijmedinf.2012.10.005.
56. Balka, E., Wagner, I. (2006). *Making things work: Dimensions of configurability as appropriation work.* Paper presented at the Proceedings of the 2006 20th Anniversary Conference on Computer Supported Cooperative Work, Banff, Alberta.
57. Dix, A. (2007). *Designing for appropriation.* Paper presented at the Proceedings of the 21st British HCI Group Annual Conference on People and Computers: HCI...but not as we know it—Volume 2, University of Lancaster, United Kingdom.
58. Carroll, J., Howard, S., Vetere, F., Peck, J., & Murphy, J. (2001). Identity, power and fragmentation in cyberspace: Technology appropriation by young people. In *ACIS 2001, the 12th Australasian Conference on Information Systems* (pp. 95–102), AISNET, Coffs Harbour.
59. Petersen, M. G., Iversen, O. S., Krogh, P. G., & Ludvigsen, M. (2004). *Aesthetic interaction: A pragmatist's aesthetics of interactive systems.* Paper presented at the Proceedings of the 5th Conference on Designing Interactive Systems: Processes, Practices, Methods, and Techniques, Cambridge, MA.
60. McCarthy, J., & Wright, P. (2004). *Technology as Experience*. Boston: MIT Press.
61. Grönvall, E., Kramp, G. (2011). *LinkLights: A modular, user adaptable system to support rehabilitation practices.* Paper presented at the Proceedings of the 4th International Conference on PErvasive Technologies Related to Assistive Environments, Heraklion, Crete.
62. Seo, K., & Ryu, H. (2014). *RehabMaster*™*': a pervasive rehabilitation platform for stroke patients and their caregivers.* In Pervasive Health: State-of-the-Art & Beyond (p. 30). New York: Springer.
63. Christensen, L. R., & Grönvall, E. (2011). Challenges and opportunities for collaborative technologies for home care work. In S. Bødker, N. O. Bouvin, V. Wulf, L. Ciolfi, & W. Lutters (Eds.) *ECSCW 2011: Proceedings of the 12th European Conference on Computer Supported Cooperative Work* (pp. 61–80), 24–28 Sept 2011, Aarhus Denmark. London: Springer. doi:10.1007/978-0-85729-913-0_4
64. Alonzo, A. A. (1979). Everyday illness behavior: a situational approach to health status deviations. *Social Science & Medicine Part A: Medical Psychology & Medical Sociology*, *13*, 397–404. doi:10.1016/0271-7123(79)90074-9.
65. Strauss, A. (1985). Work and the division of labor. *Sociological Quarterly*, *26*(1), 1–19. doi:10.1111/j.1533-8525.1985.tb00212.x.
66. WHO. (2003). *Adherence to long-term therapies*. Evidence for action: World Health Organization.
67. FCC (2012). VoIP and 911 Service. FCC. Retrieved March 20, 2013 from http://transition.fcc.gov/cgb/consumerfacts/voip911.pdf.
68. Li, Östergötland. (2002). *Informationsteknik i sjukvård och sjukvårdsanläggningar*. Linköping: Landstinget.
69. Sayadi, M. H., Trivedy, R. K., & Pathak, R. K. (2010). Pollution of pharmaceuticals in environment. *Journal of Industrial Pollution Control Paper*, *1*, 89–94.
70. Glendinning, C. (2003). *Support for carers of older people, some international and national comparisons*. London: Audit Commission.
71. Schulz, E., (2010). The long-term care system for the elderly in denmark. ENEPRI Research, Report, Vol. 73.
72. Robyn, I., Stone, R. I., & Wiener, J. M. (2001). Who will care for us? addressing the long-term care workforce crisis. The Urban Institute and the American Association of Homes and Services for the Aging. http://www.urban.org/publications/310304.html.
73. Sequeira, C. (2013). Difficulties, coping strategies, satisfaction and burden in informal portuguese caregivers. *Journal of Clinical Nursing*, *22*(3–4), 491–500. doi:10.1111/jocn.12108.

74. George, L. K., & Gwyther, L. P. (1986). Caregiver weil-being: a multidimensional examination of family caregivers of demented adults. *The Gerontologist, 26*(3), 253–9. doi:10.1093/geront/26.3.253.
75. Ornstein, K. A., Gaugler, J. E., Devanand, D. P., Scarmeas, N., Zhu, C. W., & Stern, Y. (2013). Are there sensitive time periods for dementia caregivers? the occurrence of behavioral and psychological symptoms in the early stages of dementia. *International Psychogeriatrics, 25*(9), 1453–62. doi:10.1017/S1041610213000768.
76. Thomas, P., Lalloué, F., Preux, P.-M., Hazif-Thomas, C., Pariel, S., Inscale, R., et al. (2006). Dementia patients caregivers quality of life: the pixel study. *International Journal of Geriatric Psychiatry, 21*(1), 50–6. doi:10.1002/gps.1422.
77. Silverfit. (2011). Silverfit. Retrieved May 30, 2011 from http://www.silverfit.nl/en/index.htm.
78. Van der Eerden, W., Otten, E., May, G., & Even-Zohar, O. (1999). CAREN-computer assisted rehabilitation environment. *Studies in Health Technology and Informatics, 62*, 373–378.
79. Hjälpmedelsinstitutet (2013). Digitala trygghetslarm–Ny teknik i nya infrastrukturer, Slutrapport. http://www.hi.se/publikationer/rapporter/digitala-trygghetslarm-ny-teknik-i-nya-infrastrukturer/
80. SIAT. (2013). European innovation partnership on active and healthy ageing. https://webgate.ec.europa.eu/eipaha/initiative/index/show/id/205.
81. Ballegaard, S. A., Bunde-Pedersen, J., & Bardram, J. E. (2006). *Where to, Roberta?: reflecting on the role of technology in assisted living*. Paper presented at the Proceedings of the 4th Nordic Conference on Human-Computer Interaction: Changing Roles, Oslo.
82. Bohøj, M., Borchorst, N. G., Bouvin, N. O., Bødker, S., & Zander, P. O. (2010). *Timeline collaboration*. Paper presented at the Proceedings of the SIGCHI Conference on Human Factors in Computing Systems, Atlanta, Georgia.
83. Papazissis, E. (2004). Advanced technology permits the provision of advanced hospital care in the patients' homes. In *E-Health: Current Situation and Examples of Implemented and Beneficial E-Health Applications* (pp. 190–199, Vol. 100). Hitchin: IOS Press.
84. Crossen-Sills, J., Toomey, I., & Doherty, M. E. (2009). Technology and home care: implementing systems to enhance aging in place. *Nursing Clinics of North America, 44*(2), 239–46. doi:10.1016/j.cnur.2009.03.003.
85. Harrefors, C., Axelsson, K., & Savenstedt, S. (2010). Using assistive technology services at differing levels of care: healthy older couples' perceptions. *Journal of Advanced Nursing, 66*(7), 1523–32. doi:10.1111/j.1365-2648.2010.05335.x.
86. Brand, S. (1995). *How buildings learn: what happens after they're built*. New York: Penguin.
87. Rodden, T., Benford, S. (2003). *The evolution of buildings and implications for the design of ubiquitous domestic environments*. Paper presented at the Proceedings of the SIGCHI Conference on Human Factors in Computing Systems, Ft. Lauderdale, Florida.
88. Rogers, Y. (2011). Interaction design gone wild: Striving for wild theory. *Interactions, 18*(4), 58–62. doi:10.1145/1978822.1978834

Further Reading

89. Bardram, J. E., et al. (2007). *Pervasive computing in healthcare*. Boca Raton: CRC Press.

Chapter 3
EHealth Applications for Those in Need: Making Novel Interaction Technologies Accessible

Martin Böcker and Matthias Schneider

3.1 Introduction

Recent experience with the introduction of novel user interface technologies shows a common pattern of addressing the requirements of older people and those with disabilities, but only significantly after the initial availability of these user interaction technologies. This pattern is common because new and sometimes disruptive technologies are usually developed for and targeted at mainstream consumers, or at narrow target groups of early adopters, the young, the wealthy, or the technology-aware. Therefore, new and/or disruptive interaction technologies rarely include easy accommodation of the requirements of people with disabilities. Subsequent measures for compensating these shortcomings are in many cases introduced late and at high cost.

Table 3.1 lists some examples of technologies deployed without appropriate consideration for the requirements of users with disabilities. In all cases, devices that could be used by disabled users such as blind people were replaced by a new generation of products that made it impossible for these users to migrate easily to the modern products.

The introduction of forthcoming applications and technologies such as ambient intelligence, ubiquitous communications and others enabled by Next Generation Networks (NGN) should not follow the same pattern, but adopt a true "Design for All" approach instead. This implies that the specific requirements of older users and users with disabilities should be taken into account prior to the large-scale introduction of

M. Böcker (✉)
Böcker und Schneider GbR,Konstanz, Germany
e-mail: boecker@humanfactors.de

M. Schneider
Böcker und Schneider GbR, München, Germany
e-mail: msch@usability-labs.de

A. Holzinger et al. (eds.), *Pervasive Health*, Human–Computer Interaction Series,
DOI: 10.1007/978-1-4471-6413-5_3, © Springer-Verlag London 2014

Table 3.1 Examples of accessibility gaps in consumer products (see also [1])

Technology	Accessibility weaknesses
Personal computer (PC)	The first PCs with character-based user interfaces were easily usable by blind users with a Braille-output device. The advent of graphical user interfaces (GUI) suddenly excluded blind users until screen readers became available
The Internet	The problems are similar to the ones described for the PC, as early communications services (e.g. gopher services and the first E-mail services) were text based and were later replaced by graphical interfaces such as web browsers. The web accessibility initiative (WAI) stepped in late, and took long to evolve compared to the very dynamic development of web technologies
Mobile phones	The user interfaces of early generations of mobile phones were based on a 12-key keypad and a number of softkeys. This type of interface, while not ideal for severely visually-impaired users, offered a higher degree of usability than the first generations of touchscreen-based smartphones without audio-feedback support
Document file formats	Documents produced in image-based versions of the PDF-format are not accessible to blind users
Digital music or media players	Many classic cassette players have mechanical switches and mechanisms that rely on the physical insertion and turning of a cassette to select different audio segments. However, modern digital music players are increasingly relying on on-screen interfaces with few, if any, physical controls to offer suitable feedback and are therefore unsuitable for people with poor eyesight. (After the introduction of MP3 players visually impaired people, for whom those devices offered limited usability, increasingly bought Minidisk devices and media before that technology became obsolete)
Biometric systems	Biometric applications are more and more used for supporting authorisation and access control. People with disabilities (e.g. physical or speech impairments) are likely to face barriers as users of these systems. Multimodality may contribute to accessibility in this field, as well as to higher levels of performance and user acceptance

such technologies. These requirements lead to provisions that should be made prior to or at the introduction of new technologies in order to meet the needs of all users.

Emerging user interaction technologies [2] almost certainly pose interaction challenges that still remain unaddressed by available standards on generic accessibility of ICT (information and communications technology) products and services. One of the reasons for this may be that certain modalities (e.g. haptic/tactile) have acquired an increasing importance in user interfaces, whereas previously they have been used mainly as a complement to other modalities (e.g. visual and auditory). Furthermore, new interaction paradigms (e.g. augmented reality) still lack a holistic analysis of their accessibility implications.

The European Commission (EC) therefore saw a need for an analysis that anticipates the demands of new interaction technologies and for the provision of appropriate guidance in the form of design guidelines. This documents in which ways users with different abilities will be affected by a new technology and how accessibility obstacles can be overcome. The result of this analysis, published as ETSI Guide EG 202 848 [1], is a set of user interface technology roadmaps and guidelines that help to ensure that novel interaction technologies are usable for the widest part of the population.

EG 202 848 addresses these and further issues, attempting to identify relevant future interaction technologies and appropriate Design for All provisions. Implementing the provisions in EG 202 848 can result in an immediate higher average revenue per user for eService providers and an increased customer base for device manufacturers. Ensuring that the needs of older users and users with disabilities are addressed in the initial release of a product or eService will avoid the additional re-development costs incurred by the need to address these requirements in later product releases.

Adapting new services and devices according to these provisions will result in inclusion of all users, regardless of their age and impairments. Delivering services and devices that are accessible from the start will empower users and strengthen their trust in their ability to master new technologies designed to improve their quality of life. In addition, switching to a new eService or device will be easier for users when the provisions in the present document are adopted.

Previous ETSI work has produced an excellent basis for educating device and eService designers about the requirements of older users and users with disabilities by illustrating design principles for barrier-free products and services. One example of the many ETSI publications on barrier-free design assembles a list of guidelines for the design of ICT products and services following a "Design for All" approach [3].

However, the current literature, including the documents published by ETSI, largely focuses on existing technologies. The developers of innovative new technologies may be unaware of these resources and, if they are, it may not be possible to apply guidance from these resources to the development of new technologies.

EG 202 848 addresses both the need for an analysis that anticipates the demands of new technologies and for the development of guidance that is suitable for these forthcoming technologies.

3.2 Glossary

In this chapter, the following terms are used with the indicated meaning:

Design for All design of products to be accessible and usable by all people, to the greatest extent possible, without the need for specialized adaptation.

eHealth remote health services including telecare services, remote health monitoring, access to patient data, remote diagnosis and electronic prescription services.

eService complete capability, including terminal equipment functions, for communication between users, systems and applications, according to agreed protocols.

eService cluster collection of multiple (electronic) services aggregating into one (joint, often more abstract) eService.

Innovation a new idea or invention that addresses existing market needs or new requirements or needs.

ETSI the European Telecommunications Standards Institute (officially recognised by the European Union as a European Standards Organisation).

ETSI Guide (EG) ETSI deliverable type used when the document contains guidance on handling of technical standardization activities, it is submitted to the whole ETSI membership for approval.

ICT information and communications technology (technologies that provide access to information through telecommunications).

TC HF the ETSI Technical Committee Human Factors, having a special responsibility to ensure that the needs of all users, including those who are older, younger or disabled, are considered in the standards making process.

User interaction technology any instrument, equipment, or technical system enabling a user to interact and communicate with a device or service.

3.3 State-of-the-Art

3.3.1 Patterns in the Introduction of Innovations

The introduction of innovations follows frequently-observed patterns. For example, the Henderson-Clark Model [4] differentiates innovations according the axes high/low impact on architectural knowledge and high/low impact on component knowledge leading to the categories of architectural, radical, incremental and modular innovations. Some of these types of innovation concern the underlying technology of the product or its design and creation and do not have a visible impact on the user experience.

More noticeable for the end user are disruptive technologies which, unlike sustained innovations, lead to the replacement of an established product (e.g. VCR) by a new type of product (e.g. hard disk recorder), requiring new knowledge on how to operate it.

Of particular relevance in the context of eHealth applications and services is the degree of "innovativeness" of end users as defined by Rogers [5]. According to him, relevant factors affecting the success of an innovation on the market are:

- *Relative advantage*: the subjective advantage of an innovation (e.g. the increase in prestige)
- *Compatibility*: the compatibility with an existing value system
- *Complexity or Simplicity*: the complexity or the experienced ease of use during the first contact
- *Trialability*: the possibility of experimenting with the innovation
- *Observability*: the extent to which an innovation is visible to others.

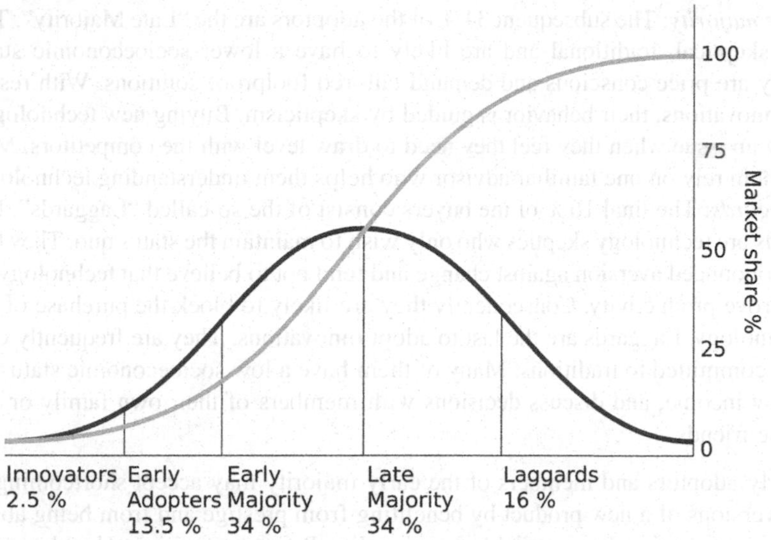

Fig. 3.1 Diffusion of innovations curve [6]

Rogers distinguishes five groups of end users according to the stage during the product life cycle at which they take up an innovative product (see also Fig. 3.1 and [5]):

- *Innovators*: The first 2.5 % of the supporters of a new product are called "Innovators". They are adventuresome and have a high level of education. They have access to various channels of information and a larger tendency to accept a risk. In addition, they are interested in technology as such and consider themselves as a source of change in their social environment. They are aware that they will possibly encounter initial problems with a new technology, but they can afford it.
- *Early adoptors*: The next 13.5 % of the buyers are "Early Adoptors". They are social leaders, popular and educated. They are visionaries on their market and interested in adapting and using new technologies in order to achieve a revolutionary breakthrough that offers them a clear competitive advantage. Early Adoptors are attracted by projects with high risks and high return, and they are not particularly price conscious if the new technology offers a better position in competition. Usually they request personalized solutions and a competent support from the manufacturer.
- *Early majority*: About 34 % of the buyers form the group of the "Early Majority". They have many informal social contacts and are more interested in evolutionary than revolutionary technical developments. Three principles guide their decisions: (1) "When it is time to move, let's all move together". (2) "When we choose a seller who leads us to a new paradigm, let's all choose the same one". (3) "Once the change begins, we believe that the sooner you notice it, the better". These principles explain why change is happening fast for these customers.

- *Late majority*: The subsequent 34 % of the adoptors are the "Late Majority". They are skeptical, traditional and are likely to have a lower socioeconomic status. They are price conscious and demand tailored foolproof solutions. With respect to innovations, their behavior is guided by skepticism. Buying new technology is only an issue when they feel they need to draw level with the competitors. Many of them rely on one familiar advisor who helps them understanding technology.
- *Laggards*: The final 16 % of the buyers consist of the so-called "Laggards". Laggards are technology skeptics who only wish to maintain the status quo. They have a pronounced aversion against change and tend not to believe that technology can improve productivity. Consequently they are likely to block the purchase of new technology. Laggards are the last to adopt innovations. They are frequently older and committed to traditions. Many of them have a low socioeconomic status and a low income, and discuss decisions with members of their own family or with close friends.

Early adoptors and members of the early majority may accept shortcomings of early versions of a new product by benefiting from prestige and from being able to make use of previously unavailable functionality. Patients requiring eHealth services may not have the choice: while not normally tending to embrace new technologies and products as early adoptors, they often end up using them for lack of alternatives. For this reason, some patients may need additional support when adopting new eHealth products and services. In addition, new interaction technologies to be employed in eHealth and other sectors should make provisions for the requirements of elderly and/or disabled users to be implemented already in first-generation products making use of those innovations. EG 202 848 documents how this can be achieved.

3.3.2 Method

The method used for EG 202 848 focused on the user, and how the user interacts with an eService. From the user's perspective, an eService can be said to consist mainly of two parts, namely functional components and interaction components (see Fig. 3.2).

When making use of an eService in order to realise a particular intention, a user has to deal with the interaction components of the communication enabling device (such as a smartphone or a terminal) in order to bring about an effect in the device's functional components which in turn enable the eService. Examples of interaction components of communication enabling devices are voice interfaces or text-entry interfaces. The functional components such as data-exchange protocols and networks have to answer to both the demands of the eService and the interaction components (however, they rarely affect the user's interaction with the eService to any great extent).

To identify the interaction technology enablers of future eServices three steps were conducted.

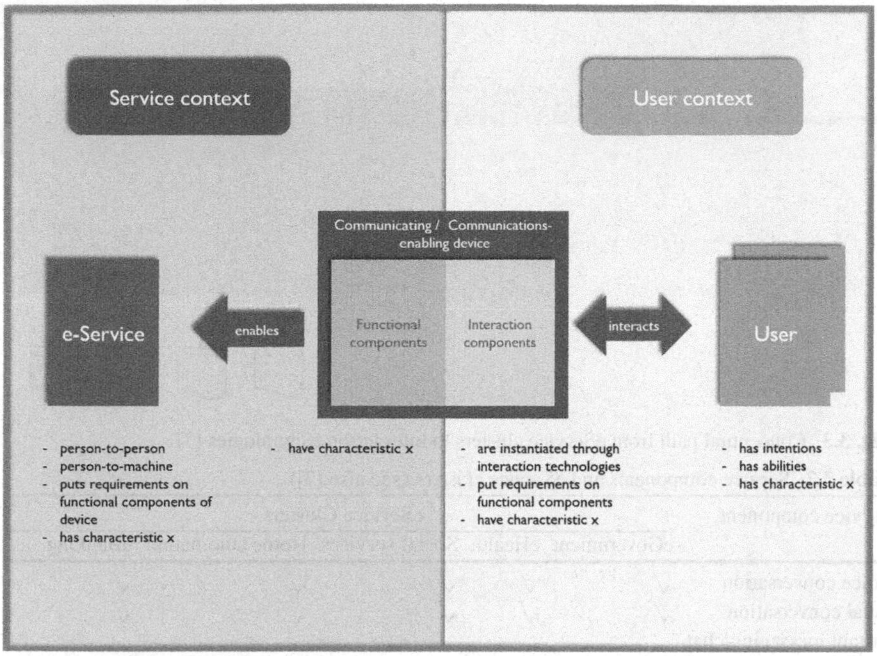

Fig. 3.2 Conceptual framework [7]

1. Identification of current and future eService clusters (e.g. eHealth), their eService components (e.g. voice conversation), and their relationship.
2. Identification of user interaction modalities, e.g. audio input and audio output, and their mapping to eService components.
3. Identification of user interaction technologies (e.g. sound beam), supporting interaction modalities.

The process of these steps is illustrated in Fig. 3.3. As a first step, current and future eService clusters (denoted "S1", "S2" ...) are identified: each of these eService clusters is making use of one or many eService components (abbreviated "SCo1", "SCo2" ...). These eService components comprise categories of communications services such as total conversation, text telephony, and file sharing.

The second step starts off by identifying interaction modalities (in Fig. 3.3 shown as "IM1", "IM2" ... for input modalities and "OM1", "OM2" ... for output modalities). Following this, the previously identified eService components are mapped onto these interaction modalities. It is now, as the last step, possible to specify the interaction technologies ("T1", "T2" ...) that support the interaction modalities identified and related to the eService components and eService clusters.

This approach allows any designer of an eService to work though the model and generate a list of the interaction technologies applicable to that eService and to review the recommendations given for preventing barriers. Here is a more detailed description of the three steps.

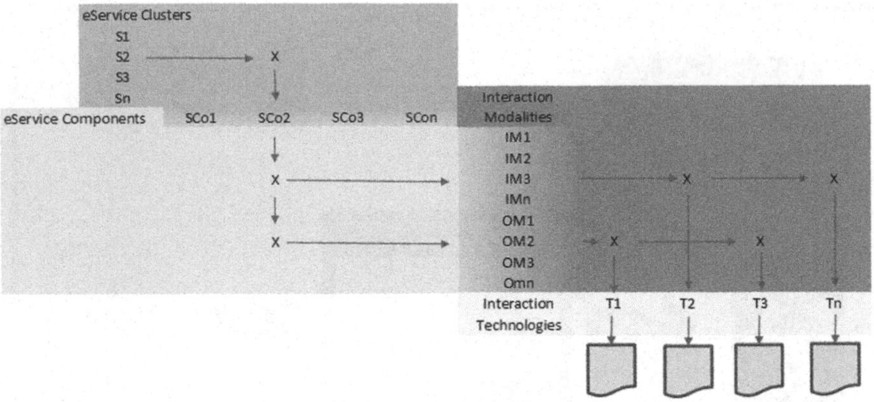

Fig. 3.3 Conceptual path from eService clusters to interaction technologies [7]

Table 3.2 Service components and eService clusters (see also [7])

Service component	eService Clusters					
	eGovernment	eHealth	Social services	Home automation	eBanking	…
Voice conversation	√	√	√	√	√	
Total conversation	√	√	√	√	√	
Instant messaging/chat			√			
Text telephony	√	√	√			
…						

1. *Analysis of current and future eServices* (*step* 1)

The analysis of existing and forthcoming services led to the selection, definition, and categorization of the eServices covered. This included services such as eHealth, eGovernment, eLearning, eCommerce, travel, and leisure, as these and other services are likely to affect older and disabled citizens and consumers. In this context, eHealth services are defined as including telecare services, remote health monitoring services, access to patient data, remote diagnosis and electronic prescription services.

The eServices within the scope were analysed in terms of their likely service components. The five types of service components include person-to-entity communication (voice conversation, total conversation, instant messaging/chat, text telephony, push to talk, and telepresence), multiparty communication (voice conferencing, video conferencing, and collaborative editing), messaging (e-mail exchange, text messaging, and multimedia messaging), content-related applications (information browsing, form filling, file sharing, application/data download/upload, and interactive digital broadcast), and context-related applications (identification-related applications, presence/context-related applications, and location-related applications).

Table 3.2 illustrates the underlying rationale of this step. For example, voice conversation, total conversation and text telephony (followed by many more) are listed as some of the service components relevant for the eHealth eService Cluster.

Table 3.3 Service components and interaction modalities (see also [7])

Service component	Interaction modalities					
	Input			Output		
	Acoustic/audio	Kinaesthetic	…	Acoustic/audio	Kinaesthetic	…
Voice conversation	√			√		
Total conversation	√		√	√		√
Instant messaging/chat		√	√			√
Text telephony		√	√			√
…						

2. *Identification of user interaction modalities, e.g. audio input and audio output, and their mapping to eService components* (*step* 2)

In the next step, interaction modalities were identified and defined. The list comprises input modalities (acoustic/audio, kinaesthetic, presence/location/ proximity based input, recognition/mood/arousal based input, smell, touch, and visual) as well as output modalities (acoustic/audio, haptic/tactile, smell, taste, and visual). These interaction modalities were then mapped onto the service components, indicating for each service component (e.g. multimedia messaging) the appropriate input interaction modalities (e.g. acoustic/audio, kinaesthetic, touch, and visual) and output interaction modalities (e.g. acoustic/audio and visual) (see Table 3.3).

3. *Identification of user interaction technologies* (*step* 3)

Roadmaps of forthcoming user interface technologies were developed by employing established R&D procedures. During this step relevant interaction technologies for the eServices defined in step 1 and the user interaction modalities defined in step 2 were identified.

The basis for this work was desk and Internet research as well as expertise from subject matter experts in the various fields. One obvious obstacle for performing such an analysis is the fact that technologies developed by commercial companies often remain classified until they are released to the market in the form of new products. Interviews with R&D staff of these companies are still worthwhile as they are usually free to discuss their view on general trends of user interface design and related technologies. Additional information can be found in conference papers and journal articles that report cutting-edge user interface technology developments.

User interaction technology roadmaps were developed to group upcoming technologies according to interaction modalities (e.g. acoustic/audio input, acoustic/audio output). Within each roadmap, technologies were organised in sub-categories where appropriate (e.g. advanced microphones and voice-input technologies are sub-categories on the roadmap for acoustic/audio input technologies). The individual technologies are positioned along a time dimension covering ten years according to their expected mass-market availability for the general consumer. Estimates of the time of mass-market availability were based on expert interviews and literature studies. As such, they represent the best estimates available at the time of writing. The indicated dates should, however, not be relied upon if making any important design or deployment decisions, as it will always be necessary to seek more current mass-market availability information before making such decisions. Sample roadmaps can be found in Figs. 3.4 and 3.5 [1].

For each user-interaction technology identified during the investigation a number of characteristics were collected:

- A description of the technology, related technologies, and expected mass-market deployment
- User requirements in terms of user capabilities required for making use of the technology
- Benefits for all users and potential benefits for users with disabilities
- Cultural issues
- Deployment pros and cons
- Solutions for overcoming the exclusion of disabled users, implementation requirements for the solution, and harmonization issues.

Table 3.4 shows the description of one of the technologies identified in the visual output technologies roadmap [1].

The services interaction profiles identified in step 2 were mapped onto the interaction technologies identified in step 3. The resulting relation between eServices and their possible interaction technologies can be used to identify solutions for design-for-all provisions required (see Table 3.5 for a representation of that process with example data). For example, an eHealth service employing gesture recognition (kinaesthetic input) as a user interface style may include passive RFID, wall-mounted cameras, and infra-red beams as UI technologies.

For each interaction technology, provisions are defined that have to be made prior to or at the introduction of each new technology in order to enable the support of emerging eServices for older and/or disabled users and citizens. Many of these provisions can be found in the literature (see e.g. [8–10]). The identified provisions were then integrated into the interaction technology tables (see Table 3.6 for a list of generic or "key" Design for All solutions that can be applied in the context of many UI technologies).

3.4 Generic Design for All Solutions for Novel UI Technologies

There are a number of generic solutions which can be applied to many accessibility problems created by the application of both existing and novel interaction technologies (see Table 3.6). In this section we will characterize the most important solutions found in the literature [8–10].

Multimodality is the most commonly used solution for many accessibility problems. Both the output of a system and the input from the user into an ICT device can be transmitted through several modalities. People who have limited abilities to use one modality get the option to use a second (independent) modality to either receive

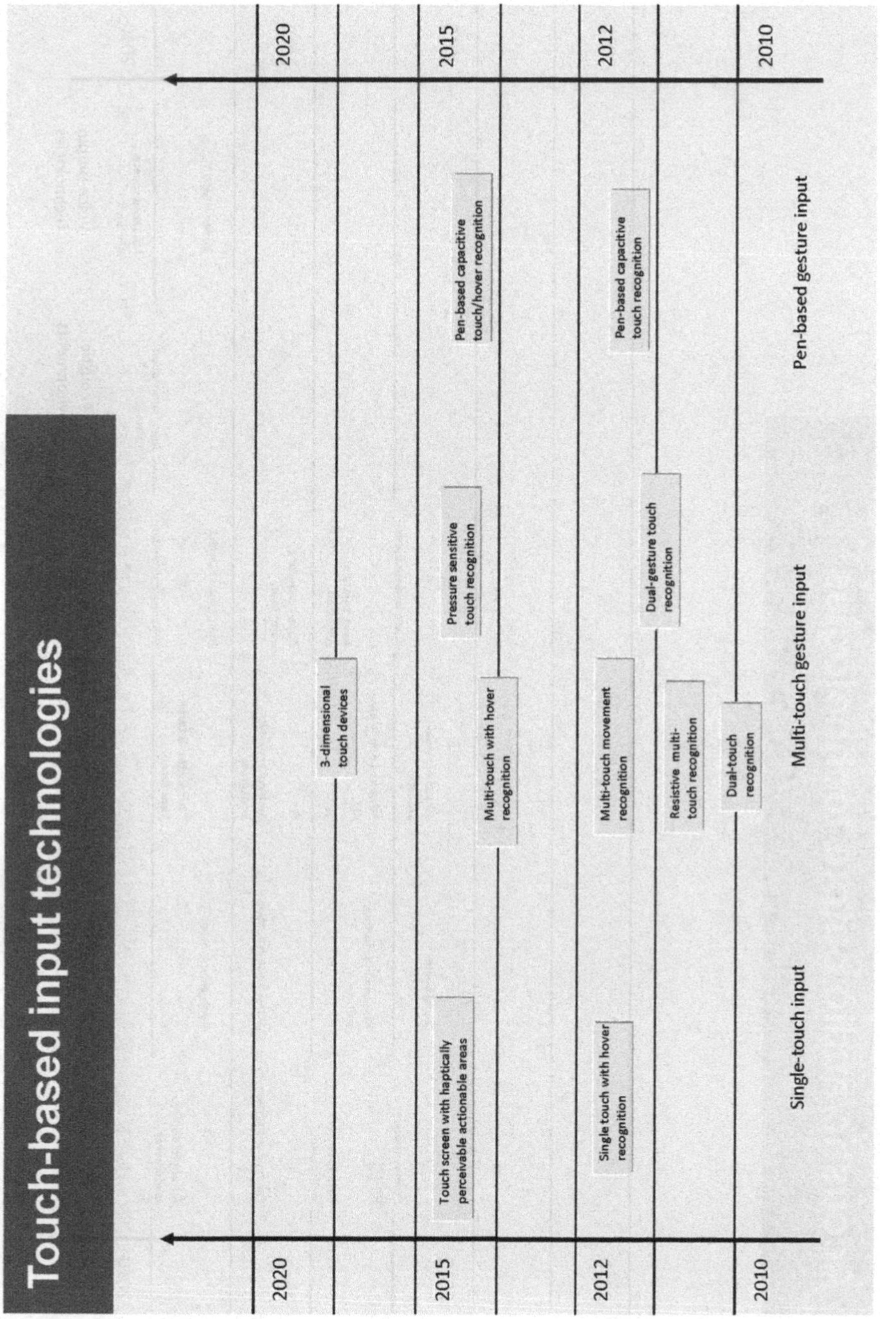

Fig. 3.4 Sample input interaction technology roadmap [1]

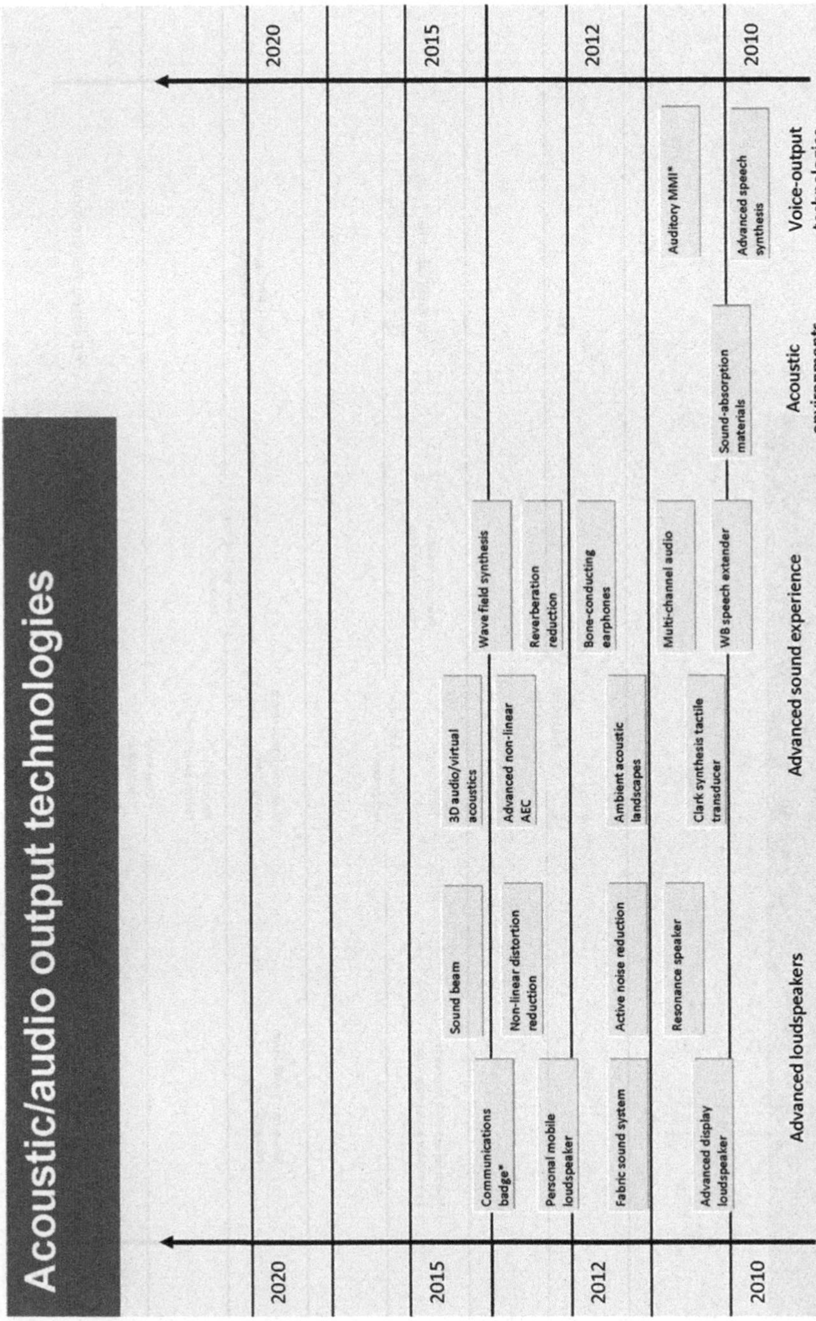

Fig. 3.5 Sample output interaction technology roadmap [1]

Table 3.4 Sample summary for an interaction technology characterization

Characteristic	Definition
Name	Direct volume display devices (DVDD)
Description	This type of display forms a visual impression in three dimensions (e.g. through rotating light spots called "Voxels") as opposed to "classical" display screens that only have an x-y planar surface and generate 3-dimensional visual impressions through visual effects
Mass market deployment	After 2015
Sub-category	2D/3D switchable
Related technology	Holographic displays
User requirements	01 Perceive visual information
	03 Perceive existence and location of actionable components
	04 Perceive status of controls and indications
	05 Perceive feedback from an operation setup
	07 Be able to complete actions and tasks within the time allowed
	08 Avoid unintentional activation of controls
	09 Be able to recover from errors 11 Not cause personal risk (e.g. seizure)
	12 Be able to efficiently operate product
	13 Understand how to use product (including discovery and activation of any accessibility features needed)
	14 Understanding the output or displayed material (even after perceived accurately)
	15 Ability to use assistive technology (AT) to control the ICT
Accessibility barriers	Displayed content might not be accessible for people with visual impairments
	3D visual effect might not be experienced by part of the user population
	Visually impaired users need to be able to perceive the existence of controls and receive feedback of operations in adequate ways
	Usage and connection of assistive devices is limited or not possible
Solutions related to accessibility barriers	Multimodal presentation: consider provision of multimodal presentation
	Multimodal control: allow for multimodal control of the device
	Object navigation: allow for navigation between displayed objects
	Selective magnification: allow for the magnification of displayed objects
	Displayed information adjustability: allow for flexible adjustment of the displayed information
	Standardized assistive device connection: provision should be made for connecting standardized assistive devices
Cultural issues	None identified
Benefit for all users	The display of 3D content can give a heightened viewing experience
Benefits for older people and people with disabilities	None identified

(continued)

Table 3.4 (continued)

Characteristic	Definition
Deployment pros	New applications/experiences of visual information displays due to the true 3D impression
Deployment cons	Stereovision (eyesight ability) is a prerequisite to perceiving 3D display effects
Implementation requirements	Fundamental problem: The number of Voxels required increases as a cubic function with resolution, requiring large amounts of data to be processed
Harmonization	None identified

Table 3.5 Matching technologies and input interaction modalities

Technologies	Input interaction modalities Acoustic/ audio	Kinaesthetic	Presence/ location/ proximity based	…
Audio input				
- Ambient noise reduction	√			
Noise cancellation	√			
…other ambient noise reduction	√			
- … other audio inputs	√			
Sensing technologies				
- Location sensing			√	
GPS tracking			√	√
Passive RFID		√	√	√
… other location sensing			√	
- Anonymous presence sensing				
PIR sensors			√	
Fixed in-device cameras			√	
Hand-held cameras			√	√
Wall-mounted cameras		√	√	
… other cameras		√	√	√
Infra-red beams		√	√	
… other anonymous sensing			√	
- … other Sensing technologies			√	
… other technologies				

information or transmit their input to the system. Examples for multi-modal communication are (i) the use of computer-generated spoken language to communicate the contents of a document to blind users or (ii) the alternative use of a touchscreen, a keyboard and a microphone for input based on gestures, keystrokes and voice for users with various disabilities.

Another generic accessibility solution is to strictly *separate the controls for different modalities* in order to allow users with motor or cognitive impairments the control of their ICT device.

Objects visualized on the display of an ICT device should be *adjustable*, i.e. the size of their visualization, their position and the colours used should be adaptable to

Table 3.6 Key design for all solutions (from [1])

Solution	Explanation	Reference
Multimodal presentation	Use different modes (visual, acoustic, tactile) for redundant presentation of information. Also support simultaneous use of different modes	[9]
Multimodal control	Use different modes (visual, acoustic, tactile) for providing control location and function information	[9]
Independent control	Provide independent controls for different output channels	[8]
Multimodal feedback	Provide effective and multi-modal feedback during and after task completion	[9]
Object navigation	Allow navigating among presented objects (e.g. visual objects, haptic/tactile)	Adapted from [8]
Object adjustability	Allow adjusting the size of displayed objects	[8]
Selective magnification	Allow magnifying portions of a visual or tactile display	Adapted from [8]
Displayed information adjustability	Allow adjusting characteristics of displayed information (e.g. contrast, volume, force, size)	Adapted from [8]
Equivalent simultaneous control	Provide equivalent control through different modes (kinaesthetic, vocal, etc.). Also support simultaneous use of different modes	Adapted from [8]
User limitation compensation	Compensate for limitations in user's actions over the system (e.g. compensate tremors, robust voice recognition systems for people with speech impairments)	Adapted from [8]
Reasonable operating forces	Use reasonable operating forces	Adapted from [8]
Sustained effort minimization	Minimize sustained physical effort	[8]
Low complexity	Eliminate unnecessary complexity	[8]
Consistency with expectations	Be consistent with user expectations and intuition	[8]
Training need minimization	Minimize the need for training	[8]
Barrier-free user education	Barrier-free provision of user-education materials (e.g. user guides)	[11]
Describability	Differentiate elements in ways that can be described (i.e. make it easy to give instructions or directions)	[8]
Standardized assistive device connection	Provide for a standardized option to connect assistive devices	[10]

users' specific requirements. This allows the modification of an interface for maximum accessibility by people with limited eyesight or colour blindness.

The *force* needed to control a mechanical or haptic control element in a user interface should be *adjustable* for people with very low strength or a lack of motor control. Also, the shape of controls should be such that they can be distinguished without vision and grasped with limited motor control and/or very small extremities.

Selective magnification allows users with limited eyesight to read display contents without changing the amount of information visualized on a screen for fully-abled users.

A number of generic solutions are directed towards limiting the complexity of user interfaces. These solutions benefit all users but are of specific importance to users with cognitive impairments: UI design should always try to *eliminate all unneeded complexity* and try to adapt to the knowledge level and expertise of the end users of an ICT device. The need for education and training should be minimized. User interaction processes should be made as simple as possible to ease the learning process of users.

All training material required (manuals, introductory documents, tutorials) should be offered in a barrier-free version, i.e. written information should be accessible through audio channels (spoken text) or Braille displays for users with limited or no eyesight (see also [11]). For training videos written descriptions of the contents allow blind users to follow the stories shown in the videos. For deaf people the audio track of videos and other audio information should be provided through captioning mechanisms.

A user interface design which uses clearly distinguishable controls and user interface elements allows for remote support (e.g. by hotline personnel) as it minimizes the information requirements for identifying specific controls and limits the cognitive load of both the support personnel and the user requiring assistance.

There will always be users with specific requirements which cannot be fulfilled by any generic accessibility solution. For these users it is important that all ICT devices have *standardized interfaces* for the connection of assistive technology to allow for special input or output devices to seamlessly work with standard user interface technology.

For novel interaction technologies it may be possible to develop alternate UI solutions to make these technologies accessible to people with special needs. As far as these solutions could be envisaged they have been mentioned in the technology descriptions in [1].

3.5 Designing the User Interface of Future Accessible Services

Given the change in population structures elderly people with age-related health problems living alone in their homes will become a large target group for eServices and eHealth applications. Obviously they will use interfaces to interact with their supporting services and the quality of interaction with required services will depend very much on how these interfaces can adapt to changing requirements of their users.

When designing user interfaces for these services a number of input and output technologies will be employed. It is important to analyse the implications of age-related accessibility problems when interacting using these technologies. Examples are:

- Touch input to control home automation components (heating, lighting, security features), possibly with multi-touch interaction
- Audio input to control a smart living environment or communication features
- Sensor input to supervise presence of persons in the environment and for medically relevant data of the person using eHealth services; sensor input for the detection of abnormal situations (such as stoves remaining turned on (heat detection) or for the detection of smoke, smell)
- PC or tablet-based user interfaces for setup, adaption and control of these interfaces through either the user or third parties and service providers
- Audio output for communication purposes
- Visual output for feedback about the state of the smart home
- Haptic output to raise awareness (e.g. use of vibration motors in tablets or smart-phones.

Using the technologies roadmaps related to these input and output technologies a service designer can decide (i) which technologies to use when developing a service component and (ii) which accessibility provisions should be foreseen to ensure that the service can be used by the largest group of potential target users.

Examples for these provisions can be:

- The design of multimodal interfaces and free selection of interface modalities according to user preferences
- Speech recognition adapting to the user's speech behaviour based on misinterpretations and user corrections
- Use of directable microphones
- Display properties adaptable to a user's limited eyesight.

3.6 How to Apply the Project Results

To explain the usage of ETSI EG 202 848 [1], we look at a typical user of eHealth services living in his "smart" home. An elderly gentleman, Peter, lives alone in his home. He is about 70 years old and uses several interfaces in his environment. His home is controlled centrally and he sets up and coordinates heating, light, security features, and his communication and entertainment systems through a number of touchscreen devices, both portable and wall-mounted. Interaction technologies employed include simple touch, multi-point touch recognition and gestures, as well as audio control. There are a number of sensors in his house which are used to identify the exact position of Peter in the building. These can be used to detect any abnormal situation or accident which might require outside attention.

Peter is currently still in good shape without major motor or sensory impairments; only his hearing has slightly deteriorated over time. He has a few health problems including arthritis in his hip joints and high blood pressure. His blood pressure measurements are taken once daily and transmitted to his medical centre.

A few years later Peter, who is still living on his own, has to deal with a number of new health issues which impact the way in which he can interact with the ICT components in his environment. His motor abilities have declined rapidly and he has developed a tremor which affects his ability to use a multi-touch gesture interface. Small buttons on a touch interface are extremely hard for him to identify—due to deteriorating eyesight—and to select and address precisely. His hearing has also deteriorated so that he is no longer able to fully understand audio output.

Fortunately, the user interface designers who developed the interfaces to his ITC environment took the possibility into account that Peter's ability to communicate with his environment might be affected by age-related deterioration of his motor and sensory abilities. Buttons on the touch screens can be enlarged to cope with limited eyesight. Multi-point gesture interaction can be replaced by a sequence of simple touch events. Audio output volumes can be adjusted to cope with limited hearing abilities. All the interfaces to his medical devices (blood pressure meter, blood sugar meter etc.) are integrated in his smart home touch panel interface and can be adapted according to his motor and sensory abilities. Moreover, the technical personnel of his health centre have the technical features to adjust the user interface of his ICT environment remotely.

The modification of the interface to adjust to these changes may not be possible for Peter without outside help but the user interface does not need any major re-programming but can simply be adjusted—by an external helper or directly by the user—to cope with different communication requirements. The fact that Peter has both portable and wall-mounted touch screen components allows him to still use his system comfortably even if he is required to use a wheel chair or walking aid to cope with his arthritis.

Taking into account the findings listed in [1] the designer was able to develop a user interface for Peter's ICT environment adapting to his specific need at any time which allows him to live for an extended time period without being forced to leave his home.

3.7 Future Outlook

There is an inherent level of uncertainty in identifying which future user interaction technologies will be available in the mainstream mass market over the next 5–10 years. In addition, identifying the dates at which such technologies will enter mainstream usage is also recognised to be an inexact science. We attempted to present the best available view that could be achieved, at the date at which the underlying research was completed, of what technologies will be relevant and when they may emerge.

What is certain is that the expectations of which technologies will reach the marketplace and when they emerge is subject to continuous change. These changes can be in the form of a gradual understanding that the development and deployment processes behind a certain technology may lengthen or shorten according to external factors such as a gradual change in the market for the related products or an increase or decrease in the costs of the materials or processes necessary to fabricate the technologies. During consultation with ICT experts from industry the exact timing of mass market penetration was contested for some of the technologies which we analysed. These experts commented that novel technologies might first only be made available in high-end product and service offerings before "trickling down" to mainstream offerings, the exact timing being dependent upon many factors difficult to foresee (such as product diversification in the market, pressure from competitors, or strategic decisions about how to develop market share). However, such changes would only result in some minor movements in the positioning of the already identified technologies on the technology roadmaps that are shown in [1]. This would mean that most of the roadmaps would continue to be of use in understanding the future of the group of technologies associated with any user interaction modality represented by the roadmap. These changes in the timescales of technology deployment should, in themselves, have no impact on the validity of the information contained in the technology properties tables presented in [1].

There may also be gradual changes in the way that the user interaction technologies are actually realised, and these may potentially cause some of the information in the technology properties tables to become less correct. However, it is likely for the normal changes that occur as technologies smoothly develop, that the majority of the information in the technology properties tables will still be very relevant and that the cases where something has changed will often be self-evident.

The emergence of new interaction technologies which were not predicted in the work on [1] will cause the findings in that document to become less relevant for services and products employing these unforeseen technologies. If these technologies are very similar to those already described in [1], the technology property tables should still prove very valuable in predicting most of the benefits, barriers and solutions that might apply to the newly emerging technology. Where the new technologies are truly unique and quite unlike any of the technologies addressed in [1], the only source of guidance that can be used to help predict benefits, barriers and solutions is by reference to the "Key Design for All Solutions" identified in our project.

In order to ensure that the value of our findings are preserved, it will be necessary to regularly update the results to ensure that they correctly reflect the most recent understanding of which technologies are likely to appear within 5–10 years, how they are likely to emerge (shown on revised roadmaps) and what benefits, barriers and solutions relate to them (shown in new and revised technology properties tables).

Acknowledgments The work reported here is the result of a team of experts. We thank the members of this team for their effort and valuable contributions: Michael Pluke, Erik Zetterström, Helge Hüttenrauch, and Alejandro Rodriguez-Ascaso. Funding for this work was provided by the European Commission.

References

1. ETSI EG 202 848 V1.1.1 (2011–02). Human factors; Inclusive eServices for all: Optimizing the accessibility and the use of upcoming user-interaction technologies.
2. Kortum, P. (Ed.). (2008). HCI Beyond the GUI: Design for haptic, speech, olfactory, and other nontraditional interfaces. Burlington, MA: Morgan Kaufmann Publishers.
3. ETSI EG 202 116 (2002). Human factors (HF); Guidelines for ICT products and services; Design for all.
4. Henderson, R. M. & Clark, K. B. (1990). Architectural innovation: The reconfiguration of existing product technologies and the failure of established firms. *Administrative Science Quarterly, 35*(1), 9–30.
5. Rogers, E. M. (1962). *Diffusion of innovations*. Florence, MA: Free Press.
6. Retrieved December 15, 2013, from http://en.wikipedia.org/wiki/Diffusion_of_innovations
7. ETSI TR 102 849 V1.1.1 (2010–11). Human factors (HF); Inclusive eServices for all; Background analysis of future interaction technologies and supporting information.
8. ISO 9241–20: Ergonomics of human-system interaction. Accessibility guidelines for information/communication technology (ICT) equipment and services.
9. The Center for Universal Design, NC State University.Retrieved December 15, 2013, from http://www.ncsu.edu/ncsu/design/cud/about_ud/udprinciplestext.htm
10. ETSI TR 102 068: Human factors (HF); Requirements for assistive technology devices in ICT.
11. ETSI EG 202 417: Human factors (HF); User education guidelines for mobile terminals and services.
12. Ahmaniemi, T. T., & Lantz, V. T. (2009). Augmented reality target finding based on tactile cues. *Proceedings of International Conference on Multimodal interfaces* (pp. 335–342).
13. Belt, S., Greenblatt, D., Häkkilä, J., & Mäkelä, K. (2006). User Perceptions on mobile interaction with visual and RFID tags. In E. Rukzio, M. Paolucci, T. Finin, P. Wisner, & T. Payne (Eds). *Proceedings of the 8th Conference on Human–Computer Interaction with Mobile Devices and Services—MobileHCI '06* (p. 295). New York: ACM Press. doi:10.1145/1152215.1152296
14. Bolzmacher, C., Hafez, M., Khoudjaa, M., Bernardonia, P., & Dubowsky, S. (2004). Polymer based actuators for virtual reality devices. *Proceedings of SPIE, 5385*, 281–289.
15. Boverie, S. (2004). Driver fatigue monitoring technologies and future ideas. *AWAKE Road Safety Workshop, Balocco, Italy.*
16. Bravo, J., Hervas, R., Chavira, G., Nava, S. W., & Villarreal, V. (2008). From implicit to touching interaction: RFID and NFC approaches. *2008 Conference on Human System Interactions* (pp. 743–748), Krakow, Poland. IEEE. doi:10.1109/HSI.2008.4581534
17. Brugnoli, M. C., Rowland, D., Morabito, F., Davide, F., & Doughty, M. (2006). Gaming and social interaction in mediated environments: The PASION project. *eChallenges e2006, Barcelona, Spain.*
18. Callaghan, M. J., Gormley, P., McBride, M., Harkin, J., & McGinnity, T. M. (2006). Internal location based services using wireless sensor networks and RFID technology. *Journal of Computer Science, 6*(4), 108–113.
19. Campbell, A. T., Eisenman, S. B., Fodor, K., Lane, N. D., Lu, H., Miluzzo, E., et al. (2008). Transforming the social networking experience with sensing presence from mobile phones. *Proceedings of the 6th ACM Conference on Embedded Network Sensor Systems—SenSys '08* (p. 367). New York: ACM Press. doi:10.1145/1460412.1460455

20. Ferris, D. P. (2009). The exoskeletons are here. *Journal of NeuroEngineering and Rehabilitation, 6*(17). Retrieved from http://www.jneuroengrehab.com/content/6/1/17
21. Furmanski, C., Azuma, R., & Daily, M. (2002). Augmented-reality visualizations guided by cognition: Perceptual heuristics for combining visible and obscured information. *Proceedings of the International Symposium on Mixed and Augmented Reality (ISMAR'02)* (pp. 215–224).
22. Gabbard, J. L., Swan, J. E., Hix, D., Si-Jung, K. & Fitch, G. (2007). Active text drawing styles for outdoor augmented reality: A user-based study and design implications. *Proceedings of the Virtual Reality Conference* (pp. 35–42).
23. Haans, A., Ijsselsteijn, W. A, & de Kort, Y. A. W. (2008). The effect of similarities in skin texture and hand shape on perceived ownership of a fake limb. *Body Image, 5*(4), 389–94. doi:10.1016/j.bodyim.2008.04.003
24. Hage, J. (2011). *Restoring the innovative Edge: Driving the evolution of science and technology*. Stanford, CA: Stanford Business Books.
25. Herr, H. (2009). Exoskeletons and orthoses: Classification, design challenges and future directions. *Journal of NeuroEngineering and Rehabilitation, 6*(21). Retrieved January 19, 2014, from: http://www.jneuroengrehab.com/content/6/1/21
26. Hightower, J., Vakili, C., Borriello, C., & Want, R. (2001). *Design and calibration of the SpotON AD-Hoc location sensing system*. Seattle: Department of Computer Science and Engineering, University of Washington.
27. Hong, Z. T., & Pentland, A. (2001). Tactual displays for sensory substitution and wearable computers. In W. Barfield, T. Caudell, & N. J. Mahwah (Eds.), *Fundamentals of Wearable Computers and Augmented Reality* (pp. 579–598). Mahwah, NJ: Lawrence Erlbaum Associates.
28. Hoshi, T., Iwamoto, T., & Shinoda, H. (2009). Non-contact tactile sensation synthesized by ultrasound transducers. *Proceedings of the Third Joint Eurohaptics Conference and Symposium on Haptic Interfaces for Virtual Environment and Teleoperator Systems* (pp. 256–260).
29. ISO/IEC TR 24714–1. *Information technology—biometrics—jurisdictional and societal considerations for commercial applications*. Part 1: General guidance (E).
30. Jaynes, C., Webb, S., & Steele, R. M. (2004). Camera-based detection and removal of shadows from interactive multiprojector displays. *IEEE Transactions on Visualization and Computer Graphics, 10*(3), 290–301.
31. Jones, L. A., & Sarter, N. B. (2008). Tactile displays: Guidance for their design and application human factors. *The Journal of the Human Factors and Ergonomics Society, 50*(1), 90–111.
32. Konomi, S. (2004). Personal privacy assistants for RFID users. *International Workshop Series on RFID* (pp. 1–6).
33. Kooper, R., & MacIntyre, B. (2003). Browsing the real-world wide web: Maintaining awareness of virtual information in an ar information space. *International Journal of Human-Computer Interaction, 16*(3), 425–446.
34. Kraft, C. (2012). *User experience innovation—user-centered design that works*. NY: Apress.
35. Langheinrich, M. (2005). *Personal privacy in ubiquitous computing tools and system support*. PhD Thesis No. 16100, ETH Zurich, Zurich, Switzerland, May 2005.
36. Laycock, S. D., & Day, A. M. (2003). Recent developments and applications of haptic devices. *Computer Graphics Forum, 22*(2), 117–132.
37. Liu, Y. C., & Wen, H. C. (2004). Comparison of head-up display (HUD) versus head-down display (HDD): Driving performance of commercial vehicle operators in Taiwan. *International Journal of Human-Computer Studies, 61*, 679–697.
38. Milgram, P., Takemura, H., Utsumi, A., & Kishino, F. (1994). Augmented reality: A class of displays on the reality-virtuality continuum. *Proceedings of SPIE, 2351*, 282–292.
39. Orr, R., & Abowd, G. (2000). The smart floor: A mechanism for natural user identification and tracking. In G. Szwillus & T. Turner (Eds.), *CHI2000 Extended abstracts conference on human factors in computing systems* (pp. 275–276). The Hague, Netherlands: ACM Press.
40. Parviz, B. A. (2009). Augmented reality in a contact lens. *IEEE Spectrum*. Retrieved from http://spectrum.ieee.org/biomedical/bionics/augmented-reality-in-a-contact-lens/0
41. Rantala, J., Raisamo, R., Lylykangas, J., Surakka, V., Raisamo, J., Salminen, K., et al. (2009). Methods for presenting braille characters on a mobile device with a touchscreen and tactile feedback. *IEEE Transactions on Haptics*, 2(1), 28–39.

42. Ruffini, G., Dunne, S., Farrés, E., Cester, I., Watts, P. C. P., Silva, S. R. P., et al. (2007). ENOBIO dry electrophysiology electrode: First human trial plus wireless electrode system. *Proceedings of the 29th Annual International Conference of the IEEE Engineering Medicine and Biology Society, Lyon, France* (pp. 6690–6694). IEEE.
43. Saffer, D. (2009). *Designing for interaction: Creating innovative applications and devices (voices that matter)*. Berkeley, CA: New Riders.
44. Stephanidis, C. (2007). Universal access in human-computer interaction ambient interaction. *4th International Conference on Universal Access in Human-Computer Interaction, UAHCI 2007*. Heidelberg: Springer.
45. Stephanidis, C. (2009). T*he universal access handbook (human factors and ergonomics)*. Boca Raton, USA: CRC Press.
46. Sun, W., Sobel, I., Culbertson, B., Gelb, D., & Robinson, I. (2008). Calibrating multi-projector cylindrically curved displays for wallpaper projection. *Proceedings of the 5th ACM/IEEE International Workshop on Projector Camera Systems* (pp. 1–8).
47. Tilton, C. (2002). Biometric standards—An overview. *Information Security Technical Report, 7*(4), 36–48. doi:10.1016/S1363-4127(02)00405-3
48. Vertegaal, R., & Poupyrev, I. (2008). Organic user interfaces: Introduction. *Communications of the ACM, 51*(6), 26–30.
49. Want, R., Fishkin, K. P., Gujar, A., & Harrison, B. L. (1999). Bridging physical and virtual worlds with electronic tags. *Proceedings of the SIGCHI Conference on Human Factors in Computing Systems the CHI is the Limit—CHI '99* (pp. 370–377). New York: ACM Press. doi:10.1145/302979.303111
50. Wunschmann, W., & Fourney, D. (2005). Guidance on tactile human-system interaction: Some statements. *Proceedings of Guidelines on Tactile and Haptic, Interactions (GOTHI'05)* (pp.6–9).
51. Xueyan, L., & Shuxu, G. (2008): The fourth biometric—vein recognition. In P.-Y. Yin (Ed.), *Pattern recognition techniques, technology and applications* (pp. 537–546). Retrieved January 19, 2014, from http://sciyo.com/articles/show/title/the_fourth_biometric_-_vein_recognition
52. Yousefi, A., Jalili, R., & Niamanesh, M. (2006). Multi-determiner protection of private data in pervasive computing environments. *IJCSNS International Journal of Computer Science and Network Security, 6*(12), 239–248.
53. Zhou, Z., Cheok, A. D., Yang, X., & Qiu, Y. (2004). An experimental study on the role of 3D sound in augmented reality environment. *Interacting with Computers, 16*(6), 1043–1068.

Chapter 4
The Innovation Binder Approach: A Guide Towards a Social-Technical Balanced Pervasive Health System

A. Jacobs, P. Duysburgh, L. Bleumers, F. Ongenae, A. Ackaert and S. Verstichel

Pervasive health systems aim to support society with the many challenges our health-care system is facing today. Embedding systematically social choices in the Research and Development process (R&D) is therefore essential. In this chapter the 'Innovation Binder' approach is presented: a procedure to confront multiple viewpoints from user/social, technology and business perspective, to make choices (e.g. target groups, practices, actors, messages, means, steps, procedures, technologies) more explicit and coordinate the team to work together to a common abstract goal (e.g. home monitoring system to support ambient assistive living) with a lot of unknown viable options. The spine of our approach is the iterative use of scenarios and personas with different finalities and discussing them iteratively in team. It enables a parallel research track of social and technical R&D activities by coordinating mutual dependencies and uncertainties. We illustrate this approach with concrete examples from past and present R&D projects in the pervasive healthcare domain. This approach can help other R&D teams, convinced of the value of interdisciplinary work, to create desired pervasive health systems for multiple users.

A. Jacobs (✉) · P. Duysburgh · L. Bleumers
iMinds—SMIT, Vrije Universiteit Brussel, Elsene, Belgium
e-mail: an.jacobs@vub.ac.be

P. Duysburgh
e-mail: pieter.duysburgh@vub.ac.be

L. Bleumers
e-mail: Lizzy.Bleumers@vub.ac.be

F. Ongenae · A. Ackaert · S. Verstichel
iMinds—IBCN, Universiteit Gent, Gent, Belgium
e-mail: Femke.Ongenae@intec.UGent.be

A. Ackaert
e-mail: ann.ackaert@intec.UGent.be

S. Verstichel
e-mail: Stijn.Verstichel@intec.UGent.be

A. Holzinger et al. (eds.), *Pervasive Health*, Human–Computer Interaction Series,
DOI: 10.1007/978-1-4471-6413-5_4, © Springer-Verlag London 2014

4.1 Introduction

As also stated in the introductory chapter of this book [25], pervasive health systems aim to support society with the many challenges our healthcare system is facing today. We search for systems that are truly supporting this transformation of healthcare organizations (e.g., self care, relying more on local teams, increase of quality with same amount of money and people). Therefore, embedding social choices systematically in the Research and Development process (R&D) is essential. These challenges are even more present in R&D of pervasive health systems. At the one, hand due to the characteristics of pervasive technologies (automation, delegating control, remote monitoring, massive big data, etc.) this embedding is pivotal, at the other hand because health is a domain dealing with vulnerable people, supported by people delivering care with scarce resources.

In this chapter, the 'Innovation Binder' approach is presented. The approach is a reaction to our need for a tool supporting interdisciplinary collaboration when developing new pervasive health systems. IT-innovation in healthcare is by default highly multidisciplinary, since innovation in healthcare requires a combination of methods and insights from multiple disciplines [24]. We wanted to create a procedure to confront multiple viewpoints, social and technical, to make choices (regarding, e.g., target groups, practices, actors, messages, means, steps, procedures, technologies) more explicit and coordinate the teamwork on a common, but abstract goal (e.g. home monitoring system to support ambient assistive living) with a lot of unknown viable options.

Our projects can be labeled as pre-competitive research to develop new health ICT systems, joining Social Sciences (Soc) with Informatics and Engineering (I&E). Besides academic researchers, these projects typically involve people from care organizations, as well as the private sector. This diversity in project partners is seen as necessary to take the complex healthcare context into consideration during development, and adequately show how pervasive technologies can add values for multiple user roles.

The spine of our approach is the iterative use of scenarios and personas with different finalities and draws on discussing them iteratively in team. These scenarios are boundary objects that organize the process (e.g., different research activities using them, referred to during meetings). The general use and creation of scenarios and personas in the Human Computer Interaction field is well described [4, 5]. In short, scenarios are narratives trying to depict the central practices in context in relation to the technology under development. In later sections we discuss them in-depth.

We try to develop an innovation process that goes beyond the current limits of user-centered design, which is currently often limited to front end research. Equally, the 'innovation binder' approach facilitates a prolongation of the continuous integration process from back-end development towards the first level of deployment (first uses of the software). In other words, the approach helps to overcome the waiting game between technical and social output. It enables a parallel research track of social and technical R&D activities by coordinating mutual dependencies and uncertainties.

We illustrate this approach with concrete examples from several past and present R&D projects in the pervasive healthcare domain. This approach can help other R&D teams, convinced of the value of interdisciplinary work, to create desired pervasive health systems for multiple users. It is a way of guiding the many choices a team should take, taking into account multiple voices, towards a valuable solution for both business and society.

4.2 Glossary: Overall Picture and Terminology

In this part a visual overview is given of the Innovation Binder approach (Fig. 4.1). The rest of the chapter revolves around this picture. Before we do that, we give a short overview of the most important terms, and how we use them.

SCOT (Social Construction of Technology Theory) it is a framework in Science and technology studies, that emphasis the role of social processes (non linearity, power, etc.) at play when developing technology [2, 19].

Boundary object an arrangement of collaboration without prior consensus between different groups. For example a concept or a drawing [22].

Pre-competitive research research aiming to develop demonstrating technology to be applied and used 5–10 years in the future [13].

Care domain and organizations the broad domain of healthcare and its organizations.

Technology providers companies developing and providing healthcare technology.

Current practices the way people are used to do things in their everyday context, the way activities are interwoven in a social domain [20].

Future practices imagined everyday practices in the future.

(Technical) components and communication software components or software modules or units in the system (also referred to as 'building blocks').

Architecture the design of how the components are connected (also: 'software architecture').

Technology roadmaps the forecast of a technological development [8].

Scenario a believable narrative, usually set in the future of a person's experience as he or she engages with a product or a service [14, p. 152].

Persona defines a persona as: 'A precise description of our user and what he wishes to accomplish'. It is a fictive character based on user research insights, which serve as characters in the scenarios

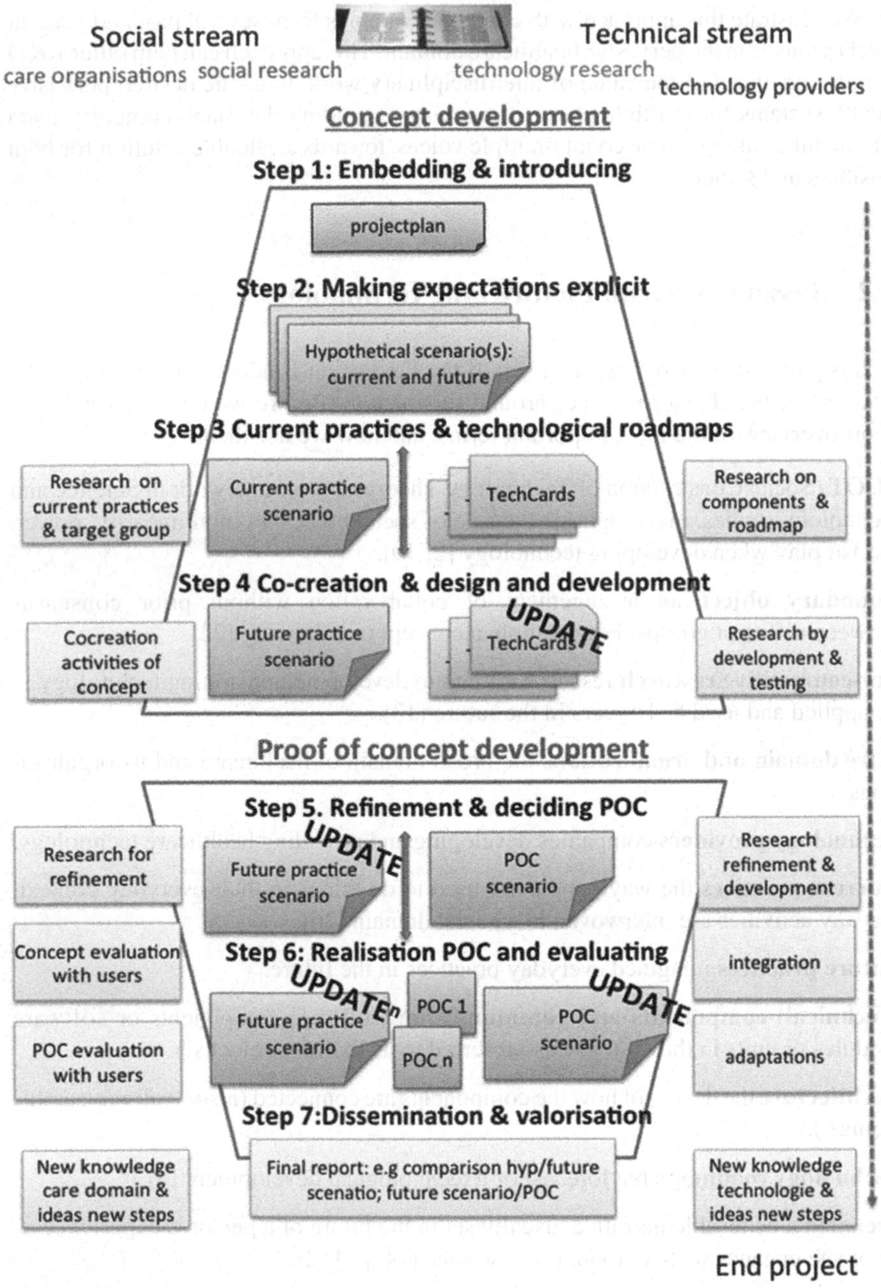

Fig. 4.1 Innovation binder approach

Use case describes user tasks and the specific functions a technology offers an end user, without detailed attention to context and experiences.

TechCards describes in a generic way the technical components that the different partners are working on.

Update the act of performing a new iteration on TechCards, scenarios, …

Concept and proof of concept (POC) A concept is an idea of the product or service, the proof of concept is the demonstration of the feasibility of a concept.

Co-creation activities in which users and stakeholders are involved in concept design.

Evaluation Concepts or POC's are evaluated together with users.

Developing and testing creating technical solutions and performing technical evaluations of the components, concepts or POC.

Continuous integration method to improve quality and delivery time of software developed in co-development teams by maintaining a common software code repository and supporting revision control.

4.3 State-of-the-Art of the Innovation Binder Approach

4.3.1 Prior Art or the Sources of Inspiration for this Approach

In this part we want to show the footage taken from previous work. First we will frame our approach within the realm of the Social Construction Of Technology theory (SCOT) within the science and technology studies. Next, the needs and problems that rise with interdisciplinary work are briefly discussed. We will situate our approach within the tools that have been developed within the fields of Human Computer Interaction (HCI) and Participatory Design (PD) over the past decades to involve the social in the design and development process. After discussing this prior art, we want to conclude this paragraph with a short discussion on the process of continuous integration. This process, with origins in the Informatics and Engineering, also copes with issues that are raised when collaboratively building software systems.

The SCOT theory explains why social context needs to be into account in IT innovation processes. In line with the SCOT perspective it becomes clear that a pervasive technology reflects different problem definitions and concerns. One has to assess the power relations; norms and values at that moment and place. A crucial idea in SCOT theory is that the outcome of a technical solution is the result of a path of choices: the solution could have been totally different, since in the development process a lot of sidetracks have been taken into consideration and abandoned. A current successful technology is a crystallization of choices that work, not the symbol of the most ultimate best solution. One best solution does not exist. For more in-depth understanding of SCOT we refer to work of e.g. Bijker [2] and Rip et al. [19].

Limonard and Koning [13] rephrase SCOT into a core tension between (i) the role and acceptance of a technology, which is primarily determined by social forces, so looking at social context is key (i.e. the 'social shaping' of technology), and (ii) the context of use (re)shapes the meaning of the technology, and how that evolves is rather unpredictable (i.e. the 'mutual shaping' of technology). Following the authors' own expertise in pre-competitive ICT development projects, they acknowledge the need for awareness of this tension and describe on an abstract level the process of critical examination one has to follow as part of the whole R&D process (Limonard and Konings, p. 169). We think the 'innovation binder approach' can be seen as an operationalization of Limonard and Koning's more generic strategy. They distinguish three dilemmas during pre-competitive ICT development projects. : (i) the starting point in configuring future use of ICT technology (the current social-technical context of use versus the future use of technology in context); (ii) the way of involving users (pro-active versus reactive); and (iii) the dilemma of the organization of interdisciplinary cooperation (the laboratory versus the development arena). Sequencing the different aspects of the dilemmas throughout the project is suggested as a solution. We will show in the description of the 'innovation binder' approach how this was achieved, and where and why we took another road than suggested by Limonard and Koning.

The investment in interdisciplinary work is driven by the need to join methods of different disciplines to answer a complex question. Van Bemmel [24] states that this is certainly the case when healthcare meets informatics. Stewart and Claeys [23, p. 2] wrapped up several difficulties from literature: epistemological differences, identity, membership conflicts and cultural capital, terminological misalignment, resistance to input from other disciplines, power issues, structural biases and management failures. To stimulate interdisciplinarity, one should take these issues into account. From their own experiences involving research with 'users' Stewart and Claeys advise (i) to invite everyone in the team to engage with users, not only social scientist or user researchers, (ii) to stimulate each team member to go beyond their own world view, and enable to have a common experience, (iii) to involve the team in the analysis (iv) to be open to the disciplines, interpretations and methods of other project partners (p. 18).

The involvement of social scientists, or experts in HCI and PD, in the development process of pervasive health systems is not new. Pagliari [18] for example described a hybrid model for interdisciplinary research in medical informatics where the goal is not only to share information, but actively design and evaluate and thus reach technologies that are *truly user-informed, fit for context, high quality and of demonstrated value* (p. 1). However, this model emphasises evaluation and excludes conceptualization, neither does scenarios play an important role as a boundary object. We think that the ambiguity in the story can indeed function very well as boundary object in the original way defined by Star [22]: an arrangement of collaboration without prior consensus between different groups.

We are not the first to see a lot of possibilities in the scenario as design tool (e.g. [11]), nor are we unique in using scenarios as the core of involving the social in software design. There is a well-documented tradition of different uses of scenarios and personas (e.g. [12, 15]), as well as an instrument to involve user involvement from evaluation to co-design [4]. Scenarios differ from use cases, which are more oriented at users tasks and specific computers functions. Scenarios are rooted in specific situations, in a certain context. They are based on knowledge on how things are done. They describe what is done, where, by who, when and by what means in what way. In contrast, use cases are generic, they describe the possibilities a technology offers to an end user, but there is no insight in the use context or the needs or preferences of the end user. As such, scenarios are better tools to integrate both a technical and social perspective than use cases. Different types of scenarios are made depending on the goal they must serve. They differ e.g. in openness, on depicting typical or critical situations, showing the extreme positive and extreme negative consequences [4]. Scenarios play a big role in the 'innovation binder' approach, and they are used in different ways throughout the process: (i) scenarios that are hypothetical or scenarios that are grounded in research on and with users; (ii) scenarios that are oriented at the current or scenarios oriented at future practices (current practice and future practice scenario); (iii) scenarios that assume the technology works flawless (sunny day) or that include technology failure (cloudy weather)[1]; (iv) scenario depicting a desired system ('desired scenario') or a system representing your worst nightmare ('horror scenario').[2] Because we do not want to be too overwhelming about variation in scenario options, we distinct in the Innovation Binder between (i) the hypothetical and the grounded dimension, and (ii) the current and the future dimension.

In line with Muller [15, p. 11], the 'innovation binder' approach serves to create a hybrid space where technology developers/researchers come together with the end-users representatives/researchers. Therefore, it is important to integrate methods that are understandable for those, non-social scientist dealing with the typical problems of making complex software systems in an interdisciplinary team. Continuous integration (CI) is one of them. It is a method advocated by Martin Fowler since 1999[3] in order to improve quality and delivery time of software developed in co-development teams. In our projects, these co-development teams often originate from different organizations and geographical locations (researchers, private companies, subcontractors) so this makes integration problems with the software building blocks even more likely. A required first step in CI is maintaining a common software code repository, supporting revision control. Having the software developers commit to these common repository on a very frequent base, contributing to an agreed mainline is essential. Automated builds and testing resolves the problems of integration testing normally done at wider time intervals. In practice, the CI process can only be successful if an 'integration manager' commits explicitly as being the problem owner of

---

[1] Inspiration from the distinction in use cases http://www.gatherspace.com/static/use_case_example.html#3.

[2] This last type is also called by Bødker [4, p. 64] minus scenarios.

[3] http://www.martinfowler.com/articles/continuousIntegration.html

the CI process. In our interdisciplinary teams, the CI process needs also to interact with the user research process. In our exploratory R&D projects there remains a high number of potential variables, both at the level of the technology and the end user. As such, the standard CI methodology can only be part of the solution for our type of interdisciplinary projects. Therefore, throughout the pervasive health projects that we worked on in recent years, a new approach was developed.

4.3.2 Situating the Context of Use in Which the Approach was Developed: When to Use the Innovation Binder

The exemplary projects presented in this chapter are all part of a demand driven research projects, partly funded by the participating companies and partly by the Flemish Government through the interuniversity and interdisciplinary knowledge center iMinds (http://www.iMinds.be). Healthcare is one of the important application domains since the conception of iMinds in 2004. The projects are pre-competitive and have a two years time-span. A project assembles different expertise to work towards a common research goal, resulting in reports and proof-of–concepts. In our examples, we will refer to experiences from several projects. These include the finished project ACCIO (2010–2012, developing a contextual nurse call system making use of ontologies and sensor data, [17]) and TransEcare (2007–2009, creating transparant ICT platforms for eCare); and to current experiences in the O'CareCloudS project (2012–2014, developing a contextual information sharing system between caregivers), Fallrisk (2013–2014, on contextual fall risk prevention and detection using sensor information) and the AAL project Care4Balance (2013–2015, on dashboard applications for elderly to coordinate care provisioning).

The 'innovation binder' approach in its current form originated from these projects. The approach tries to deal with a number of challenges that project partners were typical. A number of these are listed below.

In the first iMinds health projects, we gradually succeeded in creating more attention for user needs in IT innovation in health [6]. Interactive reflective discussions with technology developers are part of this method. However, many user researchers still had the feeling the results of their research were underutilized in the development process (e.g. [13]) and felt they were unable to substantially influence the conceptualization and implementation of the technology.

Another tension results from the difference in time spans the project partners are working on. Technical university researchers aim for a leap from the current state of the art of technical solutions, while the involved companies and care organizations are looking for mid-term reachable solutions to be valorized. Continuous integration tools are only helping to keep track of the connection and iterations of the technical components. But these tools do not help to make choices.

The user researchers typically struggled with having to research the possibilities the technology under development offers, without being able to give targeted users an experience of the future solution. Also, technical partners often considered input from social researchers as helpful, but also as delaying the process.

We developed thus the 'innovation binder' approach to guide us to make those choices collaborative, see our interdependencies and document systematically to stimulate reflection. Although it grew out our cases in pervasive health technology, we think the approach also could be useful in other domains.

4.3.3 How the Innovation Binder Approach Works Today

In the next paragraphs we discuss in detail the different steps and aspects of how we currently use the innovation binder (Fig. 4.1).

Roughly, we distinguish four types of actors: (i) social science/HCI researchers, (ii) engineering or computer science researchers, (iii) people working in (R&D departments) of private companies, and (iv) people working in (health)care organizations. These people collaborate along two types of streams: the social stream and the technical stream. Identifying oneself with one of the actors was never problematic in our projects. The different actors, their activities and expertise come together, being continuously stimulated to make choices based on the newly gained knowledge by the different partners. The leader of the process is fixed. In our cases, the project leader takes up this role, or a dedicated person who got extra effort on the planned innovation binder tasks.

As in most creativity processes, we start with a divergence phase and move subsequently to a convergence phase [9]. The divergence phase is called the 'concept development'; the convergence phase is called the 'proof-of-concept development'. During the concept development, we want to create a space for creativity by different research activities binding them together by one jointly created story. In the proof-of-concept development phase, the goal is to converge with the remaining R&D activities towards a stable proof-of-concept that demonstrates the added value. We will now describe the different steps, illustrated with some concrete examples.

4.3.3.1 Concept Development Phase: Guided Explorations for a Vision of a Future Pervasive Health System

In the concept development phase we foresee four steps: (1) introducing the method, (2) making expectations explicit, (3) documenting current practices and technological roadmaps, and (4) co-creation. The three latter steps all result in a different kind of scenario. For each step we describe the objectives, the participants, the sub steps and their outcomes, examples and reflections.

Step 1: Embedding the innovation binder approach in proposal and introducing at project kick-off

Objectives

- Structurally embed the innovation binder approach in the project, with sufficient time and effort of all partners on the task.
- Create a buy-in of all partners by explaining the goals and trajectory of the approach.

Participants/lead

All partners are involved.

Step 1.1 *Writing dedicated tasks in the proposal*
Integrate the different steps in project plan, for example in a proposal to apply for grant money. It is important to dedicate sufficient time for the different steps throughout the total timespan of the project.

Step 1.2 *Introducing approach at the kick-off of the project*
When the project starts, it is useful to spend some extra time explaining the 'innovation binder' goals to all project participants, and what the advantages and different steps are.

Example

To integrate the 'Innovation Binder' into a proposal, the steps of the Concept Development phase (step 1–4) are located in the explorative work package defined as "Requirement Analysis" or "Domain Analysis", and the Proof-of-Concept development steps (step 5–7) of the 'Innovation Binder' are defined as tasks within the "Evaluation", "Demonstrator" or "Proof-of-Concept" work package.

To explain the innovation binder goals and approach to the participants, we used in O'CareCloudS, Care4Balance and Fallrisk the 'cake baking' metaphor (as illustrated in Fig. 4.2). We deliberately opted for recognizable but unfamiliar comparison, without any relation to health or the technology in scope. Thus, attention can be triggered, in an equal and humoristic way. The approach is compared with the practice of baking a cake with different baking specialists (bakers, oven specialists, etc.) who represent the partners. Each of the partners has their own ultimate dream cake in mind. First, we make these different dream cakes explicit by creating for each partner their *hypothetical scenario*.

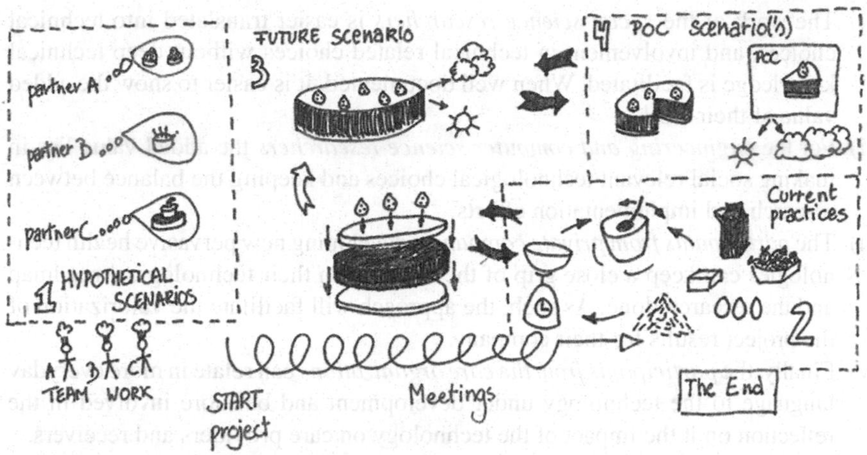

Fig. 4.2 'Baking a cake' metaphor to explain goal of approach

Secondly, we look at the current practices of making cakes, and maybe even broader practices surrounding cooking in general. We make a synthesis of these practices, by describing them in a *current practice scenario*. Thirdly, by combining the insights on current practices with the ambitions and expectations of all partners we create a *grounded future scenario* of our ideal cake. In this step of the process, it is important to come up with grounded scenarios on a sunny day when everything in our cake baking process runs smoothly (sunny day scenarios), but also to think about cloudy weather scenarios when the cake baking process have technical problems. Finally, in the fourth step we decide on which piece to make, since the total cake is too big to finish within the project time. We select the piece (big, small, a lot of cream or more fruit) considering the current needs, and the expectations/ ambitions (proof of concept scenario). Although the four steps are consecutive, there is also a lot of going back and forth between the steps, and regular meetings of all with their own skills and specialties facilitate this.

Reflections

This step is not in the learning cycle of Limonard and Koning [13], but it is essential to stimulate iteration between field and lab approach of interdisciplinary cooperation they put forward as necessary.

It is crucial to give room to the participants to discuss and doubt the approach. Next to the general added value (supra, intro), for each actor this added value is different:

(i) The work of the *social science researchers* is easier translated into technical choices, and involvement in technical related choices without deep technical knowledge is facilitated. When well documented, it is easier to show the added value of their work.

(ii) For the *engineering and computer science researchers* the added value lies in making social relevant technological choices and keeping the balance between research and implementation efforts.

(iii) The *participants from private companies* developing new pervasive health technologies can keep a close grip of the fit between their technological roadmap and the research done. As such, the approach will facilitate the valorization of the project results for their company.

(iv) Finally, the *participants from the care organizations* can relate in more everyday language to the technology under development and be more involved in the reflection on it the impact of the technology on care providers and receivers.

Step 2: Making expectations explicit towards a hypothetical scenario

Objectives

- Make ambitions, goals and expectations of each partner explicit for the other partners.
- Create hypothetical scenario(s) based on these expectations to facilitate discussion.

Participants/lead

At least one representative per partner should participate. The social science researchers take the lead, because they are more trained in making a narrative out of different points of views.

Step 2.1 *Elicit expectations and ambitions*
All project participants bring their own background and motivation to the project, next to the organization's motivations. The proposal holds clues on each partner's expectation and ambition. But due to a time gap between proposal and start of the project, changes happen. To understand the view on challenges, technologies to be used and target group, different methods for elicitations are possible: analysis of the proposal, a questionnaire, a hands-on workshop on the overarching project topic, etc. For inspiration on how to organize this elicitation, we refer to methods like Territory Maps and Stakeholder Maps [14, p. 80, 85].

Step 2.2 *Joint meeting discussing expectations and ambitions*
Similarities and differences are mapped and discussed. If a workshop type of approach is used, the workshop needs some preparation as well. Either way, creating mutual understanding needs a social process like a meeting.

Step 2.3 *Translate and synthesize in hypothetical scenario(s)*
The hypothetical scenarios (current and future practice) are based on these discussions. The number of scenarios depends on the variation in expectations amongst the project partners. In the next steps these scenarios are

challenged and reflected upon until the end (compare start with final project results). The hypothetical scenarios also help to make explicit what the project partners do not know yet and where research is required.

Example

We experimented with different ways to elicit expectations and ambitions: examining from the proposal, a questionnaire and a hands-on workshop.

(1) *Examining the proposal*
In the TransEcare project, two social researchers made an analysis of the different sub-themes of independent living that were part of the proposal, and which partners planned to work on these themes. This analysis was represented in a table, which we discussed during several joint meetings. We added other aspects of interest not that clear from the proposal. Later in the project, these tables were re-used for the prioritization of POC integration.

(2) *Open questionnaire*
In the Fallrisk project, a use case was included in the proposal, describing of the current situation of the prevention and detection system under development. Using an online questionnaire with open questions, we asked the partners to describe the actors, practices and technologies as they envisioned for the project, and to provide visuals to illustrate their vision of the future they want to support with the new system [7].

(3) *Hands-on workshop*
In the ACCIO project, we involved all project partners in an initial workshop. One goal of the ACCIO project was to develop a new way to co-create knowledge models in the care domain. The workshop explained the basics and hurdles of knowledge model engineering by performing a step-by-step exercise, actively involving all the participants. This resulted in a discussion on the opportunities we saw for this technology in our project [16]. In comparison to the use of a questionnaire, this was experienced to be a more hands on way of explaining the process.

A hypothetical scenario is based on these expectations of the project partners. Only a sunny day version is made. In Fallrisk, two hypothetical scenarios were written: a scenario on the hypothetical future, and a scenario on the assumed current practices. Thus, also assumptions and (lack of) knowledge on the current practices can be shared. A short example of a scene from the first version of a hypothetical scenario is shown in Table 4.1.

Table 4.1 First iteration on the hypothetical scenario, mapping questions

Current situation	Future situation	Comments
Scenario B installation and explanation of system		
Last week Marie walked to her sofa to watch some TV, but then trips over her carpet	Idem	
Tom discusses his concerns with his mother, Marie. Together they agree to request a PAS system	Idem	
Tom contacted a home care organization to inform about the PAS and he asked to install the system	Tom contacted a home care organization to inform about the Fallrisk system and he asked to install the system	Question: in future scenario: which kind of organization would provide support? Also home care organization? Insurer?
A couple days later…		
A couple days later, nurse Celine comes to install the PAS system and she also explains how it works to Marie and to the family care-giver(s) present	A couple days later, nurse Celine comes to install the Fallrisk system for Marie and she also explains how it works to Marie and to the family, caregiver(s) present	Question: are the children typically present in this situation? Reaction care organisation: ideal at least one formal caregiver present and he/she makes sure that the informal caregiver understand system
The PAS system comes with a small button that Marie needs to carry with her. The button can be carried as a necklace or as a bracelet. Marie can also clip the button to her bra, so it's not visible for others…	The Fallrisk system can detect falls with cameras and sensors in the house and worn by Marie (eg smart phone). It not only detect when she falls, but also warn Marie and her caregivers when her risk of falling increases after measuring over some days…	Question: in the future system: the active button is not removed? Answer social scientist: prefer to keep it optionally in to give Marie the feeling of control

Reflections

Step 2 offers an opportunity to get to know the people and organizations involved in the project more closely. This step helps to understand partners' dependencies and drivers to invest time in a certain aspect of the project, and where to find a better fit in interests. It is important that all partners realize there is no need to wait for the others to finish: both technical and social streams can start (mutual shaping).

In this phase of the project, the 'innovation binder' approach serves to build a foundation for interdisciplinary work in addition to the proposed learning cycle of Limonard and Koning [13].

Step 3: Documenting current practices and technological roadmaps: validating current practice scenario and creating future practice scenario

Objectives

- 'Ground' the hypothetical scenario by studying the current practices, the care domain, the technological opportunities and their building blocks.
- Focus on current practices with and without technologies, while reflecting on the assumptions for the future change.

Participants/lead

In this step, the activities are diverse. There is a focus on the contributions from the own discipline, but mixed teams are also formed.

Step 3.1 *Researching current practices and freedom to operate/technological roadmaps*

Different research activities are started: deepening state of the art literature, studying current user practices and examining technological roadmaps (more detail see e.g., [3]). The hypothetical current practice and future scenario can be used in this phase to probe for feedback from users. The scenario is thus challenged by reflections by potential future users. User roles are redefined and thick personas created [10].

Step 3.2 *Intermediate joint meetings*

All these inquiries finally end in reports and artifacts, but in order to create a dialectic interaction between the social and technical stream, meetings are required to enable work on intermediate results (mutual shaping). This can be facilitated by preparation of meetings by different partners depending on the main topics under discussion. These meetings can stimulate co-ownership of the output. During the process hypothetical scenarios are gradually turned into grounded scenarios of current practice and future practices with the pervasive health system. This 'future scenario' is tied to the proposed architecture. In this iterative process, spread over several meetings, the future scenario matures by the inclusion of results of the different research activities. At first, it stays focused on the sunny day version. While maturing attention to anticipate the cloudy weather version, when the technology does hamper, should increase.

This is also the moment when designing a generic architecture of the pervasive health solution is helpful. This generic architecture links the envisioned technical components and details the communication flow. The detailed architectural work can be done later.

Creating an architecture is a technical task, but by making use of TechCards it is possible to start the integration work in an interdisciplinary way as well, as such building bridges between partners and disciplines. These TechCards (see example section) describe in a generic way the technical components that the different partners are working on. In this way, an overview of the components and which components need to work together is created. Also, awareness is created about the components and links that may be missing. They are object of discussion during meetings. In contrast to the method where a "common glossary" is made for the project, e.g., in the form of a wiki, to facilitate interdisciplinary communication, this tool is more hands on and feels less like writing a burdensome dictionary.

Example

To illustrate how the different research activities interact, we present research activities from the project OCareClouds. One of the first research activities of the social scientists in the project was to perform a domain analysis on the care diary currently used to coordinate the care activities between formal and informal caregivers. This was done by means of a literature study on caregiving processes, and a series of expert interviews with different people of the care organizations involved. Concurrently, a mixed team of social and technical researchers took part in a contextual inquiry of the current formal care delivery process of the involved care organizations. In parallel, a first design of the architecture was made, making use of the technical components as mentioned in the project proposal.

In addition, and inspired by our colleagues Claeys L. and Criel J. who tested the approach out in other projects, we implemented the TechCard approach in both O'CareCloudS and Care4Balance. Each partner involved in the development of technical components had to describe their technical components in a template of the TechCard (see for an example Fig. 4.3). In the follow-up joint meeting, all partners present their component(s), and the right level of abstraction is determined. Some changes or new cards are made after this meeting. The TechCards are also mapped on the different functionalities already determined in the current iteration of the scenario. This approach enables the different partners to reflect on the responsibilities regarding the different components. It also helps to discover missed communication links and components, i.e., a missing functionality and to reflect on the complexity, scalability, usability and generic applicability of the different components.

For example, in OCareCloudS the overview of the cards triggered a new view on how to design the back-end architecture. The back-end components reason on integrated patient data to trigger alerts to the caregivers. Originally, these components were split so each covers a complete use case domain, e.g., alerts about the physical healthcare state of the patient. The TechCard exercise made aware this was not scalable nor user-friendly enough for the future software developers and not easily adaptable to future scenarios. A 'template approach' of different functionalities, e.g., a monitoring template, was the new solution. A back-end component is then built as an instantiation of such a template, e.g., a blood pressure monitoring component. As such, very scalable and small components are achieved with a very specific purpose, while user-friendliness for the software developers is assured by offering the different templates.

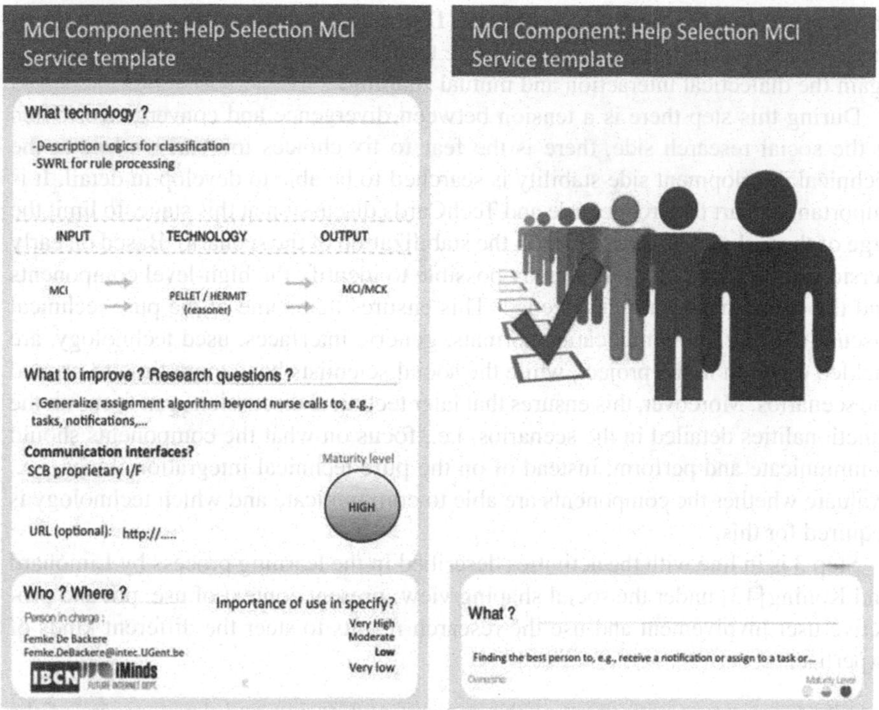

Fig. 4.3 TechCard from O'CareClouds project

In both projects the cards engaged the non-technical partners more in the technical components, but it also spurred technical groups to collaborate more. The TechCards help to make promises less vague. This improves the quality of planning towards the proof of concept.

Reflections

State of the art knowledge is necessary to formulate the research plan. But to update and collect deeper available knowledge, it is advisable to foresee some state of the art work here both from the social and technical side. The formulation of a scenario of current practices is something we recently added to the process, in order to document the evolution of the project. Also, the TechCards approach is a recent addition to the innovation binder process, which resulted from the need for a tool to facilitate communication amongst the technical partners, and between the technical and non-technical partners.

In this step the recurrent dedicated 'innovation binder' meetings are still at a low frequency. They are integrated in other general status meetings. A stepwise discussion of the scenario in a dedicated separate meeting is prepared by assigning all partners to comment on the scenarios. Depending on the skills of each partner, the comments on the scenario will be more technical or social in nature, stimulating again the dialectical interaction and mutual shaping.

During this step there is a tension between divergence and convergence. Often at the social research side, there is the fear to fix choices too early, while at the technical development side stability is searched to be able to develop in detail. It is important to start the architecture and TechCards discussion at this stage, to limit the urge of the technical partners to rush the stabilization of the scenario. Based on early versions of the scenario, it is already possible to identify the high-level components and the communication links needed. This ensures that some of the pure technical discussions, e.g., communication formats, generic interfaces, used technology, are tackled early on in the project, while the social scientists have more time to ground the scenarios. Moreover, this ensures that later technical discussions can focus on the functionalities detailed in the scenarios, i.e., focus on what the components should communicate and perform, instead of on the pure technical integration issues, i.e., evaluate whether the components are able to communicate and which technology is required for this.

Step 3 is in line with the activities described in the learning process by Limonard and Koning [13] under the social shaping view: present context of use, pre and pro-active user involvement and use the research results to steer the different kinds of expertise.

Step 4: Co-creation with users of the concept and design and development of the concept: towards an optimal ideal future scenario.

Objectives

- Organize co-creation activities to develop the concept and to stimulate technical choices.

Ensure that the future scenario reaches full maturity.

Participants/lead

The social research partners lead the co-creation with users. The care organizations are in the lead to recruit participants for the co-creation activities. The technical partners are in the lead of the technical choice process. Mixed teams are formed for the co-creation sessions.

Step 4.1 *Co-creation activities and development technical components*

Once the basic concept is made more concrete by the available technical components, we organize co-creation activities with the target user group(s). There is a wide variety of available techniques: story boarding, role-playing, paper mock up experiences, guided brainstorms, etc. One could of course start with these activities in a less technical influenced way once the context of use and user group are known (Step 3).

The first common agreed upon version of the future scenario could be integrated in this co-creation exercise. It can be used as a starting point, or as a way to offer a new point of reference, elicit openness towards the characteristics of the pervasive technology. The results of these activities are then translated into an "update" of the future scenario where the technology works flawless (sunny day scenario).

Step 4.2 *Joint meetings integrating the results and making socio-technical choices*
Open options and current choices are discussed in-group to evolve towards the realization of the "updated" future scenario. We limited the time of these meetings to a maximum of 3 hours per session, so each partner knows preparation is needed and decisions should be reached at a certain pace. Depending on the topic, the composition of the team (number and background of participants) that meets can differ. But in principle, all meetings are open for all project members.
The goal of the meeting is to match the user opportunities and needs with the technical developments. A lot of time is spent on mapping the different technical components on the scenarios, helping to determine the priority of each service and components, as well as identifying the ones that are missing. The TechCards made earlier are used to facilitate this exercise. The future scenario is split into scenes of actions and the TechCards are mapped on then. In combination with the level of maturity the priority of the further development of each component can be thus determined.

Example

During the ACCIO project we experimented with different types of co-creation workshops during the whole trajectory. A detailed description and comparison of the workshop types can be retrieved in Ongenae et al. [16, 17]. For example, the first one was a role playing workshop during which we let different stakeholders from the care field play scenes from the future scenario, offering information on both current practices, used concepts for the ontology and the envisioned future use of sensors in a ward environment.

Concurrently with the mixed team activities, the technical partners developed so called 'dummy' components and integrate them to evaluate whether the proposed architecture and communication flow is feasible and whether the proposed technologies are sufficient to reach the goals of the project. In the OCareCloudS project this integration was done with sending dummy data from one component to the other, during the ACCIO project implementing a very simple sub scene of the scenario was chosen for technical evaluation purposes. In this way continuous integration is started: stimulating the decision on the kind of data and enabling each partner to focus again on their own component.

Maturing the future scenario implies adding details on interfaces, measures for making a secure system, type of data input and output. In this way the scenarios also carry the implicit technical requirements of the new pervasive system. For example, the amount of data generated, the type of data that should be transferred between the different components to be able to transform the input to the output, where the data will be stored. Based on these requirements, technical solutions can be selected, taking into account the motivations of the partners as mapped in Step 1. For example, when one of the goals of a partner is to research the feasibility of integration of a new TV platform, it is unlikely not to use it.

Reflections

The 'innovation binder' approach appears to be more important in cases where the technical work is not that much related to the end user interaction. Without such a tool, the engagement of the technical group with non-technical research insights would remain low.

At this point in the process there are three types of scenarios: the starting hypothetical scenarios, the finished scenarios synthesizing the current practices, and rather mature future practice scenarios. Each of them is helpful to reflect on the process, as well as a tool to let new participants enter the project, as often personnel changes happen during the project time of 2 years.

In step 4 we move away from the present socio-technical context of use and focus on future use of the technology, enabling reactive user involvement which aims for visions/ambitions instead of a orientation on current problems [13, p. 175]. Step 4 can overlap and interacts with step 3. Consequently, the 'innovation binder' stimulates to look concurrently at both the current use context (step 3) and the future use context (step 4 and 5), one of the dilemmas raised by Limonard and Konings [13].

4.3.3.2 Proof of Concept Development Phase: Towards an Evaluated Proof of Concept with Value for Business and Society

The next steps describe what we have called "the convergence phase". This phase aims to bring the R&D activities to a stable proof-of-concept that demonstrates the added value of the project activities. The timing to converge is most often dictated by the project rhythm itself. It is thus a pragmatic choice. In our project rhythm of 2 years, we see the one-year project milestone as a good timing to go to the converging phase. In this phase the intensity of the joint meetings is also increased. We strive towards a rhythm of biweekly meetings.

In the proof of concept development phase, we can identify 3 steps: (1) refinement of the concept and development of proof of concept scenarios (step 6), (2) realization of the proof of concept(s) and evaluation with users (step 6) and (3) project ending and knowledge transfer towards valorization and further research (step 7).

Step 5: Refinement of concept and developing the proof of concept scenario

Objectives

- Improve the concept detailing.
- Iterative user evaluation with the material at hand: paper, mock up or in lab working prototype.
- Maintain the continuous integration: update the components, retest the internal communication.
- Test the technical requirements (e.g., scalability, performance and responsiveness).
- Select the pieces of the future practice scenario, to create a proof of concept scenario. List the development work and the evaluation options.

Participants/lead

The technical partners tend to take the lead, because of the growing focus on continuous integration and the proof of concept.

Step 5.1 *Choosing parts of the future scenario to be developed as proof of concept*
Multiple factors influence the selection of pieces. Two main points of attention are usually taken into account: (i) the proof of concept needs to illustrate innovativeness of the pervasive health system under development, and (ii) the proof of concept needs to demonstrate the added value for the different end users. The fit between those two aspects leaves some opportunities to create added value unresolved. To aid this process of choosing pieces of the future scenario, the mapping exercise on the scenario (previously done with the TechCards) can be repeated here: now the different scenes of the scenario can be rated on different aspects that are relevant for the development of the proof of concept (e.g., innovativeness, maturity, desirability, effort needed to develop, partner ambitions, etc.).

Step 5.2 *Creating proof of concept scenarios*
The difference between the proof of concept and the future scenario is that in the proof of concept scenario the future scenario is being 'translated' to the time, technical components and skills available in the project. As a result, some parts will be done with a suboptimal, but working solution. Interfaces and devices are also more fixed in detail in these scenarios. Attention for the possible flaws in the system should be explored, and are best documented in making alternative cloudy weather scenarios.

Step 5.3 *Additional research to ground proof of concept scenario where needed*
The future scenario is still on a quiet abstract level of the description of practices. To come to the level of real implementations for the proof of concept, some abstract ideas should be studied in more detail. In that way they become less based on guesswork, but are further grounded in knowledge about the care domain.

Reflections

The joint meetings are time intensive and therefore best planned in advance. For some smaller organizations, it is sometimes difficult to make this time investment. Especially for care organizations, continued presence could be hard if there is no funding for this work. The organization and the flow of the meetings also depend on the size of the group: a larger team offers more diversity in perspective, but a smaller team is more dynamic. In a larger team it is also difficult to keep everyone engaged and to determine whether everybody understands and acts his or her role in the process.

Precisely in this step, we fully embrace the mutual shaping aspects of the dilemmas described by Limonard and Konings [13]: the future context of use is the core focus, the user is involved in validation of the ideas (reactive user involvement) and testing and modifying is in the interdisciplinary cooperation mode.

Step 6: Realization of the proof of concept and evaluating it with users

Objectives

- Show one or more proof of concepts.
- Learn iteratively from in-between evaluations of the proof of concepts

Participants/lead

The task is lead by technical partners, but in close interaction with the social scientists and the care organizations providing the evaluation strategy and recruitment.

Step 6.1 *Integrating towards a working proof of concept*

In this step, continuous integration is at its highest intensity: having a central repository and testing over and over again. Testing needs to clarify how robust the proof of concept is, also if it can be set up outside the lab, and how many pieces of the test setup are feasible to make. The team works towards the demonstration moment where it tries to provide an evaluation setup as close as possible in the envisioned context of use with the targeted users. To reach this goal we advise a stepwise approach going out the lab towards the field, as described in [1].

Step 6.2 *Evaluating the proof of concept with different users*

The proof of concept scenario is also helpful to evaluate the proof of concept itself with users. In our experience, most of the time the pervasive health proof of concepts are not robust enough to go 'into the wild'. In order to obtain valuable user feedback, different solutions are available. For instance, the team can organize a role-play workshop revolving around the proof of concept, supplied with mock-ups of those features that have not yet been implemented. As such, it is possible to create an improved second proof of concept that is based on significant user tests [17].

Step 6.3 *Iterating towards new proof of concept*

During the selection of elements to include in the proof of concept, the features that need most development time are often postponed towards a next iteration of the proof of concept. However, it is also essential to foresee effort to implement the user feedback on the first version, so an improved version both on the social and technical level can be produced.

Example

In the ACCIO project, one of the goals was to show the relevance and feasibility of working with ontologies in the back end. This steered the decision to pick those scenes in the future scenario where the added value of this technology could be shown both from a user and technical perspective, illustrating a balanced use of computer reasoning and human intervention in the process [17]. In the Care4Balance project, one of the main drivers is having a demonstrator that is able to show the reciprocity between caregiver and care receiver, as well as using a new interface. These focal points guide the selection process for the proof of concept scenario.

To spur the continuous integration we had a good experience in the Care4Balance project with a co-programming one-day workshop where we looked into making a proof of concept with the components at hand for one day. This workshop was guided by the information of the TechCards and a technical partner in charge of the central platform guided the work. Short sprints are done on each component, after which each sub team explained to the rest with a mini demo what is achieved in the previous time frame.

These three steps can be repeated if the project time allows it.

Example

In step 6, the added value of the continuous integration effort becomes most clear. When using the ‘innovation binder’ approach, the technical researchers keep using the proof of concept scenarios to guide the planning, next to the preferences and skills of the developers. Technical meetings are held frequently, however, it can be recommended to have a social researcher following them as well. This person can track the changes driven from technical concerns, as well as changes in functionality that could be shown during the evaluations. As explained before, for these functionalities that have not yet been implemented, a mock-up needs to be the designed for the evaluation. During the evaluations, it is essential that a technical developer/researcher is present to support the user researchers when the system gets quirky. When doing user tests outside a lab setting and into the field, continuous technical support should also be foreseen at close distance [1].

Reflections

The proof of concept scenario has to remain rather stable, because of the interdependency of the components. However, as a result of this, developers might tend to use the proof of concept scenario as a shield, arguing against any modification of the technology under development because "it is not mentioned in the scenario". The consequences should be discussed, and if the disruption is too high one can add this change to an update of the ideal future scenario and maybe integrate it during the next proof of concept iteration. Going back to the other options left out in the proof of concept scenario is also simple, since they are documented. Alternative choices are consequently easier to make in a next iteration.

This is a continuation of giving attention to the mutual shaping cluster of the dilemmas [13] started in step 5. In step 6, we try to link back to the first step by bringing the proof of concept as close as possible to the present context of use. Acknowledging that only partial knowledge is gathered due to the unpredictability of the innovative use when the pervasive solution is appropriated in everyday practices.

Step 7: Ending the project and transferring knowledge towards valorization and new research

Objectives

- Stimulate valorization and transfer the outcomes of the project.
- Reflect on the total trajectory and the lessons learned from the interdisciplinary teamwork.
- Create grounded new research trajectories.

Participants/lead

Every partner should be involved, while the lead of this task is mostly with the project leader.

Step 7.1 *Reflecting on choices, lessons learned and starting to re-diverge*
In this step, the final update of the future scenario can be made. The reflection on the projects' process and the outcome, the demonstration of user centered designed pervasive health system can be made by comparing the hypothetical future scenario with the final future scenario. Reflections on the gap between this scenario and the demonstrator can be helpful to determine the next steps and alternative choices to make and test (re-divergence).

Step 7.2 *Final reporting of project results and transferring the knowledge*
This is the bread and butter of every R&D project, but by using the innovation binder process, the different scenarios and documentation of the process can help to show the insights and innovations in a more comprehensible way to a diverse public (funders, potential client care organizations, potential investors for further development).

Example

At the end of the ACCIO project, we held a closing event presenting the results and linking them to the broader societal debate. At this event, we illustrated the subject of a follow-up project on the use of ontologies in the home care situation by making use of an adapted format of one of the workshops we did with end users during the ACCIO project. The proof of concept scenario in ACCIO was used to contextualize the results of the technical demonstrator. In addition, we organized a final internal ideation workshop on some of the remaining research questions of the ACCIO project. Next, we also presented the research insights to the institutions that supported us during the fieldwork in step 3 (understanding the current practices). Finally, we also held a workshop with people interested in ontologies in Flemish industry to discuss their needs to use ontologies in industry.

Reflections

At the end of a project time and effort becomes scarce. Activities looking for new opportunities, beside the obligatory wrap up activities can stimulate this phase. In our experience, the pitfall is that these activities are not explicitly detailed in the work plan as discussed in step 1.

This final step is, like the first two steps, not part of the learning cycle as described by Limonard and Koning [13]. We think that this reflective step is, however, in line with their idea around interdisciplinary work and including the social in the design of new technologies.

4.4 Open Problems

In this part, we will go into some of the challenges that we were frequently faced with when using the 'innovation binder'. Since the different types of scenarios form the spine of the process, some of the open problems are related to them. Others problems are related to the teamwork and the meetings.

4.4.1 Over-Dependency on a Sunny Day Scenario

As we explained, the first scenarios are sunny day scenarios. It is often tempting to concentrate only on them, and not develop cloudy weather scenarios. It is necessary to consider the failures in the system and the non-use of the user or alternative uses throughout the process. Thinking about the 'cloudy weather' scenarios will result in another, more critical look on the technology under development.

4.4.2 Countering the Horror Scenario

During the iterations on the future scenario, the project team will experience the difficulties in finding a balance between the affordances of the pervasive health solution and the interests of the users. Often there is a moment when the future scenario turns into a description of a future experience that seems highly unwanted and not desirable for the end users. Often 'by accident' the team might have created a horror scenario. The story might for instance describe a system that results in a high loss of control. Thus, because the system gives too little freedom to the user, the quality of life tends to decrease. However, such a moment is very functional, because it lets the team question the basic assumptions made in the project. This makes it possible to delay path dependency, e.g., earlier choices dictating the path you follow [2] as long as possible. To escape the horror scenario and get back to describing a desired future, the team has to focus on the key human values the pervasive system is overruling, and insert more human agency in the system.

4.4.3 Scenarios are Not Actively Used by Partners, The Story is too Long or Detailed

The scenarios could be abandoned during the project when the feeling rises that they are too clumsy or time consuming. Typically one reduces the story to a list of requirements, losing the contextual and relational information the story offers. Again, a search for balance is the solution here. The list of functionalities or functional requirements could be tagged on the different scenes of the scenario. The scenes are parsed into one action or interaction per scene (one or two sentences). When there are changes in the scenario and scenes are added, sub numbering (e.g., 1.a, 1.b) should be used for consistency. In this way, lists and reduction is possible, without losing the connection to the story and the personas in the discussions. Another well-documented trick in literature is visualizing the personas and their stories (e.g., Pruijt and Aldin 2003, [10]).

The degree of detail of the story can also create difficulties. Especially at the start of the project, one wants to keep openness in the technical solution. Therefore, it is good to try to delay those detailed technical choices until the convergence phase, and then work them out (for example, which screens and devices are involved, how do we in detail organize the access control, what will be the procedure, etc.).

4.4.4 Balance Between Openness and Closure, and the Waiting Game

The 'innovation binder' process in its design tries to let the social and technical stream work concurrently by stimulating a pendulum between technology push and social pull into a mutual shaping process. In practice, keeping this balance is difficult. Questions that are frequently asked include the length of every step in the process, and how to determine if the scenario is sufficiently stable to start implementing. Typically, the social research stream could go on in digging deeper into the current practices and exploring other future options via co-creation. They are thus reluctant to stabilize the scenario that quickly, since this makes going back on previous choices harder or even impossible (path dependency). A scenario is after all always a condensed modeled representation of the observations and interpretations of the world, and therefore incomplete. The project team should remain aware of this shortcoming and keep the missed variation in mind during development. As such, it is fundamental in the introduction phase of the innovation binder and during the meetings to remind all partners on the dialectical mutual shaping process: choices are to be made, together each partner brings their expertise and waiting for each other should be avoided and at least made explicit.

4.4.5 No Interest in Trying the Innovation Binder Approach

Even when the 'innovation binder' approach is explicitly part of the proposal, it sometimes becomes clear that there is no genuine interest of the project partners (or even the project lead) to work in an integrated interdisciplinary way. We recommend trying to convince the other project partners at the start of the project. But when acceptance is not feasible, it is probably wiser to change from this interdisciplinary approach towards a multidisciplinary way of working (each doing their own research task next to each other) in order to lower your own degree of frustration. The 'innovation binder' alone will not suffice to work in an interdisciplinary manner. It can only be a supporting tool when project partners are willing to collaborate, but it cannot enforce it.

Another reason why people are reluctant to use the approach is when the usage domain is too large. Then there are too many practices that are part of the user domain. This usually becomes clear when the hypothetical scenarios are being written and it feels that too much ground needs to be covered. In this case, the project partners need to spend extra time on determining what the central practices are the project wants to focus on.

4.4.6 The Team, Its Scale and Different Roles

As in any collaborative undertaking, the classic team dynamics play when making use of the 'innovation binder' approach. So as the rules of thumb of a good focus group learns us, a group over 12 persons is hard to keep together. But in our experience, it is still helpful to take the different steps, although the need of one clear owner of the process is more necessary when the group is larger.

Next to the scale, there is the issue of the different roles and their targets with the project. Most researchers in the project will focus on doing research, since their performance is measured by their publications. As such, the implementation work is not as high on their agenda as it is for the participants from the companies and the care organizations. Therefore, it is important in the explication step (step 2) to allow time to understand what makes the other tick. In our experience, a hands-on workshop is more suitable for this: it can be fun, can improve other practical knowledge that is lacking on a certain topic, and it can stimulate bonding. It is important for the success of this workshop that it does not resembles a bad team building activity, which has no relation to the goal of the project.

A project can strive to involve every necessary actor, but it is unlikely to have every possible role that is needed to make it into a 'real' product. Therefore, it is also important to become aware of missing parties. This can, for instance, be a project partner that delivers content, who does the front-end design and the integration work. Expectations about the final point of the project can thus be altered and made more realistic, and actions can be started during the project to look for other alliances to fill in these gaps. Awareness about the limitations of the project team best comes as early as possible, and is important when the team has to decide which parts of the ideal future scenario should be included in the proof of concept scenario. Things high on the priority list, but unachievable with the current team in the process, should trigger a search for other parties who could help to bring the results closer to valorization in due time (during or after the project).

4.4.7 Documenting the 'Innovation Binder' Process

Making interdisciplinary choices based on grounded stories is the backbone of the process. Therefore, it is important to document them. In that way, the innovation binder process offers a tool to look back and see the accomplishments and allows going a few steps back and choosing an alternative path. Also, with new participants entering the project due to change of personnel, this documentation is important. However, it is still a challenge to log all those decisions in a good way. There are meeting reports of all meetings and different versions of the scenario are kept with comments, but this information is not that easily accessible due to its volume. As with other documenting task (e.g., code writing and documenting), it is often seen as a burden. Although documenting needs more attention, one should be careful not to loose the informal character of the meetings revolving around the boundary object of the scenario. Informality in a meeting has a function in itself [21]: finding in a free conversation inspiration and connectedness without formally having consensus on all details is one of them.

4.5 Future Outlook

Our project timeline is two years, but with another timeline and format the 'innovation binder' approach is likely to be useful as well. The whole approach is grounded in a broader tradition within HCI and PD. To be a practical approach transferable to other projects the approach needs to further mature. This can be achieved by comparing cases empirically and describing what can be altered or improved. For the future improvement of our approach, we want to improve the way we engage project partners or participants who are new to the approach. Another issue to deal with is how to simplify the visualization and documenting of the process. By doing this we do not want to loose the informality of meetings and the context of the requirements. Until now, we covered the economical, business side of the development process as part of the social stream, but we want to explore how we can make this perspective more explicit, to focus on the valorization opportunities of the project from the very start. There are certainly elements of AGILE, inspiring this approach. Systematically reviewing how strategies and tactics from this software methodology could inspire in an interdisciplinary R&D environment need also be done. Finally, we are building more experience with the use of TechCards, trying to understand when and why they work.

Searching for better pervasive health systems, with its vulnerable users and complex context of use, offered us the opportunity and the need to develop this approach and stimulate all partners to come out of their disciplinary comfort zone. If people want to endeavor in pre-competitive research in other domains, this approach could be equally useful.

We want to conclude by stating that the 'innovation binder' approach is able to support the pre-competitive research on pervasive health applications, because it is a tool which is in line with the advice given by Stewart and Claeys [23]: the innovation binder approach is inviting everyone to open up to another world as a team, providing a common ground for discussion and allowing for multiple interpretations and methods from different disciplines.

References

1. Ackaert, A., Jacobs, A., Veys, A., Derboven, J., Gils, M., Buysse, H., et al. (2009). A multidisciplinary approach towards the design and development of value+ eHomeCare services. In K. Yogesan, L. Bos, P. Brett, & M. Gibbons (Eds.), *Handbook of Digital Homecare* (pp. 243–267). Berlin: Springer.
2. Bijker, W. E. (1997). *Of bicycles, bakelites and bulbs: Toward a theory of sociotechnical change*. Cambridge: MIT Press.

3. Bleumers, L., Jacobs, A., Ongenae, F., Ackaert, A., Sulmon, N., Verstraete, M., et al. (2011). Towards ontology co-creation in institutionalized care settings. In *Proceedings of the 5th International Conference on IEEE Xplore Digital Library. Presented at the Pervasive Health, Dublin* (pp. 559–562).
4. Bødker, S. (2000). Scenarios in user-centred design–setting the stage for reflection and action. *Interacting with Computers, 13*(1), 61–75.
5. Carroll, J. M. (2000). Five reasons for scenario-based design. *Interacting with Computers, 13*(1), 43–60.
6. De Rouck, S., Jacobs, A., & Leys, M. (2008). A methodology for shifting the focus of e-health support design onto user needs: A case in the homecare field. *International Journal of Medical Informatics, 77*, 589–601.
7. Elprama, S., Duysburgh, P., Bleumers, L., & Jacobs, A. (2013). Developing assistive technology with multidisciplinary teams: a front-end procedure to stimulate collaboration and manage expectations. In *Proceedings of the 12th European Association for the Advancement of Assistive Technology in Europe Conference (AAATE), Vilamoura, Algarve, Portugal, 2013*.
8. Garcia, M. L., & Bray, O. H. (1997). *Fundamentals of technology roadmapping*. Albuquerque, NM: Sandia National Laboratories.
9. Isaksen, S. G., Stead-Dorval, K. B., & Treffinger, D. J. (2011). *Creative approaches to problem solving: A framework for innovation and change*. Los Angeles: SAGE.
10. Jacobs, A., Dreessen, K., and Pierson, J. (2008). "Thick"personas-Using ethnographic Methods for Persona Development as a Tool for Conveying the Social Science View in Technological Design. *Observatorio (OBS*), 5*, 79–97.
11. Johansson, M., & Arvola, M. (2007). A case study of how user interface sketches, scenarios and computer prototypes structure stakeholder meetings. In *Proceedings of the 21st British HCI Group Annual Conference on People and Computers: HCI... but not as we know it* (Vol. 1, pp. 177–184).
12. Karasti, H., Baker, K. S., & Bowker, G. C. (2002). Ecological storytelling and collaborative scientific activities. *ACM SIGGROUP Bulletin, 23*(2), 29–30.
13. Limonard, S., de Koning, N. (2005) Dealing with dilemmas in pre-competitive ICT. Development projects: The construction of 'The Social' in designing new technologies. In L. Haddon, E. Mante, B. Sapio, K-H. Kommonen, L. Fortunati & A. Kant (Eds.), *Everyday Innovators* (pp. 168–183). *Computer Supported Cooperative Work* (p. 32). Netherlands: Springer. http://link.springer.com/chapter/10.1007/1-4020-3872-0_11
14. Martin, B., & Hanington, B. M. (2012). *Universal methods of design: 100 ways to research complex problems, develop innovative ideas, and design effective solutions*. Beverly, MA: Rockport Publishers.
15. Muller, M. J. (2002). *Participatory design: The third space in HCI*. Cambrigde, MA: Lotus Research, Lotus Development Corporation.
16. Ongenae, F., Bleumers, L., Sulmon, N., Verstraete, M., Van Gils, M., Jacobs, A., De Zutter, S., Verhoeve, P., Ackaert, A. & De Turck, F. (2011). Participatory design of a continuous care ontology: Towards a user-driven ontology engineering methodology. In *Proceedings of the International Knowledge Engineering and Ontology Development Conference (KEOD)*, (pp. 81–90). Paris, France: SciTePress.
17. Ongenae, F., Duysburgh, P., Verstraete, M., Sulmon, N., Bleumers, L., Jacobs, A., Ackaert, A., De Zutter, S., Verstichel, S. & De Turck, F. User-driven design of a context-aware application: An ambient-intelligent nurse call system. In *Proceedings of the 6th International Conference on Pervasive Technologies for Healthcare (PervasiveHealth)*, (pp. 205–210). San Diego, CA, USA: IEEE.
18. Pagliari, C. (2007). Design and evaluation in eHealth: Challenges and implications for an interdisciplinary field. *Journal of Medical Internet Research, 9*(2), e15.
19. Rip, A., Misa, T. J., & Schot, J. (1995). *Managing technology in society: The approach of constructive technology assessment*. London: Pinter Publishers.
20. Schatzki, T. R. (1997). Practices and actions: A Wittgensteinian critique of Bourdieu and Giddens. *Philosophy of the Social Sciences, 27*(3), 283–308.

21. Sennett, R. (2012). *Together: The rituals, pleasures, and politics of cooperation*. New Haven: Yale University Press.
22. Star, S. L. (2010, January 9) This is not a boundary object: Reflections on the origin of a concept. *Science, Technology & Human Values*, *35*(5), 601–617.
23. Stewart, J., & Claeys, L. (2009). Problems and opportunities of interdisciplinary work involving users in speculative research for innovation of novel ICT applications. In S. B. (Ed.), *Presented at the COST298 The Good, The Bad and The Challenging. The user and the future of information and communication technologies* (Vol. I). Koper, Slovenia: ABS-Center.
24. Van Bemmel, J. H. (2008). Medical informatics is interdisciplinary avant la lettre. *Methods of Information in Medicine*, *47*, 318–321. doi:10.3414/ME9119
25. Ziefle, M., Röcker, C., Holzinger, A. (2014). Current trends and challenges for pervasive health technologies: From technical innovation to user integration. In *Pervasive health: State-of-the-art & beyond*, (pp. 1–18). London: Springer.

Further Reading

26. Carroll, J. M. (1995). *Scenario-based design: Envisioning work and technology in system development*. Hoboken, NJ: Wiley.
27. Nielsen, L. (2013). *Personas: User focused design*. London: Springer.

Chapter 5
The Brain Computer Interface: Barriers to Becoming Pervasive

G. Lightbody, L. Galway and P. McCullagh

5.1 Introduction

The ability to communicate one's intentions without speech or muscular engagement has been a topic of great scientific interest over the last 30 years. Such facility, which was previously within the realms of science fiction, has become achievable and arguably, at least in some sense, is becoming pervasive. In general terms this relationship between man and machine using only thought processes is termed the Brain Computer Interface (BCI). The technology offers the potential for interaction and communication without the need for explicit physical manipulation, giving rise to a powerful assistive technology [1, 11, 44, 95, 96]. By performing electroencephalography (EEG), which senses and records the electrical activity of the brain, employing some predefined cognitive activity and subsequently determining characteristic brain wave patterns by sophisticated processing, it is indeed possible to exert 'thought' control of a computer application or device.

While there have already been several decades of research in BCI, initial efforts focused on developing a suitable technology that was capable of providing a communications channel for those with the greatest level of physical disability. Consequently, the emphasis has been on finding the ultimate assistive technology for subjects who may be 'locked in' their bodies, through either neurological disease or brain injury. For such people, where residual muscular movement is limited, unreliable or no longer present, the concept of communicating their intentions via thought

G. Lightbody (✉) · L. Galway · P. McCullagh
Smart Environments Research Group School of Computing and Mathematics,
University of Ulster, Newtownabbey BT37 OQB, UK
e-mail: g.lightbody@ulster.ac.uk

L. Galway
e-mail: l.galway@ulster.ac.uk

P. McCullagh
e-mail: pj.mccullagh@ulster.ac.uk

DOI: 10.1007/978-1-4471-6413-5_5,

is an emotive research goal, opening up social inclusion and improving their overall quality of life. The importance of such social engagement on the perceived personhood is highlighted by [12]. However, the resulting technology has still not reached a significant number of subjects for which it could be most beneficial, with the systems rarely migrating out of laboratory settings and few examples of home use [81]. This is regardless of the significant progress that has been made over the years in the following technical areas; EEG signal acquisition, signal processing and classification algorithms, hardware deployment and calibration, and user application development. Significantly, BCI is still a nascent research and development area, with an expectation that BCI systems will not become a mainstream technology for at least another 5–10 years [6, 27]. While the reasons for this are many faceted, undoubtedly one of the major challenges involves the personalization of the technology, such as matching the chosen signal processing algorithms to human processing, i.e. the individual human brain. Signal quality may be affected by both external factors (e.g. electrode placement, movement artefacts, etc.) and internal factors (e.g. the physiology, mood and level of engagement of the subject), and the algorithms and devices must take such factors into account in order to provide appropriate usability.

Within BCI research there was always the quandary that the technology could often be outperformed by other assistive technologies should the user have some remaining residual movement suitable for control of peripheral devices, for example the use of an eye tracker, or puffer switch. With only a very small percentage of the population potentially benefiting from pure BCI systems, it is easy to envisage the limited global impact the technology as it once stood would have. However, in recent years the scope of BCI technology has been rapidly changing and has accelerated in a number of exciting domains. Firstly, no longer are the concepts of pure, standalone BCI systems firmly in one camp and all other assistive technologies and input modalities in the other camp. Instead, there is a merging of technologies into hybrid systems that are tailored to utilize the best parts of each creating a more personalized system for the user. BCI is now becoming a potential input modality that strengthens the overall performance of such systems by providing an additional control channel or even an alternative when other mechanisms become tiring or inaccurate.

The second exciting area is that BCI is no longer considered as purely an assistive technology. With the advancements in electronics, wearable sensors, algorithms and available software development kits (SDKs) there has been a drive towards other applications for using thought processes to interact with computing systems. BCI has gained interest within gaming [50], creativity [88] and as another non-invasive physiological observation mechanism [7]. These examples bring some interesting thoughts to the fore about the potential pervasive nature of BCI; has the underlying technology reached the point where it is indeed pervasive and we are not truly aware of its presence? Weiser [94] stated that pervasive technologies are those that weave themselves into the fabric of our everyday lives and, in effect, become invisible. Does BCI technology truly have this potential? And if so, will this take us beyond the domain of assistive technology and provide the impetus for advances that can be fed back into the roots of BCI as a communication and control mechanism for those that will gain the most impact from its use in their lives?

This chapter will provide an overview of BCI, in order to set the background of the technology, and will report the current state of the art thereby providing insight into the challenges faced in bringing BCI out of the laboratory setting for widespread adoption. The chapter will attempt to address where BCI technology sits within the domain of pervasive computing [51, 52, 86] with the emphasis on Pervasive Health. The definition for Pervasive Health is "healthcare to anyone, anytime, and anywhere by removing locational, time and other restraints while increasing both the coverage and the quality" [90]. Pervasive Health spans many domains of healthcare from prevention, home monitoring, incidence detection, emergency intervention, to treatment. BCI has a range of application areas [37] and has been investigated as a rehabilitation tool [64, 76]. However, for future BCI technology to form integral components within these health domains technical challenges and barriers preventing BCI from becoming more widespread need to be addressed. This chapter will provide discussion in this area. As will other factors such as [12] user acceptance of the technology, system complexity, safety, and, societal and ethical issues [55, 69] as they also impact widespread adoption.

There has been a recent global emphasis on mapping the brain with the US President Obama announcing a massive $100 million US led brain mapping project [73], and the European Union providing an estimated €1 billion funding for the pan European Human Brain Project [22]. The interest in harnessing and understanding the brain is evident creating a clear driving influence in BCI development.

5.2 Glossary

Active BCI Derives its outputs from brain activity consciously controlled by the user without external stimuli [99].

Reactive BCI Derives its outputs from brain activity arising in reaction to external stimuli, targeted for application control [99].

Passive BCI Derives its outputs from arbitrary brain activity without the purpose of voluntary control, for enriching a human-computer interaction with implicit information [99].

Adaptive BCI Performs online changes to the signal processing and classifier metrics in response to the continual variations in system characteristics.

Asynchronous BCI This is a self-paced BCI system which operates independently of a cue stimulus [see also Active BCI].

Ambient Intelligent (AmI) Computer based and electronic environments with built in programming to be aware and responsive to the surrounding activity. Devices may

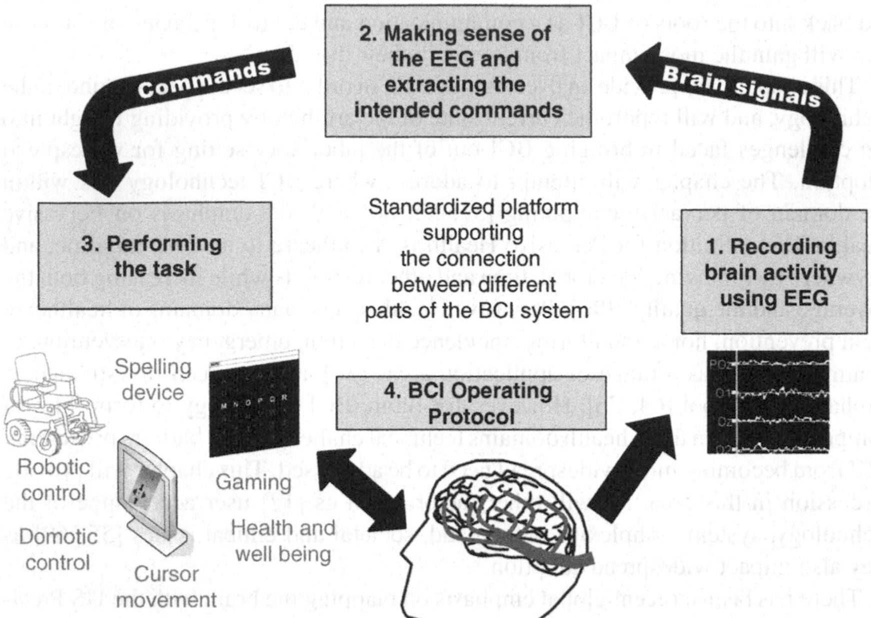

Fig. 5.1 The four major components of a BCI (based on [1, 95])

be interconnected to allow communication and interaction in performing tasks and controlling environments.

Brain-Computer Interface (BCI) This is the interaction between the brain and a computerized system using only thought processes. There are four key aspects to a BCI system: signal acquisition, signal processing, output, and operating protocol (Fig. 5.1). Signal acquisition involves the recording of Electroencephalography (EEG) data from electrodes on the surface of the scalp. These signals are enhanced using signal processing to bring out key features within the data. Classification algorithms are then used to translate the feature data from the EEG into determined meanings. These meanings can then be used to drive a user interface and enable control of an application such as a speller. The operating protocol refers to the method used to establish a communication paradigm between the user and computer. For example, visual stimulus may be used to evoke certain responses within the EEG which depend on where on the screen the user was looking. Deciphering these responses from the EEG, acts as a method to determine the intention of the user, for example, a letter choice within the speller.

Context—aware Devices are aware of their locality and the status of ongoing activities and devices that they are interacting with and they will alter their action in accordance to this environment.

Electrocardiogram (ECG) A recording over time of the electrical activity of the heart as detected by electrodes attached to the surface of the skin over the transthoracic (across the thorax or chest) region of the torso.

Electroencephalography (EEG) The recording of electrical activity within the brain using electrodes mounted on the surface of the brain. Electrodes may be intracranial but EEG captured through implanted electrodes is not discussed within this chapter.

Event related resynchronization and synchronization (ERD/S) ERD/S refers to changes within the EEG as a result of sensory, cognitive and motor activity. Such behavior can be used to determine intended movement.

Hybrid BCI BCI technology is combined with other input signals to form a complete system. Three variations were defined by [5]:

- *Pure hybrid* BCI acquires input signals from two different types of BCI input such as SSVEP and Motor Imagery.
- *Physiological hybrid* BCI acquires input signals from a primary BCI system and other physiological sensors (for example, SSVEP-BCI and ECG.
- *Mixed hybrid* BCI acquires input signals from a primary BCI system and other input modalities such as eye tracking.

P300 This is an evoked potential found within the EEG in response to the Oddball paradigm.

Pervasive Healthcare Healthcare to anyone, anytime, and anywhere by removing locational, time and other restraints while increasing both the coverage and the quality [90]. Pervasive health spans many domains of health care from prevention, home monitoring, emergency intervention, to treatment.

Repetitive Visual Stimuli (RVS) A visual stimulus that has a distinctive property in terms of frequency or phase.

Steady-state Visual Evoked Potentials (SSVEP) When a subject focuses on a repetitive visual stimulus, for example a flickering light set at a certain frequency, an evoked response may be detectable from the EEG in the visual cortex region of the brain that matches the flicker rate of the stimulus. If the user is presented with a number of simultaneous repetitive visual stimuli it may be possible to determine the one the user is focusing his/her attention on through using suitable signal processing and classification algorithms.

Synchronous BCI is a form of BCI whereby the application provides the user with stimuli to create a response in the user's EEG. The command classifications are dependent on the application providing a sequence of stimuli to the user. The application will know when it has provided the stimuli and thus when to expect the response [see also Reactive BCI].

5.3 State of the Art: BCI Overview

A BCI system comprises four primary components (As illustrated in Fig. 5.1): signal acquisition, signal processing, output, and operating protocol [1, 95]. Most BCI systems have adhered to this generally accepted model, which is typically built upon some form of standardized platform, from which EEG is extracted and analyses performed [74, 80].

Non-invasive signal acquisition involves the capture of the EEG using scalp surface mounted electrodes. For typical research projects EEG caps are used to enable identifiable and repeatable electrode positioning by the non-EEG technician. They do not provide the, convenience, aesthetics or comfort needed for long term use, as they require the application of gel to ensure good electrical contact and thus incur the need to cleanse the user's scalp and hair post use. Advances in wet [92], and dry [31], electrode technology have showed promising results and commercial companies [21] are providing examples of how BCI electrode headgear should look for widespread adoption.

Signal processing involves different stages from removing noise and artefact rejection to spatial filtering and classification algorithms to isolate the intended user commands. The BCI 'paradigm' is a term used to categorize the method of instantiating and determining a specified response from a subject's EEG. In a broad sense there are two forms. The first uses some form of external stimulus to evoke a response in a particular region of the brain. Steady-State Visual Evoked Potentials (SSVEP) Paradigm and P300 are two such examples in which visual flickering lights or icons are used to cause a visual evoked response in the EEG. The second type of BCI paradigm has no external stimuli but uses imaged movement by the subject to cause an activation and deactivation (ERS/D) of EEG patterns in sensorimotor region of the brain. Graimann et al. [28], Millán et al. [57] and Vaadia and Birbaumer [87] provide useful overviews of the state of BCI paradigm research, but the sections below give a brief overview of the three most commonly used BCI algorithms.

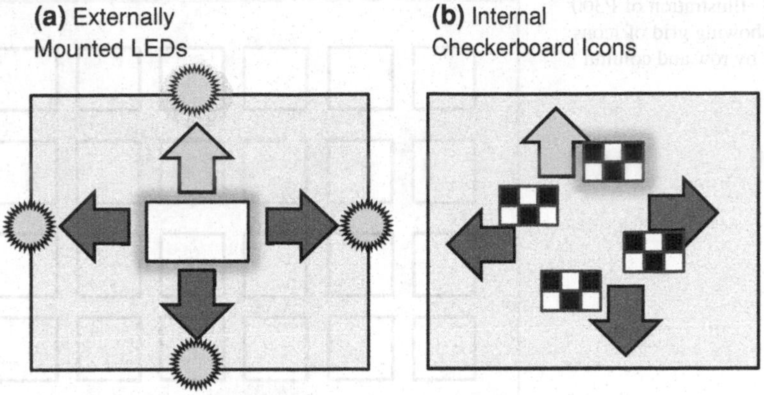

Fig. 5.2 Illustration of SSVEP set up with LEDs and Checkerboard Icons used for stimulus generation

5.3.1 Overview of BCI Algorithms

5.3.1.1 Steady-State Visual Evoked Potentials (SSVEP)

When a person is focusing attention to a continuously blinking light source, the neurons in the visual cortex synchronize their activity to the frequency of the stimulus. BCIs based on SSVEP can use a number of visual stimulations with differing frequencies to evoke respective responses in the subject's EEG matching the flicker rate of the stimulus and its harmonics. These can be detected and used to differentiate between commands. The stimulus is a flashing symbol or LED at a suitable frequency, in a region of up to 20 Hz. Higher frequency options do exist [17] whereby the flicker becomes more unnoticeable to the user. However, there is a greater difficulty in distinguishing between frequencies at these high rates. Friman et al. [25] and Piccini et al. [77] give an overview of SSVEP and [103] provide a summary of different stimulus mechanisms. External visual stimulus can be a prohibitive factor in hindering BCI adoption. Using LEDs as stimulators, requires mounting of the lights surrounding a computer screen (Fig. 5.2a) or embedding them in devices [9] or the environment. Visual stimulus can be achieved using a reversing checkerboard (Fig. 5.2b) icon on screen set to the desired unique flicker rate. This enables the stimulus to be created internally as part of the computer application.

5.3.1.2 P300

The P300 is a significant response in brain activity at around 300 ms after a rare but anticipated stimulus event, often referred to as the 'oddball' paradigm. The gTec Intendix speller [36] uses this paradigm providing a relatively stable and reliable BCI

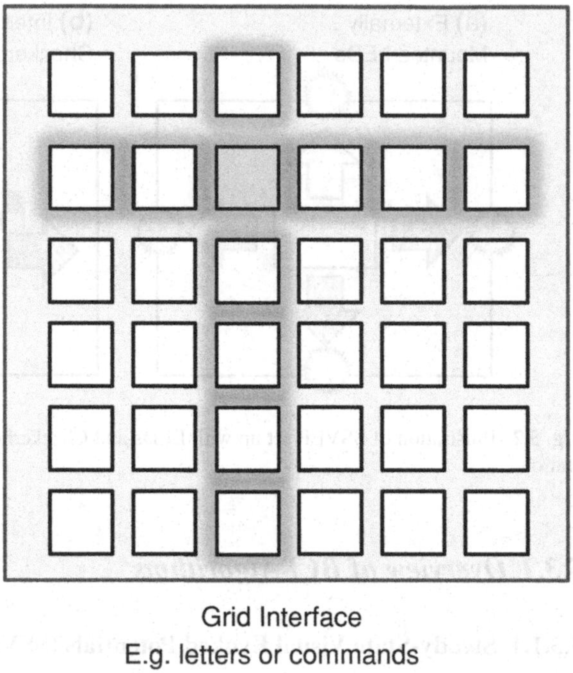

Fig. 5.3 Illustration of P300 screen showing grid of icons flashing by row and column

for those subjects with dependable P300 responses. In their application they have a grid of letters and numbers. The rows and columns flash in a randomized pattern (see Fig. 5.3 for an illustration). The user is asked to focus on the letter they want. As the row and column associated within this letter flash a response will be evoked within the subject's EEG. The software can establish on which flash the evoked response came from and hence link this to the letter of interest. The technique can be extended to other applications by changing the tiled letters and numbers to useful icons or commands.

The advantage of the P300 is the number of variables that can be decided on. However, as with all BCI paradigms [3] not all users can elicit a P300 response. Furthermore, despite being a visual evoked response the P300 requires a level of concentration and [42] found motivation to be a key factor in P300 success. A small amount of familiarization or training is needed although [30] reported a high accuracy after only 5 min of training for one of their speller algorithms.

5.3.1.3 Motor Imaginary

When performing an actual movement, amplitude changes are observable in brain activity even before the movement (due to preparation and planning). This is known as Event related desynchronization and synchronization (ERD/S). A strategy in BCIs is to imagine movement to generate brain activity, which reflects this movement. Typically a subject may imagine moving their left or their right hand, thereby giving them a two-way decision. Other possibilities would be to imagine foot movement or even tongue movement. However, imagined movement requires a significant level of training and not all subjects can master the paradigm. The level of available choices comes down to the "BCI literacy" of the subject. At best, a subject could have a 4 way decision if they can manage all 4 imagined movements (for example left hand, right hand, foot, and tongue), however, three (left hand, right hand and foot) or even just the two (hand and foot) decisions would be more typical. This limits the amount of decision choices available using imagined movement, but it is still a powerful mechanism.

Each of the BCI paradigms mentioned have their own benefits and problems, which vary from user to user. Section 5.3.2 provides a summary of hybrid BCIs, a concept in which the best components of BCI technology and possibly other input modalities can be combined to enhance operation. Following on from hybrid BCIs a section on creating BCI with adaptive properties is summarized.

5.3.2 Hybrid BCI

Irrespective of the benefits of BCI, its utilization as a pure communications channel has been shown to have a number of drawbacks. BCI systems are often unreliable, suffering from noisy, low bandwidth output, which leads to high error rates [5, 100]. Additionally, the number of recognizable mental states and subsequent range of commands is considered to be somewhat limited, thus placing constraints on associated application software [5, 98, 101]. Additionally, BCI systems that operate asynchronously typically produce a large number of false positives, resulting in a degree of frustration for the user, particular when used for control tasks. An example of such a problem could be using a Motor Imaginary paradigm to control a robotic device. The operation instantiates when the user performs the thought process established for a certain command action. The BCI system sits in a neutral state looking for such signals to signify a command, hence the added degree in complexity and risk of false positives.

Conversely, BCI systems that operate in a synchronous manner (such as a speller using visual stimulus whereby the system is looking for a response to a stimulus that it created), are restricted in the recognition of commands, resulting in the generation of spurious outputs when the user is not focused on the control task [98].

Furthermore, the choice of paradigm employed by a BCI system can also be somewhat problematic for users. Although individual paradigms may prove successful with some users, it is often the case that selected paradigms will fail for other users, thereby leading to the need for BCI systems to facilitate a range of paradigms. Consequently, such drawbacks and limitations potentially have a detrimental effect on the widespread adoption of BCI technology. In order to overcome the challenges inherent within BCI systems and respond to the overarching need for improvements in user acceptance and adoption rates, the generation of hybrid BCI systems has been proposed [4, 5, 54, 57, 78]. Allison [4] categorizes hybrid BCI systems:

- *Pure hybrid* BCI: Input signals from different types of BCI input such as SSVEP and Motor Imagery.
- *Physiological hybrid* BCI: Acquires input signals from a primary BCI system and other physiological sensors, for example, SSVEP-BCI and Electrocardiogram (ECG).
- *Mixed hybrid* BCI: Acquires input signals from a primary BCI system and other input modalities [5] (for example eye tracking and BCI).

By utilizing multiple input channels sympathetically in collaboration, signal processing can be performed either simultaneously or sequentially, with simultaneous use leading to potential improvements in the performance and accuracy of the BCI system, and sequential use leading to potential improvements in the general usage of the BCI system as it permits users to selectively engage with the associated input devices [5, 78]. However, while hybrid BCI systems open up possibilities for the creation of more intuitive and natural multimodal user interaction, it also presents a number of inherent challenges due to the integration of multiple input mechanisms and related interfaces. For example, the simultaneous use of multiple input channels for control tasks could potentially result in divergent classification outputs. Likewise, the use of multiple input devices or assistive technologies requires synchronization to be taken into consideration during both signal acquisition and processing. Consequently, in comparison to the development of a traditional BCI system, the development of a hybrid BCI system is considered to be a substantially more difficult task [5].

5.3.3 Online Adaptation

In a typical BCI system there is a calibration session to tune the classifiers to the user's characteristics. With online adaptation on-going parameters extracted from the EEG and the session is used to provide updates to the classifier. Such systems may be able to respond to some transient and temporal conditions within the EEG. A great effort is involved in choosing the optimum parameters for BCI systems and yet this calibration may quickly become outdated due external and physical factors. The ability to continually update the BCI parameters and indeed perform some level of remote monitoring of the system's performance provides a greater opportunity for offsite technical support, a necessity for widespread home use.

An error potential (errP) within the EEG is an automated evoked response by the user when they comprehend that a mistake has been made, and could be used as an automated channel to inform the BCI system that an error in the command choice has been made. Examples of it in use have been with vetoing commands and allowing a quick step back to the previous state. Other examples use the errP signal to help online adaptation of the classifiers. Allison et al. [5] provide some examples of how errPs could be used in hybrid BCI systems. Spüler et al. [82] demonstrated such a system enabling online adaptation of the classifier for a BCI using code-modulated Visual Evoked Potentials (c-VEP). The errPs detected within the subject's EEG in response to observing a decision error were used to update the classifier. They removed the data from the training set when an errP was detected since there was doubt in the true class label. Their system reports a rate of 21.3 error-free letters per minute with their speller. They compare this figure with eye trackers with typical rates ranging from 23.5 to 54.5 to letters per minute with up to 79 for the most advanced uses. The same research group also demonstrated errP use with P300 BCI [83].

Zander and Jatzev [102] highlight the differences in environment between the laboratory, clinical and home setting for BCI use. A laboratory setting is a very controlled environment and there has been a great difficulty in transitioning the complex technology out into a home environment [8, 13, 81]. Zander and Jatzev point to a context aware system as a possible solution to the transient and temporal operating conditions. They propose that BCI systems are capable of providing important contextual information which could be used to optimize operation. To fully understand the complexity of the BCI system they define the three different layers of abstraction of the states of the systems. The first of these is the status that is external and easy to observe. An example of this could be the location of the user. If they are positioned within the kitchen then the user interface that they are interacting with should take this into consideration. Another example could be the use of motion detection to signify the high risk of motion artefacts at a particular instance. The second relates to factors within the human brain including covert cognitive state. Other physiological markers could be used to signify agitation or fatigue. Lastly the third level refers to the BCI feature space, for example, the use of errPs to help in the continual training of the classifiers. There are influencing factors in each of these states that need to be addressed for a fully online and adaptable system to be developed.

5.3.4 BCI Commercialization

BCI systems have recently become a commercial concern for non-medical applications targeted at healthy users, such as brain training toys and tools, cognitive state monitors and digital entertainment controllers [45]. As pervasive computing technologies have progressed over the past two decades, from focusing on connectedness and device miniaturization within its first epoch, to device integration, sensor fusion and context awareness within its second epoch, to the current epoch's generation of highly complex, sociotechnical smart systems [24], BCI systems have embraced aspects of pervasive computing technology to become ever more ubiquitous. Indeed, the current plethora of commercially available BCI systems not only make use of technological advancements in both hardware and software, such as reductions in the size and cost of sensors and processors, wireless connectivity, and advancements in both signal processing and reasoning algorithms, they also represent another non-invasive physiological sensor for pervasive computing environments.

There are many consumer BCI systems based on the NeuroSky ThinkGear ASIC Module [67] chipset which permit wireless acquisition of EEG using passive, dry electrodes. Utilizing proprietary analysis algorithms, these NeuroSky systems (MindWave, MindWave Mobile, [59]) can be used to extract information on cognitive and physiological states including attention, mediation and eye blinks. Furthermore by enabling Bluetooth connectivity, interaction with devices for example such as Apple (iOS) and Android based tablets can be achieved. Additionally, NeuroSky provides a range of software development tools (MindSet Development Tool and MindSet Research Tools), which facilitate both BCI application and research [49] development for the ThinkGear chipsets on a wide range of software platforms, including mobile and Arduino microcontrollers [66]. Thus BCI technology is already on the road to pervasive deployment.

The NeuroSky ThinkGear ASIC Module chipset has also been leveraged within commercially available game-based toys, most notably the Star Wars Force Trainer by Uncle Milton [84], and the Mattel Mind Flex [58]. Other example consumer BCI systems that are specifically targeted for the purposes of entertainment control are given in Table 5.1.

High resolution, multi-channel EEG headsets are also commercially available (see Table 5.2) from companies such as [19, 65], which produce consumer BCI systems that are primarily targeted at research-based application development. The Emotiv EPOC and EEG headsets [19] permit 14-channel EEG signal acquisition with wireless transmission using dry electrodes. Both systems contain an embedded gyroscope, thereby permitting detection of a range of facial expressions. While supported on Windows and OS X platforms, a software development kit and suite of detection tools allows for further development of applications for a range of platforms including Windows, OS X and Linux. The Emotiv Insight [21] is a sleek headset design with 5-channel signal acquisition initially targeted at cognitive health and wellbeing. Using real-time signal analysis user metrics such as attention, focus, engagement, interest, excitement and stress can be determined. In conjunction with a built-in 6-axis inertial sensor, the Insight also permits detection of a range of facial expressions and is supported by both developer and research-based software development kits, with the latter giving access to raw EEG data in addition to proprietary analysis algorithms. Both [65] BCI systems (Enobio and Starstim) incorporate a 3-axis accelerometer and provide support software and development kits that facilitate real-time monitoring and visualization of raw EEG and power spectrum density analysis. The Enobio system is primarily targeted at EEG-based research and application development, whereas Starstim is positioned as a multi-channel transcranial current stimulator, which provides the facility for simultaneous real-time EEG signal monitoring of and transcranial stimulation, and permits custom programming and sequencing of associated protocols.

While the availability of affordable BCI hardware and associated SDKs aids in the proliferation and adoption of BCI devices and related applications, as indicated by the growing range of applications already available on both the NeuroSky and Emotiv Application Stores [20, 68], the OpenEEG Project [75] promotes the creation of homemade BCI systems, facilitating enthusiasts and researchers alike with all of the

Table 5.1 BCI systems targeted towards leisure and well-being

Product	Technical details
MyndPlay BrainBand [63]	Dual channel EEG EEG signal acquisition at 512 Hz Targeted at entertainment technology control Permits access to both raw EEG and a range of cognitive states using proprietary analysis algorithms NeuroSky Thinkgear ASIC Module Chipset
InteraXon Muse [62]	4-channel EEG signal acquisition using a dry sensor-based headband Bluetooth connectivity Built-in 3-axis accelerometer Provides raw EEG, accelerometer data, raw power spectrum data, and analyzed cognitive states, such as focus and relaxation based on common EEG power spectrum bands Provides a range of proprietary tools, SDKs and software libraries targeted at both application developers and researchers NeuroSky Thinkgear ASIC Module Chipset
Melon Headband [56]	Three-channel EEG headband Integrated accelerometer Provides personalized attention and activity tracking using an iOS or Android-based smartphone application. SDKs available for both iOS and Android platforms Access to both raw EEG and a range of cognitive states Can permit Bluetooth connectivity NeuroSky Thinkgear ASIC Module Chipset
BCINet Neural Impulse Accelerator Game Controller [10]	Wireless BCI headband and controller Gestures, intentions and eye movements translated to standard input device control signals. SDK and set of proprietary libraries supported on the Windows platform

resources required to create EEG-based hardware using off-the-shelf components. Consequently, the ModularEEG [75] system provides a low-cost, multi-channel EEG signal acquisition device that is supported by a community of developers and enthusiasts. In a similar manner, there is a growing interest in the modification of existing, commercial BCI-based games, such as the Uncle Milton Star Wars Force Trainer and the MyndPlay, for the creation of low-cost BCI systems [26, 35, 46]. Although predominantly the preserve of enthusiasts, such hardware 'hacking' suggests a growing interest in both the availability and potential application space of BCI systems, albeit at in an affordable manner. Indeed, the recent trend that may be observed in the success of crowd funding to support the development of BCI systems, such as the Emotiv Insight [40], Melon Headband [41] and InteraXon Muse [34],indicates a growing desire for lightweight BCI technology focused on mobile

Table 5.2 Emotiv and Neuroelectrics research grade BCI products

Product	Technical details
Emotiv EPOC	14-channel EEG signal acquisition at a sample rate of 128 Hz Transmission over proprietary wireless using dry electrodes Contains an embedded gyroscope
Emotive EEG	14-channel EEG signal acquisition at a sample rate of 128 Hz Transmission over proprietary wireless using dry electrodes Contains an embedded gyroscope Also permits output of raw EEG signal values
The Emotiv Insight	5-channel signal acquisition at a sample rate of 128 Hz Transmitted over Bluetooth 4.0 LE to a range of platforms including iOS and Android-based smartphones and tablet devices Built-in 6-axis inertial sensor
NeuroElectrics Enobio	High resolution 24-bit signals from (up to) 20 channels Sample rate of 500 Hz: Provides a frequency response in the range 0–250 Hz Transmitted over Bluetooth
NeuroElectrics Starstim	High resolution 24-bit signals from 8 channels sample rate of 500 Hz: Provides a frequency response in the range 0–250 Hz Transmitted over Bluetooth

"lifestyle" applications. Thus, such endeavors, while somewhat removed from the roots of BCI research, can only add to the increasing ubiquity and acceptance of BCI systems.

5.4 Open Problems: Barriers to Being Pervasive

Despite recent progress much more needs to be achieved before BCI can become a truly *pervasive health solution* that can be 'woven into the fabric of our everyday lives' as envisioned by [94] without the user needing to focus on its presence and use. The challenges to adoption of pervasive technology represent a significant issue for the field of human computer interaction (HCI), and this is clearly brought under the magnifying glass when dealing with a low bit rate and error-prone interface channel, as manifested in BCI technology. Supporting smart sensors and actuators and clever software which can learn from experience and context, are needed to make up for the deficiencies in the communication channel. This section will address some of the key challenges that have hindered BCI progression. These factors can be partitioned into several groups, namely:

- Scientific challenges
- System complexity and support infrastructure
- User acceptance and fitness for purpose
- Ethical issues associated with adoption and uptake.

5.4.1 Scientific Challenges

Advancements have been made on all technical aspects of a BCI system resulting in aesthetically headsets with advanced electrodes that can catapult BCI from a 'hospital' intervention to a desirable gaming device. Their potential extends to use in a home based setting to achieve a more pervasive solution. Applications that users want to use will play a role here. These can range from entertainment and leisure activities through to rehabilitation. Indeed 'gamification' has the potential to encourage more prolonged usage of the headset, and hence allow for calibration data to be recorded without further inconveniencing the user. The potential for rehabilitation using BCI can be inferred from the uptake of Wii, Playstation and Xbox applications. The appetite for health and wellbeing application can be confirmed by the large number of apps available for mobile platforms.

Enhanced algorithms, and user interfaces [53], will also play a key role in making up for the deficit of the communication channel. There are improvements to be made with classification accuracy of algorithms and with personalization of an algorithm to the individual. However context aware software has the ability to reduce the reliance on command accuracy by using knowledge from the wider 'environment' and user habits (status of devices, e.g. which TV channel is the user watching, at 6pm switch to the news channel except at weekend etc.) to reduce the number of explicit BCI commands needed to complete a task. This can provide a general improvement where interaction is trigger by the BCI but comprising autonomous elements.

Yet still more intelligent software is needed to create a robust and usable BCI system optimized for individual use. Each user reacts differently to each form of BCI and parameters may need to be adjusted to enhance the algorithm to the characteristics of the user (positioning of electrodes, usable stimulating frequency, filters etc.). This can be thought of as individual calibration and hence personalization and of the BCI system. Online adaptable systems are also a means to further personalize and enable on-going calibration [82, 83].

One of the main challenges that the technology faces is that it requires a high level of user personalization and on-going calibration if it is to become a useful and reliable assistive technology for that user. Personalization begins with the optimum choice in BCI paradigm [2]. Determining a potential BCI alone can be a hindrance and may require substantial commitment and engagement of the user with the process. For SSVEP only certain frequencies may provide adequate accuracy and a limited number will impact the navigation controls for the user interface, and as the number of frequencies used increases so does the challenge in distinguishing between them successfully within the signal processing. The P300 based BCI relies on flashing images or icons. Yet again for some their P300 features will be weak and difficult to determine. They may require more repetitions to enhance clarity and naturally this will impact performance and usability (i.e. a slower bit transfer rate). The BCI based on imagined movement requires extensive training and interaction with the research team to determine the best imagined strategies that will instigate a measurable and distinguishable response in their EEG. Optimum electrode placement may also be needed to tailor the system to the user. Temporal changes in the user's BCI ability are also an issue requiring a review of system over time. In summary there is a need to:

- Screen users for BCI ability
- Personalize BCI technology and also the applications
- On-going calibration to account for temporal changes in BCI ability.

It is essential for any BCI system that in some stage the target user or user group is involved but this leads to many more challenges that need to be overcome. An initial development for BCI typical involves user trials with research colleagues and in general subjects without any physical or neurological impairment. However, trials have shown [32, 61, 93] that there is a performance gap between users with and without brain injury. Investigations are needed into the signal processing algorithms, BCI systems to help close this gap. However, the initial designs are tailored to users with different characteristics than the target user group, yet to involve said target user group too early poses other ethical issues. The involvement of a lead user can be one option [47] but the choice of this user can have impact on both the course of development (as user characteristics can be so individual) and on them too if a successful outcome does not happen.

A major challenge is still the development of a friendly, straightforward tutorial or 'wizard' [18] that will walk each user through a series of tests to determine optimal parameters. This affords a degree of personalization; matching user (brain) with the (computer) algorithms, protocols and set up, and interface. Such a wizard should be adaptive, and as automated as possible. For example, the wizard should determine the best stimulus timing and display parameters for P300 BCIs, or change the operating frequencies for SSVEP. To evaluate ERD/S BCIs, the wizard will ask the user to imagine different movements across different feedback types. In addition, for each BCI approach, software will determine the best electrode sites and spatial filters. The user may also choose to answer questions about training, application parameters, and other personal preferences. Based on this information, an expert system will then determine the best BCI approach and parameters for each subject. While this challenge has been addressed by a number of research projects (e.g., [13, 14]), the sheer complexity posed by a large number of experimental variables, the daily somewhat unpredictable rhythm of the EEG, and exacerbated by people with disparate (and hence personalized) brain impairments has meant that a solution has not been found. Prolonged use of a BCI with passive measurement building up a knowledge base may yet offer a personalized solution.

5.4.2 System Complexity and Support Infrastructure

Scientific challenges are not the only challenges in BCI becoming pervasive as the scientific 'black box' needs to be enhanced to productize, standardize and commercialize the technology. System complexity and user acceptance have been reported as key barriers to BCI use [12]. Furthermore, device portability, battery life and technical support are also important as with any evolving technology eager for widespread adoption.

A true cost in terms of financial investment for BCI as a medical assistive technology can only be made if compared with the support needed for other assistive solutions. There will always be an overhead in terms of tailoring the tools to the needs and characteristics of the user, requiring an occupation therapist, to support this process. But with BCI there are additional technical challenges in terms of on-going calibration and tailoring to the user's varying characteristics. Relatively, in the future the BCI tool may cost little (say, a few hundred pounds) but the support package will still remain very costly (a few hundred pounds per week!).

If BCI technology can prove its worth as an assistive technology, there will be no technological barrier, just a medical one. At that stage BCI will have succeeded. At present however, long term BCI use requires a significant level of technical support [81] and also the unwavering support of carers and family. An established and standardized framework is needed to ensure that as time progresses there can be a guarantee of the permanency of support packages that matches current assistive technology solutions. The complexity of the science needs to be invisible to the user, leaving them the only technical challenges of downloading their desired applications from whatever library or resource they have purchased them from.

5.4.3 User Acceptance, Fitness for Purpose and the BCI Nirvana

Traditionally the physical look of BCI systems has been discouraging but headsets such as those by Emotiv and NeuroSky give a modern and fashionable appeal. But for widespread adoption wearing the headset needs to become an acceptable, even cool, thing to do. With increased technology acceptance and the extension of the self with mobile devices it is feasible that BCI technology may become the 'next thing' to connect with for the techno-savvy 'early adopter'. However, applications will have moved far from the origins of communication devices for the physically impaired.

A key challenge is in developing usable systems that meet the accuracy needs thus limiting user frustration [93]. The key area is the balance between 'embedded intelligence' and 'ease of use' creating an 'ambient solution'. As the system becomes more intelligent the HCI should become easier to use. The domain of assistive technology requires adequate accuracies and an increased degree in complexity. Furthermore, there is a performance gap between healthy users and those with brain injury [61]. Failure in achieving this nirvana of BCI as an assistive device does not rule BCI out of a range of other possible useful applications in industry, gaming and 'lifestyle BCI'. Industry applications could be monitoring user states while driving/flying [33], operating as a city trader or in hazardous environments. Less demanding applications may lead the way in technology acceptance and adoption.

5.4.4 Ethics

Ethical issues [55] range from those concerned with rights of users in trials to a broader sense of the use of BCI in society, or indeed lack of use, that is technology that could improve the quality of life is not reaching those who could benefit the most. Nijboer and Broermann [69] highlight this later point when they discuss the limited choices of assistive technology that some sufferers of ALS have when deciding whether or not to accept life prolonging respiratory help. Involvement of users in research also becomes a complex ethical challenge when the users are vulnerable, unable to give consent, require long training sessions, or have high expectations of how the technology may impact their lives. Grübler [29] explores the issues of responsibility and liability; where are the boundaries of responsibility when someone is using BCI? Selective enhancement and social stratification [4] are also concerns. Vlek et al. [91], comment on the possible pressure to enhance one's brain to keep up with society. BCI is no longer a research only tool. The Intendix is a commercially available speller is available from gTec, but due to lack of expertise and support BCI may not be available to complex cases such as people with 'locked in' syndrome, ironically the people who could benefit most. The ethical discussions are the subject of a report from the Nuffield Council on Bioethics [72]. This will aid the awareness, understanding and hopefully further acceptance of the technology [91].

5.5 Future Outlook: Promoters to Being Pervasive

As previously discussed, one of the emerging trends in BCI is the rise of more simplistic consumer BCI systems that are predominately targeted at healthy users and "lifestyle" applications, with interest growing in BCI being used as a control mechanism within digital games [38, 50]. While such uses of BCI will inevitably help promote BCI as a pervasive technology, systems that incorporate BCI must also advance in terms of user behavior and context-awareness, particularly if they are to provide pervasive applications within the healthcare domain [23].

5.5.1 Augmented Channels for Both Entertainment and Serious Games

The application of BCI for interaction within the application area of digital games is becoming increasingly common in research studies. Due to the advances in computational power, increasingly available low-cost BCI hardware and rising number of published peer-reviewed research papers, the number of studies incorporating BCI within games has grown over the last decade, with over 50 studies having been published since 2007 alone [16, 50, 71, 79, 89]. While such studies have predominantly focused on the use of BCI within games for entertainment purposes, the past decade has also witnessed an analogous increase in research into "serious games", which has produced a diverse range of approaches to the applied use of games and game-related technologies within the healthcare domain [39]. Indeed, BCI-based serious games are considered to provide a more interesting and effective approach to healthcare education and treatment than traditional methods, particularly in cases where the patient fails to engage with therapeutic interventions [85].

Although passive BCI has been employed within both serious and entertainment games in order to improve or utilize the affective state of the user [70, 71, 79, 97], within the research literature BCI paradigms are primarily considered as an adjunct or replacement for traditional control modalities. Currently, the most frequently used BCI paradigm, as a control mechanism in games, is Motor Imagery as it permits a continuous level of control along with a reasonable level of proficiency in its usage [50]. The P300 paradigm is also considered as a suitable control mechanism, due to high levels of accuracy and minimal training requirements, however the need for a static set of stimuli may subsequently prevent widespread adoption [38]. Likewise, the SSVEP paradigm provides high levels of accuracy without the need for preliminary training, however the stimuli required is considered to be too fatiguing to be used over long periods of time [15, 50]. Furthermore, it was observed that the need for the user to refocus concentration between the stimuli and the game itself led to a distraction, thus breaking the user's level of engagement and immersion [15, 89] .

In order to encourage the widespread adoption of BCI as a game-related technology, which indirectly advances the provision of BCI as a pervasive technology applicable to healthcare-based serious games, the limitations inherent in the individual paradigms must be overcome. For example, it has been suggested that BCI-based control should be simplified and users adequately trained in the use of the chosen paradigm using inbuilt tutorials [50, 79]. Indeed, issues associated with a user's proficiency in a given paradigm often result from constraints within the underlying software, hence may be countered by taking the modality into consideration during the design of the software [15, 50, 79, 89]. Consequently, while a variety of challenges associated with the use of BCI within either serious or entertainment games remain, these often mirror the challenges faced when incorporating BCI within other domains, such as healthcare. Subsequently, such challenges must be addressed in order for BCI to be considered as a pervasive technology.

5.5.2 Towards Personalized Hybrid-BCI Systems

In order to create a truly pervasive BCI system, which is both context-aware and personalized to the user, new hybrid-BCI architectures are required. For example, the architecture illustrated in Fig. 5.4 depicts how a graphical user interface, such as that developed within the BRAIN project provides the central component of a personalized hybrid-BCI architecture that also comprises a Multimodal Interaction Platform, an Affective Computing Platform and an Ambient Intelligence Platform

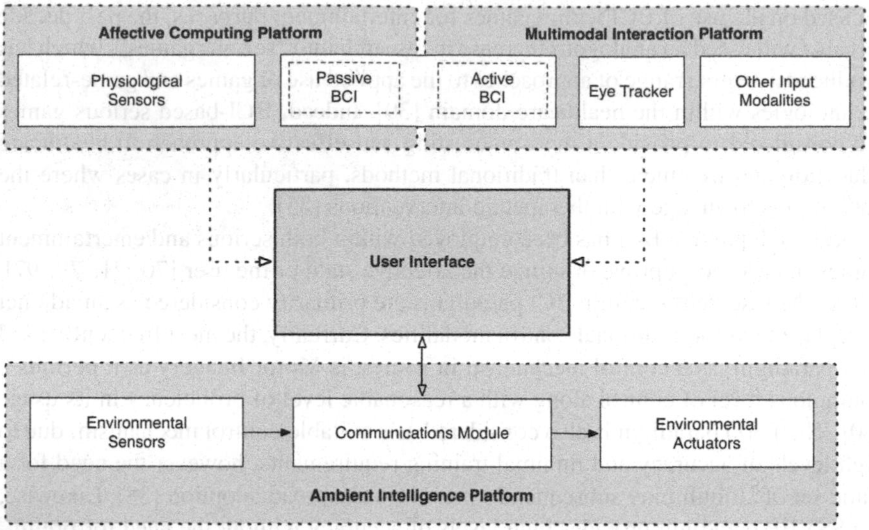

Fig. 5.4 Personalized hybrid-BCI system architecture

[4, 54]. By utilizing BCI as one of a number of input modalities, multimodal interaction permits a potential increase in the overall bandwidth of information available for control of the system. A wide range of input devices should be made available to the user in a seamless and intuitive manner, thereby facilitating a synergy between input modalities that takes into consideration user capability, preference and application context. In order to successfully realize the Multimodal Interaction Platform, a number of existing research challenges must be addressed, including the selection of effective approaches to signal processing for the complementary integration of input modalities [5], and improvements in the robustness and reliability of the input modalities during operation [60, 70]. Subsequently, by employing a Multimodal Interaction Platform that contains BCI as a potential input channel, the possibilities for new heterogeneous forms of user interaction may arise.

While the locus of a Multimodal Interaction Platform is the explicit interaction of the user with the system, an Affective Computing Platform forms a complementary input modality that utilizes purely implicit user input, in the form of physiological information acquired from a range of biometric and activity-orientated sensors. BCI systems may also be incorporated within a suite of sensors for the purpose of passive EEG signal acquisition, thereby providing additional information regarding the cognitive state and load of a user when interacting with the system. By eliciting a range of physiological and cognitive information, the affective state of the user may be modelled, which subsequently permits aspects of the graphical user interface, or other output modality, to be personalized according to the implicit reactions observed. Additionally, by operating sympathetically with the Multimodal Interaction Platform, the implicit selection of appropriate input modalities may be possible, thus permitting the automated transfer of control between input devices according to the current physical and cognitive capability and capacity of the user. However, a number of existing research challenges must be overcome in order to successfully develop the Affective Computing Platform. These include the reliable identification and classification of the user's affective state from both physiological information and supplementary brain signals, and the subsequent integration of such contextual information with the interaction platform [71, 79].

Contemporaneous to the Affective Computing Platform, in terms of implicitly monitoring user interaction with the system, is the need for an Ambient Intelligence Platform, which focuses on the implicit acquisition of information pertaining to the environment of the user and explicit control of connected facilities within the environment. Through the use of sensors and actuators employed within the environment, factors external to the user may be utilized in order to help inform the context of the user's interactions, which, in turn, provides additional information that can be used to generate a more personalized user experience. Similar to the Affective Computing Platform, the existing research challenges that must be addressed for the successful development of the Ambient Intelligence Platform include the identification and classification of situational context from heterogeneous data sources, and the creation of a corresponding ontology suited to subsequent reasoning [43]. Thus, by providing the hybrid-BCI system architecture with a degree of context-awareness, the overall system may learn to adjust to the commonly observed usage patterns and needs of the user, thereby facilitating greater autonomy by helping to reduce the cognitive load associated with daily tasks.

Although aspects of the individual high-level components of the proposed architecture may be currently considered as open research problems, their effective integration also poses a number of additional research challenges. Primarily, a communication architecture is required that is capable of underpinning the dataflow between each high-level component in the overarching hybrid-BCI system. In addition, the communication architecture must also permit effective and robust dataflow between a variety of disparate subcomponents and the corresponding high-level component, such as the acquisition and transmission of both data and status signals between individual physiological sensors, including the passive BCI, and the Affective Computing Platform. In order to establish a suitable communication architecture, a data exchange protocol and associated schema is required. Such a schema must take into consideration the myriad data types that may be potentially utilized by the system, particularly as new input modalities and sensor platforms become available. The data exchange schema must be flexible and robust in order to handle both propriety and open data formats, whilst supporting lightweight and efficient communications. As a consequence of the integration of high-level system components, in conjunction with the integration of subcomponents within each individual high-level component, the selection of suitable and effective data fusion techniques presents an additional challenge that must also be addressed. Through the successful resolution of these challenges, it is clear that future BCI systems may be endowed with a degree of "awareness" of the user, thereby facilitating the provision of a bespoke, personalized experience that can adapt to the capabilities and needs of a broader spectrum of users.

Indeed, by aligning and combining BCI with existing physiological and environmental sensors, not only will it potentially benefit from the additional information that becomes available, it will conceivably gain a level of ubiquity through acceptance and adoption as simply another sensor device.

5.6 Closing Arguments

As the previous discussions throughout this chapter have hopefully indicated, the widespread delivery of a BCI system is a challenge, regardless of the application domain. In order to further the adoption and subsequent ubiquity of BCI the following suggested enablers need to be addressed:

- Technology ease-of-use: all systems should be supplied with good documentation, appropriate training and on-going technical support. Multiple components of a BCI system should be housed within single units whenever possible to simplify system setup and usage
- Battery life and system ergonomics: during the development of BCI applications and associated user interfaces, existing, successful assistive technologies should be closely examined for guidance on apposite HCI design
- Choice of electrodes: dry and water-based electrodes, and the aesthetics of the BCI headset, may provide a significant advantage for technology adoption as an appropriate choice can enable a good set of EEG signals to be recorded within minutes of engaging the user
- Optimized user experience: the user experience of the BCI system should be designed with careful consideration for the input modality
- The Wizard approach should be further expanded.

Although delivery of a *fully functional* personalized BCI may still be some way off, we should take encouragement by recent trends that have seen BCI systems become available commercially. These consumer systems are typically restricted in terms of EEG acquisition and analysis capabilities; however crucially provide accessible, low-cost BCI hardware. In particular, BCI technology is now being extended beyond the core scientific community, due to the availability of headsets with software development kits that are supported on a wide range of desktop and mobile computing platforms. Within the next five years we are set to witness BCIs being used in many research projects that previously employed acquisition of simpler bio-signals as viable measures. Further research combining BCI, eye tracker technology and user experience modelling could be used to help optimize user interaction, however such research requires a stable BCI system (in terms of both hardware and software) that operates with an acceptable level of accuracy. Indeed, hybrid systems [48] have been highlighted as having great potential for the future of BCI, whereby the BCI input forms only one possible control path allowing, for example, other input modalities or bio-signals to be combined with the BCI in order to provide a more personalized approach that meets the needs of the user. This opens many avenues for research and

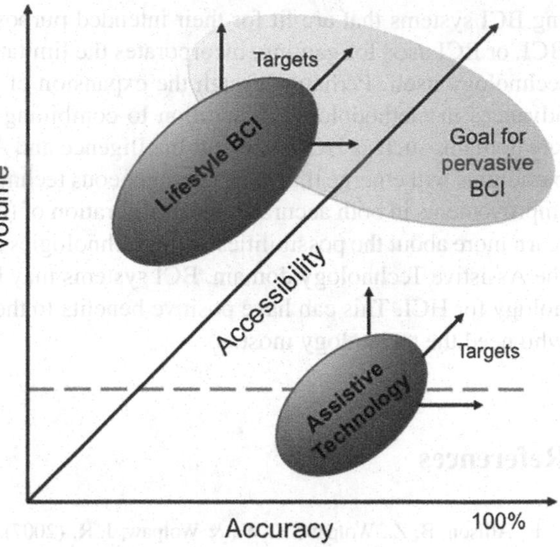

Fig. 5.5 Volume versus Accuracy and Accessibility in BCI Technology

development, enabling the strengths of different control mechanisms to be harnessed in one system. It also helps to broaden the potential application domain of BCI from assistive technology, to therapeutic tool, to interactive entertainment and creative medium.

Figure 5.5 illustrates the required trade-off between the BCI system accuracy and respective volume of proliferation and usage.

As can be seen, for BCI systems that are used within the Assistive Technology domain, the accuracy must high, which subsequently results in a relative low volume of actual systems in use. For example, BCI systems deployed for the purposes of assistive technology currently number in the tens of units sold (i.e. 20–30), whereas chipsets, such as that produced by NeuroSky, which are employed in a wide range of consumer BCI systems have shown sales in the millions [4]. Conversely, with the rise of Lifestyle BCI systems, a high volume of systems being proliferated is expected, yet these typically contain a much smaller number of EEG channels, hence tend towards lower accuracy and corresponding frequency response. Consequently, a trade-off must be made between robust, high-volume production of BCI systems and their inherent capabilities to ensure the proliferation of BCI systems. Ideally, to improve the accessibility of BCI systems, thus moving BCI towards a pervasive technology, both volume and accuracy must be simultaneously increased.

At the outset of this chapter, the question of whether or not the drive beyond the domain of assistive technology will provide advances to the roots of BCI was posed. As we have seen, both the hardware and software challenges of BCI exist regardless of the application domain, however by utilizing BCI in domains other than assistive technology new modes of thought towards overcoming these challenges have taken root in the wider scientific community and industrial sector. At the very least, designing BCI systems that are fit for their intended purpose, as is the case with lifestyle BCI, or BCI used for gaming, incorporates the limitations and challenges within the technology itself. Perhaps through the expansion of computational techniques and advances in methodology, in addition to combining aspects and approaches from key domains such as HCI, Ambient Intelligence and Affective Computing, new BCI paradigms will emerge that take heterogeneous technologies into account, leading to improvements in both accuracy and proliferation of (hybrid) BCI technology. As we learn more about the possibilities of the technologies and expand their usage beyond the Assistive Technology domain, BCI systems may become a truly pervasive technology for HCI. This can have positive benefits to the pervasive healthcare of those who need the technology most.

References

1. Allison, B. Z., Wolpaw, E. W., & Wolpaw, J. R. (2007). Brain computer interface systems: progress and prospects. *British Review of Medical Devices*, *4*(4), 463–474.
2. Allison, B. Z., Luth, T., Valbuena, D., Teymourian, A., Volosyak, I., & Graser, A. (2010a). Bci demographics: how many (and what kinds of) people can use an ssvep bci? *IEEE Transactions on Neural Systems and Rehabilitation Engineering*, *18*(2), 107–116.
3. Allison, B. Z., & Neuper, C. (2010). Could anyone use a BCI? In *Brain-Computer Interfaces* (pp. 35–54). London: Springer.
4. Allison, B. Z. (2011). Future BNCI: A roadmap for future directions in Brain / Neuronal computer interaction research. [Online] http://future-bnci.org/images/stories/Future_BNCI_Roadmap.pdf [Accessed: December 2013]
5. Allison, B. Z., Leeb, R., Brunner, C., Müller-Putz, G. R., Bauernfeind, G., Kelly, J. W., et al. (2012). Toward smarter bcis: extending bcis through hybridization and intelligent control. *Journal of Neural Engineering*, *9*(1), 013001.
6. Allison, B. Z., Dunne, S., Leeb, R., Millán, J. D. R., & Nijholt, A. (2013). Recent and upcoming BCI progress: Overview, analysis, and recommendations. In *Towards Practical Brain-Computer Interfaces* (pp. 1–13). Berlin, Heidelberg: Springer.
7. Aspinall, P., Mavros, P., Coyne, R., & Roe, J. (2013). The urban brain: Analysing outdoor physical activity with mobile EEG. *British Journal of Sports Medicine*. doi:10.1136/bjsports-2012-091877
8. BackHome. (2013). Brain-neural computer interfaces on track to home—Development of a practical generation of BNCI for independent home use, EU FP7 Project. [Online] http://www.backhome-fp7.eu/ [Accessed: May 2013]
9. BCI Appliance. (2013). INCF neuro informatics 2012, BCI appliance presented at CeBit 2012. [Online] http://www.neuroinformatics2012.org/abstracts/bci-appliance [Accessed: August 2013]
10. BCInet. (2013). *BCInet NIA game controller*. [online] http://www.bcinet.com/products/ [Accessed December 2013]
11. Birbaumer, N., & Cohen, L. G. (2007). Brain-computer interfaces: communication and restoration of movement in paralysis. *The Journal of Physiology*, *579*(3), 621–636.
12. Blain-Moraes, S., Schaff, R., Gruis, K. L., Huggins, J. E., & Wren, P. A. (2012). Barriers to and mediators of brain-computer interface user acceptance: focus group findings. *Ergonomics*, *55*(5), 516–525.
13. BRAIN. (2011). *BCIs with rapid automated interfaces for nonexperts EU FP7 (ICT-2007-224156)*. [online] http://www.brain-project.org/ [Accessed December 2013]

14. Brainable. (2012). *Autonomy and social inclusion through mixed reality Brain-Computer Interfaces*. [online] http://www.brainable.org/ [Accessed December 2013]
15. Chumerin, N., Manyakov, N. V., van Vliet, M., Robben, A., Combaz, A., & Van Hulle, M. M. (2013). Steady-state visual evoked potential-based computer gaming on a consumer-grade eeg device. *IEEE Transactions on Computational Intelligence and AI in Games*, *5*(2), 100–110.
16. Coyle, D., Principe, J., & Lotte, F. (2013). Nijholt, A. Brain/neuronal computer games interfaces and interaction: Guest editorial.
17. Durka, P., Kus, R., Zygierewicz, J., Milanowski, P., & Garcia, G. (2009). High-frequency SSVEP responses parametrized by multichannel matching pursuit. In *Frontiers in Neuroinformatics. Conference Abstract: 2nd INCF Congress of Neuroinformatics*.
18. Ehlers, J., Volosyak, I., & Lüth, T. (2010). "toward a bci wizard", in methods and applications in automation. *Publication Series of the Institute of Automation: Shaker Verlag, 2010*, 65–73.
19. Emotiv. (2013). *Home page for Emotiv*. [Online] http://www.emotiv.com [Accessed August 2013]
20. *Emotiv App Store*. (2013). [Online] http://www.emotiv.com/store [Accessed August 2013]
21. Emotiv Insight. (2013). *Emotiv insight*. [Online] http://emotivinsight.com/ [Accessed December 2013]
22. EU. (2013). *The human brain project*. [online] https://www.humanbrainproject.eu/ [Accessed December 2013]
23. Favela, J. (2013). Behavior-aware computing: applications and challenges. *Pervasive Computing*, *12*(3), 14–17.
24. Ferscha, A. (2012). 20 yeas past weiser: what's next? *Pervasive Computing*, *11*(1), 52–61.
25. Friman, O., Lüth, T., Volosyak, I., & Gräser, A. (2007). Spelling with steady-state visual evoked potentials. *Proceedings of the 3rd International IEEE EMBS Conference on Neural Engineering Kohala Coast*, Hawaii, USA, May 2–5, 2007.
26. Frontier Nerds. (2010). [Online] http://frontiernerds.com/brain-hack [Accessed August 2013]
27. Gartner. (2011). *Gartner's 2011 hype cycle special report evaluates the maturity of 1,900 technologies*. [Online] http://www.gartner.com/newsroom/id/1763814 [Accessed May 2013]
28. Graimann, B., Allison, B., & Pfurtscheller, G., (Eds). (2010). *Brain-computer interfaces: Revolutionizing human-computer interaction (The Frontiers Collection)*. Springer.
29. Grübler, G. (2011). *Beyond the responsibility gap. discussion note on responsibility and liability in the use of brain-computer interfaces* (pp. 1–6). AI & Society.
30. Guger, C., Daban, S., Sellers, E., Holzner, C., Krausz, G., Carabalona, R., et al. (2009). How many people are able to control a p300-based brain-computer interface (bci)? *Neuroscience Letters*, *462*(1), 94–98.
31. gTec Sahara. (2013). *gTec sahara dry electrodes*. [Online] http://www.gtec.at/Products/Electrodes-and-Sensors/g.SAHARA-Specs-Features [Accessed August 2013]
32. Hill, J., Brunner, P., & Vaughan, T. (2011). Interface design challenge for brain-computer interaction. In *Foundations of Augmented Cognition. Directing the Future of Adaptive Systems* (pp. 500–506). Berlin Heidelberg: Springer.
33. Hood, D., Joseph, D., Rakotonirainy, A., Sridharan, S., & Fookes, C. (2012, October). Use of brain computer interface to drive: preliminary results. In *Proceedings of the 4th International Conference on Automotive User Interfaces and Interactive Vehicular Applications* (pp. 103–106). ACM.
34. Indiegogo. (2013). *Muse*. [Online] http://www.indiegogo.com/projects/muse-the-brain-sensing-headband-that-lets-you-control-things-with-your-mind [Accessed August 2013]
35. Instructables. (2013). [Online] http://www.instructables.com/id/How-to-hack-EEG-toys-with-arduino/ [Accessed August 2013]
36. Intendix. (2013). [Online] http://www.intendix.com/ [Accessed August 2013]
37. Jackson, M. M., & Mappus, R. (2010). Applications for brain-computer interfaces. In *Brain-Computer Interfaces* (pp. 89–103). London: Springer.
38. Kaplan, A. Y., Shishkin, S. L., Ganin, I. P., Basyul, I. A., & Zhigalov, A. (2013). Adapting the p300-based brain-computer interface for gaming: a review. *IEEE Transactions on Computational Intelligence and AI in Games*, *5*(2), 141–149.

39. Kharrazi, H., Lu, A. S., Gharghabi, F., & Coleman, W. (2012). A scoping review of health game research: past, present, and future. *Games For Health Journal*, *1*(2), 153–164.
40. Kickstarter. (2013a). *Emotiv insight.* [Online] http://www.kickstarter.com/projects/tanttle/emotiv-insight-optimize-your-brain-fitness-and-per [Accessed August 2013]
41. Kickstarter (2013b). *Melonheadband.* [Online] http://www.kickstarter.com/projects/806146824/melon-a-headband-and-mobile-app-to-measure-your-fo?ref=live [Accessed August 2013]
42. Kleih, S. C., Nijboer, F., Halder, S., & Kübler, A. (2010). Motivation modulates the p300 amplitude during brain-computer interface use. *Clinical Neurophysiology*, *121*(7), 1023–1031.
43. Kokar, M. W., & Endsley, M. R. (2012). Situation awareness and cognitive modeling. *IEEE Intelligent Systems*, *27*(3), 91–96.
44. Kübler, A., Kotchoubey, B., Kaiser, J., Wolpaw, J. R., & Birbaumer, N. (2001). Brain-computer communication: unlocking the locked in. *Psychological Bulletin*, *127*(3), 358.
45. Lance, B. J., Kerick, S. E., Ries, A. J., Oie, K. S., & McDowell, K. (2012). Brain-computer interface technologies in the coming decades. *Proceedings of the IEEE*, *100*, 1585–1599.
46. Lifehacker. (2011). [Online] http://lifehacker.com/5842991/make-your-own-mind+control-headgear-with-a-star-wars-toy [Accessed: August 2013]
47. Lightbody, G., Ware, M., McCullagh, P., Mulvenna, M., Thomson, E., & Martin, S. (2010). A user centred approach for developing brain-computer interfaces. *2010 4th International Conference on Pervasive Computing Technologies for Healthcare (PervasiveHealth)*, pp. 1–8.
48. López, J. F., Muñoz, J., Henao, O., & Villada, J. F. (2013). BKI: Brain Kinect Interface, a new hybrid BCI for rehabilitation. In *Games for Health* (pp. 233–245). Wiesbaden: Springer Fachmedien.
49. Luo, A., & Sullivan, T. (2010). A user-friendly ssvep-based brain-computer interface using a time-domain classifier. *Journal of Neural Engineering*, *7*, 1–10. doi:10.1088/1741-2560/7/2/026010.
50. Marshall, D., Coyle, D., Wilson, S., & Callaghan, M. (2013). Games, gameplay, and bci: the state of the art. *IEEE Transactions on Computational Intelligence and AI in Games*, *5*(2), 82–99.
51. McCullagh, P.J., Ware, M., Mulvenna, M., Lightbody, G., Nugent, C. D., & McAllister, H. G. (2010a). Can brain computer interfaces become practical assistive devices in the community? In: Medinfo 2010. *Studies in Health Technology and Informatics, 160*, 314–318.
52. McCullagh, P. J., Ware, M., Lightbody, G., Mulvenna, M., McAllister, H. G., & Nugent, C. D. (2010b). Can brain computer interfaces become personal health devices? In *7th International Conference on Wearable Micro and Nano Technologies for Personalized Health*, May 26–28, 2010, CD Conference Proceedings.
53. McCullagh, P., Ware, M., McRoberts, A., Lightbody, G., Mulvenna, M., McAllister G., González J. L., and Medina, V. C. (2011). Towards standardized user and application interfaces for the brain computer interface. In *Universal Access in Human-Computer Interaction. Users Diversity* (pp. 573–582). Berlin, Heidelberg: Springer.
54. McCullagh, P.J., Galway, L., & Lightbody, G. (2013a) Investigation into a mixed hybrid using SSVEP and eye gaze for optimising user interaction within a virtual environment. In *Universal Access in Human-Computer Interaction. Design Methods, Tools, and Interaction Techniques for EInclusion* (pp. 530–539). Berlin, Heidelberg: Springer.
55. McCullagh, P., Lightbody, G., Zygierewicz, J., & Kernohan, W.G. (2013b). Ethical challenges associated with the development and deployment of brain computer interface technology. *Neuroethics*, 1–14.
56. Melon. (2013). *Melon headband for improving focus*. [online] http://www.usemelon.com [Accessed December 2013]
57. Millán, J., Rupp, R., Müller-Putz, G. R., Murray-Smith, R., Giugliemma, C., Tangermann, M., et al. (2010). Combining brain-computer interfaces and assistive technologies: state-of-the-art and challenges. *Frontiers in Neuroscience*, *4*, 161.

58. MindFlex. (2013). *Mind flex duel from mattel incorporated*. [online] http://mindflexgames.com/ [Accessed December 2013]
59. MindSet. (2013). *NeuroSky mindSet*. [online] http://www.neurosky.com/products/mindset.aspx [Accessed December 2013]
60. Müller-Putz, G. R., Breitwieser, C., Cincotti, F., Leeb, R., Schreuder, M., Leotta, F., et al. (2011). Tools for brain-computer interaction: a general concept for a hybrid bci. *Frontiers in Neuroinformatics*, *5*, 30. doi:10.3389/fninf.2011.00030. NULL
61. Mulvenna, M., Lightbody, G., Thomson, E., McCullagh, P., Ware, M., & Martin, S. (2012). Realistic expectations with brain computer interfaces. *Journal of Assistive Technologies*, *6*(4), 233–244.
62. Muse. (2013). *Interaxon muse brain sensing headband*. [online] http://www.interaxon.ca/muse/ [Accessed December 2013]
63. *MyndPlay*. (2013). *MyndPlay*. [online] http://www.myndplay.com/products.php [Accessed December 2013]
64. Neuper, C., & Pfurtscheller, G. (2010). Neurofeedback training for BCI control. In *Brain-Computer Interfaces* (pp. 65–78). Berlin, Heidelberg: Springer.
65. NeuroElectrics. (2013). *Neuro electrics*. [online] http://www.neuroelectrics.com [Accessed December 2013]
66. NeuroSky. (2009). *Instruction Manual NeuroSky MindSet*. [Online] http://developer.neurosky.com/docs/doku.php?id=mindset_instruction_manual [Accessed: August 2013]
67. NeuroSky. (2013). *NeuroSky incorporated website*. [online] http://www.neurosky.com/ [Accessed December 2013]
68. NeuroSky App Store. (2013). [Online] http://store.neurosky.com/collections/applications [Accessed: August 2013]
69. Nijboer, F., & Broermann, U. (2010). Brain-computer interfaces for communication and control in locked-in patients. In *Brain-Computer Interfaces* (pp. 185–201). Berlin, Heidelberg: Springer.
70. Nijholt, A., van Erp, J. B. F., & Heylen, D. K. J. (2008). BrainGain: BCI for HCI and Games. In *Symposium Brain Computer Interfaces and Human Computer Interaction: A Convergence of Ideas at the AISB 2008 Convention "Communication, Interaction and Social Intelligence"*, Aberdeen, UK, 32–35, 2008.
71. Nijholt, A., Plass-Oude Bos, D., & Reuderink, B. (2009). Turning shortcomings into challenges: brain-computer interfaces for games. *Entertainment Computing*, *1*, 85–94.
72. Nuffield Council on Bioethics. (2012). Novel neurotechnologies: Intervening in the brain. [Online] http://www.nuffieldbioethics.org/neurotechnology [Accessed: April 2013]
73. Obama. (2013). *Obama proposes brain mapping project*. [online] http://www.bbc.co.uk/news/science-environment-22007007 [Accessed December 2013]
74. OpenBCI. (2013). [Online] http://bci.fuw.edu.pl/wiki/OpenBCI_system [Accessed: August 2013]
75. OpenEEG. (2013) *OpenEEG project*. [online] http://openeeg.sourceforge.net/doc/ [Accessed December 2013]
76. Ortner, R., Ram, D., Kollreider, A., Pitsch, H., Wojtowicz, J., & Edlinger, G. (2013). Human-Computer Confluence for Rehabilitation Purposes after Stroke. In *Virtual, Augmented and Mixed Reality. Systems and Applications* (pp. 74–82). Berlin, Heidelberg: Springer.
77. Piccini, L., Parini, S., Maggi, L., & Andreoni, G. (2005). A Wearable Home BCI system: preliminary results with SSVEP protocol. *Proceedings of the 2005 IEEE Engineering in Medicine and Biology 27th Annual Conference Shanghai*, China, September 1–4, 2005.
78. Pfurtscheller, G., Allison, B. Z., Brunner, C., Bauemfeind, G., Solis-Escalante, T., Scherer, R., et al. (2010). The hybrid bci. *Frontiers in Neuroscience*, *4*, 42. doi:10.3389/fnpro.2010.00003
79. Plass-Oude Bos, D., Reuderink, B., van de Laar, B., Gürkök, H., Mühl, C., Poel, M., et al. (2010). Brain-computer interfacing and games. In D. S. Tan & A. Nijholt (Eds.), *Brain-computer interfaces, human-computer interaction series* (pp. 149–178). London: Springer.

80. Schalk, G., McFarland, D. J., Hinterberger, T., Birbaumer, N., & Wolpaw, J. R. (2004). BCI2000: A general-purpose brain-computer interface (BCI) system. *IEEE Transactions on Biomedical Engineering*, *51*(6), 1034–1043.
81. Sellers, E. W., Vaughan, T. M., & Wolpaw, J. R. (2010). A brain-computer interface for long-term independent home use. *Amyotrophic Lateral Sclerosis*, *11*(5), 449–455.
82. Spüler, M., Rosenstiel, W., & Bogdan, M. (2012a). Online adaptation of a c-vep brain-computer interface (bci) based on error-related potentials and unsupervised learning. *PloS One*, *7*(12), e51077.
83. Spüler, M., Bensch, M., Kleih, S., Rosenstiel, W., Bogdan, M., & Kübler, A. (2012b). Online use of error-related potentials in healthy users and people with severe motor impairment increases performance of a p300-bci. *Clinical Neurophysiology*, *123*(7), 1328–1337.
84. Star Wars. (2013). *Uncle Milton industries incorporated star wars force trainer*. [online] http://unclemilton.com/star_wars_science/#/the_force_trainer/ [Accessed December 2013]
85. Sung, Y., Cho, K., & Um, K. (2012). A development architecture for serious games using bci (brain computer interface) sensors. *Sensors*, *12*, 15671–15688.
86. Tan, D. S., & Nijholt, A. (Eds.). (2010). *Brain-computer interfaces—Applying our minds to human-computer interaction*. Springer.
87. Vaadia E. & Birbaumer, N. (2009). Grand challenges in brain computer interface. *Frontiers in Neuroscience*, *3*(2).
88. van de Laar, B. L. A., Brugman, I., Nijboer, F., Poel, M. & Nijholt, A. (2013). BrainBrush, a multimodal application for creative expressivity. In *Sixth International Conference on Advances in Computer-Human Interactions (ACHI 2013)*, pp. 62–67.
89. van de Laar, B., Gürkök, H., Poel, M., & Nijholt, A. (2013). Experiencing bci control in a popular computer game. *IEEE Transactions on Computational Intelligence and AI in Games*, *5*(2), 176–184.
90. Varshney, U. (2007). Pervasive healthcare and wireless health monitoring. *Mobile Networks and Applications*, *12*(2–3), 113–127.
91. Vlek, R. J., Steines, D., Szibbo, D., Kübler, A., Schneider, M. J., Haselager, P., et al. (2012). Ethical issues in brain-computer interface research, development, and dissemination. *Journal of Neurologic Physical Therapy*, *36*(2), 94.
92. Volosyak, I., Valbuena, D., Malechka, T., Peuscher, J., & Gräser, A. (2010). Brain-computer interface using water-based electrodes. *Journal of Neural Engineering*, *7*(6), 066007.
93. Ware, M. P., McCullagh, P. J., McRoberts, A., Lightbody, G., Nugent, C., McAllister, G., et al. (2010). Contrasting levels of accuracy in command interaction sequences for a domestic brain-computer interface using SSVEP. In *2010 5th Cairo International Biomedical Engineering Conference (CIBEC)* (pp. 150–153). IEEE.
94. Weiser, M. (1991). The computer for the 21st century. *Scientific American*, *265*(3), 94–104.
95. Wolpaw, J. R., Birbaumer, N., McFarland, D. J., Pfurtscheller, G., & Vaughan, T. M. (2002). Brain computer inter-faces for communication and control. *Clin Neurophysiol*, *113*(6), 767–791.
96. Wolpaw, J. R., & Wolpaw, E. (Eds.). (2012). *Brain-computer interfaces: Principles and practice*. USA: Oxford University Press.
97. Yoh, M. -S., Kwon, J., & Kim, S. (2010). NeuroWander: A BCI game in the form of interactive fairy tale. In *Proceedings of the 12th ACM International Conference Adjunct Papers on Ubiquitous Computing*, New York, USA, pp. 389–390.
98. Yong, X., Fatourechi, M., Ward, R. K. & Birch, G. E. (2011). The design of a point-and-click system by integrating a self-paced brain-computer interface with an eye-tracker. *IEEE Journal on Emerging and Selected Topics in Circuits and Systems*, *1*(4), 590–602.
99. Zander, T. O., Kothe, C., Welke, S., & Roetting, M. (2008). Enhancing human-machine systems with secondary input from passive brain-computer interfaces. In *Proceedings of the 4th International BCI Workshop and Training Course (Graz, Austria, 2008)*. Graz University of Technology Publishing House.
100. Zander, T. O., Kothe, C., Jatzev, S., & Gaertner, M. (2010). Enhancing human-computer interaction with input from active and passive brain-computer interfaces. In D. S. Tan & A. Nijholt (Eds.), *Brain-computer interfaces* (pp. 181–199). London: Springer.

101. Zander, T. O., Gaertner, M., Kothe, C., & Vilimek, R. (2011). Combining eye gaze input with a brain-computer interface for touchless human-computer interaction. *International Journal of Human-Computer Studies*, *27*, 38–51.
102. Zander, T. O., & Jatzev, S. (2012). Context-aware brain-computer interfaces: exploring the information space of user, technical system and environment. *Journal of Neural Engineering*, *9*(1), 016003.
103. Zhu, D., Bieger, J., Molina, G. G., & Aarts, R. M. (2010). A survey of stimulation methods used in SSVEP-based BCIs. *Computational Intelligence and Neuroscience*, 1.

Further Readings

104. Allison, B. Z. (2011). *Future BNCI: A roadmap for future directions in brain/Neuronal computer interaction research.* [Online] http://future-bnci.org/images/stories/Future_BNCI_Roadmap.pdf [Accessed: September 2012]

Chapter 6
'RehabMaster^{TM}': A Pervasive Rehabilitation Platform for Stroke Patients and Their Caregivers

Kyoungwon Seo, Jieun Kim, Hokyoung Ryu and Seongho Jang

6.1 Introduction

As aging society is coming, concern about long-term disability (e.g., stroke, dementia, and so forth) is dramatically increasing [19]. Especially, stroke is the leading cause of long-term disability that hinders post-stroke patients going back to their normal life [16, 17, 21]. In their normal treatment process, i.e., post-stroke rehabilitation process, the hospitalization period (N.B. the state-covering insurance in Korea accepts only 8 weeks hospitalization for stroke patients) is over, most of inpatients get back to their homes and are prescribed with a home exercise therapy program. However, the outpatients are getting usually worse than their hospitalization period when they get back to the medical center for check-ups in every 4 weeks. One of the major reasons for the deterioration is their weakened determination compared to the compulsory exercise program in their hospitalization period. In this context, a number of researches have done about serious games, to foster post-stroke patients' motivation in performing the home exercise therapy [3, 11, 29].

K. Seo
Department of Industrial Engineering, Hanyang University,
Wangsimni-ro, Seongdong, Seoul 133-792, Korea
e-mail: cseo@hanyang.ac.kr

J. Kim · H. Ryu (✉)
Graduate School of Innovation and Technology Management, Hanyang University,
Wangsimni-ro, Seongdong, Seoul 133-792, Korea
e-mail: hryu@hanyang.ac.kr,

J. Kim
e-mail: jkim2@hanyang.ac.kr

S. Jang
Department of Physical Medicine and Rehabilitation, Hanyang University College of Medicine,
Wangsimni-ro, Seongdong, Seoul 133-792, Korea
e-mail: systole77@hanmail.net

A. Holzinger et al. (eds.), *Pervasive Health*, Human–Computer Interaction Series,
DOI: 10.1007/978-1-4471-6413-5_6, © Springer-Verlag London 2014

Though the game-based rehabilitation programs (e.g., Nintendo Wii Fit™ or Microsoft Xbox Your Shape™ Fitness Evolve) have been highly welcomed in this regard, they seem controversial on the clinical staffs' view [6, 9]. This is mostly because the medical staffs feel inconvenient to adopt the off-the-shelf games into their current work practices (i.e., prescribing an exercise therapy with Nintendo Wii Fit). Indeed, the rehabilitation procedure in Korea, post-stroke patients should heavily interact with either physiatrists or occupational therapists. However, only a few rehabilitation platforms have considered these interactions, so the usefulness of serious games is not much appraised for the current rehabilitation practices of what clinical staffs are doing.

To address these problems, this chapter provides a comprehensive description of studies that discuss serious game for not only stroke patients but also other key stakeholders (e.g., physiatrists, occupational therapists, and family members). In this context, firstly, we will review edutainment issues for motivating patients to further engage in the exercises [2, 3, 8–10, 25], e.g., deploying multimedia gaming module like [26], and suggest how a serious game platform can be integrated into institutionalized medical treatments in the current work practices in Korea. After that, our design experiences in implementing and installing such a platform in the homes of patient and across institutions, under an umbrella program called 'Ubiquitous Health Korea', will be shared. The clinical and usability test is conducted to verify the usefulness of our rehabilitation platform—RehabMaster™. Finally, lessons learned that can inform methodological and practical approaches to designing a clinical-level serious game will be highlighted and new approaches for reaching patients and providing support to promote health, goals which require understanding the mobile learning process will be outlined. This chapter includes a number of Human-Computer Interaction (HCI) issues [12], a larger overview of societal changes in the last decades [26], and how many issues raised by caregivers (e.g., medical staff, family members, authorities concerned) have been addressed, from user studies to finalizing the high fidelity prototypes.

6.2 Glossary

Declaration of Helsinki The Declaration of Helsinki is a set of ethical principles regarding human experimentation developed for the medical community by the World Medical Association (WMA). It is widely regarded as the cornerstone document of human research ethics.

Edutainment Edutainment is the compound word that is formed from the words "education" and "entertainment". This refers to content that is designed to both educate and entertain.

Natural user interface (NUI) Natural user interface is the interface that is based on nature or natural elements like gesture, multi-touch, voice, and sensory stimuli (e.g., Kinect-like depth camera). Unlike current computer interfaces that use artificial control devices (e.g., keyboard or mouse) whose operation has to be learned, users are able to learn how to use NUI naturally.

Occupational therapist An occupational therapist works with a patient to help them achieve a fulfilled and satisfied state in life through the use of "purposeful activity or interventions". These purposeful interventions are to a greater extent developed by physiatrists and designed to achieve functional outcomes that promote health and restore the highest possible level of independence.

Physiatrist Physiatrists specialize in restoring optimal physical function to people with injuries to the muscles, bones, tissues, and nervous system (such as stroke patients). In the clinical setting, physiatrists are the people who stroke patients meet firstly. Physiatrists identify stroke patients' symptoms and prescribe proper therapy.

Rehabilitation Rehabilitation is a treatment or treatments designed to facilitate the process of recovery from injury, illness, or disease to as normal a condition as possible. In this chapter, we specifically focus on "long-term" physical therapy which is primarily concerned with the remediation of impairments and disabilities and the promotion of mobility, functional ability, quality of life and movement potential.

Serious game A serious game is a game that has a primary purpose other than pure entertainment. The adjective 'serious' generally refers to domains such as education, health care, engineering, training, and scientific exploration.

Stroke A stroke is the rapid loss of brain function due to a sudden interruption in the blood supply of the brain. It can cause loss of sensation or difficulty with speaking, seeing, sensing, or walking.

Upper extremity (UE) functional deficits The upper extremity or upper limb refers to the region in our body extending from the deltoid region to the hand, including the arm, axilla, and shoulder. This region is closely related to our everyday life activity, so functional deficits in the upper extremity can cause severe decline in someone's quality of life.

Usability Usability refers to ease of use as well as learnability of objects like software applications, websites, books, tools, machines, or anything a human interacts with.

6.3 State-of-the-Art

6.3.1 Supporting Stroke Patients in a Clinical Setting

Stroke is the leading cause of severe, long-term disability among adults in many countries, including the United States, the UK, Canada, and Korea [16]. Approximately 80 % of stroke survivors have significant motor impairment [17], including upper extremity (UE) functional deficits. In the last decade (2002–2012), for instance, about 1.6 million patients have been hospitalized in Korea, and the number of stroke inpatients has been continuously increasing at a compound annual growth rate of 6.4 % [16].

Evidence shows that the effectiveness of a rehabilitation training program depends upon both the intensity and frequency of the program [17] however, simple and uniform repetitive training has been viewed as very unmotivated for stroke patients, especially in home-based stroke rehabilitation systems. Adherence to rehabilitation programs at home is significantly affected by the motivation of stroke patients [8]. Many studies have thus questioned how to boost motivational power (or at the very least, the will-power to complete exercises) of stroke patients for a long-term rehabilitation process at home [2, 3, 8, 11, 25]. In this regard, research into serious games (i.e., edutainment) has been done to determine their effectiveness in rehabilitation as well as to motivate stroke patients while they train at home. This might be an important contribution of the Human-Computer Interaction (HCI) discipline to the medical field [26].

Current game-based rehabilitation systems using off-the-shelf fitness programs (e.g., Nintendo Wii Fit™ or Microsoft Xbox Your Shape™ Fitness Evolve) are mostly used in nursing facilities and at home and are not often employed in clinical settings. This is partly because there is no strong validation of the clinical effects and because medical staffs are still reluctant to insert off-the-shelf games into their conventional rehabilitation programs. Indeed, in clinical rehabilitation sessions, stroke patients should interact with either physiatrists or occupational therapists, and these interactions remain as the core part of successful rehabilitation. However, few motion-based rehabilitation programs have considered the interactions between the stroke patient and the clinical staff, and the usefulness of serious games (except their ease of use) was not considered appropriate to current clinical practices of physiatrists and occupational therapists. This lack of consideration regarding such interactions prevents clinical staff from being more effective and helpful to stroke patients [6, 9].

In this context, the key challenges for a new pervasive rehabilitation platform in clinical settings are twofold: (1) to design a motion-based rehabilitation that not only benefits stroke patients but also simulates occupational training (OT) sessions of the clinical staff; and (2) to validate the clinical advantages and usability from the perspectives of three stakeholders' (i.e., stroke patients, physiatrists, occupational therapists).

6.3.2 Current Game-Based Rehabilitation Program

In stroke rehabilitation, a motion-based rehabilitation program is gaining a strong ground in that its repetitive training can achieve functional improvement in the upper extremities (UE). In this context, game-based rehabilitation programs are now widely deployed in institutionalized environments and/or homes to enhance training effects as well as to motivate stroke patients.

As Table 6.1 shows, many game-based rehabilitation programs are widely installed in not only institutionalized environments but also in patients' homes and used to

Table 6.1 List of the current game-based rehabilitation programs

Place of usage	Game-based rehabilitation program	Description
Institutionalized environments	Rabbit chase, bubble trouble, arrow attack [10]	Games for upper limb rehabilitation which integrates 3D virtual environments, sensor, and camera technology
	The butterfly game [15]	Interactive game for mentally and physically disabled at residential home
Home	Helicopter, pong, and baseball catch [3]	Games for upper limb rehabilitation which uses Wii remotes, and a web camera
	Games for physical therapy [25]	Games for recovering arm movements which uses Wii remotes, color detection software to track a colorful glove
Both	Nintendo and Xbox game titles [3, 6]	Using commercial video games to motivate patients, develop skills and serve as a distractor in pain management

rehabilitate as well as motivate stroke patients; however, most game-based rehabilitation programs only concern the end user (i.e., stroke patients) and overlook the roles of other stakeholders, e.g., the clinical staff.

6.3.3 'RehabMaster^{TM}': A Pervasive Rehabilitation Platform for the Stroke Patients

Hanyang University Medical Center is one of the most advanced rehabilitation facilities in Korea. Approximately two hundreds of stroke patients stay at this center as inpatients, and more than five hundreds of patients are regularly treated by the 60 clinical staff every day. During rounds, physiatrists test the physical function of stroke patients and properly modify occupational therapy sessions. Stroke patients have to participate in this therapy session during their hospitalization period. Occupational therapists help patients attend therapy sessions and motivate them to rehabilitate.

After the hospitalization period is over, inpatients go back to their homes and become outpatients. As outpatients, they are prescribed home therapy and have to visit the medical center twice a month to check their progress. However, after 2 weeks, outpatients are usually worse when they present to the medical center for their checkup. The major reason for this deterioration is the lack of therapy sessions while outpatients are at home compared to their hospitalization period. In addition, physiatrists have difficulty prescribing further home therapy sessions, because there is no information about the progress of outpatients.

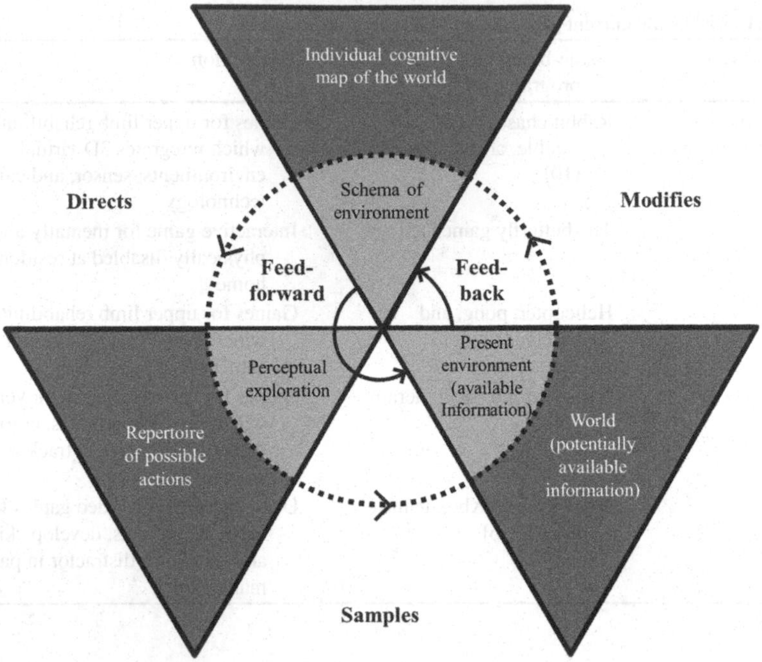

Fig. 6.1 The perceptual cycle model (PCM) [20, 22]

To solve these problems (less motivation for home therapy, lack of proper information about patient's progress at home), Hanyang University and Medical Center joined together under umbrella program called 'Ubiquitous Health Korea' and tried to build a rather pervasive rehabilitation platform. In this platform, a serious game was used as a major home therapy session to motivate outpatients while training at home. As we discuss above, these serious games were verified as sufficient motivators for rehabilitation at home [3, 6, 25]. The remaining major issues are how we can gather an outpatient's progress information and how to use this information effectively as well as efficiently. In this context, we pay attention to Nessier's "perceptual cycle model (PCM)" [20] as a conceptual approach to developing information systems that might help the pervasive usage of rehabilitation platforms.

PCM is a model that refers to the idea of a reciprocal and cyclical relationship between a person (i.e., rehabilitation stakeholders) and the world (i.e., rehabilitation environment) as in Fig. 6.1. According to this model, people seek out certain kinds of information and develop world knowledge (schema) with this information (feedback in Fig. 6.1). These schema then leads to anticipation about certain information (feedforward in Fig. 6.1) [20, 22]. These interactions (i.e., developing schema and anticipation) can be seen as feedback and feedforward in our decision making process. Feedback about world information (e.g., patient's progress and states, therapist's opinion) as well as feedforward for anticipation (e.g., game-based program

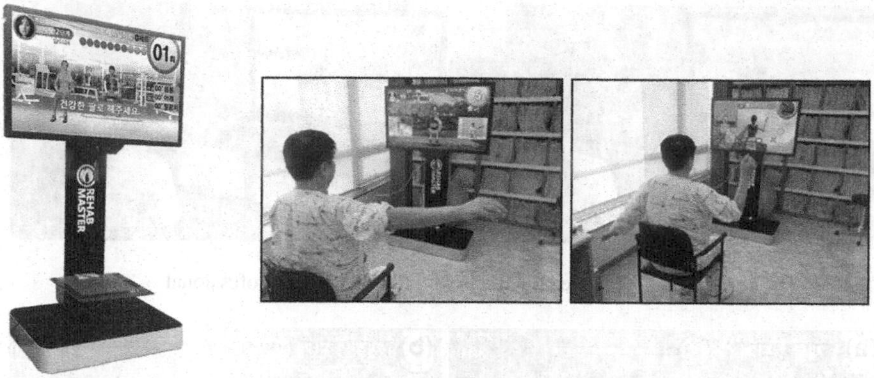

Fig. 6.2 RehabMaster™: a pervasive rehabilitation platform for the stroke patient

recommendation) can solve these issues about gathering an outpatient's progress data and effective information usage by the clinical staff. We hypothesized that feedback and feedforward ultimately help the pervasive usage of a rehabilitation platform in institutionalized environments as well as at home in addition to focused feedback and feedforward through our rehabilitation platform.

These information transmissions (i.e., feedback and feedforward) help clinical staff to keep up on rehabilitation progress and make schema about each patient according to their progress data. With these schema, the clinical staff can prescribe proper and customized therapy sessions for each patient and this can be linked to comprehensive usage of the rehabilitation platform. In particular in the clinical setting, the clinical staff has to deal with more than twenty patients per day, so a rehabilitation platform that can help the clinical staff's decision making process with both feedback and feedforward might be useful. For instance, if a rehabilitation platform provides progress information about patients (feedback in Fig. 6.1), this reduces the amount of time needed to understand a detailed medical record of the stroke patients, chronicle the serious game practice, and record notes by occupational therapists. Also, if a rehabilitation platform can recommend the game-based therapy that is the most proper for a current patient's state (feedforward), this can relieve a cognitive burden from clinical staff. These rehabilitation platform's functions (i.e., feedback and feedforward) can be seen as the clinical staff's distributed cognition [14], which helps their cognitive decision making process while treating stroke patients in the clinical setting. In this context, we designed RehabMaster™ as shown in Fig. 6.2, which addresses not only the motivation of stroke patients but also the feedback and feedforward of rehabilitation information for the clinical staff, which might be related to pervasive usage of the rehabilitation platform.

This rehabilitation program consists of two functional stages for rehabilitating the stroke patient. In the first stage (Fig. 6.3), the patients are given a pre-defined training set by healthcare professionals (generally, physiatrists). A total of 36 types of motor skill exercises are included, and the information gathered from the exercises is fed

Fig. 6.3 The first stage: a predefined training set by the healthcare professional

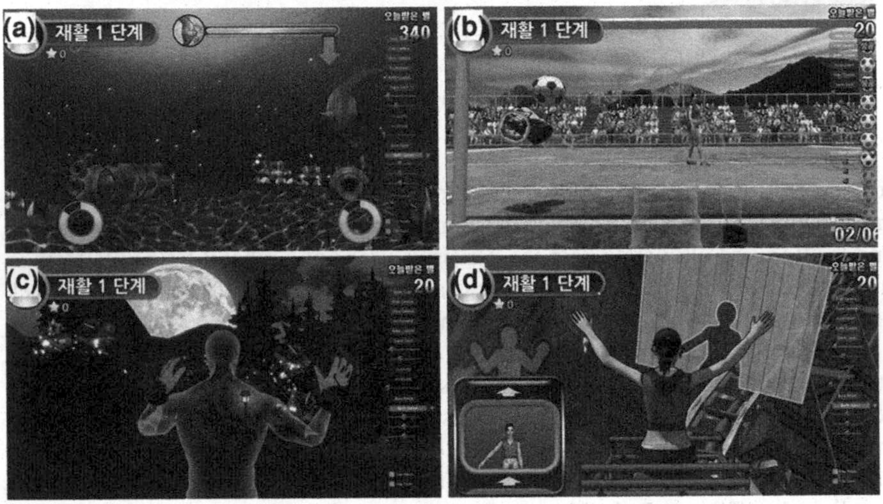

Fig. 6.4 Game-based learning content: swimming with dolphins (**a**), goal-keeping (**b**), catching flies (**c**), and a roller-coaster (**d**)

Table 6.2 Different physical exercises for each game-based learning content

Contents	Different physical exercises			
	Shoulder	Elbow	Wrist	Grasp/release
Swimming with dolphins	O		O	
Goal-keeping	O		O	O
Catching flies	O	O		O
A roller-coaster	O	O		

into the game-based training exercises in the second stage. The game-based learning contents (Fig. 6.4) include many different types of physical exercises (Table 6.2) such as swimming with dolphins, goal-keeping, catching flies, and a roller-coaster, and each one is specially designed to promote relevant motor skills for the stroke patients to enjoy exercise.

Table 6.3 Difference in ELO-rating and its corresponding expected chance of winning [4]

Rating difference	Expected chance of winning	Difference	Chance	Difference	Chance
$0 \geq dif \leq 3$	0.50	$122 \geq dif \leq 129$	0.67	$279 \geq dif \leq 290$	0.84
$4 \geq dif \leq 10$	0.51	$130 \geq dif \leq 137$	0.68	$291 \geq dif \leq 302$	0.85
$11 \geq dif \leq 17$	0.52	$138 \geq dif \leq 145$	0.69	$303 \geq dif \leq 315$	0.86
$18 \geq dif \leq 25$	0.53	$146 \geq dif \leq 153$	0.70	$316 \geq dif \leq 328$	0.87
$26 \geq dif \leq 32$	0.54	$154 \geq dif \leq 162$	0.71	$329 \geq dif \leq 344$	0.88
$33 \geq dif \leq 39$	0.55	$163 \geq dif \leq 170$	0.72	$345 \geq dif \leq 357$	0.89
$40 \geq dif \leq 46$	0.56	$171 \geq dif \leq 179$	0.73	$358 \geq dif \leq 374$	0.90
$47 \geq dif \leq 53$	0.57	$180 \geq dif \leq 188$	0.74	$375 \geq dif \leq 391$	0.91
$54 \geq dif \leq 61$	0.58	$189 \geq dif \leq 197$	0.75	$392 \geq dif \leq 411$	0.92
$62 \geq dif \leq 68$	0.59	$198 \geq dif \leq 206$	0.76	$412 \geq dif \leq 432$	0.93
$69 \geq dif \leq 76$	0.60	$207 \geq dif \leq 215$	0.77	$433 \geq dif \leq 456$	0.94
$77 \geq dif \leq 83$	0.61	$216 \geq dif \leq 225$	0.78	$457 \geq dif \leq 484$	0.95
$84 \geq dif \leq 91$	0.62	$226 \geq dif \leq 235$	0.79	$485 \geq dif \leq 517$	0.96
$92 \geq dif \leq 98$	0.63	$236 \geq dif \leq 245$	0.80	$518 \geq dif \leq 559$	0.97
$99 \geq dif \leq 106$	0.64	$246 \geq dif \leq 256$	0.81	$560 \geq dif \leq 619$	0.98
$107 \geq dif \leq 113$	0.65	$257 \geq dif \leq 267$	0.82	$620 \geq dif \leq 735$	0.99
$114 \geq dif \leq 121$	0.66	$268 \geq dif \leq 278$	0.83	$dif \leq 736$	1.00

Due to the chronic nature of symptoms in the stroke patient, the rehabilitation program in RehabMaster^{TM} needs to be effective for improving the daily life of stroke patients. This would further engage the stroke patient to such a long-term and consistent rehabilitation activity, because only intensive as well as frequent training can improve the physical performance of stroke patients. To make stroke patients willingly engage in long-term and consistent rehabilitation activity, usability by a rehabilitation system's stakeholders is an important matter. In this regard, dynamic difficulty adjustment (DDA) is applied to suit the different types of stroke patients by offering an alternative to match a patient's skill (in particular, limb movement) and the game challenges. An important goal is to make sure the stroke patient experience the right level of challenge, so they can fully concentrate and avoid discouragement. Our DDA algorithm is based on the ELO-rating system [4], which ranks players depending on their in-game performance. The ELO system makes use of the deviation of the actual rehabilitation performance outcome (win, loss, or tie with other player) from the expected outcome for each of two players. For instance, if player 1 (P1: ELO-rating 1,000) meets player 2 (P2: ELO-rating 800), an ELO-rating difference of 200 corresponds to a specific chance of winning (according to Table 6.3, P1 wins of 76 %). If P1 wins, its new ELO-rating is updated according to this formula (P1 new ELO-rating = P1 old ELO-rating + $(1 - 0.76) * 100$). For P2, as its initial rating is lower than P1, its decrease in rating is smaller than that of P1 (P2 new ELO-rating = P2 old ELO-rating + $(0 - 0.24) * 100$). This balanced rating system adjusts each player's rehabilitation performance level and helps them to compete with proper contestants. Through competition with other stroke patients who have

a similar level of capability, patients can intensely concentrate on a rehabilitation program.
To calculate ELO-ratings, this table is used after each contest. For each rating difference between two contestants, it gives the corresponding expected chance of winning for the one with the highest rating. Graphically, this table resembles a logistic curve. Since our game is played alone, the player gets to "compete against the game". Thus, a "skill level" that reflects difficulty is associated with each level. Then, the result from the ELO-rating gives us a difficulty ratio, which represents the expected level of challenge that will be experienced by the player for the completion of this level. The player's rank is automatically adjusted throughout the game, with an increase if he or she completes tasks easily and a decrease if he or she repeats errors and needs assistance. To maximize limb movement of the stroke patient, RehabMaster^{TM} employs a Kinect-like depth camera. As the patients lift their arms following the instructions on the display, the depth camera detects the movements and measures their absolute angles in 3D space with an error tolerance of approximately 2–5 degrees at the shoulders, elbows, and wrists. The performance and training data collected by the system are sent back to the physiatrists (feedback), so they know the conditions or states of the patients. Based on this knowledge about the patients (schema), physiatrists are able to prescribe rehabilitation therapy for the stroke patient that is mostly recommended by RehabMaster^{TM} (feedforward).

6.3.4 The Present Study

Rehabilitating stroke patients need ongoing, long-term treatment. In particular, motivating them to continuously engage in treatment is key to success. In practice, such an approach has been widely applied in institutionalized environments (e.g., hospitals), but it has been less successful when patients return home, which underscores the importance of pervasive health. That being said, when designing an effective rehabilitation program, it is important to consider not only the patients but also their caregivers, including physiatrists, occupational therapists, and their family members, to name just a few. This follows, because effective and efficient rehabilitation for the stroke patient relies heavily on coordinated, integrated, and long-term care from all relevant stakeholders.

Within the purview of this chapter, we present our experiences in developing a pervasive interaction based rehabilitation program—'RehabMaster^{TM}'—for stroke patients, inserting rather different requirements from clinical staff. By deploying a rehabilitation program not only for the motivation of stroke patients but also for information gathering about a patient's state and progress, this program can be used as distributed cognition by the clinical staff [14]. Thus, by reducing clinical staff's cognitive burden, clinical staff can concentrate on the rehabilitation itself, and this might lead to improved quality of rehabilitation programs.

The following sections include an HCI design process consisting of three sessions: (1) understanding the clinical setting; (2) extracting usability factors for different stakeholders; and (3) designing a pervasive motion-based rehabilitation system. The quantitative and qualitative results of the empirical study are then interpreted. Finally, lessons learned about an overarching perspective, including both stroke patients and clinical staff, and the potential contribution of serious games in the rehabilitation program, are further discussed.

6.4 Methods

6.4.1 Session 1: Understanding the Clinical Setting

In order to understand how the rehabilitation process for stroke patients works, the contextual inquiry method were employed, including focus group interviews, individual interviews, and observation in a clinical setting. We first held focus group interviews in order to understand how the rehabilitation process for stroke patients works. Four stakeholders (i.e., stroke patients, their caregivers, physiatrists, and occupational therapists) were then interviewed in a clinical setting for 2 weeks. We also carried out a 1 week observation session of how stakeholders interact one after another. Below is an illustrative example of the interaction between a stroke patient, Bob (anonymous), the physiatrist and the occupational therapist at the clinic.

> Bob was diagnosed with an upper extremity (UE) functional deficit after a stroke. After having recovered from the operation to some extent, Bob visited a rehabilitation clinic. The physiatrist tested Bob's upper limb motor function and prescribed an occupational therapy program best suited for Bob's symptoms. With this prescription, Bob had a training session every two days with the therapist at the clinic. At first, Bob hardly moved his right arm, so the therapist often paused training until Bob completed a particular movement. Sometimes Bob's condition was good with the ability to complete wide and fast movements; however, his condition could also deteriorate suddenly, such that some days he could not even move his arm up and down. In response to this rapid changing in condition, the therapist modified the level of prescriptive training program. After a 2 weeks training session, Bob visited the physiatrist again. She checked the progress report and prescribed new occupational therapy for the next exercise.

As above, clinical staff closely interact with patients in order to ask patients to perform the most effective and efficient rehabilitation program. These interactions between clinical staff and patients were discretely analyzed (Fig. 6.5, Table 6.4). A critical requisite for success is thus information on how each patient was treated and progressed along with their prescribed exercise program; however, we found that most off-the-shelf serious games (e.g., Nintendo and Xbox game titles) for stroke patients are not available for clinical staff to obtain such critical information. Of particular interest here was the lack of a proper information acquisition system from the games; consequently the physiatrist cannot prescribe the best possible rehabilitation program for different symptoms. Further, as a perpetual contact point for the rehabilitation program, therapists need to be able to fully control serious game-based exercises. For instance, when the patient complains of severe pain, or there is an

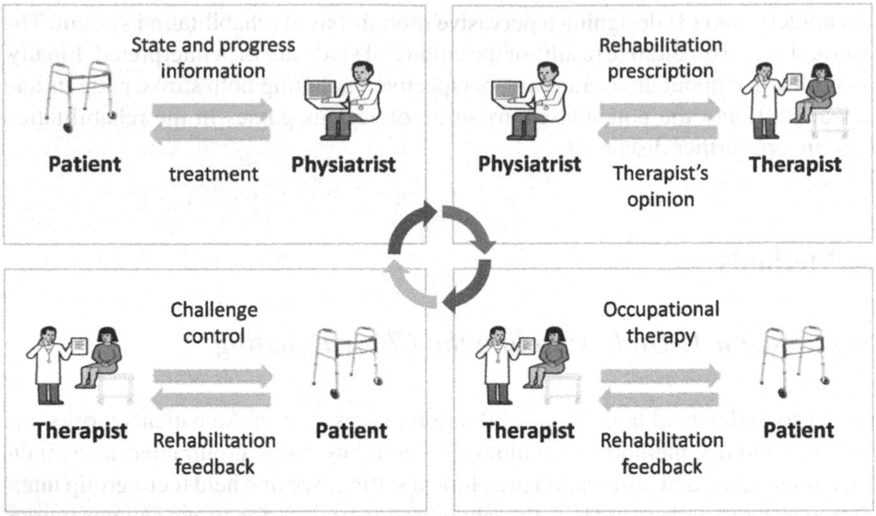

Fig. 6.5 Interaction between stroke patients, physiatrists and occupational therapists in the clinical setting

abrupt change in the stroke patient's state (which is quite common), the therapists should have some authority to control the rehabilitation program. These differences between the clinical process and current serious games available for stroke patients have to be integrated into a new game-based rehabilitation program (Table 6.4).

6.4.2 Session 2: Extracting Usability Factors for Different Stakeholders

Next, we developed a core set of usability factors for each stakeholder. In order to elicit usability factors, we first had a focus group interview to analyze the entire rehabilitation process in a clinical setting. After that, a 2 weeks interview session in the clinical setting with four stakeholders (i.e., stroke patients, their caregivers, physiatrists and occupational therapists) was carried out to formulate the proper course of rehabilitation and to determine critical usability issues. Table 6.5 illustrates relevant design factors and potential effects for each user group in the actual clinical setting, which were retrieved from our early usability studies and the existing literature [2, 3, 6, 8–12]. First, many studies related to home-based rehabilitation games have emphasized the importance of 'meaningful play' and 'challenge' of the stroke patient. Meaningful play emerges from a game through the relationship between a player's actions and outcomes that are closely related to the purposes of rehabilitation. This, of course, leads the stroke patient to have increased motivation and enjoyment [8, 9]. Challenge is also important because it affects a player's on-going enjoyment

Table 6.4 Difference between the clinical process and a serious game

Clinical process	Serious game	Difference
1. State and progress information	X	Physiatrist check patient's motor capability (clinical setting); mostly not available to get progress information (serious game)
2. Treatment	X	Useful information for treatment (clinical setting); no information through serious game (serious game)
3. Rehabilitation prescription	O	Prescribe occupational therapy program (clinical setting); prescribe serious game for home therapy (serious game)
4. Therapist's opinion	X	Therapist can discuss with physiatrist about therapy session (clinical setting); no discussion through serious game (serious game)
5. Occupational therapy	O	Therapy session with therapist (clinical setting); playing serious game with caregiver (serious game)
6. Rehabilitation feedback	X	Patient discuss with therapist about their condition or state (clinical setting); no feedback (serious game)
7. Challenge control	X	Therapist control challenge according to patient's feedback (clinical setting); mostly hard to control challenge (serious game)
8. Rehabilitation feedback	X	Patient discuss with therapist about their condition or state (clinical setting); no feedback (serious game)

Table 6.5 Usability factors for different stakeholders. Potential outcomes are also identified by both interviews and a literature review

User group	Usability factor	Proposed outcomes
Stroke	Meaningful play	Increased motivation and enjoyment [8, 9]
Patients	Challenge	Continuous enjoyment [8, 9]
Physiatrists	Information acquisition	Get the information of patient's progress [6, 7]
	Meaningful prescription	Proper prescription for patient's symptom [6, 8]
Occupational	Easy to use	Easy to configure and start a serious game [6]
Therapists	Challenge	Easy to control challenge while playing [6, 8–10]

and engagement on the horizon of experience [8]. For instance, if challenges are too high for the player, he or she becomes easily frustrated, which can result in the player quitting [10].

Second, the physiatrists asked to easily obtain reliable information about a patient's state as well as his or her progress from the serious games. In particular, they wanted an occupational prescription module that could easily manage meaning-

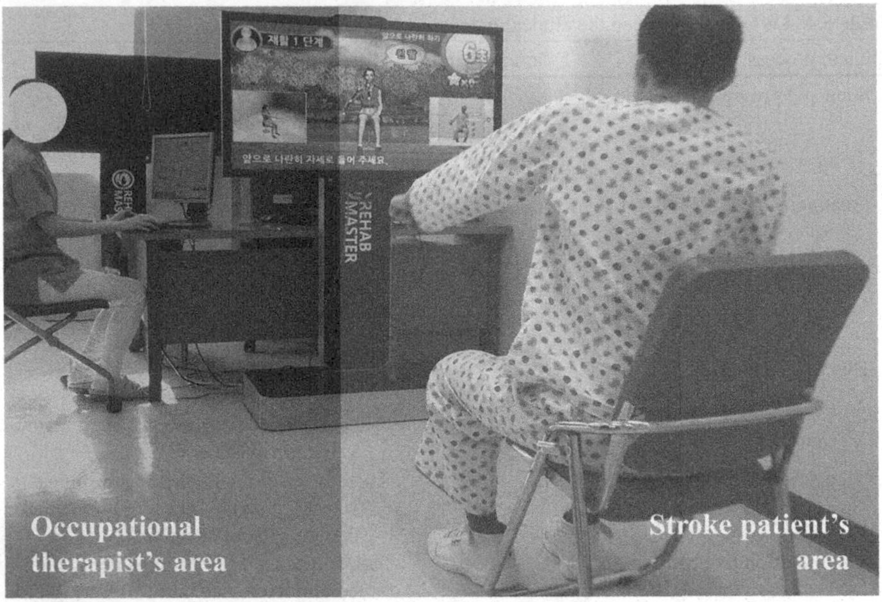

Fig. 6.6 RehabMaster^{TM}: upper extremity (UE) rehabilitation training

ful serious games for UE rehabilitation. In contrast, in their current work practices, occupational therapists tend to meet with more than one patient at a time. Normally, they deal with three or four patients at a time. Due to the massive and frequent use of serious games, occupational therapists asked for a serious game to be easily configurable. For instance, they suggested an appropriate level of therapy to be easily set or improvised while playing, depending on the current state as well as the progress of the patients.

6.4.3 Session 3: Designing a Motion-Based Rehabilitation System

Based on the above rather different user requirements, we developed a high-fidelity prototype with a motion-based serious game, called RehabMaster^{TM}. Its rehabilitation training simulates arm movements to restore specific functional deficits as shown in Fig. 6.6, in which the patients attempt to mimic motions pre-recorded for perfect limb movements [12].

In a practical setting, occupational therapists can manage 36 different training exercises that are based on the motion of Fugl-Meyer Assessment (FMA) at different levels of difficulty [13]. While the stroke patient plays with RehabMaster^{TM}, occupational therapists also provide physical assistance, verbal feedback, and emotional encouragement. This clinical trial generally took the entire 2 weeks period, around

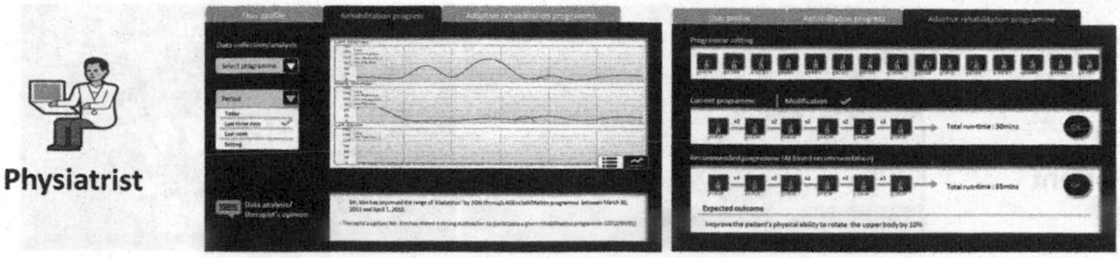

Fig. 6.7 Physiatrists: user management UI (*left*) and prescription UI (*right*)

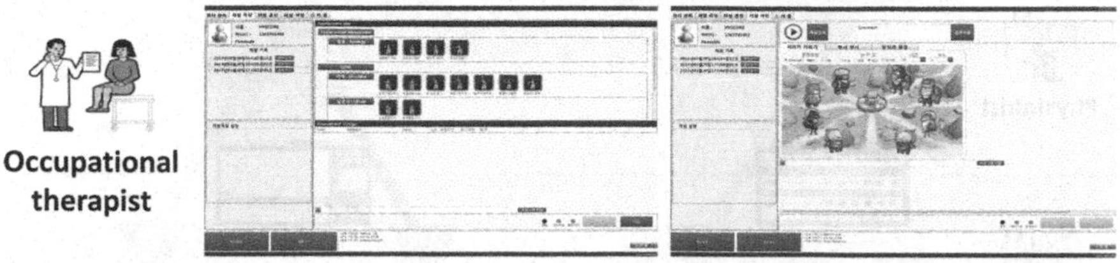

Fig. 6.8 Occupational therapists: editable UI for rehabilitation training (*left*) and rehabilitation game editing UI (*right*)

once a day for 20 min. All the training data were transferred into the main database, and physiatrists were able to use these data to diagnose as well as further prescribe customized exercise treatment.

Based on our usability factors (See Table 6.5), the RehabMaster^{TM} is aimed at not only the stroke patient, but also the clinical staff in their actual working environment. Thus, we developed three different types of user interfaces (UIs) (e.g., physiatrists UI, occupational therapists UI, and patients UI).

First, the interface for physiatrists consists of two key elements: a user management UI that contains information about the stroke patient (i.e., a detailed medical record of the stroke patients, a chronicle of the RehabMaster^{TM} practice, and notes recorded by occupational therapists); and a prescription UI that helps physiatrists coordinate meaningful rehabilitation training or relevant serious games (See Fig. 6.7).

Second, the occupational therapist's interface consists of four key elements: a user management UI that is exactly the same as the physiatrist's UI; an assessment UI that evaluates the rehabilitation progress; an editable UI for rehabilitation training that can assign personalized limb training exercises (Fig. 6.8, left); and a rehabilitation games editing UI that allows them to manage a series of best games for the current state of the stroke patient (Fig. 6.8, right). All the occupational therapist's UIs are easy to configure (e.g., pause, start, and stop) and the level of difficulty is easy to control while in use in the clinical setting.

Third, the UI for the stroke patient relies on an assessment of their limb movements, and the calculated scores against the perfect limb movement are presented on a display as in Fig. 6.9. Our system RehabMaster^{TM} consists of the three different user interfaces below (Figs. 6.7, 6.8 and 6.9), and these independent interfaces help each stakeholder interact with each other for successful rehabilitation.

Fig. 6.9 Patients: Rehabilitation training (*left*) and rehabilitation game (*right*)

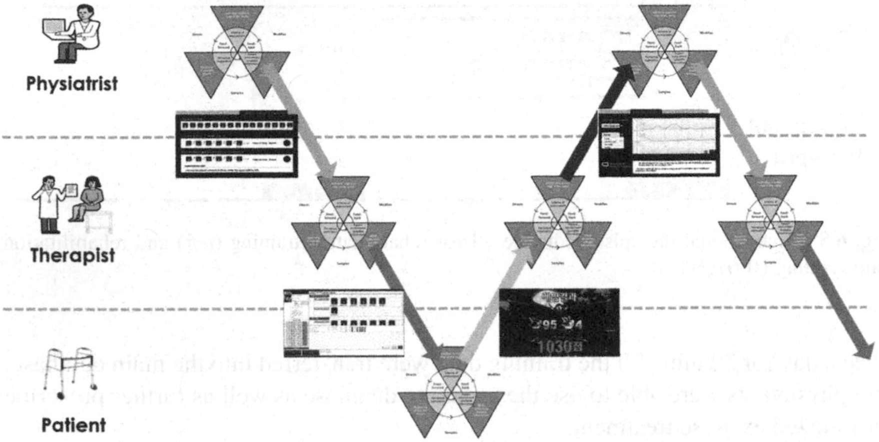

Fig. 6.10 Interaction between each stakeholder's perceptual cycle models through RehabMaster^{TM}

The integration and interaction between the three distinct user interfaces along with perceptual cycle model (PCM) is shown in Fig. 6.10. Each different stakeholder (i.e., physiatrists, occupational therapists, and patients) can update their own PCM while interacting with each other through their own UI in the RehabMaster^{TM}. For instance, unlike previous off-the-shelf game-based rehabilitation program, the RehabMaster^{TM} can help physiatrists to easily prescribe meaningful rehabilitation training or serious games at their own UI (a user management UI, and a prescription UI). The user management UI helps physiatrists to understand (i.e., make their own schema) about stroke patients through a detailed medical record and a history of the RehabMaster^{TM} practice (i.e., feedback information about patients). Based on these two types of personal information, RehabMaster^{TM} can suggest appropriate rehabilitation programs on the prescription UI that helps physiatrists to decide what training or relevant serious games would be (i.e., feedforward from the RehabMaster^{TM}). The prescribed rehabilitation training or serious games are delivered to the occupational therapist's UI, and therapists only need to guide patients toward the appropriate personalized limb training exercises. While training, an editable UI for rehabilitation training and a rehabilitation games editing UI are used to manage a series of best exercises for the current state of the stroke patient. Stroke patients can easily follow the therapist's guidance with RehabMaster^{TM}, and information about progress and states is automatically transmitted to the therapist's UI (the assessment UI; feedback information for occupational therapists). According to this information, therapists can easily configure (e.g., pause, start, and stop) and control the level of difficulty. Finally, all the rehabilitation information and notes recorded by occupational therapists are gathered and delivered to physiatrists (through the user management UI) to check information about the stroke patients, again.

Thanks to our RehabMaster^{TM}, both clinical staff and stroke patients can be easily connected with each other. They (i.e., clinical staff and stroke patients) can understand each other through feedback information from the RehabMaster^{TM}, and this helps them easily making their own schema about rehabilitation environment. Also, their cognitive burden can be reduced through our platform's feedforward about what to do (e.g., meaningful prescription for physiatrists, dynamic difficulty adjustment for therapists and patients). This natural flow of information enables RehabMaster^{TM} to be used pervasively in institutionalized environments as well as the home.

6.5 Design

One of the main objectives of the study was to see whether consideration of the three different kinds of user interfaces (UI) would ensure the success of RehabMaster^{TM} in an actual clinical setting. Clinical tests with the three user groups (i.e., physiatrists, occupational therapists, and stroke patients) were thus carried out. RehabMaster^{TM} was installed in a rehabilitation hospital for 2 weeks, and a clinical test and a usability test were performed. A total of seven physiatrists and three occupational therapists employed RehabMaster^{TM} for their actual work practices, and we wanted to see whether RehabMaster^{TM} could fit into their actual work practices. All of them had never used any motion-based rehabilitation program and they were trained to use RehabMaster^{TM} for two hours before the clinical test.

6.5.1 Part 1: Clinical Test

First, the clinical test was performed with sixteen 'acute-to-subacute' stroke patients (7 acute and 9 subacute/ 8 men and 8 women/ mean age = 49.6, standard deviation = 10.1). All the participants had suffered hemiparetic upper limb dysfunction resulting from first time strokes. They provided written informed consent, and this study was conducted in accordance with the Declaration of Helsinki and approved by the Institutional Review Board of the author's institute. A total of seven physiatrists and three occupational therapists employed the RehabMaster^{TM} for their actual work practices.

Stroke patients were randomly assigned to two groups (OT only group: a conventional occupational therapy (OT) for 20 min; RehabMaster^{TM}+OT group: 10 min

RehabMaster^{TM} training plus 10 min conventional OT). Each group was assigned to ten sessions over 2 weeks. All sessions were administered by the trained occupational therapists, who were blinded to the protocol. The baselines of the two groups were compared using a Mann–Whitney U test before the main experiment to verify homogeneity of the participants. Then, a Fugl-Meyer Assessment (FMA) for upper limb motor function (0 = lowest score; 66 = highest score) [13] and the Modified Barthel Index (MBI) (0 = lowest score; 100 = highest score) for global function evaluation [23] were used at the baseline (T0), the fifth session (T5), and the last session (T10). We conducted univariate analyses using Mann-Whitney tests to compare the FMA and MBI score changes between the 'OT only' group and the 'RehabMaster^{TM}+OT' group. All analyses were performed using SPSS statistical software, and statistical significance refers to a $p \leq 0.05$.

6.5.2 *Part 2: Usability Test*

The patients and clinical staff rated usability-related statements after using the RehabMaster^{TM} for 2 weeks. The statements included separate concerns for each user group. For instance, the patients assessed whether the RehabMaster^{TM} was able to make them immerse in the rehabilitation procedure. The physiatrists rated the system from a rather different viewpoint, regarding whether it would be helpful to acquire patients' information or whether it was meaningful to prescribe exercises for the stroke patients. The occupational therapists also evaluated usability differently such as whether the RehabMaster^{TM} was designed for easy control during rehabilitation or whether it could flexibility control the challenge levels depending on the patient's state.

6.6 Results

6.6.1 *Part 1: Clinical Test*

To verify differences between the two groups (i.e., OT only group and RehabMaster^{TM}+OT group), baseline data were compared using the Mann-Whitney test and Fisher's exact test. All analyses were performed using SPSS statistical software (version 21.0), and the statistical significance level was set at $P \leq 0.05$. Table 6.6 shows that there were no significant differences in the baseline characteristics between the two groups, which are considered a homogeneous group at baseline (T0). After ten sessions for 2 weeks, the upper limb motor function improvement of the participants was measured by the Fugl-Meyer Assessment (FMA) as well as the Modified Barthel Index (MBI).

Table 6.6 Baseline characteristics

Outcome	OT only (n=7)	RehabMaster™+OT (n=9)	p-value
Age, years	46.6 ± 5.8	52.0 ± 11.9	0.54
Male (%)	3 (42.9)	5 (55.6)	0.[a]
Right-side lesion (%)	2 (28.6)	4 (44.4)	0.[a]
Days after onset	76.6 ± 28.5	67.1 ± 45.3	0.30
Modified rankin scale	3.7 ± 0.5	3.2 ± 1.0	0.40
Fugl-Meyer assessment score	34.4 ± 12.4	39.4 ± 10.7	0.46
Modified barthel index	44.7 ± 9.1	59.9 ± 17.6	0.10

All values are mean ± SD
SD standard deviation, *FMA* Fugl-Meyer Assessment, *MBI* Modified Barthel Index
p-values by Mann–Whitney test
[a] p-values by Fisher's exact test

Table 6.7 FMA and K-MBI results

Outcome	OT only (n = 7)		RehabMaster™+OT (n = 9)	
	Pre	Post	Pre	Post
FMA	34.4 ± 12.4	40.7 ± 9.8	39.4 ± 10.7	51.1± 17.8
K-MBI	44.7 ± 9.1	51.0 ±8.8	59.9 ± 17.6	71.2 ± 15.4

All values are mean ± SD
SD Standard Deviation, *FMA* Fugl-Meyer Assessment, *MBI* Modified Barthel Index

In Table 6.7, the Fugl-Meyer Assessment (FMA) results show significant ($p=0.07$) improvement observed in the RehabMaster™+OT group compared to the OT-only group. Improvement in the Modified Barthel Index (MBI) ($p=0.16$) was greater in the RehabMaster™+OT group (11.6±6.5) than in the OT-only group (7.7±4.6). Considering these results, serious games and motion-based rehabilitation programs presented by our RehabMaster™ could contribute to a patient's upper limb motor function improvement.

6.6.2 Part 2: Usability Test

Seven physiatrists assessed the RehabMaster™ based on two factors: information acquisition and meaningful prescription, as shown in Table 6.8.

It can be seen that most physiatrists were able to acquire proper information about the patients through the RehabMaster™ (mean 4.6 for statement 1). The RehabMaster™ also helped the physiatrists to manage diverse occupational therapy (4.3 for statement 2), and this could be customized for each patient; thus, they found the therapy meaningful for different levels of patients (4.7 for statement 3). Three occupational therapists were also asked to rate the following two statements: "I was easily able to manage the therapy prescription with RehabMaster™" and "I was able to improvise the rehabilitation program with RehabMaster™ depending

Table 6.8 Usability ratings by physiatrists

Statements	Mean ± SD**
1. RehabMaster™ was able to provide relevant information of how a patient has been improved or not	4.6 ± 0.5
2. RehabMaster™ was effective to administer occupational therapy	4.3 ± 0.8
3. RehabMaster™ was able to design the whole rehabilitation process customizable for a particular patient	4.7 ± 0.5

All values are mean ± SD
**All p-values for the two-tailed test were less than 0.01

Table 6.9 Usability ratings by stroke patients

Statements	Mean ± SD[a]
1. When using RehabMaster™ I thought about other things	1.3 ± 0.6
2. RehabMaster™ was fun for me to use	4.5 ± 1.1
3. I felt that I had no control over my training process with RehabMaster™	1.3 ± 0.6
4. When using RehabMaster™ I was frustrated with what I was doing	1.9 ± 1.1

All values are mean ± SD
[a] All p-values for the two-tailed test were less than 0.01

on the actual performance of each patient." All occupational therapists strongly agreed with both statements, but no further analyses were made due to the ceiling effect.

Table 6.9 gives the mean ratings across four main contributors (attention focus, pleasant to use, meaningful play, and challenge to motivation). All the patient stated that the RehabMaster™ made them highly attentive to the rehabilitation procedure (mean 1.3 for Statement 1). They also enjoyed the rehabilitation program (4.5 for Statement 2), and they viewed the RehabMaster™ as meaningful (1.3 for Statement 3) as well as appropriately challenging (1.9 for Statement 4). As a whole, the sixteen patients would recommend the RehabMaster™ to other patients. One-sample t-tests against the neutral value (3.0) supported the interpretations above.

Taken together, the RehabMaster™ might be said to achieve satisfaction from all the relevant rehabilitation stakeholders, and it could easily be employed in a clinical rehabilitation setting. Design factors for each individual rehabilitation stakeholder and different user interface (UI) forms make it possible to encourage all user groups (physiatrists, occupational therapists, and stroke patients) to actively see the benefits of serious game-based rehabilitation. In particular, physiatrists, who are considered to be the main hurdle to adopting motion-based rehabilitation, also showed that the way game-based rehabilitation is presented is key to accepting new interactive systems replacing their current work practices.

6.7 Open Problems

The clinical and usability tests above demonstrated the usefulness of RehabMaster^{TM} in an actual clinical setting, which has not been widely experimented on in the Human-Computer Interaction (HCI) and design communities. In particular, an application of the user interface (UI) design process (e.g., focus group studies and interview, usability testing) in the medical field would be an important contribution. From this, we draw out three lessons learned that can inform methodological and practical approaches to designing a clinical-level serious game as follows: use of a high fidelity prototype in the early design process; effective and efficient information design by handing a large amount of patient data recorded; and ease of customizing a system to maintain a suitable degree of challenge for an individual patient undergoing stroke therapy.

6.7.1 Use of a High-Fidelity Prototype in the Early Design Process

In the early design process, it is important to extract usability factors of physiatrists and occupational therapists specifically. In our case study, various methods (e.g., focus group studies, interview, and observation) were used to grasp usability issues between stroke patients and clinical staff while using the rehabilitation program in the medical field. However, it was hard to understand which usability factors need to be supplemented or reinforced in order to make a pervasive rehabilitation platform. Various usability ideas were generated; however, they were never fully developed and changed frequently.

Thus, we developed a high-fidelity prototype based on usability factors derived from the contextual inquiry session, and we used this prototype to communicate with clinical staff. It is commonly agreed that the early use of a high-fidelity prototype may place a restriction on the early design ideation. However, our experience with clinical staff suggests that the high-fidelity prototype may need to help our stakeholders (e.g., stroke patients, physiatrists, occupational therapists) more effectively express their usability issues relative to an imaginative game-based rehabilitation system in the clinical setting. This approach was particularly useful when combined with a series of contextual inquiry sessions. In line with our findings, the issue identified by [1] in the field of product design supports that a concrete prototype may be more suitable than a low fidelity prototype to provoke functional creativity. Whilst the use of a high-fidelity prototype was mostly positive in our particular experiment, we also assume negative impacts, including the time-consuming and costly nature of the system and difficulty for in-house designers and HCI researchers, which can be critical in some cases.

6.7.2 *Effective and Efficient Information Design for Handling a Large Amount of Recorded Patient Data*

Plenty of data (e.g., training sessions done by stroke patients, patients' performance data and game scores) are gathered while using RehabMaster^{TM} in institutionalized environments or at home. From a physiatrist and occupational therapist perspective, one of the most important benefits of integrating a motion-based rehabilitation system instead of using a conventional occupational therapy (OT) alone is the fact that the system is capable of recording the upper limb motor function of the individual patient spontaneously. Large amounts of patient data (e.g., training time, performance, and game score) can be recorded for the short- and/or long-term so that progress in stroke recovery can be objectively measured, which is often hard to track in the current clinical environment [3]. In handling these large medical records, an information design issue arises which is how can a patient's progress be effectively and efficiently conveyed to the patient and the clinical staff. Apparently, the patient and clinical staff have different concerns for their rehabilitation treatment as shown in Table 6.5. For example, in our case study, physiatrists preferred to examine a patient's progress chart on a weekly or monthly basis instead of a daily basis. The potential for effective information design creates interesting design challenges that need significant study.

6.7.3 *Ease of Customizing a System to Maintain a Suitable Degree of Challenge for an Individual Patient Undergoing Stroke Therapy*

Finally, in the clinical setting, the most persistent request of physiatrists and occupational therapists was that the clinical serious game design provide adequate freedom to customize the program such that an appropriate level of challenge for individual patients undergoing stroke therapy could be maintained. This includes speed of movement, movement ranges, the number of sets, and repetitions. One reason could be that the physiatrist and occupational therapist can set a personal goal based on her/his progress in stroke recovery, so that they can help the patient maintain motivation [3, 8]. Most importantly, clinical staff need to control and prevent unexpected physical problems of patients, which is an essential part of clinical treatment. For example, in our case study, while one stroke patient played RehabMaster^{TM} with his occupational therapist, he suddenly complained of severe pain in his left hand. Occupational therapists directly modified the rehabilitation program to only use the right hand and then added a supplemental rehabilitation program dedicated to his left hand at a low level of challenge.

Also, in RehabMaster^{TM}, dynamic difficulty adjustments (DDA) are applied to suit the different kinds of stroke patients by offering a proper therapy session based on the ELO-rating system [4]. Through this automated competition with other stroke patients who have similar capabilities, both patients not only intensely concentrate on rehabilitation programs but also maintain a suitable degree of challenge when undergoing stroke therapy.

6.8 Future Outlook

Apart from physical treatments, stroke patients seek support to cope with the psychological effects of living with any level of disability. The process of recovering from a stroke usually includes treatment, spontaneous recovery, rehabilitation, and the return to community living. The same applies to patients who suffer from a stroke and many age-related diseases who need long-term rehabilitation in both mental and physical activities. For instance, the support groups facilitated by healthcare professionals also seem to be a valuable means of working through the fear of long-term disability by sharing detailed stories, gaining a positive outlook, and seeking practical information [18].

However, at present, the communication activity between physiatrists and patients through RehabMaster^{TM} is not allowed, which would be critical for the home-based rehabilitation program. This lack of communication of how to use RehabMaster^{TM} and information about which treatments would be further needed discouraged stroke patients and slowed their rehabilitation progress. Hence, it became crucial to develop a new system that is able to support information sharing, communication activity, and emotional support from other users of RehabMaster^{TM}, which falls exactly into the realm of learning technology. In addition, understanding further usability design factors for patients and caregivers (e.g., medical staff, family members, authorities), is one of the key elements that could facilitate communication by setting a context for the common ground of the group and instilling credibility. Hence they shared credible information and resources, which accordingly facilitated help seeking by the users. Information seeking, giving encouragement, and sharing personal experiences are the main reasons people would use RehabMaster Mobile^{TM} to obtain support from others with similar conditions, and our mobile learning also sought to include these context-based advantages [5].

Changes in health care delivery encourage healthcare providers to seek new approaches for reaching patients and providing support to promote health, goals which require understanding the mobile learning process. As such, the meaning of patient education may be changing, as well as the power and control of this information. Information is no longer accessible to a privileged few. This is an important factor for healthcare professionals to keep in mind as an alternative to actual face-to-face support groups. As patients and healthcare professionals increase their mobile device usage, research on the most appropriate way to use mobile communication is critically important to improve the provision of healthcare. Patients also need to be given the opportunity to more fully participate in the process of care. This requires a change in the structure and goals of rehabilitation of stroke patients and a reengineering of practices to capitalize on technology.

Acknowledgments This work was supported by the Industrial Strategic Technology Development Program (10042694, Socio-Cognitive Design Technology for Convergence Service) funded by the Ministry of Knowledge Economy (MKE, Korea). The authors acknowledge that one version of the manuscript has been presented at the International Association of Societies of Design Research, Tokyo, August 2013. This chapter was then improved with feedback from the editor and anonymous reviewers and through discussions with Nadia Berthouze, Chris Vincent, and Carole Bouchard.

References

1. Acuna, A., & Sosa, R. (2010). The complementary role of representations in design creativity: Sketches and models. *Design creativity* 2010 (p. 265–270). London:Springer. NULL
2. Alankus, G., & Kelleher, C. (2012). *Reducing compensatory motions in video games for stroke rehabilitation*. Paper presented at the CHI 2012 Conference, Austin University, Texas, 5–10 May 2012.
3. Alankus, G., Proffitt, R., Kelleher, C., et al. (2011). Stroke therapy through motion-based games: a case study. *ACM Transactions on Accessible Computing*, *4*, 1–35.
4. Albers, P. C. H., & De Vries, H. (2001). Elo-rating as a tool in the sequential estimation of dominance strengths. *Animal Behaviour*, *61*, 489–495.
5. Alnanih, R., Ormandjieva, O., & Radhakrishnan, T. (2014). A new methodology (CON-INFO) for context-based development of a mobile user interface in healthcare applications. In: *Pervasive health: State-of-the-art & beyond* (pp. 317–344).
6. Annema, JH., Verstraete, M., & Vanden Abeele, V., et al. (2010). Videogames in therapy: A therapist's perspective. Paper presented at the 2010 Fun and Games Conference, Leuven University, Belgium, 15–17 September 2010.
7. Axelrod, L., Fitzpatrick, G., & Henwood, F., et al. (2011). Data recording in primary care field studies: Patient records enhancement project. Paper presented at the 2011 PervasiveHealth Conference, Dublin, Ireland, 23–26 May 2011.
8. Balaam, M., Rennick Egglestone, S., & Fitzpatrick, G., et al. (2011). Motivating mobility: Designing for lived motivation in stroke rehabilitation. Paper presented at the CHI 2011 Conference, Vancouver Convention Centre, Vancouver, 7–12 May 2011.
9. Burdea, G. C. (2003). Virtual rehabilitation-benefits and challenges. *Methods of Information in Medicine*, *42*, 519–523.
10. Burke, J. W., McNeill, M. D., Charles, D. K., et al. (2009). Optimising engagement for stroke rehabilitation using serious games. *The Visual Computer*, *25*, 1085–1099.
11. Deci, E. L., & Ryan, R. M. (2004). *Handbook of self-determination research*. New York: Rochester.
12. Egglestone, SR., Axelrod, L., & Nind, T., et al. (2009). A design framework for a home-based stroke rehabilitation system: Identifying the key components. Paper presented at the 2009 PervasiveHealth Conference, City University of London, UK, 1–3 April 2009.
13. Fugl-Meyer, A. R., Jääskö, L., Leyman, I., et al. (1975). The post-stroke hemiplegic patient. 1. a method for evaluation of physical performance. *Scandinavian journal of Rehabilitation Medicine*, *7*, 13–31.
14. Hutchins, E. (1991). The social organization of distributed cognition. In: Lauren B. R. John, M. L. & Stephanie, D. T. (Eds.), *Perspectives on socially shared cognition* (pp. 283–307). Washington, DC: American Psychological Association.
15. Kramp, G., Nielsen, P., & Møller, AS. (2010). *Particapatory Interaction in Therapeutical Strategies*. Paper presented at the 2010 NordiCHI Conference, Reykjavik, Iceland, 16–20 October 2010.
16. Kwon, Y. D., Chang, H., Choi, Y. J., et al. (2012). Nationwide trends in stroke hospitalization over the past decade. *Journal of the Korean Medical Association*, *55*, 1014–1025.
17. Langhorne, P., Coupar, F., & Pollock, A. (2009). Motor recovery after stroke: a systematic review. *Lancet Neurology*, *8*, 741–754.

18. Lasker, JN., Sogolow, ED., & Sharim, RR. (2005). The role of an online community for people with a rare disease: Content analysis of message posted on a primary biliary cirrhosis mailing list. *Journal of Medical Internet Research* 7(1), e10. doi:10.2196/jmir.7.1.e10.
19. Muramatsu, N., & Akiyama, H. (2011). Japan: super-aging society preparing for the future. *The Gerontologist*, *51*, 425–432.
20. Neisser, U. (1976). *Cognition and Reality*. Freeman and Co: San Francisco, W.H.
21. Nichols-Larsen, D. S., Clark, P. C., Zeringue, A., et al. (2005). Factors influencing stroke survivors' quality of life during subacute recovery. *Stroke*, *36*, 1480–1484.
22. Plant, K. L., & Stanton, N. A. (2013). What is on your mind? using the perceptual cycle model and critical decision method to understand the decision-making process in the cockpit. *Ergonomics*, *56*, 1232–1250.
23. Shah, S., Vanclay, F., & Cooper, B. (1989). Improving the sensitivity of the barthel index for stroke rehabilitation. *Journal of Clinical Epidemiology*, *42*, 703–709.
24. Stokes E (2014) The Ongoing Development of a MultimediaGaming module to aid speech, language and communication. In: *Pervasive health: State-of-the-art & beyond* (pp. 255–288).
25. Wang, AY. (2012). *Games for physical therapy*. Paper presented at the 2012 CHI Conference, Austin University, Texas, 5–10 May 2012.
26. Ziefle, M., Röcker, C., & Holzinger, A. (2014). Current trends and challenges for pervasive health technologies: From technical innovation to user integration. In: *Pervasive health: state-of-the-art & beyond* (pp. 1–8).
27. Cama, R. (2009). *Evidence-based healthcare design*. Hoboken: John Wiley & Sons.
28. Groopman, J. E., & Prichard, M. (2007). *How doctors think*. Boston: Houghton Mifflin.
29. Heritage, J., Maynard, DW. (2006). Communication in medical care: Interaction between primary care physicians and patients. Cambridge: Cambridge University Press.
30. Maharatna, K. & Bonfiglio, S. (2014). Systems Design for Remote Healthcare. New York: Springer.
31. Miller, RL., Swensson, ES. (2002). *Hospital and healthcare facility design*. New York: WW Norton & Company.
32. Roter, D., Hall, JA. (2006). Doctors talking with patients/patients talking with doctors: Improving communication in medical visits. Portsmouth: Greenwood Publishing Group.
33. Silverman, J., Kurtz, SM., & Draper, J., et al. (2005). *Skills for communicating with patients*. Oxford, UK.
34. Sixsmith, A., & Gutman, GM. (2013). Technologies for Active Aging. New York: Springer.
35. Troshani, I., & Goldberg, S. (2013). *Pervasive health knowledge management*. New York: Springer.

Chapter 7
Managing Telehealth and Telecare

Kenneth J. Turner

7.1 Introduction

This chapter expands on one theme of the overall book [65]: how to support flexible and automated management of care at home. This requires techniques that allow people to effectively interact with a home care system. The chapter describes the work of ACCENT (Advanced Component Control Enhancing Network Technologies [52]) as an extensible infrastructure that allows home care devices to be readily integrated. ACCENT also supports the definition of how the system should react to various circumstances. This is achieved through user-friendly interfaces that permit easy interaction with the system. The advantage of the approach presented here is that the logic of a home care system is exposed and made available for easy modification. When it comes to customisation and adaptation of the system, this largely removes the need for specialised technical knowledge and programming ability.

The world population is ageing, with the percentage of older people (over 65) gradually rising. In the UK, for example, this percentage was 24.4 % in 2000 and is expected to become 39.2 % by 2050 [44]. In Europe, the number of older people is expected to grow from 75 million in 2004 to 133 million in 2050 [6]. A similar situation applies in other developed countries, with much higher percentages forecast for some areas (e.g. 71.3 % by 2050 in Japan). Clearly this will increase the demand for care of older people. Technology for home care has been enthusiastically embraced as part of the solution for the ageing population.

Although people are living for longer, many have to deal with long-term, age-related conditions. The growing percentage of older people, coupled with pressure on social and health care budgets, means that care providers will be increasingly

K. J. Turner (✉)
Computing Science and Mathematics, University of Stirling, Stirling FK9 4LA, UK
e-mail: kjt@cs.stir.ac.uk

A. Holzinger et al. (eds.), *Pervasive Health*, Human–Computer Interaction Series,
DOI: 10.1007/978-1-4471-6413-5_7, © Springer-Verlag London 2014

challenged to cope. As a result, it will not be feasible to provide sufficient care homes as these are much more expensive than looking after someone in their own home.

Technology to support home care delivery has been identified as part of the solution. Home care technologies offer significant benefits. Particularly in rural settings, the ability to support care at a distance can save substantial travel. Many health authorities are promoting self-care at home rather than relying exclusively on centrally provided care. Trends, anomalies and alert conditions can be identified and reported to a central location such as a health centre or a call centre. Family members can be reassured that the user is being monitored for undesirable situations. Professional carers can also be relieved of low-level monitoring tasks. Older people can therefore be assisted to stay longer in their own homes, where they are in familiar surroundings and near to the people and the area they know.

A home care system aims to help users to live independently at home, supporting their care and wellbeing. A home care system can also monitor the extent to which people are living normally. For example, non-intrusive sensing can confirm that the individual is complying with medical advice, is sleeping well, and is dealing with personal hygiene and toileting. The system can also check for potentially hazardous situations such as the user falling or forgetting to take medicine. More advanced systems can help with activities of daily living [60] through speech-based or visual prompting, and by reminders for medication, appointments, etc. Trends and anomalies can be noticed in user health and reported to carers for further investigation. This work is important for all users of home care technologies: the end users themselves (the residents), their informal carers (family and friends), and their formal carers (health and social care professionals). It allows users to customise and adapt home care technologies to their individual and evolving needs.

7.2 Glossary

ACCENT (Advanced Component Control Enhancing Network Technologies) a component framework and policy-based management system used in a variety of applications including home care.

Android an open-source operating system developed by Google for mobile devices such as phones and tablets.

APPEL (Adaptable and Programmable Policy Environment and Language) a policy language used in a variety of applications including home care.

Goal a computer-supported objective for what the user wishes to achieve. In the context of home care, this defines a user aim for care (e.g. complying with medication or avoiding allergens).

Home Care System a computer-based system for supporting delivery of health and social care in the home.

iOS an operating system developed by Apple for mobile devices such as phones and tablets.

Policy a computer-supported rule that governs how a system reacts to external events. In the context of home care, this defines the reaction to normal occurrences (e.g. going to the toilet or taking exercise) as well as to abnormal occurrences (e.g. having a fall or forgetting to take medicine).

Telecare (also called **Assisted Living**) remote support of social care at home. This includes monitoring for undesirable situations (e.g. falls, flooding or night wandering) as well as services for the less able (e.g. curtain openers, door entry phones or home automation).

Telehealth (also called **Telemedicine**) remote support of health care at home. This includes remote consultation and diagnosis as well as monitoring health parameters (e.g. blood pressure, heart rate or seizure risk).

7.3 State-of-the-Art

7.3.1 Related Work on Home Care Systems

7.3.1.1 Telehealth and Telecare

Health care and social care have traditionally been organised and funded differently. However, it has been recognised that there is an important interplay between these two aspects of care [23]. Social problems (e.g. a stay-at-home attitude or missing meals) can have health implications (e.g. depression or dietary problems). Conversely, health problems (e.g. dementia or a heart condition) can have social implications (e.g. forgetfulness or lack of sociability). The work reported in this chapter therefore aims to cover the intersection of health care and social care.

Home care can be supported by purpose-designed computer-based systems [55]. Typically some kind of home platform is provided to collect, analyse, react to, and forward care data collected from a variety of sensors or other input devices. Besides sensor inputs, a home care system can receive data from software services (e.g. for verification of a fall or for analysis of cardiac data). A home care system is able to respond through a variety of actuators to signal alert conditions, to give the user advice, to remind the user of medical appointments, etc. Services can also perform output actions. More sophisticated systems have a degree of programmability, allowing customisation for individual user needs and adaptation to changing circumstances.

Data can be collected from sensors worn around the body in what are called Body Sensor Networks [64]. Mobile sensors have also been used, for example to help people with mental health problems [28]. Multimodal interfaces allow users to interact with a home care system in ways that suit the person's needs, preferences and environment [32]. For example, audio and speech are alternatives to visual communication. Touch and gestures can also be used, and even smell can be useful—say, to remind the user to cook a meal.

Home care data can become voluminous. The challenge is then to draw meaningful conclusions from it. In general, analysis and interpretation of care data has received considerable attention [3]. A common approach is to build models that can be analysed for trends and anomalies in health and lifestyle, and can be presented in a way that is meaningful to carers [20].

There are many commercial solutions for telehealth, telecare, and increasingly both aspects. The Continua Health Alliance [11] has more than 220 members including well-known companies such as Cisco, Intel, Oracle, Philips and Samsung. Continua aims to promote interoperability, particularly among health care devices, and also certifies devices for compliance.

For concreteness, the following gives a few examples of commercial home care solutions. Docobo [16] provide a home hub that allows the user to record vital signs, medication use and lifestyle information. Information from this and other sources such as tablets and smartphones is collected securely and made available to care practitioners. Just Checking [24] offer a home monitoring system that records activities of daily living. This is used for non-intrusive assessment of how independently a user can live at home. Mirth [34] is unusual in offering an open-source solution for collection and distribution of home care data. Mirth Connect allows interfacing of devices using common standards such as Dicom and Health Level 7. OmniQare [37] supply a modular and extensible home care system. A touch screen interface offers capabilities in areas such as health, safety, communication and household planning. Tunstall [49] support assisted living through a home hub that interfaces to a variety of sensors and actuators. This underpins telecare, health monitoring and lifestyle assessment.

There have also been numerous research projects in telehealth and, to a lesser extent, telecare. For concreteness, the following gives a few examples. The Bath Smart Home project [38] has investigated how assisted living can support people with dementia. The e-HealthCare project [18] has investigated the spectrum from hospital-based home care to community-based home care. The Motivating Mobility project [2] has investigated how to motivate people who have had a stroke to undertake rehabilitation exercises at home. The SAPHIRE project [22] created an intelligent health care monitoring solution that integrates wireless sensor data with hospital systems. The Veterans Association [13] has extensive experience of using telehealth and remote health monitoring.

The COBALT project (Challenging Obstacles and Barriers to Assistive Living Technologies [10]) is investigating obstacles to the uptake of assisted living technologies. The DREAMING project (Elderly-Friendly Alarm Handling and Monitoring [17]) conducted a large-scale pilot to demonstrate and evaluate new services to support independent living. The MATCH project (Mobilising Advanced Technologies for Care at Home [61, 63]) has focused on telecare and its intersection with telehealth. The PERSONA project [41] has worked on a common semantic framework for integrating solutions that support independent living.

Despite the enthusiasm for home care technologies, a number of barriers to their uptake have been identified [8, 47]. Design is perceived as important for making home care devices acceptable and desirable. Attention is also needed to interfaces that non-technical users can easily learn and use. Personalisation and adaptation are essential to make sure that the home care system reflects actual care needs. Ethics and privacy may be sensitive issues, with some users being concerned that home care systems carry out 'surveillance' [46]. Awareness of home care technologies among care professionals is currently low, and will require accessible information and training materials [62].

7.3.1.2 Home Care Infrastructure

Pervasive (or ubiquitous) computing deals with how computer-based solutions pervade all aspects of daily life. Unsurprisingly, pervasive computing has found many applications in health care (e.g. [59]) and in social care (e.g. [40]).

Context-aware systems aim to make a system reactive to context, and have been used in home care applications. Gaia [42] supports 'active spaces' that rely heavily on contextual information including presence. EasyLiving [5] is designed to support intelligent environments through dynamic interconnection of a variety of devices. This middleware offers mechanisms such as inter-system communication, location tracking for objects and people, and visual perception.

This chapter focuses on the use of OSGi ('Open Services Gateway initiative' [39]) as it has proven popular as a home platform to support home automation, telehealth and telecare. A well-known example is Atlas [26] that started as an academic project to support sensor-actuator networks in a service-oriented manner, but was later made available commercially. Among other applications, the Atlas middleware has been used for smart homes and healthcare.

OSGi was developed as a dynamic module system for Java. OSGi modules are called bundles, and have a simple interface. They can communicate via an event bus using the Event Admin service. This allows bundles to be created in a loosely coupled way, and yet to cooperate in support of higher-level services.

However, the basic bundle interface needs to be augmented for easy configuration and integration. SODA (Service-Oriented Device Architecture) provides a framework for uniform development of OSGi device bundles [14]; this has been enhanced with data semantics [21]. Other work has aimed to make bundles self-describing, thereby easing their management and allowing arbitrary bundles to be controlled by a rule-based system [30, 31].

Standards for home care technologies are still emerging. Organisations such as the Continua Health Alliance [11] are working towards interoperability of equipment. Standards similar to Health Level 7 [1] will also have to be created or adapted for home care data. Until standards appear, commercial home care systems are forced to use proprietary designs and protocols. As a result, it is important to work towards a common infrastructure that can accommodate a variety of manufacturer's equipment and third-party devices.

7.3.1.3 Policy-Based Management of Home Care

Policies are computer-interpreted rules that are automatically executed when events occur. Policies have been used in applications such as access control, network/system management and quality of service. Most policy languages are in ECA form (Event-Condition-Action). As a typical example, Ponder [12] is a general-purpose policy approach. It offers a mature methodology for handling policies in applications such as system management and sensor networks (including body sensor networks).

However, nearly all policy approaches are designed for technical applications. A different kind of policy approach is therefore needed for the 'softer' management tasks found in human-oriented applications such as home care. This is the focus of the ACCENT work reported in this chapter.

A few systems employ rules for managing the home. Leong et al. [27] describe a rule-based system for smart homes. However, this is a rather heavyweight solution that expects home devices to be interconnected via an Ethernet. Although the system supports basic rules, these do not seem to be defined by end users. Gadgetware [25] achieves a similar result, though not in a recognisably rule-based way. Physical objects are given a digital representation with 'plugs' that can be connected via 'synapses'.

7.3.1.4 Home Care Interfaces

User-friendly interfaces for home care systems are receiving increasing attention. Multimodal interfaces show promise in allowing the use of audio, speech, touch, gesture, smell, etc. [32]. In fact, most work on home applications has been in the field of end-user programming using techniques such as programming by demonstration, tangible programming and visual programming.

The acceptability of home care systems is slowly being improved. Users are reluctant to use devices that are difficult to learn or that stigmatise them as needing specialised equipment. Participative design (or co-design) of home system interfaces is an important part of making such systems acceptable [10, 57]. Collaborative technologies such as Augmented Binders have been investigated as a solution for supporting care at home [7]. Home care devices need to offer easy interactions, and should be personalisable for the individual's needs [8]. This is particularly important if the user has physical, sensory or learning impairments. Someone with a degenerative health condition will need solutions that can be adapted (or automatically adapt) over time. In home systems, the interfaces should be simple enough for novice users, but should also allow for efficient interaction by more experienced users [33].

The following are concrete examples of interfaces that have been designed for home systems. A CAPpella [15] allows a situation to be set up and then an appropriate response to be demonstrated. ACHE [35] offers limited support for home goals (user comfort and cost), with the emphasis being on learning how best to meet these goals. Alfred [19] uses demonstration to capture macro-like rules, making particular use of speech interaction. Accord [43] uses jigsaw-like pieces to assemble rules. Although the approach ensures that the rules are meaningful, the range of possible rules is very restrictive. CAMP [48] allows end users to define requirements using words drawn from a 'magnetic poetry' set, but with a rather limited set of concepts. Media Cubes [4] allow rules to be defined by placing action requests next to devices (read from the cube faces using infrared). iCAP [45] permits new devices to be added through icons that are then used to identify conditions and actions. Oscar [36] provides a visual environment for selecting and interconnecting components, but only for home media.

The focus of this chapter is on how to manage telehealth and telecare more effectively. The user interface issues that arise are therefore related to how goals and policies can be easily defined and used.

7.3.2 The ACCENT Home Care System

To explore the issues in managing home care systems and interfacing with them, the remainder of this section covers one approach in depth. ACCENT (Advanced Component Control Enhancing Network Technologies [52]) is an approach and a set of tools for managing systems through goals and policies. ACCENT and its accompanying policy language APPEL (Adaptable and Programmable Policy Environment and Language [53]) were designed as a general-purpose solution for managing systems. Originally developed for control of telephony, ACCENT has been evolved to support home care.

7.3.2.1 Home Care System Users

There are many potential users of a home care system, and also many stakeholders in how home care is automated.

The end users are those receiving telehealth or telecare, i.e. the home residents. These people are likely to have limited involvement with the system, e.g. to take regular measurements of blood glucose or oxygen levels. Other functions of the home system should be largely automated and invisible to end users.

Although the ACCENT system is of general applicability, it is expected to be used by older people who wish to prolong independent living at home. Such people may have a long-term health condition (or conditions) or may simply need extra support in their daily living. They may therefore need to have their health and lifestyle monitored for onward transmission to a health centre. They may also need help with normal activities such as reminders to attend medical appointments or to prepare meals, encouragement to take exercise and to eat well, etc.

A particular challenge for home care systems is multiple occupancy: the end user receiving care may live with family or have visitors. As a result it may be difficult to distinguish the activities of the cared-for person from those of other residents. For health measurements, say, end users can use a personal identifier or can wear

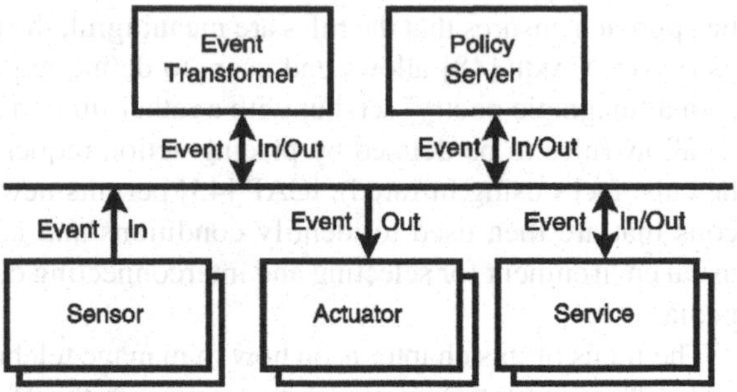

Fig. 7.1 High-level ACCENT system architecture [50]

individual sensors. Pendants or active badges can also identify individuals and their locations, though compliance with wearing these can be problematic.

The home system is likely to be configured and monitored by health care professionals (e.g. nurses, doctors) and social care professionals (e.g. social workers, occupational therapists). These people will have a more active involvement with the system, and will regularly check the data that is collected. It should be possible to collect and analyse data without actual visits to the home. It should also be possible to (re)configure the system from a remote location.

Family and neighbours could also be users of a home care system. For example, they may need reassurance that an older person is taking medication regularly and is not showing any deterioration in health. With the end user's consent, these informal carers may be allowed to see a summary of care data and to receive alerts that may require a home visit.

Other stakeholders in telehealth and telecare include technicians who have to install and maintain the equipment, policy makers who decide on care service provision, and politicians who allocate funding for this.

7.3.2.2 ACCENT Architecture

Figure 7.1 shows the high-level architecture of the ACCENT system. When used to support care, this operates in a home environment: the end user's home and its wider context, including when the user is out of the home. Sensors provide input signals from the home: medication use, heart rate, fall indications, etc. Actuators perform output actions in the home: sending alerts, providing reminders, managing devices, etc. Services are potentially bidirectional providers and consumers of information: communications in and out, weather forecasts in, care summaries out, etc. The policy server achieves high-level user goals by executing appropriate lower-level policies. The event transformer supports a mapping between low-level triggers/actions and high-level ones.

All components are implemented as OSGi bundles, linked via the OSGi event bus. This conveys inputs and outputs among all components, but particularly to/from the policy server. Usually the policy server receives inputs from sensors (and services) that trigger one or more goals and policies. These determine how the system should react to the input. The resulting output actions are then performed by the relevant actuators (and services).

The event transformer can intercept one or more inputs and transform them into high-level signals for the policy server. This is normally called sensor fusion and can be used, for example, to combine several information sources into a reliable fall indication. Conversely, the event transformer can take a high-level output from the policy server and convert it into several low-action actions. For example, a reminder might choose the most appropriate modality: on-screen message, spoken output, text message, etc. Sensors, actuators and services normally communicate only with the policy server or event transformer. However they can also communicate directly with each other to build higher-level capabilities.

To support easy integration of components, home care events in ACCENT have a uniform structure that carries the message type, the entity name and instance involved, a message qualifier (for timing or confidence information) and message parameters. This uniformity makes it easier to support new kinds of devices since only a simple message interface has to be implemented. It also makes the policy server extensible for new devices, allowing policies to be written for these.

The components provide a range of care services in the home. These can be defined in isolation or through hierarchic combination of simpler capabilities. A variety of services is offered, including health care, social care, safety, security, communication, entertainment and household management. ACCENT supports a wide range of devices including:

- telehealth and telecare devices, e.g. from Tunstall and BM Innovations
- mains-controlled appliances, e.g. lights, heating and blinds using the X10 standard for mains control or Plugwise modules
- infrared-controlled appliances, e.g. audio-visual equipment and air conditioning
- environmental monitors, e.g. from Oregon Scientific
- security and home sensors, e.g. from Visonic
- user-friendly interface devices, e.g. iOS and Android phones/tablets, as well as Internet buddies like the Nabaztag 'rabbit' and the Tux Droid 'penguin'
- readers, e.g. for barcodes and RFID (Radio Frequency Identification)
- messaging services, e.g. email, SMS (Short Message Service) and speech synthesis.

As noted earlier, ACCENT is designed so that new devices can be easily added. Besides the components shown in Fig. 7.1, there are also infrastructure bundles. For example an ontology server provides domain-specific information about home care, and policy wizards make it easy to define goals and policies.

Security and confidentiality are important aspects of any care system. Information collected and distributed by ACCENT is therefore protected by standard mechanisms. The ACCENT database and associated files are protected by passwords and appropriate permissions. When data is sent over a network connection, HTTPS (HyperText Transfer Protocol Secure) is used to encrypt the data. This includes remotely logging into the home care system to check the user's status or to configure the system. Home care data is therefore protected while being managed by ACCENT, though its external use (in a health or social care centre) is beyond the control of ACCENT.

The policies that govern the use of information (e.g. sending an alert or reporting user status) are agreed in consultation with the end user as part of a care assessment. This ensures that information is passed to only those individuals that the end user approves. Obtaining informed consent is in fact a key part of the care assessment that determines what facilities are provided by the home care system.

7.3.2.3 Management of Home Care

Goals and policies are the primary way for users to interact with and manage the ACCENT home care system. Only a brief overview is provided here of the APPEL policy language; see [56] for full details. Although APPEL is XML-based, it is designed for human-oriented management tasks such as in home care. For readability, examples of APPEL are provided below in near-natural language following the style of the web wizard discussed later.

Among other things, APPEL is used to define goals and policies of various kinds. Although these can be created from scratch, a library has been developed with over a hundred predefined templates for ease of use. The user usually just needs to select a template, defining key values such as an emergency telephone number or the user's normal bedtime.

7.3.2.4 Goals for Home Care

Goals are high-level user objectives. An optional condition specifies the circumstances in which the goal applies. Only two types of actions are used: to maximise or to minimise some measure of a goal, defined in terms of how various factors affect its achievement. Most approaches to goals are based on logic, but ACCENT treats goal achievement as an optimisation problem. This allows goals to be realised in a dynamic way depending on current circumstances (which may vary over time). It is also pragmatic in that goals are achieved as far as is possible, and do not need to be completely fulfilled in some absolute sense.

As an example, Fig. 7.2 illustrates a health goal of avoiding allergens. Goals can have conditions such as dates or times, though here 'unconditionally' means that there are none. A goal is high-level and not executable. To give the goal meaning, the user has to specify the factors that contribute to the goal (i.e. to its measure). Figure 7.2 states that avoiding allergens depends on minimising pollen exposure and avoiding additives in food. These are both negative factors to be minimised.

Each of these factors is internally associated with a weight that is automatically determined by the system so that the factors make similar contributions. The goal system includes automated sensitivity analysis to check how its behaviour depends on the choice of weights. It has been found in practice that weights are not critical

Fig. 7.2 Goal: avoid allergens

```
goal Avoid allergens
if unconditionally
do optimise
    pollen level as negative
    additive intake as negative
```

Fig. 7.3 Prototype policy: encourage summer-time walk

```
prototype Encourage summer-time walk
preference prefer
when always
if the hour is 17:00:00 and
    afternoon excursion is false and
    exterior temperature is warm
do send a message to lounge loudspeaker about
    'You need exercise so please go for a walk'
Effect social contact += 1 and
    pollen level += 3
```

to goal achievement: the outcome is usually the same even if the weights vary over a ratio of 10:1.

A user can define multiple goals, each of which has a relative importance assigned by the user. For example, the user may decide that being active is three times more important than avoiding allergens. The weighted combination of goal measures constitutes an overall evaluation function to be optimised dynamically by the system.

7.3.2.5 Policies for Home Care

Goals are achieved by special policies called prototypes. Like all policies, prototypes normally have a trigger, a condition and an action (each of which may be composite). The strength of a policy can be indicated through a preference (must, should, prefer, and negative forms of these); this is one way of resolving conflicts among policies. Policies can also be associated with profiles such as 'at home' or 'on holiday'. Unlike other kinds of policies, prototypes indicate how they affect goals through their effect on the factors in goal measures.

As an example, the prototype in Fig. 7.3 encourages the user to go for a walk in summer-time. There is no trigger, or rather the policy is triggered when 5PM arrives. The policy applies if the user has not taken an excursion during the afternoon and the exterior temperature is warm. In this case, a message is spoken to the user on the lounge loudspeaker encouraging them to go for a walk. The prototype has the effect of increasing social contact by one level (due to getting out) and increasing pollen exposure by three levels (due to being outside in warm weather). If this policy conflicts with another one, the user would *prefer* this policy to be followed.

Using precise values in policies (such as an exterior temperature of 25 °C) can be unrealistic as users may not know quite which values to use. Fuzzy values like 'warm' or 'cool' are therefore allowed, making it easier for users to formulate policies. Fuzzy

Fig. 7.4 Regular policy: night light

policy Night light
preference must
when the bed reports it is unoccupied
if the time is 11PM to 7AM
do turn on the toilet light
else
when the bed reports it is occupied
if the time is 11PM to 7AM
do turn off the toilet light

sets are defined in each domain ontology for use by the policy wizard and the policy server. The policy server supports fuzzy logic for making inexact decisions. It is also possible to use probabilistic or confidence values. This is useful if the sensor input is not known precisely. For example, a thermometer may have an accuracy of ±1 °C or a weather forecast may have a confidence of 70 %.

A regular policy is similar to a prototype policy but does not identify an effect on goals. This is used for policies that should always apply irrespective of the current goals. As an example, older people may need to go to the toilet more frequently at night; this carries the risk of falling in the darkness. Figure 7.4 shows a policy that addresses this problem. When an occupancy sensor reports that the user has got out of bed at night, the toilet light is switched on. When the bed becomes occupied again, the toilet light is switched off. The two policy rules are tried in sequence, checking first for an unoccupied bed and then for an occupied bed.

When triggers occur, they cause regular policies and goal-related (prototype) policies to be activated. Prototype policies are selected to maximise the overall evaluation function, and are then combined with regular policies. This allows the system to react appropriately and dynamically to changing circumstances.

7.3.2.6 Conflicts in Home Care

Goals can conflict with each other (e.g. avoiding allergens might conflict with a goal of getting fresh air). Policies can also conflict with each other (e.g. one policy might wish to close the windows while another wishes to open them). To handle this situation, resolution policies are used. These are rather specialised and can be defined only by the system administrator (most likely being selected from the system library). Resolutions define what conflicts should be detected, and also state how to resolve them. This means that conflict handling is not hard-wired into the policy system—it can be adjusted according to the user's preferences and circumstances.

Conflicts usually arise with goals and policies that are defined by different stakeholders. For example, a doctor's goals for the user (e.g. to stay warm in winter) might run counter to a social worker's goals (e.g. to maintain social contact by getting out). When there are multiple occupants in the home, their wishes as expressed in goals and policies may also not agree. Even the wishes of one user can contradict each

Fig. 7.5 Resolution policy: ventilation conflict

resolution Ventilation conflict
when perform open at window **and**
perform close at window
if the entity instances are the same
do choose the policy with the stronger preference

other, perhaps because the conflict was not anticipated or because an older definition (that should have been removed) conflicts with a newer one.

The triggers of resolution policies are the actions of normal policies. Conditions may also apply to resolution policies. A generic resolution action chooses one of the conflicting policies (e.g. the most recently defined one or the one with the stronger preference). A specific resolution action is a regular policy action such as giving a reminder or activating a device.

As an example, the resolution in Fig. 7.5 deals with conflicts over ventilation for health reasons. Suppose one policy wishes to open a window (for fresh air) while the other wishes to close the window (to reduce pollen). If the entity instances are same (i.e. the actions are for the same window), the policy with the stronger preference is chosen.

7.3.2.7 Interfaces for Home Care

It has been seen that telehealth and telecare are managed through goals and policies that define how the home care system reacts to events. The focus of this subsection is therefore on interfaces that make it easy and convenient for users to define goals and policies.

The user needs to be able to configure the house easily. This is achieved by an Android application that allows rooms and their contents to be defined visually. Figure 7.6 shows the contents of a sample bedroom. The passive (unmanaged) objects are a bed, a bedside cabinet, a chest and a chair. The active (managed) objects are a bedside lamp, a TV, a pendant alarm and a movement sensor. The window and the door are fitted with opening sensors. In the figure, the user has tapped on the window to display a pop-up where the window sensor details can be edited. As rooms and their contents are edited, a home system database is updated. This determines what the system manages and the kinds of policies that can be written.

Although APPEL policies internally use XML, this has to be presented in a user-friendly way. A variety of wizards and interfaces have been created for this purpose. An important aspect of the approach is providing convenient interfaces for definition of goals and policies. This allows the home care system to be customised for the end-user's needs, and also to be evolved as these change over time. This is particularly relevant for people with long-term and perhaps degenerative conditions.

The web wizard allows local or remote editing using near-natural language. This is the most comprehensive of the wizards as it supports full creation and editing of goals and policies. The other wizards are more conventional in aim, being used only for initial creation. The web wizard is illustrated here as it supports all aspects of APPEL, including definition of resolution policies, policy variables, availability and

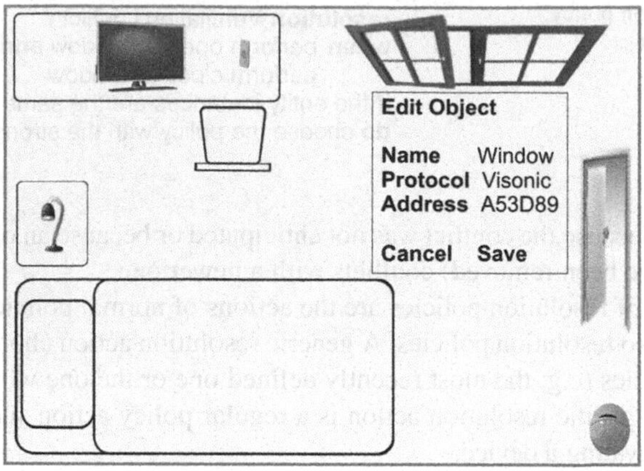

Fig. 7.6 Home configuration

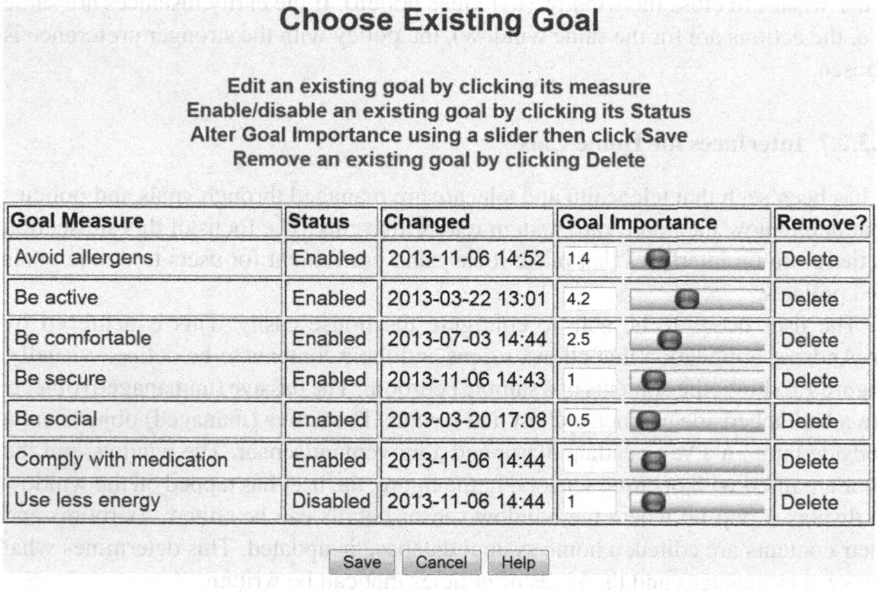

Choose Existing Goal

Edit an existing goal by clicking its measure
Enable/disable an existing goal by clicking its Status
Alter Goal Importance using a slider then click Save
Remove an existing goal by clicking Delete

Goal Measure	Status	Changed	Goal Importance	Remove?
Avoid allergens	Enabled	2013-11-06 14:52	1.4	Delete
Be active	Enabled	2013-03-22 13:01	4.2	Delete
Be comfortable	Enabled	2013-07-03 14:44	2.5	Delete
Be secure	Enabled	2013-11-06 14:43	1	Delete
Be social	Enabled	2013-03-20 17:08	0.5	Delete
Comply with medication	Enabled	2013-11-06 14:44	1	Delete
Use less energy	Disabled	2013-11-06 14:44	1	Delete

Fig. 7.7 Web wizard: editing a list of goals

presence. An advantage of the web wizard is that it can be used from any location and by any (authenticated) user. This means that it can be used in the home and also remotely, say from a health or social work centre. Care data can also be accessed in the same way from outside the home. The web wizard is multilingual, being currently localised in English, French and German.

Figure 7.7 shows an example list of goals defined by a user. Goals can be editing by clicking on their labels, can be disabled and can be removed. More importantly,

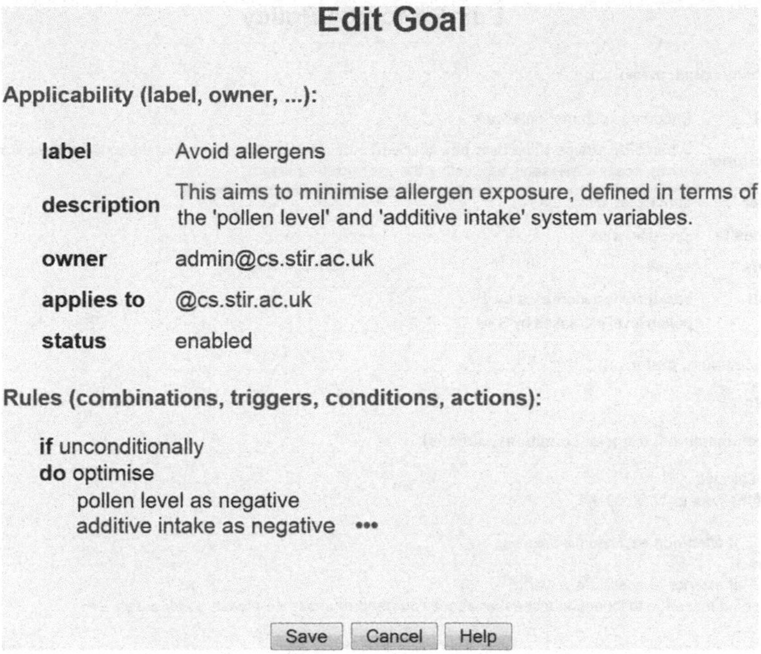

Fig. 7.8 Web wizard: editing a goal

the relative importance of each goal can be set by dragging a slider; the range is from 0.1 to 10.0.

Figure 7.8 shows what happens when the 'Avoid allergens' goal in the list is clicked for editing; this is the same goal as was described in Fig. 7.2. Although goals and policies have individual owners, they can apply to a whole domain—here, to all people falling under cs.stir.ac.uk (Computing Science, Stirling). This is useful for, say, a block of sheltered housing where the warden can define goals for all the residents. Domains are hierarchic, so definitions can also be created for higher-level groups such as stir.ac.uk (all Stirling). This can be used for, say, all homes operated by a housing provider.

All elements presented by the web wizard are active links. Clicking such a link allows that element to be edited. Where multiple instances of an elements are allowed (e.g. a condition or a factor in a goal measure), clicking the '···' symbol allows a new one to be added.

Figure 7.9 shows one of the prototypes that contribute to the 'Avoid allergens' goal; this is the same prototype as was described in Fig. 7.3. Other prototypes affecting this goal include one to cool the house by opening windows (thus bringing in pollen during summer-time), and one that encourages a choice of low-additive foods (thus reducing allergen intake).

As an alternative way of creating policies, Fig. 7.10 shows the Android wizard that can run on a phone or a tablet. A drop-down list at the top left gives the names

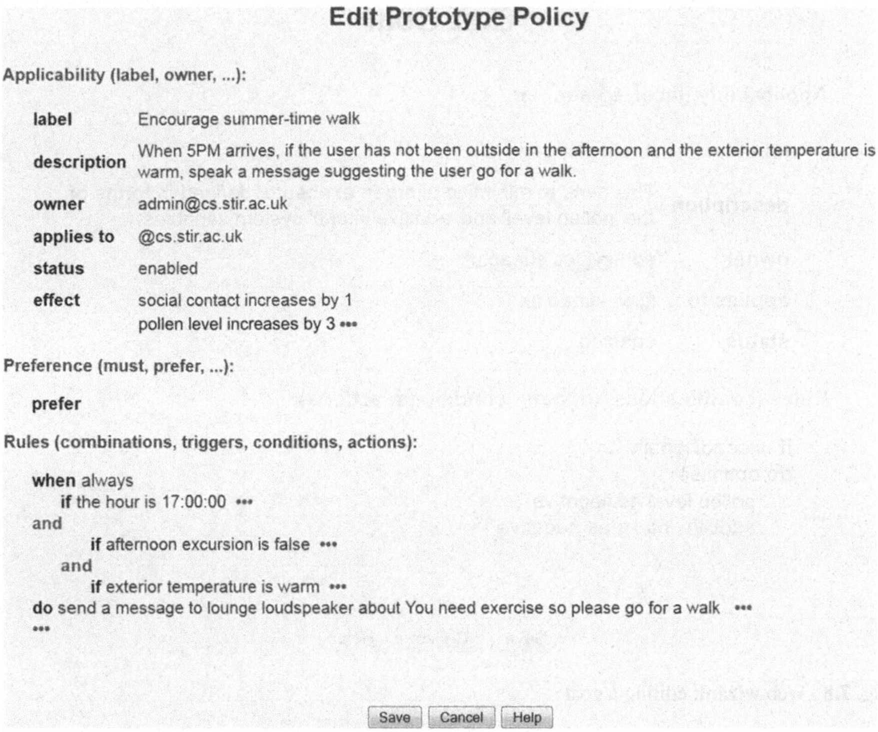
Edit Prototype Policy
Applicability (label, owner, ...):
label
Encourage summer-time walk
description
When 5PM arrives, if the user has not been outside in the afternoon and the exterior temperature is warm, speak a message suggesting the user go for a walk.
owner
admin@cs.stir.ac.uk
applies to
@cs.stir.ac.uk
status
enabled
effect
social contact increases by 1
pollen level increases by 3 •••
Preference (must, prefer, ...):
prefer
Rules (combinations, triggers, conditions, actions):
when always
if the hour is 17:00:00 •••
and
if afternoon excursion is false •••
and
if exterior temperature is warm •••
do send a message to lounge loudspeaker about You need exercise so please go for a walk •••
•••
Save
Cancel
Help

Fig. 7.9 Web wizard: editing a prototype Policy

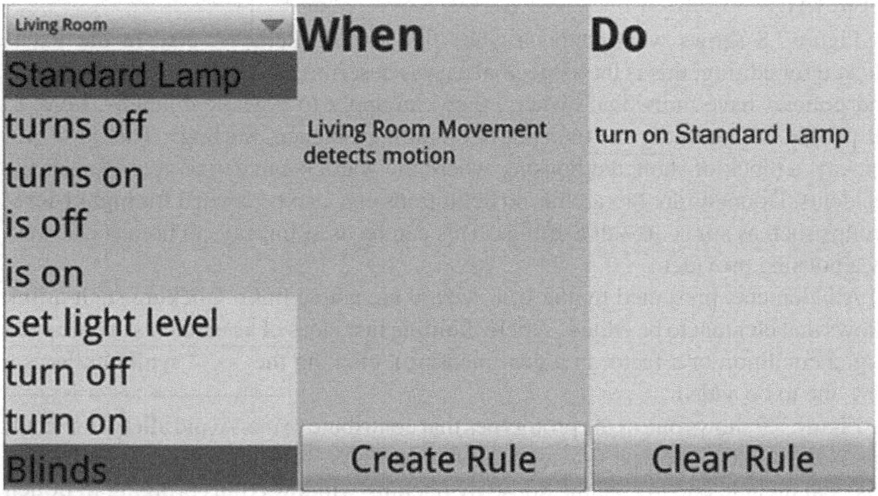

Fig. 7.10 Android wizard: editing a policy

of all rooms. Selecting the living room then lists devices in this room such as the standard lamp. Choosing a device displays its triggers (shown in darker grey) and actions (shown in lighter grey). These can be dragged onto the **when** (trigger) and **do** (action) columns to create a policy rule. The policy currently states that when movement is detected in the living room then the standard lamp should be turned on.

The digital pen wizard allows simple definition of policies by ticking items on a form. This uses predefined forms for specific scenarios such as what to do when the house is unoccupied. The user ticks choices such as ‘at home’ or ‘out shopping’ to define the context. Other selections define policy triggers (e.g. ‘**when** the user falls’), conditions (‘**if** it is 9 AM to 5 PM’) and actions (e.g. ‘**do** alert the health centre **else** alert a neighbour’). The pen records where exactly on the form each tick was placed. This information is then read by docking the pen and converting its input into policy form.

The speech-based wizard creates policies using spoken dialogues. This employs VoiceXML [58], originally designed for Interactive Voice Response in telephony but used here with standard computer audio facilities. This wizard is also limited to specific scenarios. Since the wizard is speech-based, it is suitable for those with a visual impairment. A spoken dialogue leads the user through various choices in a VoiceXML ‘form’, ultimately generating a policy from the values entered into the form ‘fields’.

Other interfaces have been developed, e.g. to provide Twitter feeds about activities in the home (for peace of mind). Overall, the aim has been to give users a range of interface choices so they can select whatever suits them best when managing telehealth and telecare.

7.3.2.8 Usability Evaluations

The ACCENT system has been extensively tested in an experimental setting—a home care lab at the author’s institution. This is a small flat where volunteer users attend on a day basis to evaluate the capabilities in controlled circumstances. The robustness of ACCENT has also been assessed through short-term deployments in two actual homes over a combined total of nine months [51]. The main practical issues in home deployments were avoiding disruption (by using wireless devices and existing wiring), accessing the home system remotely (by using Dynamic DNS), and occasional unreliability of X10 control (now rectified using the SerialIO driver for Java).

Policy-based management of home care was evaluated to discover if users can relate to this [29]. It was found that users are enthusiastic about this approach. The study involved 71 volunteer users ranging in age from 18 to 75, with an average age of 37. 94 % of the users were competent in at least basic computer usage, though they had no knowledge of home care technologies. Users were asked to rate their computing skills from weak to expert so that this could be correlated with the survey results.

The participants were asked to go through a number of exercises supported by an online tool: understanding existing policies, creating policies from natural language descriptions, and creating user-selected policies from scratch. This was followed by collecting responses to key research questions. It was expected that the survey would take 15–30 min to complete.

A number of hypotheses were formulated before the survey and were then statistically assessed after the survey had been completed. Focusing only on the question of accuracy, the main results were as follows. Across all levels of computing skill, users were able to describe existing policies with 93 % accuracy. For translating natural language objectives into policies, the accuracy across all user levels was 98 %; this higher figure can be attributed to users learning how to use policies in the first stage of the survey. When creating unconstrained policies from scratch, users achieved an accuracy of 88 %; this lower figure can be attributed to having no prior guidance as to what should appear in the policies.

In a much more limited but more technically intense study, the usability of detailed policy features was investigated [51]. Five householders were recruited, ranging in age from 40 to 70 with an average age of 55. These people received an average of 41 min individual training in use of the web-based policy wizard. They were then asked to define a range of five increasingly more complex policies for home care; this stage was performed unaided. On average, all these policies were completed in 16 min with an accuracy of 90 %.

The participants were then asked to rate five questions about the approach on a scale from 1 (strongly disagree) to 5 (strongly agree). The average score for this part of the study was 3.8, indicating agreement that the approach was usable. A number of weaknesses in the usability of the policy wizard were identified that have largely now been rectified. For example, the selection of policy elements is now governed by the home configuration rather than being free-form text as originally.

Following the evaluation of policies for home care, a study was undertaken of the usability of goals [9]. This time a group of care managers was recruited as these are the kinds of user most likely to be involved in defining home care goals. Although goals are supported by the web-based policy wizard, the focus was on the conceptual issues rather than on the usability of tools. The nature of goals and policies was first explained verbally using examples on paper. Participants were given a half-page scenario that described the situation of a hypothetical older couple. The participants were then asked to formulate three home care goals for this couple, and to define policies that could be used to realise these. As a more open-ended exercise, participants were also asked to devise goals and policies that might apply to themselves. Finally, they were asked to answer a number of questions about how easy it was to formulate goals and policies, and the way in which these might be used for home care.

All participants were able to come up with plausible goals for home care. Perhaps more surprisingly (because it is a more technically challenging task), all participants successfully thought of policies that could be used to achieve the goals. This is significant because it requires two levels of thinking that could be expected to be difficult for non-computing people. Goals require relatively abstract and declarative thinking, while policies require relatively concrete and operational thinking. In a few cases the goals that were defined were too operational and closer to policies, but over 90 % of the goals were high-level and abstract. It had been anticipated that some of the devised policies would be technically infeasible, requiring a device that could not be realistically built. In fact all the policies assumed devices that either exist or could reasonably be created.

A further study has examined whether the ACCENT system is able to satisfactorily explain its operation [54]. A potential issue with an automated system such as this is that it behaves like an impenetrable black box. Even though it respects the goals and policies defined by users, there was a question of whether its operation would be understandable. Again, a number of care managers were recruited to participate as these are likely to be the major system users.

These participants were given individual training of 40 min in the basics of defining policies using the web-based wizard, and in how to use this to check the operation of policies. The home care system was then put into a known state in which a number of triggers had been received, resulting in a number of policies being executed and the corresponding actions being undertaken. The participants were then asked to undertake an unaided exercise concerning nine questions about policies, to be answered in 20 min. Using the wizard, the participants were able to answer these questions with 94 % accuracy.

The first set of questions asked whether particular policies were being used by the system and how. Some of these were prototype policies contributing to goals, and some were regular policies. The participants had to distinguish a range of reasons as to why a policy had (or had not) been executed depending on triggering, validity of conditions, and optimality for goals.

The second set of questions asked what the system would do in the event of certain events or changes in system environment. This required using the wizard to simulate the outcome of these triggers, the participants being asked to explain what the resulting actions would be (and why these would happen).

The final set of questions asked the participants to explain whether the system had (or had not) performed certain actions. This relied on the activation history built into the policy server, the participants being asked to explain when and why certain policies were causing these actions. This was potentially the most complex part of the exercise. In reporting the status of actions, the system can report that they were later overridden. For example, when asked why an alert had been raised the system might report that it *had* been raised but was later cancelled due to the intervention of another policy. It was anticipated that questions about inactions would be hard to formulate (e.g. why has the user not been reminded about taking medication?). However, all the participants were able to successfully answer questions about system actions and inactions.

Overall, it is believed that the robustness and usability of ACCENT approach have been adequately evaluated for managing telehealth and telecare through goals and policies. In the trials so far, the ACCENT system has run independently of existing care arrangements so as not to place users at risk. It is acknowledged that further practical evaluation is needed through longer-term deployments in a range of actual homes.

7.4 Open Problems

Interfaces have been discussed for management of home care, using goals and policies to customise the system for individual user needs and preferences. The approach has been successfully used in a lab setting and, on a limited basis, in actual homes. This has validated the usefulness of the research. However, as noted in Sect. 7.3.1.1 a number of pragmatic issues need attention.

Standardisation in home care systems is the most obvious problem. At present, there are few standards for equipment interoperability and data interchange in this field. As a result it is not practicable to mix and match solutions from different suppliers, and isolated 'data islands' are preventing effective combination of information from multiple sources—particularly the separate data about health care and social care.

Developers tend to focus on functionality, so the physical design of home care devices may need improvement. This is important in achieving user acceptance and 'buy in'. Users are resistant to devices that do not fit well into the home, are inconvenient to use, or are seen as stigmatising (marking users out as needing special support) [10, 33]. Developers should therefore work with designers to ensure that their solutions are acceptable and indeed desirable [57]. The ACCENT work has been complementary to this by creating an infrastructure that is open to new devices.

Personalisation and customisation remain important issues. Although research efforts such as ACCENT have made this possible, many commercial solutions for home care are still relatively inflexible and require specialised expertise to modify [55]. It is easier for commercial developers to create and to maintain fairly fixed solutions. However, practitioners often comment that 'one size fits all' solutions are not appropriate.

Improved user interfaces will also be required for home care systems. Again, developers may tend to concentrate on functionality rather than on how people can easily interact with the system. Although ACCENT has produced a number of usable interfaces for managing home care, further innovations are required in how this can be made as easy as possible.

Ethical and privacy concerns can arise because of the (misguided) perception among users that they are under surveillance [46]. It will be necessary to continue improving guidelines for deployment of home care systems, providing reassurance to users that the system is behaving in an acceptable way. It will also be important to develop technical standards for appropriate transmission and use of data collected by home care systems.

Care professionals need more training materials to increase their awareness and understanding of home care technologies. In the author's experience, there is enthusiasm and a strong demand for this information. Professionals need impartial advice on what is available, and what the costs and benefits are. Technology also needs to be more closely integrated into care assessments and daily practices.

7.5 Future Outlook

A number of developments are addressing the problems identified in Sect. 7.4. Through the work of industrial organisations such as the Continua Health Alliance [11], developers are putting more effort into standardisation—though there is still a long way to go. Further efforts are needed on co-design of devices and services for home care, involving users as well as service providers [33]. Customisation has been explored through the work of ACCENT, but this needs wider adoption. There is an encouraging trend towards use of multiple interface modalities for users with sensory impairment or simply different preferences [32]. Legislation and practitioner guidelines are progressively clarifying issues around ethics, privacy, confidentiality and informed consent. More courses, training and case studies are becoming available to inform care professionals about the potential of home care technologies.

From a research perspective, an area that needs particular attention is learning what the end user actually needs. There has been a little work on this in home automation [35], but more is needed specifically for home care. In fact this is planned as a future development of ACCENT.

Although telehealth and telecare are not yet mainstream, there is substantial support for them by Governments, and by health and social care authorities in many countries. Many trials have been and continue to be conducted, establishing a firm evidence base for future developments and deployments. A successful future can be predicted for home care systems that will be cost-effective, manageable, customisable and acceptable to users.

References

1. American National Standards Institute. (1999). *Health level seven: An application protocol for electronic data exchange in healthcare environments*. Washington, DC, USA: American National Standards Institute. NULL
2. Axelrod, A., et al. (2011). A toolkit to explore lived experience of motivation: When words are not enough. In *Proceedings of 5th International Conference on Pervasive Health* (pp. 32–39). Los Alamitos, California, USA: IEEE Computer Society.
3. Barger, T. S., Brown, D. E., & Alwan, M. (2005). Health-status monitoring through analysis of behavioural patterns. *IEEE Transactions on Systems, Man and Cybernetics, Part A: Systems and Humans*, *35*(1), 22–27.
4. Blackwell, A. F., & Hague, R. (2001). AutoHAN: An architecture for programming the home. In *Proceedings of Symposium on Human Centric Computing Languages and Environments* (pp. 150–157). New York, USA: ACM Press.
5. Brumitt, B., Meyers, B., Krumm, J., Kern, A., & Shafer, S. (2000). Easyliving: Technologies for intelligent environments. In P. J. Thomas & H.-W. Gellersen (Eds.), *Proceedings of 4th International Symposium on Handheld and Ubiquitous Computing. Lecture Notes in Computer Science* (Vol. 1927, pp. 12–29). Berlin, Germany: Springer.
6. Carone, G., & Costello, D. (2006). Can Europe afford to grow old? *Finance and Development Magazine*, *43*(3), 8–31.
7. Chistensen, L. R., & Grönvall, E. (2011). Challenges and opportunities for collaborative technologies for home care work. In S. Bødker, N. O. Bouvin, W. Wulf & L. Ciolfi (Eds.),

Proceedings of 12th European Conference on Computer-Supported Cooperative Work (pp. 61–80). Berlin: Springer.
8. Clark, J. S., & McGee-Lennon, M. R. (2011). A stakeholder-centred exploration of the current barriers to the uptake of home care technology in the UK. *Assistive Technologies*, *5*(1), 12–25.
9. Clark, J. S., & Turner, K. J. (2013). Usability of goals for home care, Assistive Technologies (in preparation).
10. Cobalt Consortium. (2013). The Cobalt project. Retrieved November 2013, from, http://cobaltproject.org
11. Continua Health Alliance. (2013). Connected health standards. Retrieved August 2013, from, http://www.continuaalliance.org
12. Damianou, N., Lupu, E. C., & Sloman, M. (2001). The Ponder policy specification language. In M. Sloman, J. Lobo & E. C. Lupu (Eds.), *Proceedings of Policy Workshop. Lecture Notes in Computer Science* (Vol. 1995). Berlin, Germany: Springer.
13. Darkins, A., Ryan, P., Kobb, R., Foster, L., Edmonson, E., Wakefield, B., et al. (2008). Care coordination/home telehealth: The systematic implementation of health informatics, home telehealth, and disease management to support the care of veteran patients with chronic conditions. *Telemedecine and E-Health*, *14*(10), 1118–26.
14. de Deugd, S., Carroll, R., Kelly, K., Millett, B., & Ricker, J. (2005). Soda: Service oriented device architecture. *Pervasive Computing*, *5*(3), 94–6.
15. Dey, A. K., Hamid, R., Beckmann, C., Li, I., & Hsu, D. (2004). A CAPpella: Programming by demonstration of context-aware applications. In: E. Dykstra-Erickson & M. Tscheligi (Eds.), *Proceedings of Conference on Human Factors in Computing Systems* (pp. 33–40). New York, USA: ACM Press.
16. Docobo. (2013). Home health solutions. Retrieved November 2013, from, http://www.docobo.co.uk
17. Dreaming Consortium. (2013). The Dreaming project. Retrieved November 2013, from, http://ec.europa.eu/information_society/apps/projects/factsheet/index.cfm?project_ref=225023
18. e-HealthCare. (2013). Advanced home healthcare environment. Retrieved November 2013, from, http://ehealth.sourceforge.net
19. Gajos, K., Fox, K. H., & Shrobe, H. (2002). End user empowerment in human centered pervasive computing. In F. Mattern & M. Naghshineh (Eds.), *Proceedings of 1st International Conference on Pervasive Computing. Lecture Notes in Computer Science* (Vol. 2414, pp. 134–140). Berlin, Germany: Springer.
20. Gil, N. M., et al. (2007). Data visualisation and data mining technology for supporting care for older people. In: *Proceedings of 9th International Conference on Computers and Accessibility* (pp. 139–146). New York, USA: ACM Press.
21. Gouvas, P., Bouras, T., & Mentzas, G. (2007). An OSGi-based semantic service-oriented device architecture. In R. Meersman, Z. Tari & P. Herrero (Eds.), *On the move to meaningful Internet systems. Lecture notes in computer science* (Vol. 4806, pp. 773–782). Berlin, Germany: Springer.
22. Hein, A., Nee, O., Willemsen, D., Scheffold, T., Dogac, A., & Laleci, G. N. (2006). Intelligent healthcare monitoring based on semantic interoperability platform: The homecare scenario. In *Proceedings of 1st European Conference on eHealth*, Fribourg, Switzerland.
23. Hine, N. A., Stewart, N. M., Arnott, J. L., Cipars, A., & Martin, C. J. (2012). Supporting the dialogue of care. In K. J. Turner (Ed.), *Advances in home care technologies: Results of the* MATCH *project* (pp. 183–202). Amsterdam, Netherlands: IOS Press.
24. Just Checking. (2013). Home monitoring solutions. Retrieved November 2013, from, http://www.justchecking.co.uk
25. Kameas, A., Mavrommati, I., & Markopoulos, P. (2005). Computing in tangible: Using artifacts as components of ambient intelligence environments. In G. Riva, F. Vatalaro, F. Davide, & M. Alcañiz (Eds.), *Ambient intelligence: The evolution of technology, communication and cognition* (pp. 121–42). Amsterdam, Netherlands: IOS Press.
26. Kind, J., Bose, R., Yang, H.-I., Pickles, S., & Helal, A. (2006). Atlas: A service-oriented sensor platform. In *Proceedings of Workshop on Practical Issues in Building Sensor Network Applications*. Los Alamitos, California, USA: IEEE Computer Society.

27. Leong, C., Ramli, A. R., & Perumal, T. (2009). A rule-based framework for heterogeneous subsystems management in smart home environment. *IEEE Transactions on Consumer Electronics*, *55*(3), 1208–13.
28. Magill, E. H., & Blum, J. M. (2012). Personalised ambient monitoring: Supporting mental health at home. In K. J. Turner (Ed.), *Advances in home care technologies: Results of the* MATCH *project* (pp. 67–85). Amsterdam, Netherlands: IOS Press.
29. Maternaghan, C. (2012). *Can People Program Their Home?* Technical Report CSM-191. Stirling, UK: Computing Science and Mathematics, University of Stirling.
30. Maternaghan, C., & Turner, K. J. (2011). Pervasive computing for home automation and telecare. In S. I. A. Shah, M. Ilyas & H. T. Mouftah (Eds.), *Pervasive communications handbook* (pp. 17.1–17.25). Boca Raton, Florida, USA: CRC Press.
31. McBryan, A., & Gray, P. D. (2012). Dynamic configuration of home services. In K. J. Turner (Ed.), *Advances in home care technologies: Results of the* MATCH *project* (pp. 86–105). Amsterdam: IOS Press.
32. McGee-Lennon, M. R., Gray, P. D., & Brewster, S. A. (2012). Multimodal interaction and technologies for care at home. In K. J. Turner (Ed.), *Advances in home care technologies: Results of the* MATCH *project* (pp. 106–117). Amsterdam, Netherlands: IOS Press.
33. McGee-Lennon, M. R., Smeaton, A., & Brewster, S. A. (2012). Designing home care reminder systems: Lessons learned through co-design with older users. In *Proceedings of 6th International Conference on Pervasive Computing Technologies for Healthcare*. Los Alamitos, California, USA: IEEE Computer Society.
34. Mirth Corporation. (2013). Healthcare solutions. Retrieved November 2013, from, http://www.mirthcorp.com
35. Mozer, M. C. (1998). The neural network house: An environment that adapts to its inhabitants. In M. Coen (Ed.), *Proceedings of AAAI Symposium on Intelligent Environments* (pp. 110–114). Menlo Park: AAAI Press.
36. Newman, M. W., Elliott, A., & Smith, T. F. (2008). Providing an integrated user experience of networked media, devices, and services through end-user composition. In *Proceedings of Symposium on Human Centric Computing Languages and Environments. Lecture Notes in Computer Science* (Vol. 5013, pp. 213–227). Berlin, Germany: Springer.
37. OmniQare. (2013). Home care solutions. Retrieved November 2013, from, http://www.omniqare.com
38. Orpwood, R., Adlam, T., Evans, N., & Chadd, J. (2008). Evaluation of an assisted-living smart home for someone with dementia. *Assistive Technologies*, *2*(2), 13–21.
39. OSGi Alliance. (2003). OSGi system. Retrieved August 2013, from, http://www.osgi.org
40. Osman, K. A., Ashford, R. L., & Oldacres, A. (2007). Homecare hub: A pervasive computing approach to integrating data for remote delivery of personal and social care. In *Proceedings of 2nd International Conference on Pervasive Computing and Applications* (pp. 348–353). Los Alamitos, California, USA: IEEE Computer Society.
41. Persona Consortium. (2013). The Persona project: Perceptive spaces promoting independent ageing. Retrieved November 2013, from, http://cordis.europa.eu/projects/rcn/80532_en.html
42. Román, M., Hess, C. K., Cerqueira, R., Ranganathan, A., Campbell, R., & Nahrstedt, K. (2001). Gaia: A middleware infrastructure for active spaces. *Pervasive Computing*, *1*(4), 74–83.
43. Rodden, T., Crabtree, A,. Hemmings, T., Humble, B. K. J., Åkesson, K. P., & Hansson, P. (2004). Configuring the ubiquitous home. In *Proceedings of 6th International Conference on the Design of Cooperative Systems* (pp. 215–230). Amsterdam, Netherlands: IOS Press.
44. Stationery Office Limited. (2003). *Aspects of the economics of an ageing population*. London, UK: Stationery Office Limited.
45. Sohn, T., & Dey, A. K. (2003). iCAP: An informal tool for interactive prototyping of context-aware applications. In *Proceedings of International Conference on Human Factors in Computing Systems* (pp. 974–975). New York, USA: ACM Press.
46. Sorell, T., & Draper, H. (2012). Telecare, surveillance, and the welfare state. *American Journal of Bioethics*, *12*(9), 36–44.

47. Taylor, K., & Yadav, A. (2013). *Telecare and telehealth: A game changer for health and social care*. London, UK: Deloitte Centre for Health Solution.
48. Truong, K. N., Huang, E. M., & Abowd, G. D. (2004). Camp: A magnetic poetry interface for end-user programming of capture applications for the home. In N. Davies, E. Mynatt, I. Siio (Eds.), *Proceedings of Ubiquitous Computing. Lecture Notes in Computer Science* (Vol. 3205, pp. 143–160). Berlin, Germany: Springer.
49. Tunstall. (2013). Health and social care solutions. Retrieved November 2013, from, http://tunstall.co.uk
50. Turner. K. J. (2010). Device services for the home. In K. Drira, A. H. Kacem, M. Jmaiel (Eds.), Proceedings of 10th International Conference on New Technologies for Distributed Systems (pp. 41–48). Los Alamitos, California, USA: IEEE Computer Society.
51. Turner, K. J. (2011). Flexible management of smart homes. *Ambient Intelligence and Smart Environments*, *3*(2), 83–110.
52. Turner, K. J. (2013). Accent (Advanced Component Control Enhancing Network Technologies). Retrieved August 2013, from, http://www.cs.stir.ac.uk/accent
53. Turner KJ (2013) Appel (Adaptable and Programmable Policy Environment and Language). Retrieved August 2013, from, http://www.cs.stir.ac.uk/appel
54. Turner, K. J. (2013). Explaining the operation of a home care system, Assistive Technologies (in preparation).
55. Turner, K. J., & Maternaghan, C. (2012). Home care systems. In K. J. Turner (Ed.), *Advances in home care technologies: Results of the* MATCH *project* (pp. 21–9). Amsterdam, Netherlands: IOS Press.
56. Turner, K. J., Reiff-Marganiec, S., Blair, L., Campbell, G. A., & Wang, F. (2013). *Appel: Adaptable and Programmable Policy Environment and Language*. Technical Report CSM-161. Stirling, UK: Computing Science and Mathematics, University of Stirling.
57. Vines, J., Clarke, R., Wright, P., McCarthy, J., & Olivier, P. (2013). Configuring participation: On how we involve users in design. In *Proceedings of Conference on Human Factors in Computing Systems* (pp. 429–443). New York, USA: ACM Press.
58. VoiceXML Forum. (2010). *Voice eXtensible Markup Language*. Piscataway, New Jersey, USA: VoiceXML Forum.

Further Readings

59. Bardram, J. E., Mihailidis, A., & Wan, D. (2006). *Pervasive computing in healthcare*. Boca Raton: CRC Press.
60. Katz, S. (1983). Assessing self-maintenance: activities of daily living, mobility, and instrumental activities of daily living. *Journal of The American Geriatrics Society*, *31*(12), 721–7.
61. MATCH Consortium. (2013). MATCH (Mobilising Advanced Technologies for Care at Home). Retrieved August 2013, from, http://www.match-project.org.uk
62. Oudshoorn, N. (2011). *Telecare technologies and the transformation of healthcare*. Basingstoke, UK: Palgrave Macmillan.
63. Turner, K. J. (Ed.). (2012). *Advances in home care technologies: Results of the* MATCH *project*. Amsterdam, Netherlands: IOS Press.
64. Yang, G.-Z. (2006). *Body sensor networks*. Berlin, Germany: Springer.
65. Ziefle, M., Röcker, C., & Holzinger, A. (2014). Current trends and challenges for pervasive health technologies: from technical innovation to user integration. In A. Holzinger, M. Ziefle, & C. Röcker (Eds.), *Pervasive health: State-of-the-art and beyond*. Berlin: Springer.

Chapter 8
Personal Assistive Devices for Elderlies

Executing Activities of Daily Living Despite Natural Ageing-Related Changes

Lorenzo T. D'Angelo, Joachim F. Kreutzer, Jakob Neuhaeuser, Samuel Reimer and Tim C. Lueth

8.1 Introduction

In industrialized countries, the population's average life expectancy has been growing continuously over the last decades. This development, although being positive in itself, poses new challenges to the society, as ageing is always associated with natural changes in the human body which can only be minimized to a given extent.

In this chapter we introduce and describe personal assistive devices for elderlies as technical devices aimed at compensating for these changes by technical means. We will first examine the consequences of the demographic change. We mainly focus on the development in Germany, but the situation in other industrialized countries in Europe but also outside, e.g. Japan, is very similar. For a larger overview of the context of societal changes in the last decades refer to [77]. We will then define the target group for personal assistive devices for elderlies more in detail. For the description of the main applications and of the state of the art we will use a new classification by technical type of support, rather than by concerned body part. At the end of the chapter we will give a qualitative comparison of the presented systems and elaborate the challenges laying ahead.

8.1.1 Demographics

In Germany and other industrialized countries the population's average life expectancy has been rising for many decades as a consequence of better medical supply, availability of food, higher safety and comfort standards at home and at work as well as sport programs and their promotion. On the other hand, the amount of children per couple started to sink rapidly after the 1960s.

L. T. D'Angelo (✉) · J. F. Kreutzer · J. Neuhaeuser · S. Reimer · T. C. Lueth
Institute of Micro Technology and Medical Device Technology (MiMed), TU München, Garching, Germany
e-mail: Lorenzo.DAngelo@tum.de

A. Holzinger et al. (eds.), *Pervasive Health*, Human–Computer Interaction Series,
DOI: 10.1007/978-1-4471-6413-5_8, © Springer-Verlag London 2014

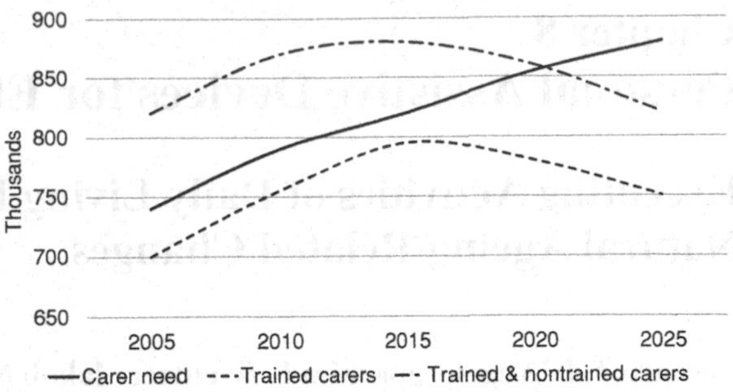

Fig. 8.1 Statistics and projection of caregiver need (*continuous line*) and available caregivers (*broken lines*) over time in Germany. Based on [1]

As a consequence, the mean age in Germany is over 40 and thus the highest in Europe. The so-called ageing pyramid has become rather an ageing column with a bulge at the level of the 1960s-born baby-boomer generation. These people, currently the society's top-performers, will go into retirement within two decades and be part of a large amount of elderly people that the younger generation will have to support, both from a social economical and from a personal perspective. While in 2009 every fifth person was over 65 (17 of the total 82 Million inhabitants), in 2030 it will be every third, amounting to 22 Million people. In the same timespan the amount of people over 85 will more than double, from 1.5 to 4 Million [22]. This trend is nonreversible, even if birth rates started rising today, and leads to a number of challenges.

As the care quota over age shows, due to the natural changes in old age, the number of people in need of care rises with the population's mean age. The statistics record people in need of care only according to the long-term care insurance act (Pflegeversicherungsgesetz, SGB XI), but even this group included 2.3 Million people in 2009 (two third being over 75) and is expected to rise to 3.4 Million in 2030 [53] only. These people will not be able to continue practicing their profession if they haven't reached their retirement age yet. In addition, the assistance then necessary will have to be provided by family members or professional caregivers, leading to additional financial and/or time burden for the person concerned or for his relatives. Even with economical means available, however, a remaining challenge is the sinking amount of relatives available for assistance nearby and the increasing gap between supply and demand of professional caregivers (Fig. 8.1). In 2005 there was a shortage of 39,000 full-time care personnel already, which is expected to increase to 193,000 by 2025. This shortage is currently being compensated by employing untrained personnel or personnel in training, but even this personnel will only be sufficient to fill the gap until 2018. Furthermore, the personnel shortage, including untrained personnel and personnel in training, will still amount to 112,000 people by 2025 [1].

In conclusion, the demographic change is leading to an increasing amount of people in need of assistance and to a decreasing amount of people available to provide or finance assistance, both on a professional and on a personal level.

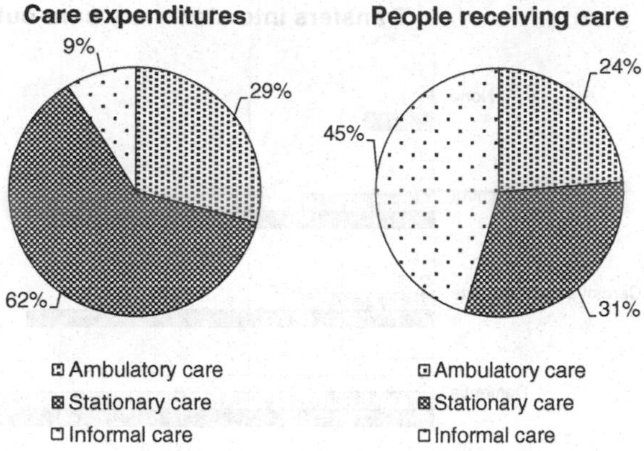

Fig. 8.2 Comparison of the distribution of care expenditures in 2010 and people receiving care in 2009 on informal care, ambulatory care and stationary care in Germany. Based on [53, 64], respectively

8.1.2 Target Group

In the last section we learned that there is a demand for personal assistive devices for elderlies based on the growing gap between people in need of care and available caregivers. In this section, we will examine the target group, i.e. who are the future users of these devices and what do they expect from them? What is the common goal all personal assistive devices must achieve in order to be worth their price?

In respect to the way and by whom they are administered, care services can be subdivided in three types: informal care (by relatives, friends etc.), ambulatory care (by professional caregivers, including services provided at the concerned person's home) or stationary care (inpatient care). Of course, also mixed types are possible and common. In Germany in 2009, 45 % of people in need of care received informal care at home accounting for the majority of people in need of care. Another 24 % received ambulatory care, i.e. at home by professional caregivers or informal caregivers supported by professionals. The remaining 31 % of people in need of care received help in a stationary facility [53]. The distribution of care costs, however, is different. In 2010, costs for care and therapies amounted to 69 Billion € and made up 24 % of all healthcare expenditures. Of this sum, 62 % went to stationary and 29 % to ambulatory facilities, while only 9 % went to private households [64]. The comparison of these figures quickly shows that stationary care determines higher costs than ambulatory or informal care per person taken care of. Therefore, there is a big potential in cost savings if people treated in stationary institutions could be shifted to ambulatory care or even informal care (Fig. 8.2).

Most importantly, we also know that the majority of elderly people have the wish to remain living in their home as long as possible [39]. As the care insurance doesn't cover all the expenses for stationary care, usually the concerned person or his relatives have to pay in addition to finance the stay. Thus, if a device can help to avoid or postpone the transition from care at home to stationary care without increasing

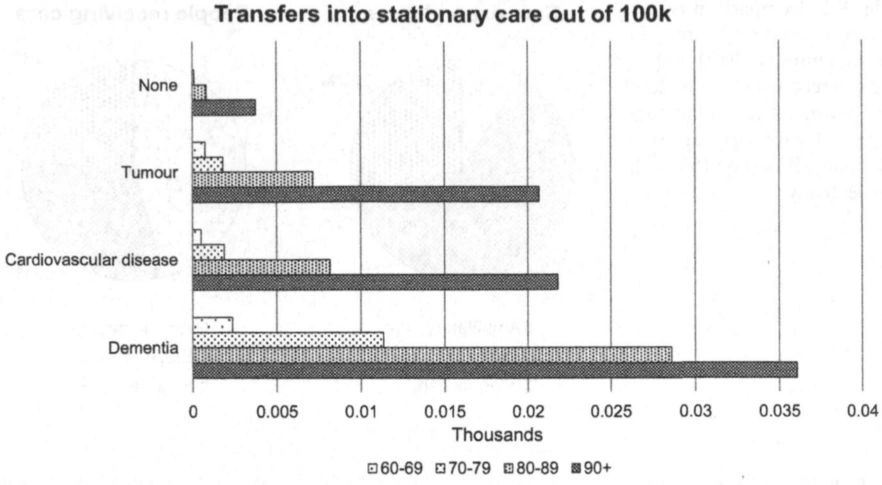

Fig. 8.3 Transfers into a stationary care facility out of 100,000 insured people depending on the diagnosis 2 years before transfer. Based on [70]

other societal or economical costs, not only will it fulfill an unmet need, but it will also offer a valuable service.

Personal assistive devices for elderlies must therefore primarily address elderly people who want to live independently in their home but have difficulties doing so because of age-related changes. The common goal of these devices, i.e. the decisive factor for their acceptance and for the willingness of the user to buy and use them is whether or not they actually enable them to compensate these changes and thus stay independent. From a User-Centered Design (UCD) point of view, therefore, the primary persona is the elderly person and the primary use case involves supporting the elderly person by compensating an age-related change.

8.1.3 Technical Classification

Personal assistive devices for elderlies have the common goal to enable elderly people to stay independent despite age-related changes. What applications derive from this premise, and how can we classify them from a technical point of view?

Why do we need a technical classification in the first place? Age-related changes, but also other classifications in the nursing sciences or medical literature list deficits according to the affected part of the human body, e.g. deficits linked to heart diseases are separated from deficits linked to lung diseases [38]. Any therapy, rehabilitation or compensation strategy is listed according to this classification, including available technical solutions. It can thus be the case that the same or similar technical solutions or techniques is repeated for every deficit for which it is applicable. Also most statistics deliver the medical origin for the transfer into a stationary facility, but not the required functionality to avoid the transfer (Fig. 8.3).

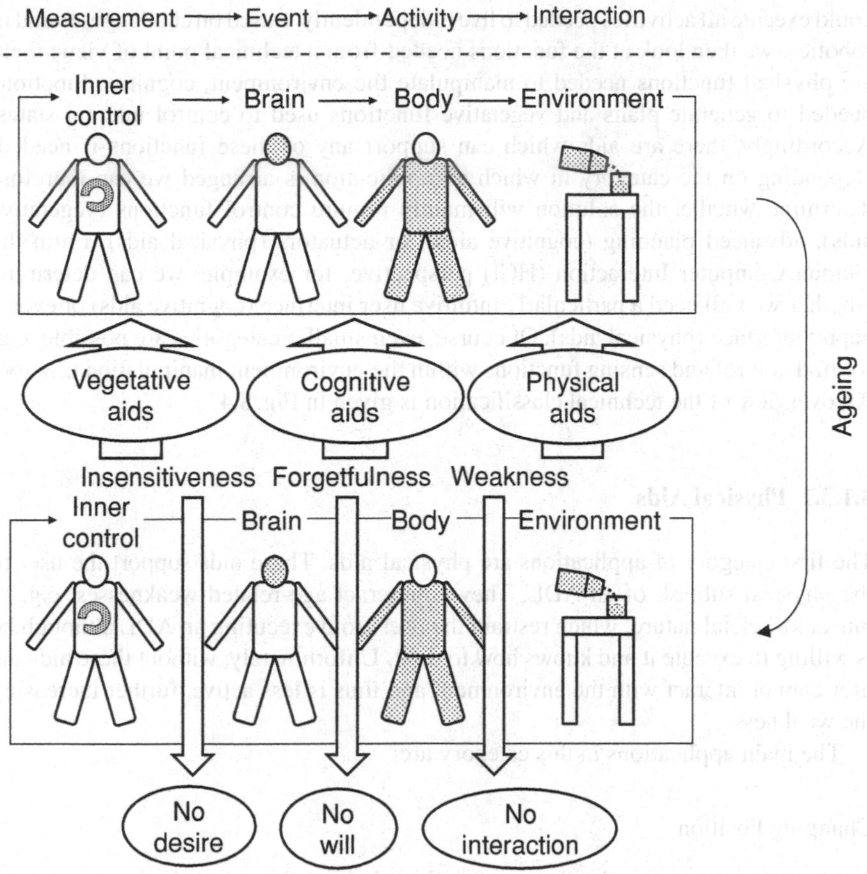

Fig. 8.4 Technical classification of personal assistive devices for elderlies into vegetative, cognitive and physical aids (*middle*). Their goal is to compensate possible functional age-related changes (shift from *top* to *bottom* half). These can be of vegetative (change in inner control leading to a decrease of desire), cognitive (change of brain processes leading to a decrease of will) or physical (changes in the body leading to a decrease of interaction) nature

A technical classification, on the other hand, lists applications according to the required technical functionality independently from the biological origin of the need, i.e. it groups solutions which are similar in respect to the expected requirements and involved technical field. We will use this classification to be able to find common technical challenges for similarly classified support tasks and will introduce this classification in the following.

We start from the activities of daily living (ADL), which are used in caregiving processes to assess a person's independence level using scales such as the Katz ADL scale [25]. ADLs are a good tool to break the goal of ensuring the independence at home into subgoals which, once achieved, would make sure that an elderly person could execute all activities needed to live independently. Based on challenges found in robotics, we then look at the functions needed from a technical point of view: there are physical functions needed to manipulate the environment, cognitive functions needed to generate plans and vegetative functions used to control internal states. Accordingly, there are aids which can support any of these functions if needed. Depending on the category in which an application is arranged we can therefore determine whether the solution will mainly require control functions (vegetative aids), advanced planning (cognitive aids), or actuators (physical aids). From the Human Computer Interaction (HCI) perspective, for example, we can determine whether we will need a particularly intuitive user interface (cognitive aids) or even a haptic interface (physical aids). Of course, even smaller categories are possible, e.g. we find control and sensing functions within the environment manipulation task too. An overview of the technical classification is given in Fig. 8.4.

8.1.3.1 Physical Aids

The first category of applications are physical aids. These aids support the user in the physical subtask of an ADL. They counteract age-related weaknesses, e.g. of musculoskeletal nature, which restrain the user from executing an ADL although he is willing to execute it and knows how to do it. Unfortunately, without these aids the user cannot interact with the environment and thus is less active, further increasing the weakness.

The main applications in this category are:

Changing Position

Applications supporting the change of position help walking-impaired users to move inside their home or outside of it, at least in an area corresponding to a 5 min walk. In urban environments, this is the minimum movement radius for independent living, as it enables handling daily routines or reaching the own car or local public transport [70].

Changing Posture

Applications supporting the change of posture enable users to change their body posture between lying, sitting and standing who are otherwise unable or impeded in doing so. These pose changes are a common need in everyday life: sitting down and standing up is required to take a meal, using the toilet, using a vehicle or a mobility aid while lying down and getting up is needed to move in and out of bed.

Manipulating the Environment

Applications supporting the manipulation of the environment enable the user to lift or move objects (e.g. a crate of water bottles or groceries) or operating devices through physical interaction. They mainly support movements of the upper body, arms and hands.

8.1.3.2 Cognitive Aids

The second category are cognitive aids. These aids support the user in cognitive subtasks of an ADL, i.e. remembering or recognizing the need of executing an ADL in the first place, or generating a plan to execute it. They counteract age-related forgetfulness or dementia, i.e. recognize events based on available information about the user and his environment and generate a will to execute ADLs which are required for independent living. These aids, too, have a stabilizing function as forgetting to execute ADLs can have further deterioration as a consequence.

The main applications in this category are:

Single Events

Applications supporting the will to pursue single activities enable users to better remember important appointments, e.g. a visit to the doctor. Although these are usually time-based, event-based applications are conceivable, e.g. an application could suggest a visit to an orthopedist upon measuring a slowdown of the user's movements.

Recurring Events

Applications supporting the will to execute recurring ADLs ensure that the user remembers everyday vital activities such as drinking, eating, using the toilet, shopping for groceries, cooking etc.

Plans

Applications supporting the execution of plans support the user in executing complex activities which require the execution of several tasks in a fixed or condition-dependent order. Examples for such complex activities are cooking or navigating between two locations by foot or using one or several vehicles.

8.1.3.3 Vegetative Aids

The third category are vegetative aids. These aids support the user's vegetative functions, compensating control mechanisms regulating parameters of his body which do not function as well as in younger age, e.g. the insurgence of thirst when the body is dehydrating. They counteract age-related insensitiveness, i.e. the capacity of recognizing a feeling or a bodily need and thus to generate a desire to fulfill this need. These aids must be able to monitor body parameters directly or indirectly and to detect or predict whether they are getting out of control. Drinking reminders are a good example for the stabilizing effect of these aids, as dehydration can lead to dementia-similar states.

The main applications in this category are:

Thirst

Applications compensating thirst decrease support the user in keeping track of his liquid intake and outtake and warn him in case he is not drinking enough. A loss of water of 3 % referred to the body mass can lead to tiredness, weakness, nausea, movement disorders and temperature, while a loss of 11 % can lead to dementia, seizures and delirium. A loss of 20 % can be lethal [30]. While in younger age the body detects risk for dehydration and feels thirst, in older age this control mechanism can be disturbed.

Appetite

Applications compensating appetite decrease support the user in keeping track of his food intake and energy consumption and warn him in case he is not eating enough or too much. Especially the risk of starvation is a problem in older age. The need to eat can be damped by adverse effects of medications or by the natural reduction of the taste sensation in older age. A regular monitoring of the body weight is a standard measure when such a risk exists.

Urge to Urinate/Defecate

Applications compensating the decreasing urge to urinate or defecate support the user in noticing the body's need to do so ahead of time. In older age, the ability to sense these needs in time, especially when continence is impaired or visiting a toilet takes longer, is important. The consequences of a loss of control are not lethal but have still a great impact on the social level and on the ability to live independently. Obstipation, on the other hand, can have serious consequences too, making its detection another important application field.

8.2 Glossary

ABA scheme Evaluation method for assistive devices consisting of three testing phases without (A), with (B) and without (A) the device.

Care quota Statistical figure indicating the ratio of people in need of care within a given population.

Care, informal Care administered at home by non-professional caregivers.

Care, ambulatory Care administered at home by professional caregivers.

Care, stationary Care administered in a residential facility by professional caregivers.

Cognitive aids, event-based Reminding aids relying on events to generate reminders.

Cognitive aids, time-based Reminding aids relying solely on time to generate reminders.

Event Relevant occurrence in the user or in his environment.

Exoskeleton In this context, wearable robot which empowers the user.

Forgetfulness In this context, the inability or impaired ability to recognize events and generate the will to execute activities needed for the daily living.

Haptic user interface User interface involving touch.

HCI Human Computer Interaction.

Insensitiveness In this context, the inability or impaired ability to recognize a bodily need.

Position change Locomotion.

Posture change Changing e.g. from standing to sitting or lying.

UCD User Centered Design.

Weakness In this context, bodily impairments (e.g. musculoskeletal or neurological) which prevent a person of moving, changing posture or manipulating the environment or which lead to early fatigue.

8.3 State-of-the-Art

In the following we will survey the state of the art for selected applications out of the described classes of personal assistive devices for elderlies. In each section we will describe, where applicable, devices already in use clinically (3.3.2) or in care settings (3.1.1, 3.1.2, 3.3.1), clinical studies (3.2.1), and results in research (3.1.3, 3.2.2, 3.2.3,

3.3.3). Section 8.3.3. will give an overview of our past results in monitoring serving as a base to develop assistive devices. In Sect. 8.4 we will then give an overview, qualitative comparison and analysis of open problems.

Methodology and Topical Boundaries

For the collection of the following state of the art we followed various approaches depending on the type of solutions we were looking for.

We mainly used textbooks or regulations to search for solutions or methods already in use in care or in clinical settings, e.g. [30] for standard care procedures.

The results on exoskeletons are researched starting from the systems described in [26, 55], out of which we selected the empowering systems. The research on cognitive aids was conducted starting from the reviews by Meiland et al. [35, 37] and selecting systems which were evaluated with real people and actually provided reminders. IEEE Xplore and PubMed search were used additionally to find newer developments and additional details about the selected works.

The research on systems for thirst decrease compensation was conducted in IEEE Xplore using the keywords "fluid/liquid", "intake", "monitoring", and "reminder".

In selecting research results we limited our search to personal assistive devices for elderlies as described in the Sects. 8.1.2 and 8.1.3. This means in particular that we looked for systems who support the elderly person in the first place and only address relatives or caregivers as backup solutions, if at all. Therefore, for instance, pure (tele-) monitoring, alarming or diagnosis systems were excluded in the first place.

Other chapters of this book explore topics excluded here. Non-functional-related challenges in home-based healthcare are addressed in [21], while management of Telehealth and Telecare systems is described in [68]. Specific chapters focus on the topics of rehabilitation [61] and barrier-free usability [7].

8.3.1 Physical Aids

While there are a wide range of products supporting the change of position and posture available on the market, little help is available for manipulation of the environment.

The most international research groups working on physical aids do so by working on the advance of exoskeletons. These are wearable robots consisting of a structure supporting both its own weight and the wearer's movements. Depending on the actuated limb(s), exoskeletons can be applied both for position change, posture change or manipulating the user's environment.

Therefore, in this section we will survey mainly devices available on the market for support of position and posture change and give an overview of research work on exoskeletons.

8.3.1.1 State of the Art in Care (Changing Position)

The German National Association of Statutory Health Insurance Funds (GKV Spitzenverband) maintains a list of medical aids (Hilfsmittelverzeichnis). The costs for aids on this list are met by the statutory health insurance, although not being legally binding. Products are included in the list upon request of the manufacturer if they meet certain criteria. This list therefore gives a good overview over devices available on the market and their characteristics and functionalities.

Frame-based devices supporting position change include walkers and walking frames. These devices consist of a frame which the user can hold up to and have wheels allowing the frame to move on an even surface and to transfer part of the weight force onto the ground at the same time. This type of device increases the safety of the position change, e.g. lowering the risk of falls. Additionally they have racks allowing the transport of goods like groceries. These devices do not offer an active locomotion support counteracting fatigue. They are available both for indoors and outdoors.

Another class of position change supporting devices are wheelchairs. The target group here are people who are impaired to walk temporarily or definitely. They offer an active locomotion support, either through the user's own upper-arm force or through electrical engines in case of electrical powered wheelchairs. Electrical wheelchairs are operated through an input device, mostly a joystick, and are usually conceived for indoor and outdoor use.

For use in bathrooms or under the shower, there are specially designed waterproof walkers or wheelchairs. They offer a safer handling on wet surfaces or with wet hands.

Electromobiles or electric cars are devices which are used by mobility impaired people to cover middle-long distances outdoors. Their target group are people who can walk by themselves but have a high risk of falls or fatigue. The user can sit on these four-wheeled devices and steers them using a steering column, similar to a motor scooter. These devices are typically driven by electrical engines and also offer racks for transporting goods.

8.3.1.2 State of the Art in Care (Changing Posture)

Devices supporting the change of posture are listed in the German National Association of Statutory Health Insurance Funds' list of medical aids too (see previous Sect. 8.3.1.1).

Strictly speaking there are no devices on the market supporting the user in changing his posture by himself but rather devices supporting caregivers in doing so. These lifters are available in several forms and are used to lift a person out of a bed, wheelchair or seating accommodation and lowering them back into another one. They consist of a C-shaped wheeled structure which is moved under the bed and has belts attached to the upper arm. The belt system embraces the transferred person and supports primarily his thighs, hip and back. It is lifted manually or with electrical support, until the person hangs in the belts. It is then moved and the person is subsequently lowered in the new seating accommodation or bed.

In addition to the mentioned lifters there are especially designed mobilization wheelchairs which support transfers. Their target group are immobile or obese people (bariatric aids). These devices support a posture change from seated into lying by moving the back, leg and seat rest in respect to the base frame. This pose is then rotated while the user is retained by belts until he is standing and is used to stress the cardiovascular system for training purposes. Some of these devices include a stand-up aid which lifts and rotates the seat rest slightly as a support. They can be operated manually or driven by electrical engines or pneumatic springs.

8.3.1.3 Research on Exoskeletons

The development of exoskeletons started for military purposes with the "Hardiman", a wearable structure given into commission for development by the US Department of Defense to the Cornell Laboratories and then for construction to General Electric [33]. The system was operated using the master-slave principle, meaning that it consisted of two exoskeletons and the outer exoskeleton (slave) followed the movements of the inner exoskeleton (master). Since these beginnings many groups started working on exoskeletons worldwide for various applications and tested them with humans. While whole-body exoskeletons are mainly advanced in Japan and in the USA, projects for the development of orthotic exoskeletons for single limbs are found in Europe too.

The Hybrid Assistive Limb (HAL) is a grounded exoskeleton which is able to carry its own and the user's weight. It was developed for both empowering and rehabilitation applications. It is articulated at the knee, hip, shoulder and elbow, is actuated by direct current motors with harmonic drive gearboxes and uses electromyography to detect the user's muscular activity. It employs position sensors as well as pressure sensors to measure ground reaction forces. Two control systems read the EMG signals to actuate the engines and estimate the future movements, respectively. In 2012 a HAL version for a single leg was presented for rehabilitation of people with neuronal dysfunctions. For this application HAL was expanded with a cane with embedded movement and pressure sensors to determine the gait cycle phase, as in patients with neuronal dysfunctions EMG signals cannot be used as operating input [24].

The Kanagawa Power Suit is a grounded exoskeleton developed to support nurses in carrying patients. It actuates the elbow, hip and knee joints using pneumatic rotary engines. The air is compressed by an electrical pump supplied with energy by an accumulator. Pressure sensors are employed to measure the change in muscle volume and determine the muscle strain. The control's goal is to provide half of the required torque by the exoskeleton [74].

The Roboknee is a non-grounded exoskeleton attached to the knee which has one degree of freedom. It is actuated by a linear series elastic actuator positioned behind the knee spreading thigh and shank. Gyroscopes and pressure sensors under the shoes are used to detect the user's intention with the scope of amplifying the torque he applies [56].

The Berkeley Lower Extremity Exoskeleton (BLEEX) is an exoskeleton with three degrees of freedom on the hip, one degree of freedom on the knee and three degrees of freedom on the ankle. The rotations of knee and hip in the sagittal plane and of the hip in the frontal plane are actuated. The rotations of the ankle in the frontal plane and of the hip in the transversal plane are pre-loaded with springs. It is driven by linear hydraulic actuators. The walking motion is controlled by the exoskeleton autonomously while the user only has to state the desired direction as the system is designed for use by paraplegics. In 2011 a version for rehabilitation was developed which actuates rotations of hip and knee in the sagittal plane. Sensors on the arm and under the shoes are used to coordinate the exoskeleton's movements with the crutches' movements [12].

LOPES is an exoskeleton for gait rehabilitation which supports the rotation of hip and knee in the sagittal plane. Both joints are actuated by direct current motors. These are not linked to the joint directly but through a drive belt in the hip and bowden cables and a spring in the knee. In the knee this corresponds to a rotatory series elastic actuator. This actuator allows controlling the force between exoskeleton and body by controlling the angle difference between actuator and joint [17].

The EXO-UL supports movements of the upper limbs and has seven degrees of freedom. The system was developed considering everyday activities' movements. It is driven by direct current motors. While four of them are in a fixed position, the three motors for the distal degrees of freedom are positioned onto the exoskeleton. The driving torque is transmitted onto the exoskeleton by wire cables [52].

The NEUROExos is an exoskeleton developed to combine robotics and neurosciences. It actuates the flexion and extension of the elbow and is characterized by four more degrees of freedom used to compensate translational and rotational movements between user and exoskeleton and thus reduce friction on the skin. It uses Bowden cables driven by hydraulic actuators (flexor and extensor) placed outside the exoskeleton. Sensors measure length and force changes on the Bowden cables. Two control strategies allow either selecting a desired home position and joint stiffness (passive-compliance control) or a desired joint torque (torque control) [58].

The elbow exoskeleton developed by Yano and colleagues was developed for rehabilitation. It has four degrees of freedom of which flexion and extension are actuated. The pressure between exoskeleton and user is measured by eight force sensing resistors. It is presumably actuated by direct current motors. The control strategy estimates the user's movement and supports it. The basic assumption for the estimation is that each movement's speed course over time resembles a bell-shaped curve, making an estimation of the whole movement possible already shortly after the movement start [75].

The orthesis developed by Tomizuka and colleagues is used for knee rehabilitation. The actuator is a rotatory series elastic actuator composed by a direct current motor, a worm drive and a torsional spring. The torsional spring acts both as energy buffer and, together with a rotary encoder, as a torque sensor [29].

The walking support exoskeleton (WSE) is an exoskeleton for the lower limbs supporting walking with crutches. It uses servo drives to actuate the knee and hip rotation in the sagittal plane [51].

8.3.2 Cognitive Aids

Several cognitive aid systems can be found in the international scientific literature. In the following, we will distinguish between time-based and event-based systems.

Time-based cognitive aids give the user a hint about executing an activity to a specific point in time. The point in time and the hint content are mostly predetermined. On the other hand, event-based cognitive aids sense the user's environment and detect events enabling them to automatically detect when the user needs a hint and what the hint content should be. Thus it also has the ability to detect extraordinary events and notify relatives or caregivers if needed.

Time-based cognitive aids are therefore suitable for cognitive aids applications involving single-events, while event-based cognitive aids are also applicable on recurring events or plans.

Time-based cognitive aids comprehend devices like timer clocks, timers or intelligent drug containers reminding the user of the drug intake. Additionally, electronic systems like dictating machines, time-controlled acoustic signals in watches, alarm clocks or mobile phones are used. The latter, as well as smartphones and PDAs, are also used as reminding aids based on their internal calendar function. Mobile phones and pagers are also being used to send out reminders to given points in time as messages.

Event-based cognitive aids are being developed in research. They also employ mobile phones as hint output devices, or newly developed portable or stationary systems.

8.3.2.1 Clinical Studies With Time-Based Systems

Various commercially available time-based systems have been scientifically evaluated concerning their usability as cognitive aids. In fact, more studies have been conducted on these devices in comparison with event-based systems, as the former are readily available on the market.

A Dictaphone was used as a simple and cost-effective reminder tool for five people with memory dysfunctions originating from brain injuries. It was shown that the device could improve the prospective memory in all participants [69]. The NeuroPage system is based on using a pager which sends the user textual reminders to fixed points in time and is managed by a service provider [73]. It has been evaluated multiple times, lastly in a randomized study with 143 participants between 8 and 83 years of age with different memory problems. An improvement in executing activities of daily living could be demonstrated in 80 % of the participants [72].

A mobile phone based system was developed and evaluated with five people with memory impairment showing an increase in the percentage of activities the participants remembered executing from 38 to 96 %. It sent reminders as phone calls with prerecorded messages [71].

Organizers showed good results too: three out of five people with memory impairments testing them for four weeks found them to increase their quality of life [4]. In other studies, the use of an organizer as cognitive aid convinced the majority of the participants [27, 28]. Cognitive aid software for organizers or smartphones is also commercially available (Fable Link Technologies, Colorado Springs, USA), but not evaluated yet.

8.3.2.2 Research on Time-Based Systems

Some systems also enable a stronger interaction between user and caregiver or relatives. The MEMOS System is a portable computer receiving reminders from a server. Both the user and the caregiver can change the reminder's time and content. It was evaluated for two weeks with nine participants and compared with a system based on a mobile phone. The MEMOS system achieved better results [60]. Memojog is a similar system which uses a PDA to output textual reminders to given points in time. The system is developed specifically for elderlies and here, too, they can change the reminders at their will. The system was tested twice with six people for 12 weeks to demonstrate its ease of use [66].

The MPVS (Mobile Phone Video Streaming) is a system able to output video-reminders on a mobile phone. These can be recorded by caregivers and shown to the user automatically timed. It was developed in multiple iterations with the aid of 27 users and evaluated with nine. They stated that the system is a valuable aid in the execution of daily tasks [16, 50]. ISAAC is a portable device, attachable to the belt, which can output reminders graphically or textually over a touchscreen or even acoustically. Caregivers can input the reminders and the device is able to determine the user's success. The system was evaluated with two users over one year. According to the participants, the system is useful for their daily routines and can increase their quality of life [20].

8.3.2.3 Research on Event-Based Systems

With Autominder, a robot was developed which is able to output reminders and attend the user in fulfilling his tasks. It is able to detect to which activities the user needs to be reminded and to which he needs assistance by observing him. It was not evaluated systemically yet [54].

The COGKNOW system was developed within the scope of an EU project and is the only system known in the international scientific literature which employs ambient-embedded sensors especially for use within elderly people's home environment. The reminder output takes place on a PDA coupled to a stationary computer within the user's home. Multiple sensors like contact sensors, movement sensors and cameras detect which activities are carried out by the user. The system was evaluated within the homes of 12 people (average age over 70) over periods of 3–8 weeks. The system's acceptance was good, however a statement about its impact on the user's quality of life was not possible [37].

8.3.3 *Vegetative Aids*

In this section we will limit our examination of the state of the art on available systems compensating thirst decrease as there are few results in the domains of compensating decrease in appetite or urge of bathroom use in research.

We will first examine in which way this is done by professional caregivers. We will then present methods used in clinical examinations and devices developed for personal use in research.

8.3.3.1 State of the Art in Care (Liquid Intake Monitoring)

According to compulsory recommendations of the Medical Review Board of the Statutory Health Insurance Funds, nursing homes in Germany must conduct spot tests to identify persons at risk of dehydration. When a person is at risk, a liquid balance protocol must be kept on a daily basis [8, 59].

As liquid dispersion is usually harder to observe in the course of the day, these protocols are simplified to a liquid intake protocol which is then compared to a calculated demand. The latter is determined based on person-independent guidelines or calculated using standard methods [10, 23, 63].

Liquid intake protocols are taken based on observations of caregivers about how often they refill glasses. These observations are then written down on a list, mostly rounded, and added up. When a discrepancy between intake and demand is detected, actions like reminding, motivating to drink more or even infusions are taken.

8.3.3.2 State of the Art in Clinical Examinations (Dehydration Detection)

In clinical settings, e.g. hospitals, dehydration is diagnosed based on several symptoms which comprehend standing skin folds, rifty tongue, dry mucosae, blood pressure drop when standing up or low filling of the throat veins when lying.

In unclear situations, the central venous pressure and the pressure inside the left ventricle can be measured or a radiography of the chest can be done [57]. When observing the hydration status over few days changes in body mass can be examined, as changes of more than 0.5 kg per day are related to liquids [3]. There are other methods for determining the hydration status, however they are not very relevant in clinical practice [62].

8.3.3.3 Research on Aids for Thirst Decrease Compensation

Research on personal assistive devices for compensation of thirst decrease aim at automating the detection of the hydration state and increasing the accurateness of measurements.

One of the first approaches was to integrate a weighting scale into a thermos flask and connecting it to a computer analyzing the data. It was tested with two elderly people [67].

A similar system was developed, using a bottle cooler as a base which is able to detect the weight of its filling and to give an acoustic warning in case the user is drinking too few [65].

Playful Bottle allows connecting a special cup to mobile phones. The software running on the phone detects the cup's filling level with its camera and markings on the cup upon movement of the cup. Games on the phone can be used to motivate to drink more. It was evaluated with 16 caregivers [11].

Another system combines movement sensors attached to the wrist and an electromagnetic inclination indicator attached to the shoulder to detect drinking movements and quantity. It was tested on six students [2].

8.3.4 Past Results

In the past years, our group's main focus lied on developing monitoring devices which can be used to assess parameters allowing an inference on the user's physical and cognitive state in various settings [32]. These devices serve as a base to develop personal assistive devices for elderlies supporting in physical, cognitive or vegetative tasks.

In this section, we will shortly give an overview on the main results in the applications of assessing human motion, detecting human interactions and collecting these data on a platform for the home setting.

For all the devices, one common HCI approach to simplify the usability for examiners was to use memory cards for data storage and set up of the recording parameters. Data is saved on the cards as comma separated value format, which can be opened with a variety of third party software. Setting up the parameters can be done by changing a text file, thus no specific software or knowledge is needed. The meaning and supported ranges for the parameters is explained in the same text file. Also, the device configuration can thus be changed by exchanging the memory card, which is a fast and easy operation even for the user. In case the examiner or user erase the configuration file by error, the device generates a new one with standard setting automatically.

Direct feedback about the device operation is given to the user through three LEDs. Their configuration is kept consistent through all the devices as one LED indicates battery status (loading, loaded or almost empty), one LED indicates the recording status (recording in progress or not), and one LED indicates errors (lights

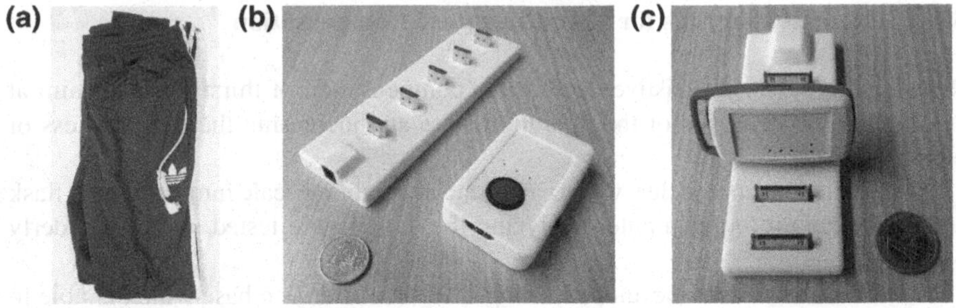

Fig. 8.5 **a** Textile Logger pants with embedded acceleration sensors. **b** Textile Logger electronic unit (*right*) for data logging on SD Card and reprogramming with charging station for up to 5 units (left). **c** EventLogger for detection of interaction with daily life objects on charging station

up on error). The specific error message is then recorded on an error text file on the memory card.

8.3.4.1 Textile-Integrated Movements Recording: Textile Loggers

The goal of the measurement textile project was to have a non-obtrusive, non-stigmatizing device usable for the recording of bodily movements (for several limbs) in everyday life, at home or underway. From a HCI perspective, the goal was to embed the sensing device in the user's daily workflow as much as possible. Therefore we integrated the system into a piece of clothing which can be put on in the usual way, without having to attach additional wires or straps. For the same reason, it must also be possible to wash the system into a normal washing machine, to avoid an increase in the maintenance effort.

The resulting "Textile Loggers" are a combination of sweater and pants (Fig. 8.5a) with embedded acceleration sensors. These do not differ optically from other sweaters or pants and are washable in a washing machine with a washing temperature of up to 40 °C. All sensors are connected to an electronics unit via a watertight connector. The electronics unit (Fig. 8.5b) is placed in a pocket of the textile and must be removed before washing. It contains a processing unit (μC), 2.4 GHz radio chip, real time clock, SD card, accumulator as well as a beeper and various status LEDs and electronic power management components.

With the Textile Loggers it is possible to record and digitalize acceleration data of 8 (sweater) or 5 (pants) sensors with a sampling frequency of up to 20 Hz, within a measuring range of ±2, ±4 or ±8 g in three spatial directions and with a resolution of 10 bit. The acceleration data can be time-stamped and processed on the device, saved on the removable SD card (in a comma separated text file) or exported via radio to receivers distant up to 5 m (see Sect. 8.3.4.5). The device has an energetical autonomy of 8 h.

We implemented and evaluated applications aimed at detecting falls [45], activity level of upper and lower body [46, 47] as well as tremor [48] and freezing of gait [49, 76] in Parkinson's patients.

8.3.4.2 Portable Movement Recording: MotionLogger

The goal of this project was to develop a portable, small and lightweight device usable for the recording of bodily movements on one body position in everyday life, at home or underway. It must be similar to a key fob in size, and allow application-specific data analysis, similarly to the measuring textiles. The user interface is kept to a minimum, as there are only the mentioned LEDs. There are no buttons: the device is always on and recording, except when it is not in motion.

The MotionLogger is a device which can be worn in a trouser or shirt pocket or attached to a necklace. It contains a single acceleration sensor, a processing unit (μC), 2.4 GHz radio chip, real time clock, μSD card, an accumulator, various status LEDs and electronic power management components.

With it, it is possible to record and digitalize acceleration data at the wearing spot with the same specification as the Textile Loggers. The device has an energetical autonomy of 4 h.

On this device we implemented and evaluated an application for the detection of movement [14].

8.3.4.3 Event Recording: EventLogger

The goal of this project was to develop a portable, small and lightweight device usable for the recording of events in everyday life at home. An important requisite was to preserve the user's privacy as much as possible, which lead to excluding cameras, microphones, and motion or door contact sensors in order to avoid the recording of video, audio or location information about the user. As Events we define interactions with objects of daily use, which can be used to infer the activities the user executes. It must be possible to install the system in a home without modifications to the building, the detection of events must be person-specific and the detection range must be specifiable for each object.

The result was the EventLogger: it works on the same hardware platform as the MotionLogger (Fig. 8.5c). However, it is both worn by the user and attached to daily use objects. The user-worn EventLogger detects entering a specifiable radius of EventLoggers attached to daily life objects and records it as an event.

Events can be recorded with a sampling frequency up to 2 Hz for detection radii which can be varied in 63 steps up to 5 m. Events are time-stamped and saved on the removable μSD card (in a comma separated text file) or exported via radio to receivers distant up to 5 m (see Sect. 8.3.4.5). The device has an energetical autonomy of 4 h. A similar device "RFID-Logger" has been developed as a wrist-worn device

Fig. 8.6 **a** Embedded network gateway server for wireless data reception, storage and distribution over LAN. **b** Home care unit for central data storage and user interaction

used to detect events as interactions with daily use objects tagged with UHF RFID tags.

With this device we implemented and evaluated applications for the detection of activities of daily living [15, 40, 42–44].

8.3.4.4 Software Development Environment

One requirement to the development of the mentioned devices was their openness for easy reprogramming for the development of new applications or optimization of the implemented applications by updating their firmware. In addition to reprogramming, they should also allow the fine-tuning of application specific parameters for people who are not experts in programming.

For this purpose, the devices contain a μSD or SD card which can be used for data storage. On these cards, there is also a config file which can be opened with any text editor and which allows changing the application parameters, e.g. the sampling frequency in the Textile Loggers. If the user happens to erase the config file, it is automatically restored with standard parameters as soon as the card is inserted into the device.

The cards can also be used for updating the device's firmware. Once modified, the binary file of the new firmware is stored onto the card, the card is inserted into the device and it will automatically update its firmware upon reset. Thus, no programmer devices or additional hardware is needed for developers.

8.3.4.5 Communication and Data Collection Infrastructure

Monitoring devices for daily life use must be able to export collected data in a safe, power-saving and automatic way. It must also be possible to store and further process or display the collected data in a central device within the user's home.

For this purpose, we developed a communication infrastructure consisting of "Embedded Network Gateway Servers" (Fig. 8.6a) and a central data collection hub, the "Home Care Unit" (Fig. 8.6b).

The EventLogger, Textile Loggers and MotionLogger can export collected data up to 5 m distance in a batch or stream, as long as a radio receiver using their power-saving 2.4 GHz protocol is nearby. The Home Care Unit contains such a receiver as well as an embedded computer with a 7″ touchscreen, speakers, microphone, Local Area Network (LAN), Wireless LAN (WLAN) and Universal Mobile Telecommunications System (UMTS) interfaces. It is thus possible to export data to the Home Care Unit and process or visualize it there, as long as the user is in the same room. The Home Care Unit was developed with feedback about early prototypes from potential users. For example, users suggested making the display tiltable in order to adjust it to the personal point of view and to give an auditory feedback for every registered touch input [13]. The Embedded Network Gateway Server, on the other hand, contains a radio receiver and a LAN interface, thus it can receive data over the 2.4 GHz radio network while the user is in another room and forward it to the Home Care Unit via the home LAN [41].

8.4 Open Problems

In this section, we will examine the suitability of the presented solutions for the mentioned applications as far as currently known, give a qualitative overview and analyze them in respect to room for improvement.

8.4.1 Physical Aids

In the category of physical aids, mobility aids are well established devices for the support of position changes. Passive, stabilizing mobility aids like walking frames help reducing the risk of falls, but they do not support the user amplifying his strength. On the other hand, active mobility aids like electromobiles help decreasing the risk of fatigue but they increase the risk of accidents as their operation requires faster reaction times then walking. Also, the user interface which is mostly a joystick might not be intuitive enough to steer the vehicle.

The currently employed methods and devices for supporting the change of body posture also offer room for improvement: Several studies show that caregivers are exposed to an increased risk of musculoskeletal injuries [9, 36] which oftentimes leads to working inability. This risk is correlated with the often lifting tasks associated with the job, for example when lifting people from (wheel) chairs [6]. The available lifters on the market, on the other hand, are not used often enough. Studies show that such systems are used only in 2 % of all transfer tasks [19]. Reasons for this are their big size and weight, difficult handling, high time effort needed for their used in comparison with manual transfers and finally safety issues, as problems with the belt systems can lead to serious injuries [5, 18]. Bariatric aids which combine position change and posture change support are mostly developed for obese people, but we

Table 8.1 Physical aids listed by application and method

Method	Device	Changing position (stabilization/ support)	Changing posture (stabilization/ support)	Manipulating the environment (stabilization/ support)	Example
Manually	Relative/ caregiver	+/0	+/0	−/0	Nursing home
Rolling	Frame	+/−	−/−	−/−	Walking frame
Rolling	Vehicle	+/−	−/−	−/−	Wheelchair
Electrical drive	Vehicle	0/+	−/−	−/−	Electromobile
Lever/pneumatic drive or spring	Frame	−/−	−/0	−/−	Lifter
Electrical drive	Whole body exoskeleton	0/0	0/0	0/0	Kasaoka and Sankai [24]
Pneumatic drive	Whole body exoskeleton	0/0	0/0	0/0	Yamamoto et al. [74]
Linear series elastic actuator	Knee exoskeleton	0/0	0/0	−/−	Pratt et al. [56]
Rotary series elastic actuator	Lower body exoskeleton	0/0	0/0	−/−	Ekkelenkamp et al. [17, 29]
Electrical drive	Upper limb exoskeleton	−/−	−/−	0/0	Perry and Rosen [52], Yano et al. [75]
Hydraulic drive	Shoulder exoskeleton	−/−	−/−	0/0	Sarellitti et al. [58]

Support empowering, e.g. strength or endurance increase; Stabilization: risk factor, e.g. reduction of fall risk while changing position or empowering without risk increase; *Example* Specific environment, product or reference employing the method; + Device is well applicable; 0 Device is fairly applicable (in research/evaluated for different application or users); − Device is not applicable

know that even with people of normal weight (50 Kg) and using the optimal transfer technique there are still risks for injuries in the lower back [34].

Table 8.1 gives a qualitative comparison of available physical aids.

8.4.2 Cognitive Aids

Small electronic devices portable on the user's body such as pagers, mobile phones, organizers or smartphones have been shown to achieve good results in supporting users in reminding single events, e.g. important appointments.

A typical evaluation method is the ABA scheme, in which the evaluation period is divided into three phases, typically lasting 3–4 weeks each. In the first phase (A, baseline) the amount of activities the user executes or forgets is observed and noted.

Table 8.2 Cognitive aids listed by application and method

Method	Device	Single events (time/event)	Recurring events (time/event)	Plans (time/event)	Example
Vocal	Relative/ caregiver	+/+	0/0	0/0	Nursing home
Audio	Portable device	+/−	0/−	−/−	van den Broek et al. [69], Wade and Troy [71]
Video	Portable device	+/−	0/−	−/−	Donnelly et al. [16], Gorman et al. [20], O' Neill et al. [50]
Text	Portable device	+/−	0/−	−/−	Baddeley and Wilson [4], Kim et al. [28], Schulze [60], Szymkowiak et al. [66], Wilson et al. [72]
Video/Audio	Mobile robot	0/0	0/0	−/−	Pllack et al. [54]
Video/Audio	Sensors smartphone stationary computer	0/0	0/0	−/−	Meiland et al. [37]

Plans complex activities involving a specific sequence of actions, e.g. cooking; *Example* Specific environment, product or reference employing the method; + Device is well applicable; 0 Device is fairly applicable (in research/evaluated for different application or users); − Device is not applicable

In the second phase (B), the user is supported by the device and again the executed and forgotten activities are monitored. The third phase (A), similar to the first, is conducted to determine whether the use of the device has some effects even after the device has been stopped using.

Unfortunately, newer event-based systems which are applicable for recurring events or support in executing plans have not been evaluated quantitatively with these scheme yet, leaving the question of their practical impact in everyday life beyond secondary requirements like usability.

Table 8.2 gives a qualitative comparison of available cognitive aids.

8.4.3 Vegetative Aids

Using tables or calculations to determine the amount of liquid needed per person is an established method in practice. The method used to take note of liquid intake,

Table 8.3 Vegetative aids for thirst decrease compensation listed by method

Method	Device	Thirst decrease (intake measurement /dehydration prevention)	Example
Observation/ documentation	Relative/caregiver	0/0	Nursing home
Weighting scale	Thermos flask	0/0	Steinbeck et al. [65], Tamura et al. [67]
Optical sensor	Portable device/bottle	0/−	Chiu et al. [11]
Orientation sensor	Portable device	+/−	Amft et al. [2]

Dehydration prevention involves intake measurement, comparison with required intake, and drinking reminder before a dehydration occurs. *Example* Specific environment, product or reference employing the method; + Device is well applicable; 0 Device is fairly applicable (in research/evaluated for different application or users); − Device is not applicable

however, can be improved. It is subjective and has accuracy limitations [31]. In addition to this, it requires a high time effort. Also, the last step, i.e. determining whether there is a discrepancy between intake and acting is not executed regularly or too late in the day to prevent dehydration from happening

Devices for the automated detection or prediction of dehydration and warning are still needed and are being developed. However, they need to integrate seamlessly into the user's daily activities and not require more attention or care than an ordinary water bottle or drinking cup.

Table 8.3 gives a qualitative comparison of the mentioned solutions for compensation of thirst decrease.

8.5 Future Outlook

As we have seen in the last sections, considerable work has been done on assistive devices for elderlies. Nevertheless, only few devices are actually in the market and are being used, effectively supporting elderly people in staying home as long as possible.

For the presented device categories, in the following we will shortly present future goals and priorities we think are of importance to make sure that useful solutions will get onto the market and be accepted.

8.5.1 Physical Aids

Observing the open problems in the devices for the support of physical applications, it becomes clear that there is a need to improve them by increasing their adaptation to the user and their level of individualization.

Devices for position change need to be improved in order to allow stabilization and support at the same time, i.e. both increasing the user's movement radius and lowering the risk for accidents and falls. Electrical powered wheelchairs amplifying the user's force input are a good example of how this support is possible in combination with an intuitive user interface which still gives the user a good control over the vehicle.

Devices for posture changes need to solve the problems of being too big in size, weight and needing too much time for handling. A good approach is integrating them directly into a chair, wheelchair or mobility aid to make them available where they are needed. In the next steps, these devices also must be adaptable to the user, in order to reduce their size and weight to the minimum needed to support this specific user.

For manipulation, until now only exoskeletons are being developed to increase the strength in the upper body. Here, too, the adaptability to the individual need is crucial to avoid friction, high pressure or too loose connection between the exoskeleton and the user, and to optimize the exoskeleton's dimensions.

Physical aids are a category of assistive devices for elderlies which will require the development of new mechatronic aids, as well as methods for their adaptability to the user movement tasks and dimensions for every single device. We believe that the current growth of rapid prototyping technology combined with automated kinematic synthesis and dimensioning methods have a high potential in this field. Ultimately, an empowerment of the user or a clear load reduction for caregivers must be proven for this category of devices to become accepted.

8.5.2 Cognitive Aids

The category of cognitive aids still hasn't arrived on the market except for very basic devices which were primarily intended for other uses. Automated solutions for the event-based reminding of activities of daily living or even execution of plans which work in a robust way and have shown to have an impact on people's daily lives are still missing. There is, however, an increasing demand not only for people with cognitive impairments but ultimately for much more people who can use them as comfort devices, or personal electronic butlers.

In this category, in future it will be important to develop, optimize further and evaluate methods for the inference of activities of daily living from sensor readings and events, and learning to use a sensor combination which is effective but easy to install, to maintain, robust and affordable. The focus must also be laid on helping the user help himself first, e.g. sending reminders to him first and including third parties only in emergencies.

These systems will have to show quantitatively, i.e. using evaluation schemes such as the ABA scheme but also developing benchmark tests to compare them, that they offer a real improvement and added value in the user's life.

8.5.3 Vegetative Aids

There is little research in the category of vegetative aids yet, especially in compensating decrease in appetite and urge of bathroom use. These fields still offer a great potential in increasing the quality of life of elderly people and making their independent living safer.

In the field of compensation of thirst decrease sensing technology will have to become more pervasive, power-efficient and robust (e.g. dish-washer safe), as well as interconnected with devices on the user which will warn him when he should drink more. Ultimately, such devices must prove to be able to increase the amount of daily liquid intake and decrease the risk of dehydration for their users to be accepted and used.

Acknowledgments The authors would like to thank all the people involved in the work of the AgeTech group at the department of Micro Technology and Medical Device Technology of the TU Muenchen.

We thank Prof. Tim C. Lueth for his valuable input and discussions about the technical classification, open problems and future outlook, as well as Samuel Reimer, Jakob Neuhaeuser and Joachim F. Kreutzer for their input regarding the state of the art in physical, cognitive and vegetative aids, respectively.

We would also like to thank the KWA Kuratorium Wohnen im Alter gAG, especially Dr. Stefan Arend and Michael Pfitzer for the interesting discussions and for letting us visit their nursing home and observe the caregivers in their daily work.

Last but not least, we are very grateful to the Alfried Krupp von Bohlen und Halbach-Stiftung for its financial support of our work.

References

1. Afentakis, A., & Maier, T. (2010). Projektionen des Personalbedarfs und-angebots in Pflegeberufen bis 2025. *Wirtschaft und Statistik, 11*, 990–1002.
2. Amft, O., Bannach, D., Pirkl, G., Kreil, M., & Lukowicz, P. (2010). Towards wearable sensing-based assessment of fluid intake. In *2010 8th IEEE International Conference on Pervasive Computing and Communications Workshops (PERCOM Workshops)* (pp. 298–303).
3. Armstrong, L. E. (2005). Hydration assessment techniques. *Nutrition Reviews, 63*, S40–54.
4. Baddeley, A. D., & Wilson, B. A. (1995). *Handbook of memory disorders*. Chichester: Wiley.
5. Bell, F. (1987). Ergonomic aspects of equipment. *International Journal of Nursing Studies, 24*, 331–337.
6. Black, T. R., Shah, S. M., Busch, A. J., Metcalfe, J., & Lim, H. J. (2011). Effect of transfer, lifting, and repositioning (TLR) injury prevention program on musculoskeletal injury among direct care workers. *Journal of Occupational and Environmental Hygiene, 8*, 226–235.
7. Böcker, M., & Schneider, M. (2014). EHealth applications for those in need: Making novel interactions technologies accessible. In A. Holzinger, M. Ziefle & C. Roecker (Eds.), *Pervasive health: State-of-the-art & beyond*, Human-Computer Interaction Series. Springer (To be published).
8. Brüggemann, J., Jung, C., Kreck, C., Kurzmann, K., Lucke, M., Schulte, C., & Wermann, O. R. (2003). Grundsatzstellungnahme Ernährung und Flüssigkeitsversorgung älterer Menschen (Abschlussbericht No. P39). Medizinischer Dienst der Spitzenverbände der Krankenkassen e.V. (MDS), Essen.

9. Cheap, D. (1987). Low back injuries in nursing staff. *Occupational Medicine, 37*, 66–70.
10. Chernoff, R. (1994). Meeting the nutritional needs of the elderly in the institutional setting. *Nutrition Reviews, 52*, 132–136.
11. Chiu, M.-C., Chang, S.-P., Chang, Y.-C., Chu, H.-H., Chen, C. C.-H., & Hsiao, F.-H., et al. (2009). Playful bottle: a mobile social persuasion system to motivate healthy water intake. In *Proceedings of the 11th International Conference on Ubiquitous Computing, Ubicomp '09* (pp. 185–194). New York, NY: ACM.
12. Chu, A., Kazerooni, H., & Zoss, A. (2005). On the biomimetic design of the Berkeley lower extremity exoskeleton (BLEEX). In *Proceedings of the 2005 IEEE International Conference on Robotics and Automation. ICRA 2005* (pp. 4345–4352).
13. Czabke, A., Loeschke, J., & Lueth, T. C. (2011a). Concept and modular telemedicine platform for measuring of vital signs, ADL and behavioral patterns of elderly in home settings. In *Annual International Conference of the IEEE Engineering in Medicine and Biology Society, EMBC* (pp. 3164–3167).
14. Czabke, A., Marsch, S., & Lueth, T. C. (2011b). Accelerometer based real-time activity analysis on a microcontroller. In *5th International Conference on Pervasive Computing Technologies for Healthcare (PervasiveHealth)* (pp. 40–46).
15. Czabke, A., Neuhauser, J., & Lueth, T. C. (2010). Recognition of interactions with objects based on radio modules. In *4th International Conference on Pervasive Computing Technologies for Healthcare (PervasiveHealth)* (pp. 1–8).
16. Donnelly, M. P., Nugent, C., McClean, S., Scotney, B., Mason, S., Passmore, P., et al. (2010). A mobile multimedia technology to aid those with Alzheimer's disease. *IEEE Multimedia, 17*, 42–51.
17. Ekkelenkamp, R., Veneman, J., & van der Kooij, H. (2005). LOPES: selective control of gait functions during the gait rehabilitation of CVA patients. In *9th International Conference on Rehabilitation Robotics. ICORR 2005* (pp. 361–364).
18. Garg, A., & Owen, B. (1992). Reducing back stress to nursing personnel: An ergonomic intervention in a nursing home. *Ergonomics, 35*, 1353–1375.
19. Garg, A., Owen, B. D., & Carlson, B. (1992). An ergonomic evaluation of nursing assistants' job in a nursing home. *Ergonomics, 35*, 979–995.
20. Gorman, P., Dayle, R., Hood, C.-A., & Rumrell, L. (2003). Effectiveness of the ISAAC cognitive prosthetic system for improving rehabilitation outcomes with neurofunctional impairment. *NeuroRehabilitation, 18*, 57–67.
21. Grönvall, E., & Lundberg, S. (2014). On challenges designing the home as a place for care. In A. Holzinger, M. Ziefle & C. Roecker (Eds.), *Pervasive health: State-of-the-art & beyond*, Human-Computer Interaction Series (pp. 19–46). London: Springer.
22. Haustein, T., & Mischke, J. (2011). *In the spotlight: Older people in Germany and the EU*. Wiesbaden: Statistisches Bundesamt.
23. Institute of Medicine Staff. (1989). *Recommended dietary allowances*. Washington: National Academies Press.
24. Kasaoka, K., & Sankai, Y. (2001). Predictive control estimating operator's intention for stepping-up motion by exo-skeleton type power assist system HAL. In *Proceedings 2001 IEEE/RSJ International Conference on Intelligent Robots and Systems, 2001* (Vol. 3, pp. 1578–1583).
25. Katz, S., Ford, A. B., Moskowitz, R. W., Jackson, B. A., & Jaffe, M. W. (1963). Studies of illness in the aged. The index of ADL: A standardized measure of biological and psychosocial function. *JAMA Journal of the American Medical Association, 185*, 914–919.
26. Kazerooni, H. (2008). Exoskeletons for human performance augmentation. In B. S. Prof & O. K. Prof (Eds.), *Springer handbook of robotics* (pp. 773–793). Berlin: Springer.
27. Kim, H. J., Burke, D. T., Dowds, M. M., & George, J. (1999). Utility of a microcomputer as an external memory aid for a memory-impaired head injury patient during in-patient rehabilitation. *Brain Injury (BI), 13*, 147–150.
28. Kim, H. J., Burke, D. T., Dowds, M. M, Jr, Boone, K. A., & Park, G. J. (2000). Electronic memory aids for outpatient brain injury: Follow-up findings. *Brain Injury (BI), 14*, 187–196.

29. Kong, K., Bae, J., & Tomizuka, M. (2010). A compact rotary series elastic actuator for knee joint assistive system. In *IEEE International Conference on Robotics and Automation (ICRA)* (pp. 2940–2945).
30. Köther, I. (2005). THIEMEs Altenpflege. Zeitgemäß und zukunftsweisend, 1. A. ed. Thieme, Stuttgart.
31. Kreutzer, J., Pfitzer, M., & D'Angelo, L. T. (2013). Accuracy of caring personnel in estimating water intake based on missing liquid in drinking vessels. In *Annual International Conference of the IEEE Engineering in Medicine and Biology Society, EMBC* (Accepted for publication).
32. Lüth, T. C., D'Angelo, L. T., & Czabke, A. (2010). TUM-AgeTech: A new framework for pervasive medical devices. In A. Coronato & G. De Pietro (Eds.), *Pervasive and smart technologies for healthcare* (pp. 295–321). Hersey: IGI Global.
33. Makinson, B. J. (1971). Research and development prototype for machine augmentation of human strength and endurance. Hardiman I Project, PN.
34. Marras, W. S., Davis, K. G., Kirking, B. C., & Bertsche, P. K. (1999). A comprehensive analysis of low-back disorder risk and spinal loading during the transferring and repositioning of patients using different techniques. *Ergonomics, 42*, 904–926.
35. Mason, S., Craig, D., O'Neill, S., Donnelly, M., & Nugent, C. (2012). Electronic reminding technology for cognitive impairment. *British Journal of Nursing Mark Allen Publication, 21*, 855–861.
36. Maul, I., Laubli, T., Klipstein, A., & Krueger, H. (2003). Course of low back pain among nurses: A longitudinal study across eight years. *Occupational and Environmental Medicine, 60*, 497–503.
37. Meiland, F. J. M., Bouman, A. I. E., Sävenstedt, S., Bentvelzen, S., Davies, R. J., Mulvenna, M. D., et al. (2012). Usability of a new electronic assistive device for community-dwelling persons with mild dementia. *Aging Mental Health, 16*, 584–591.
38. Menche, N. (2011). *Pflege heute*. München: Urban & Fischer, .
39. Motel-Klingebiel, A., Wurm, S., & Tesch-Römer, C. (2010). *Altern im Wandel. Befunde des Deutschen Alterssurveys (DEAS)*. Stuttgart: Kohlhammer.
40. Neuhaeuser, J., Czabke, A., & Lueth, T. C. (2011a). First steps towards a recognition of ADLs with radio modules. In *13th IEEE International Conference on E-Health Networking Applications and Services (Healthcom)* (pp. 225–228).
41. Neuhaeuser, J., & D'Angelo, L. (2013). Collecting and distributing wearable sensor data: An embedded personal area network to local area network gateway server. In *35th Annual International Conference of the IEEE Engineering in Medicine and Biology Society (EMBC)* (pp. 4650–4653).
42. Neuhaeuser, J., Diehl-Schmid, J., & Lueth, T. C. (2011b). Evaluation of a radio based ADL interaction recognition system in a day hospital for old age psychiatry with healthy probands. In *Annual International Conference of the IEEE Engineering in Medicine and Biology Society, EMBC* (pp. 1814–1818).
43. Neuhaeuser, J., Proebstl, D., D'Angelo, L. T., & Lueth, T. C. (2012a). First application of behavoir recognition through the recording of ADL by radio modules in a home. In *Annual International Conference of the IEEE Engineering in Medicine and Biology Society (EMBC)* (pp. 5841–5845).
44. Neuhaeuser, J., Wilkening, M., Diehl-Schmid, J., & Lueth, T. C. (2012b). Different sADL day patterns recorded by an interaction-system based on radio modules. In R. Wichert & B. Eberhardt (Eds.), *Ambient assisted living* (pp. 95–105). Berlin: Springer.
45. Niazmand, K., Jehle, C., D'Angelo, L. T., & Lueth, T. C. (2010). A new washable low-cost garment for everyday fall detection. In *Annual International Conference of the IEEE Engineering in Medicine and Biology Society (EMBC)* (pp. 6377–6380).
46. Niazmand, K., Neuhaeuser, J., & Lueth, T. C. (2012). A washable smart shirt for the measurement of activity in every-day life. In R. Wichert & B. Eberhardt (Eds.), *Ambient assisted living* (pp. 333–345). Berlin: Springer.
47. Niazmand, K., Somlai, I., Louizi, S., & Lueth, T. C. (2011a). Proof of the accuracy of measuring pants to evaluate the activity of the hip and legs in everyday life. *Lecture Notes Institute of Computer Science Society Information Telecommunication Engineering*, 55, 235.

48. Niazmand, K., et al. (2011b). A measurement device for motion analysis of patients with Parkinson's disease using sensor based smart clothes. In *5th International Conference on Pervasive Computing Technologies for Healthcare (PervasiveHealth)* (pp. 9–16).
49. Niazmand, K., et al. (2011c). Freezing of Gait detection in Parkinson's disease using accelerometer based smart clothes. In *IEEE Biomedical Circuits and Systems Conference (BioCAS)* (pp. 201–204).
50. O'Neill, S. A., Mason, S., Parente, G., Donnelly, M. P., Nugent, C. D., McClean, S., et al. (2010). Video reminders as cognitive prosthetics for people with dementia. *Ageing International, 36*, 267–282.
51. Onen, U., Botsali, F. M., Kalyoncu, M., Tinkir, M., Yilmaz, N., & Sahin, Y. (2013). *Design and actuator selection of a lower extremity exoskeleton*. Early Access Online: IEEEASME Transaction Mechatronics.
52. Perry, J. C., & Rosen, J. (2006). Design of a 7 degree-of-freedom upper-limb powered exoskeleton. In *The First IEEE/RAS-EMBS International Conference on Biomedical Robotics and Biomechatronics. BioRob 2006* (pp. 805–810).
53. Pfaff, H. (2011). Pflegestatistik 2009. Pflege Im Rahm. Pflegeversicherung-Deutschlandergebnisse Wiesb.
54. Pollack, M. E., Brown, L., Colbry, D., McCarthy, C. E., Orosz, C., Peintner, B., et al. (2003). Autominder: An intelligent cognitive orthotic system for people with memory impairment. *Robotics and Autonomous Systems, 44*, 273–282. doi:10.1016/S0921-8890(03)00077-0.
55. Pons, J. L. (2008). Wearable robots: Biomechatronic exoskeletons (1st ed.). Berlin: Wiley.
56. Pratt, J. E., Krupp, B. T., Morse, C. J., & Collins, S. H. (2004). The RoboKnee: An exoskeleton for enhancing strength and endurance during walking. In *2004 IEEE International Conference on Robotics and Automation. Proceedings ICRA '04* (Vol. 3, pp. 2430–2435).
57. Rüchardt, A., & Lydtin, H. (1999). Störungen des Natrium- und Wasserhaushaltes Diagnostik und Therapie. *Internist, 40*, 861–871.
58. Sardellitti, I., et al. (2006). Description, characterization and assessment of a bioInspired shoulder joint-first link robot for neurorobotic applications. In *The First IEEE/RAS-EMBS International Conference on Biomedical Robotics and Biomechatronics. BioRob 2006* (pp. 112–117).
59. Schulin, B. (2001). *SGB XI - Soziale Pflege-Versicherung*. München: Dt. Taschenbuch-Verl.
60. Schulze, H. (2004). MEMOS: A mobile extensible memory aid system. *Telemedicine Journal of E-Health (Office Journal of American Telemedicine Association), 10*, 233–242.
61. Seo, K., & Ryu, H. (2014). RehabMaster: A pervasive rehabilitation platform for stroke patients and their caregivers. In A. Holzinger, M. Ziefle, & C. Roecker (Eds.), *Pervasive health: State-of-the-art & beyond*, Human-Computer Interaction Series (pp. 131–156). London: Springer.
62. Shirreffs, S. M. (2000). Markers of hydration status. *Journal of Sports Medicine and Physical Fitness, 40*, 80–84.
63. Skipper, A. (1998). *Dietitian's handbook of enteral and parenteral nutrition*. Sudbury: Jones & Bartlett Learning.
64. Statistisches Bundesamt (2012). Gesundheit Ausgaben 2010 Fachserie 12 Reihe 7.1.1.
65. Steinbeck, F., Klieber, T., Grimmert, T., Stürenburg, H. J., & Staemmler, M. (2008). Erinnerungs- und Monitoringsystem zur Flüssigkeitsaufnahme. Presented at the Jahrestagung der Deutschen Gesellschaft für Medizinische Informatik, Biometrie und Epidemiologie e.V., Stuttgart.
66. Szymkowiak, A., et al. (2004). Memojog: An interactive memory aid with remote communication. Cambridge: Access and Assistive Technology (CWUAAT).
67. Tamura, T., Miyasako, S., Ichinoseki, N., Nambu, A., & Suenaga, T. (2002). A water supply telemonitoring system as a assistive device for the nurses and caregivers. In *Engineering in Medicine and Biology. 24th Annual Conference and the Annual Fall Meeting of the Biomedical Engineering Society EMBS/BMES Conference. Proceedings of the Second Joint* (Vol. 3, pp. 1857–1858).
68. Turner, K. J. (2014). Managing telehealth and telecare. In A. Holzinger, M. Ziefle & C. Roecker (Eds.), *Pervasive health: State-of-the-art & beyond*, Human-Computer Interaction Series (pp. 157–180). London: Springer.

69. Van den Broek, M. D., Downes, J., Johnson, Z., Dayus, B., & Hilton, N. (2000). Evaluation of an electronic memory aid in the neuropsychological rehabilitation of prospective memory deficits. *Brain Injury (BI), 14*, 455–462.
70. Voges, W. (2007). Soziologie des höheren Lebensalters: Ein Studienbuch zur Gerontologie, 1, Aufl. ed. Maro Verlag.
71. Wade, T. K., & Troy, J. C. (2001). Mobile phones as a new memory aid: A preliminary investigation using case studies. *Brain Injury (BI), 15*, 305–320.
72. Wilson, B., Emslie, H., Quirk, K., & Evans, J. (2001). Reducing everyday memory and planning problems by means of a paging system: A randomised control crossover study. *Journal of Neurology, Neurosurgery and Psychiatry, 70*, 477–482.
73. Wilson, B. A., Evans, J. J., Emslie, H., & Malinek, V. (1997). Evaluation of NeuroPage: A new memory aid. *Journal of Neurology, Neurosurgery and Psychiatry, 63*, 113–115.
74. Yamamoto, K., Hyodo, K., Ishii, M., & Matsuo, T. (2002). Development of power assisting suit for assisting nurse labor. *JSME Japan Society of Mechanical Engineers International, 45*, 703–711.
75. Yano, K., Hashimura, J., Aoki, T., & Nishimoto, Y. (2009). Flexion-extension motion assistance using an upper limb motion-assist robot based on trajectory estimation of reaching movement. In *Annual International Conference of the IEEE Engineering in Medicine and Biology Society. EMBC 2009* (pp. 4599–4602).
76. Zhao, Y., et al. (2012). Online FOG identification in Parkinson's disease with a time-frequency combined algorithm. In *2012 IEEE-EMBS International Conference on Biomedical and Health Informatics (BHI)* (pp. 192–195).
77. Ziefle, M., Roecker, C., & Holzinger, A. (2014). From computer innovation to human integration: Current trends and challenges for pervasive health technologies. In J. Karat & J. Vanderdonckt, (Eds.), *Pervasive health: State-of-the-art & beyond* (pp. 1–17). London: Springer Verlag.

Further Reading

78. Bardram, J. E., Mihailidis, A., & Wan, D. (2007). *Pervasive computing in healthcare*. Boca Raton: CRC Press.
79. Coronato, A., & De Pietro, G. (2010). *Pervasive and smart technologies for healthcare: Ubiquitous methodologies and tools*. Hershey: Medical Information Science Reference.
80. Lesnoff-Caravaglia, G. (2007). *Gerontechnology: Growing old in a technological society*. Springfield, Ill: Thomas.
81. Pons, J. L. (2008). *Wearable robots: Biomechatronic exoskeletons*. Chichester: Wiley
82. Rocon, E., & Pons, J. L. (2011). *Exoskeletons in rehabilitation robotics tremor suppression*. Berlin: Springer.
83. Winter, D. A. (2009). *Biomechanics and motor control of human movement*. Hoboken, NJ: Wiley.

Chapter 9
Sleep Quality Monitoring with the Smart Bed

Daniel Waltisberg, Bert Arnrich and Gerhard Tröster

9.1 Introduction

Sleep has a paramount effect on our physical and mental health in many aspects. Without sufficient high quality sleep, we feel tired, without energy, and are less productive at work, at school or in sports. These subjective impressions have been consistently confirmed in literature. In studies it has been shown that sleep deprivation has negative effects on cognitive performance with no significant difference between acute sleep deprivation [29, 36] or the cumulative effects of chronic sleep restriction to less than 7 h per night [9, 18]. Other studies have even shown that sleep deficiency harms the driving ability as much as being drunk [38, 47].

For a clinical sleep examination one has to visit a sleep laboratory and to undergo a sleep study. In a sleep study with polysomnography (PSG), several body functions such as brain activity, eye movement, heart rhythm are recorded and evaluated, giving evidence of the quality and quantity of sleep. In sleep medicine, PSG is the 'gold standard' to determine sleep stages, sleep quality and the diagnosis of sleep disorders [5, 21, 28]. However, traditional PSG has several drawbacks. First of all, the patients need to sleep with obtrusive sensors in an unfamiliar environment which can make it difficult to fall asleep. Additionally, the setup is cumbersome and during the whole night an assistant needs to ensure that no problems occur, i.e. no wires break loose. Together with the required equipment, this makes an overnight study expensive, and usually only one night is recorded per patient. As alternative,

D. Waltisberg (✉) · G. Tröster
Electronics Laboratory, ETH Zürich, Zürich, Switzerland
e-mail: daniel.waltisberg@ife.ee.ethz.ch

G. Tröster
e-mail: troester@ife.ee.ethz.ch

B. Arnrich
Department of Computer Engineering, Bogazici University, Istanbul, Turkey
e-mail: bert.arnrich@boun.edu.tr

A. Holzinger et al. (eds.), *Pervasive Health*, Human–Computer Interaction Series,
DOI: 10.1007/978-1-4471-6413-5_9, © Springer-Verlag London 2014

unattended portable monitoring (PM) with at least 4 physiological channels was described in literature [16, 28] to be used in selected cases if PSG is not applicable. This reduces operation cost, but doesn't solve the problem with the cumbersome setup and is not applicable for routinely checkups or continuous recordings over an extended period of time.

While the information gained from PSG and PM is important for certain types of evaluations, it may not be essential to know the specific sleep stages or to record all physiological parameters, but primarily the information about the sleep-wake rhythm is required [42]. In actigraphy a portable device, usually worn at the wrist, records movements during several days and nights and estimates these sleep-wake patterns. Actigraphy is an accepted alternative for the healthy population or for patients with certain disorders such as circadian rhythm disorders or insomnia [30, 42]. When more detailed information is required, there is no way around the traditional recordings.

In the case of elderly people the most prevalent sleep complaints are circadian rhythm changes, sleep-disordered breathing, period limb movements, medical illness or medication use [6] and the sleep can be further affected by various reasons like pain or other age-related changes. The sleep quality does not only influence the daily receptiveness and cooperation, but can also lead to pressure ulcers when there are not enough self-induced movements during the night [11]. Traditionally, the risk of pressure ulcers is assessed with a questionnaire and a person with a high risk is relocated every few hours in a night based on a predefined schedule. However, since the risk assessment with a questionnaire does not represent the actual movements during the sleep but only the subjective observation, questionnaires might over- or under-estimate the actual risk [34]. With actigraphy, the sleep-wake rhythm could be described and help to identify certain sleep disorders, but it is not suitable for pressure ulcer prevention since it is not sensitive enough for the distinction between position shifts or other smaller movements.

The described situation is only one of many where the objective of the current research is to measure sleep quality and sleep movements for several days. To be accepted by the users such a system should be user-friendly and truly unobtrusive, i.e. not require to attach electrodes or to wear devices.

In this chapter we will focus on intelligent bed systems which measure relevant signals and give insight into sleep quality and sleep disturbances. After an overview of related state-of-the-art sleep monitoring systems, we focus on the Mobility Monitor as a particular example of a monitoring system developed for the support of elderly care facilities. To demonstrate the application of the Mobility Monitor, we describe two case examples from nursing homes. We further present a recent observational study in a nursing home and a geriatric hospital and show how the insights were used to adopt individual measures and to improve the care quality. We conclude the chapter with a review of open problems and challenges and give an outlook on the current research.

9.2 Glossary

Pressure ulcer Pressure ulcers, also known as bedsores, are dermal injuries which occur when pressure or pressure in combination with shear and/or friction is applied to skin for a longer time, resulting in a completely or partially obstructed blood flow. Elderly and immobile people are at highest risk of developing pressure ulcers.

Relocation, Repositioning In order to avoid the development of pressure ulcers, the patient's position needs to be changed every few hours by nursing staff.

Polysomnography Polysomnography (PSG) is a type of sleep study in a sleep laboratory where a number of physiological body signals is recorded. A minimum of 12 channels is required, including brain activity (EEG), eye movement (EOG) and heart rhythm (ECG), airflow, respiratory effort and oxygen saturation.

Sleep Staging Based on the PSG record, sleep is classified into 5 stages (Wake, REM, NREM1-3) according to the AASM standard [21]. This sleep staging is done visually by sleep experts which classify the whole night in 30 s time windows.

Actigraphy A small portable sensor which is usually worn at the wrist, records movements over several days and nights. Using the fact that during sleep there is little movement and during wake phase there is an increased movement, it computes sleep-wake patterns and the total sleep time.

Ballistocardiography Ballistocardiography (BCG) is a measure of the ballistic forces of the heart. It can be recorded by noninvasive methods from the surface of the body and has been used in bed systems to estimate the heart rate.

9.3 State-of-the-Art

In the past decades, a wide range of methods for the contact-free measurement of sleep-related parameters has been developed. We present related work from literature and some commercially available systems from the last decade, but the main focus of this section will be on the Mobility Monitor, a newly developed monitoring system for elderly care facilities. We present an observational study with nine patients from a nursing home and a geriatric hospital, and based on selected application examples, we will highlight the use of a modern monitoring system for nursing homes and their employees.

9.3.1 Related Work

In the past, the bed has often been used as a place for the recording of physiological signals [4], but the focus was rarely on contactless and unobtrusive recordings. With miniaturization and the increased computational power available in the twentieth century, such unobtrusive systems have become feasible and interesting for the consumer market [20].

9.3.1.1 Scientific Studies

Physiologically, a person lying in a bed generates signals corresponding to body movements, respiration rhythm and heart rhythm which overlay each other. In literature different sensor technologies have been integrated into beds, i.e.

- Force sensors: Strain gauges [14], load cells [2, 8, 43, 44] or more sophisticated force measuring systems [12] are placed under bedposts, integrated into the bed frame, or placed under the bed mattress.
- Piezoelectric sensors: The piezoelectric effect describes the internal generation of electrical charge when a force is applied to the material. The material is usually a thin and flexible film [23, 25, 31, 37] which is placed under the bed mattress, a piezoelectric film sensor under the mattress topper [33], or a solid piezoceramic sensor [32, 41] placed under the bedposts.
- Pressure sensors: Sensors are placed under the pillow [49] or the bed mattress [17, 27, 46], or integrated directly into tubes of an air filled bed mattress [22].

In contrast to traditional PSG [21], no standards or best practices for contactless and unobtrusive bed sensing have been established. Although PSG is usually used as reference for unobtrusive measurements, only few papers have compared the different sensor systems between each other. In [40], a comparison between an air-mattress, load cell and EMFi-film system was done, but focussed only on the automatic beat detection in the ballistocardiogram with similar results for all systems. As to our knowledge, a detailed comparison including respiration and movements has not been done yet. This can be partially explained by the complex and sophisticated system setup. A comparison should further not only evaluate the accuracy but also include practical parameters like feasibility, costs and usability.

In the following we describe some of the most advanced systems in more detail.

Force Sensors

At the biomedical engineering division of the Oregon Health and Science University, a system with force sensors under the bedposts was developed and used in various publications. The system was used to detect movements [1, 2] with a low error rate of 3.22 %. It was further developed to classify lying positions [7], and to classify disordered breathing segments with a sensitivity of 0.77 and a specificity of 0.91 [8].

A similar system with load cells under the bedposts was presented in [48] for the detection of movements and for sleep/wake staging. It was further improved in [43] and [44] to detect BCG peaks and to estimate slow wave sleep episodes (deep sleep stages) with a sensitivity of 0.81 and a specificity of 0.94.

Brink et al. describe in [12] specialized system with high-resolution force sensors under the bedposts. They evaluated body movements, respiration rate and heart rate and achieved an agreement of about 2–3 bpm for the heart rate, and a similar accuracy for the respiration rate. In the following, the system was used in studies to detect the influence of aircraft noise on these physiological sleep parameters [13].

Bruser et al. [14] focused on the detection of the BCG signal and accurate beat-to-beat (RR) intervals. Strain gauges were mounted on one slat of a bed frame and an advanced algorithm was applied to detect single heart beats. The evaluation showed low false positive and false negative rates (0.12 and 0.41 %) and the mean absolute error of the RR intervals was 16.61 ms.

Piezoelectric Sensors

In [32] and [41] ceramic sensors were placed under the bed posts and were used to measure heartbeat, respiration, turning movements and scratching. They showed a good signal to noise ratio for the heartbeat (40 dB) and respiration (14 dB), but no clinical evaluation was done yet.

A thin and flexible film called EMFi has been used in various publications. In [3], measurements of the ballistocardiographic signal in sitting and horizontal positions have shown that the acquired waveform is highly position- and person-dependent. However, Kortelainen et al. showed in [25] that classification of REM and NRM sleep based on the estimated heart-beat interval and movements is achievable with a total accuracy of 79 %. For a more detailed review on cardiorespiratory signals in PVDF and EMFi materials see [37].

Pressure Sensors

In Watanabe et al. [45, 46] an air cushion under the bed mattress was used to measure simultaneously heartbeat, respiration and body movement, and they created a mathematical sleep model which included a sleep stage estimator. Several bench tests and feasibility studies were carried out and showed a good agreement with the reference measurements. The system was further developed in [26] and [27] to distinguish REM sleep and sleep depth based on heartbeat and body-movement signals.

Pressure pads on top of the bed mattress were used in the noninvasive analysis of physiological signals (NAPS) system presented in Mack et al. [17]. In overnight studies with 40 healthy subjects, the heart and breathing rates were evaluated. The deviation from reference was 2.72 beats per minute for the heart rate and 2.10 breaths per minute for the respiration rate.

In Shin et al. [22, 39] the differential output of two balancing tubes of an air-mattress system was used for the estimation of heart and respiration rates and for the detection of snoring, sleep apnea events and body movements.

With a water-filled vinyl tube placed under a pillow, a long-term monitoring system was developed and presented in various publications [15, 49, 50]. The system allows an unobtrusive recording of heart rate, respiration rate and body movements during a long period.

9.3.1.2 Commercial Systems

There is a number of companies which have seen the bed as a suitable place for the measurement of various sleep parameters.

The company EMFIT[1] is the developer of the piezoelectric film EMFi, which has been used in several publications [23, 25, 37]. The film creates a charge which is proportional to the applied force. The sensitivity of the material is sufficient to measure physiologic parameters like movement activity, heart and respiration rhythm. Products with applications ranging from bed exit and activity detection to vital monitoring and sleep quality monitoring were developed and put on the market.

The company BAM Labs[2] uses a pressure mattress below the bed mattress to determine movements, bed exits, heart and breathing rates, and sleep statistics. With this platform, healthcare professionals and caregivers can monitor a group of people while performing their daily duties.

The EarlySense system[3] is a similar device which consists of a flat sensing unit placed under the mattress, a bedside monitor that processes and presents the measured data, and a central unit at the nurse station that presents the information. Selected case studies with applications from pain management, fall prevention to cardiac arrhythmia detection are presented on their homepage and show a wide application range. In a study with 49 volunteers, heart and respiration rate were compared with reference measurements and showed an absolute relative error of 4 % for both the heart and respiration rate.[4]

While most of the commercial systems are developed for the use in nursing homes or hospitals, Beddit[5] is a system for the consumer market. With long experience in ballistocardiography, they developed a thin sensor that is placed between the bed sheet and the bed mattress [33]. In combination with environmental sensors, they present the sleep information like heart rate, breathing rhythm, movements and sleep quality through an appealing visualization. For their final production they recently raised a half million dollar at indigo.[6]

In the following we will focus on the Mobility Monitor, a commercial product which was developed for the use in elderly care facilities, nursing homes or hospitals.

9.3.2 Mobility Monitor

In elderly care facilities, the requirements for the care are increasing steadily and with it the workload for the nursing personnel. To relieve the nursing staff and to ensure a high nursing quality, intelligent solutions will be needed.

[1] http://www.emfit.com

[2] http://www.bamlabs.com

[3] http://www.earlysense.com

[4] http://www.earlysense.com/clinical-evidence/white-papers/

[5] http://www.beddit.com

[6] http://www.indiegogo.com/projects/beddit-automatic-sleep-and-wellness-tracker-turn-your-bed-into-a-smart-bed

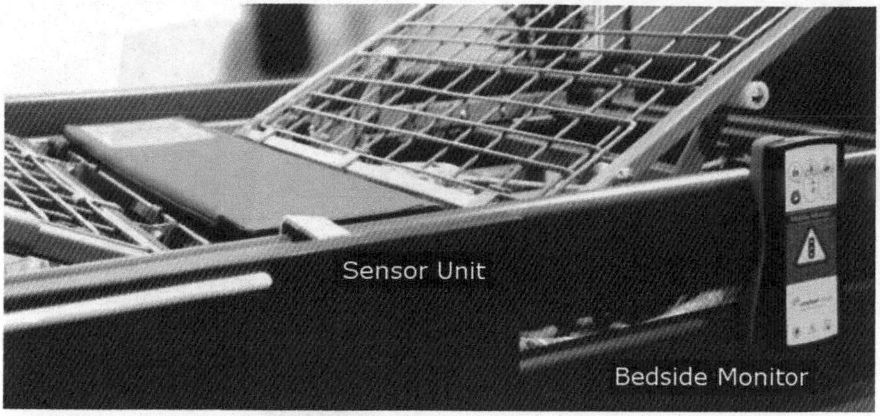

Fig. 9.1 Mobility monitor with sensor unit and bedside monitor installed on a hospital bed

The Mobility Monitor of compliant concept[7] was specifically designed for this goal, i.e. to support the nursing staff in their daily operations. To be accepted by the nursing staff it was important to integrate the system in their daily working routine and to verify that the interaction with the system is simple and convenient. The primary use of the Mobility Monitor is the risk assessment and prevention of pressure ulcer as well as the documentation. Furthermore, the Mobility Monitor can be used to monitor bed exits, to check the influence of medication on the sleep pattern or to evaluate the duration of bed occupancy for rehabilitation reasons.

The system consists of a sensor unit with integrated force sensors and a bedside monitor, see Fig. 9.1. The sensor unit is placed below the bed mattress and records the signals of a person lying inside the bed. The bedside monitor processes the signals to distinguish between small movements like leg movements and relevant, pressure relieving position changes. For the visualization of the movement pattern there are two interfaces with different resolution. A simple traffic light on the bedside monitor allows the nurse to check if any further interactions are necessary. For a detailed analysis, the movement pattern during the night can be reviewed and discussed on a personal computer.

In Sect. 9.3.2.1 we describe why nightly movements are important for the pressure ulcer prevention and how the Mobility Monitor can help to avoid unnecessary relocations. In Sect. 9.3.2.2 we present selected case examples of a nursing home and present the offline analysis and visualization on a personal computer. Finally, we describe the bedside monitor in Sect. 9.3.2.3 and present the traffic light as an example of simple human-computer interaction (HCI).

[7] http://compliant-concept.ch/en/

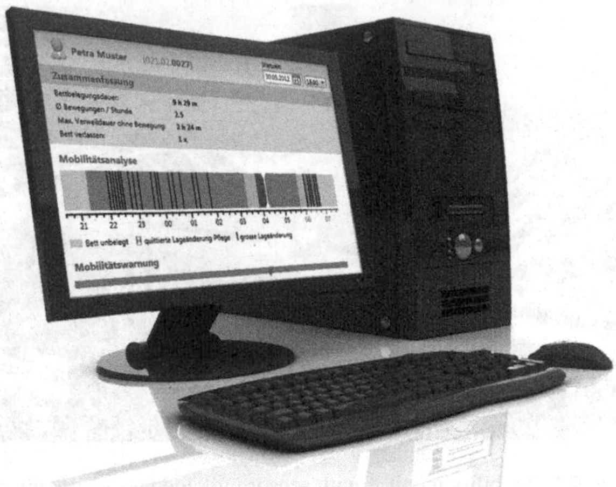

Fig. 9.2 The individual mobility profile including sleep statistics can be displayed on a personal computer. Copyright compliant concept

9.3.2.1 Background

Young and also healthy elderly people move themselves unconsciously about two to four times per hour during the night [24]. These nightly movements are a natural protection to avoid pressure ulcers. However, this movement pattern can be altered by medication or diseases which can lead to immobility and increases the risk of pressure ulcers. Traditionally, patients with pressure ulcer risk are identified based on the experience of the nursing staff and an assessment questionnaire [11]. In order to avoid pressure ulcers during the night and to ensure that all body parts are relieved, risk patients are manually relocated every few hours based on a fix schedule. These relocations are cumbersome for the patient since he has to be wakened up and the position has to be changed [19].

With the Mobility Monitor, self-induced movements of the patient are detected and the care personnel is informed through the nurse call when relocations are required. In comparison to the traditional method with a fix relocation schedule, the relocations are only carried out when necessary. This not only relieves the nursing personnel, but also improves the patient's sleep quality. Furthermore, the relocations are recorded together with the movement pattern which simplifies the documentation.

9.3.2.2 Mobility Analysis

The movement pattern and the registered relocations are automatically stored for a detailed review on a personal computer, see Fig. 9.2. Below, we describe the mobility graph based on a typical movement pattern of a healthy adult and show its practical use with two case examples of a nursing home.

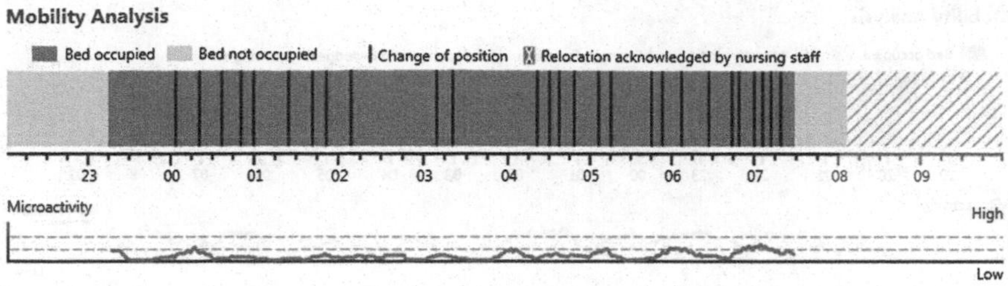

Fig. 9.3 Typical movement pattern of a healthy adult with regular movements during the night

Healthy Adult

In Fig. 9.3, the mobility analysis of a healthy male adult is shown. The bed was occupied for 8 h 15 min and position changes, indicated on the plot with black bars, were detected with an average of 3.3 movements per hour. This observation agrees well with literature, where an average of 3.6 movements per hour for an 18–24 years old person is described [24]. Additionally to the bed occupancy and position shifts, the 'microactivity' index is shown on the bottom line. The index corresponds to the occurrence of smaller movements which are not pressure relieving position changes. If the index is high, the person is restless and probably not sleeping.

Case 1: Persisting Pain

With increasing age, the average number of movements tends to reduce to about 2.1 movements per hour for a 65–80 year old person [24]. However, the movement pattern can be significantly altered by persisting pain. In Fig. 9.4, the mobility analysis of a 76-years old male patient is shown. His anamnesis showed that he has fallen at home and incurred several bruises. In the nursing home, he hid his pain from the nursing staff to avoid a longer stay. Due to his pain, he moved about 5.5 times per hour and showed an increased microactivity. Moreover, based on the assessed risk of pressure ulcers, he was relocated three times by a caregiver, indicated in the mobility analysis with white bars.

In the subsequent treatment, he received an analgesic which reduced the patient's pain and his movement activity lowered to a normal level in the following nights. Based on the mobility analysis, the risk of pressure ulcer was shown to be low and no more relocations were necessary.

Case 2: Medication

Similarly, the influence of sedatives can be observed. In Fig. 9.5, an 80-years old male patient received a sedative to reduce posture-dependent pain. The influence of the sedative can be seen when the occurrence of movement and the microactivity index

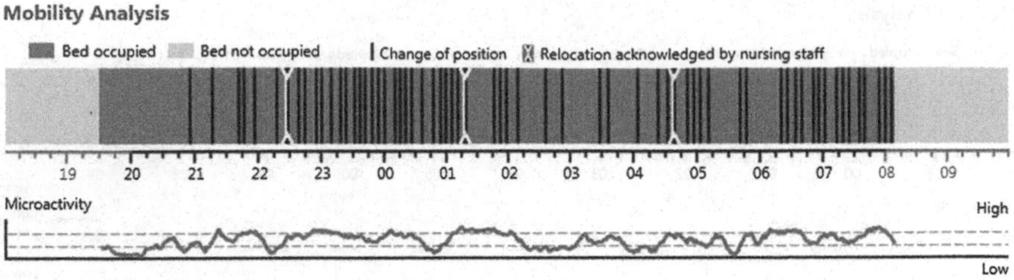

Fig. 9.4 Movement pattern of an elderly patient with increased pain-induced movements. Furthermore, the patient was repositioned three times during the night

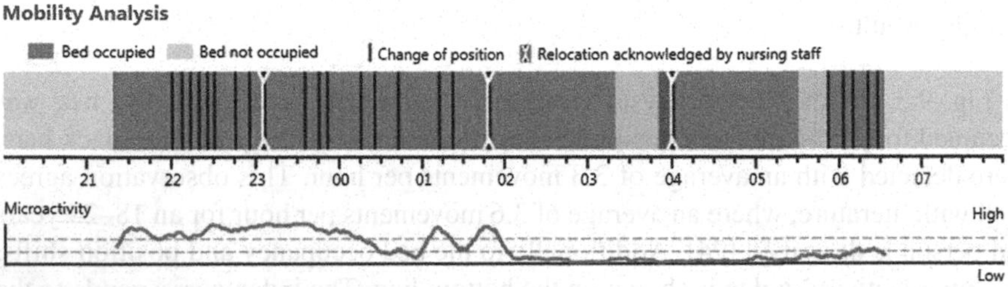

Fig. 9.5 Movement pattern of an elderly patient with a reduction of movement after a sedative was administered

drops at about 2 o'clock. In order to prevent pressure ulcers, the Mobility Monitor informed the nursing staff when no movement occurred during two hours and the patient's position was changed manually by a caregiver.

9.3.2.3 Bedside Monitor

The bedside monitor is used to adjust settings, to register relocations and to give a quick overview to the nursing personnel to check if further interactions are required. With the use of a simple traffic light (see Fig. 9.6), the complex information of the movement pattern is reduced to the crucial information if the patient has enough self-induced movements: green for normal mobility, orange for reduced mobility and red for critical mobility.

During the night shift, the responsible nurse is not overwhelmed by the information of this simple HCI interface, but instead has an overview about the crucial data at this time. For a detailed review in the morning, it is still possible to have a closer look at the detailed mobility analysis on a personal computer.

Fig. 9.6 A simple traffic light helps the nurse to know if the patient has had enough self-induced movements in the previous hours

9.3.3 Observational Study

To show the usability and benefit of a sleep monitoring system for elderly care, an observational study with the Mobility Monitor has been conducted recently [35]. The study included nine patients of a nursing home and a geriatric hospital which were observed during five days and nights with the Mobility Monitor. The risk of pressure ulcers was assessed by the nursing staff based on their expertise. This is the normal assessment method in these care facilities. Additionally, restrictions of mobility and activity were objectively assessed with items of the Branden Scale [10] which describes the type and severity of the restrictions.

The recorded movement pattern and other sleep parameters like the total bed occupancy and the number of bed exits were discussed for each patient with the nursing staff. The results were compared with the risk estimation of the traditional assessment and the subjective assumption of the patient's nightly activity.

The nurse staff was interviewed with a standardized questionnaire concerning usability and functionality. The Mobility Monitor was described as simple and intuitive. In three of the nine cases, the mobility analysis could confirm the expected movement activity. In these cases, the Mobility Monitor could be used to give a general overview of the movement activity which is particular useful if a nurse doesn't know the patient well.

New insights could be gained in six of the nine patients, i.e.

- Unexpected low movement during the night in two cases,
- Excessive bed occupation during the day,
- Unexpected low microactivity,
- Very high movement activity,
- Unnecessary and too frequent relocations.

Based on these new objective insights, individual measures were discussed in team meetings. Applied measures varied from nightly demands for position change, an adjustment of sleeping pills, the request to do more daily activity or the adjustment of the relocation interval.

It was concluded that the system allows to measure movements objectively and in an unobtrusive way. The nurse staff sees the application of the Mobility Monitor in the routinely assessment of new patients, in a relief for night shifts, in the definition and review of adequate measures for the pressure ulcer prevention and for the continuous surveillance of patients with a high risk of pressure ulcers.

9.3.4 Discussion

From a demographic perspective, the need for intelligent solutions which support the nursing staff in their daily operations is obvious. The people get older which results in an increased need for nursing personnel and appropriate care equipment. With the presented case examples and the results from the observational study, the use of sleep quality assessment using movements could be demonstrated for elderly care facilities. It shows that unobtrusive bed sensing can relieve the nursing staff, give additional objective information about movement patterns and improve the care quality of a nursing home.

The technological review has shown that bed systems are well suited for movement detection, heart rate and respiration rate estimation and that they show a good agreement with reference measurements. For commercialization it is the question about the choice of the sensor technology, the required accuracy, device size, design choice and the human interface. Several companies have seen a business opportunity for sleep analysis with bed systems and have put products on the market. Their focus is mainly on nursing homes and hospitals, but with the new system from Beddit the general population which wants to improve sleep quality is also addressed.

In contrast to the available commercial systems, the Mobility Monitor is focusing on movements and movement patterns. This has to do with the adapted sensor technology. While the sensors used in the Mobility Monitor are force sensors, the sensors from EMFI, Early Sense and Beddit are based on the piezoelectric effect. An applied force change is transformed into an electric charge which can then be measured. Since these sensors are able to measure small and dynamic force changes, they are well suited for the measurement of sources like the ballistocardiogram. However, this goes with the drawback that the value of a constantly applied force can't be measured directly and could only be estimated from an inaccurate integration method. With force sensors like the ones used in the Mobility Monitor, the total applied mass and the pressure distribution can be measured directly.

This advantage of the Mobility Monitor allows distinguishing small movements from pressure relieving position changes which would look similar on a piezoelectric system. As shown in the previous pages, health changes are reflected in the movement pattern and it is therefore important to monitor and distinguish these movements. The drawback of measuring with force sensors is that the interesting waveforms of heart and respiration are overlaid by the constant applied mass. For high accuracy, a good resolution over a large measurement area is required and estimation of heart and respiration rate is more challenging than with piezoelectric systems.

It can be concluded that the aim of the Mobility Monitor and the other bed monitoring systems is not the replacement of polysomnography. They should be seen as unobtrusive tools to measure selected physiological parameters, to describe the current health state and to monitor health trends.

9.4 Open Problems

9.4.1 Technical Challenges

With different approaches and sensor technologies, researchers have developed intelligent bed systems for sleep monitoring, whereas each sensor technology has its advantages and disadvantages. For instance, strain gauges and load cells are able to measure the applied mass, whereas piezoelectric sensors can't be used to determine the total applied mass, but achieve a better performance for small signals like the heart beat movement.

Therefore, the selection of the sensor setup depends on the use case of the system. To achieve the best results, a combination of different sensors technologies seems promising.

9.4.2 HCI Challenges

The challenge for any new tool is to move from a technological innovation to a system which is accepted by the users [51]. In the case of the Mobility Monitor the primary user is the nursing staff. The handling and design is always critical and it was particularly helpful to get direct feedback in an early development stage. The feedback from the users showed the importance of simple HCI elements like the traffic light display which was used for reduction of the mobility information. But although the interaction with the Mobility Monitor was described as simple and intuitive, the experience has shown that training sessions are unavoidable to verify the correct handling and to help with the interpretation of the visualized data.

Additionally, the communication with all employees in an elderly care home is important and arguments have to be selected carefully according to their function. The new tool should be seen as helpful and not as a threat for their job.

An issue which we have not focused here is how the patients themself conceive the product. The design and implementation issues concerning the acceptance of wireless and unobtrusive sleep monitoring would be interesting for further research.

9.5 Future Outlook

As illustrated in the previous examples, the display and notification of bed occupancy and movement pattern help the nursing staff to assess and minimize the risk of pressure ulcers and to adjust the dose of medication. From these dedicated applications for the elderly care, we would like to move towards a sleep quality monitoring system for everyone including more physiological signals and a correlation with sleep quality. From the technological viewpoint, we have seen that additional physiological signals from respiration and heart rate can be recorded with such an unobtrusive monitoring system and further studies will help to correlate sleep quality with these physiological signals.

Gadgets like the Fitbit One,[8] the Jawbone Up[9] wristband, or smartphone applications allow us to track our daily activities and to quantify ourselves, but all those devices only deliver limited information about our sleep. Smartphone applications placed on our bed sheets promise to track our sleep[10] and wake us up in the best time,[11] but have limited accuracy and validity. The funding success of the recently promoted Beddit sensor shows that there is interest for specialized tool for consumer market.

Unobtrusive sleep monitoring systems like the Mobility Monitor open new research possibilities, since these systems can be used to measure over several days or weeks and with minimal sleep interference. Moreover, in combination with daily monitoring systems, influences of daily activities and life style could be shown, and could suggest activities or other guidance in order to improve the quality of live.

References

1. Adami, A. M., Adami, A. G., Hayes, T. L., Pavel, M., & Beattie, Z. T. (2012). A Gaussian model for movement detection during sleep. In Annual International Conference of the IEEE Engineering in Medicine and Biology Society, (vol. 2012, pp. 2263–6). Jan 2012.
2. Adami, A. M., Pavel, M., Hayes, T. L., & Singer, C. M. (2010). Detection of movement in bed using unobtrusive load cell sensors. *IEEE Transactions on Information Technology in Biomedicine*, *14*(2), 481–90.
3. Alametsä, J., Viik, J., Alakare, J., Värri, A., & Palomäki, A. (2008). Ballistocardiography in sitting and horizontal positions. *Physiological Measurement*, *29*(9), 1071–87.
4. Alihanka, J., & Vaahtoranta, K. (1979). A static charge sensitive bed. A new method for recording body movements during sleep. *Electroencephalography and Clinical Neurophysiology*, *46*, 731–4.
5. American Academy of Sleep Medicine. (2005). *International classification of sleep disorders (ICSD-2)* (2nd ed.). Westchester: American Academy of Sleep Medicine.

[8] http://www.fitbit.com/

[9] https://jawbone.com/up

[10] https://sites.google.com/site/sleepasandroid/

[11] http://www.sleepcycle.com/

6. Ancoli-Israel, S. (1997). Sleep problems in older adults: Putting myths to bed. *Geriatrics, 52*(1), 20–0.
7. Beattie, Z. T., Hagen, C. C., & Hayes, T. L. (2011) Classification of lying position using load cells under the bed. In Annual International Conference of the IEEE Engineering in Medicine and Biology Society, (vol. 2011, pp. 474–7). Jan 2011.
8. Beattie, Z. T., Hagen, C. C., Pavel, M., & Hayes, T. L. (2009). Classification of breathing events using load cells under the bed. In Annual International Conference of the IEEE Engineering in Medicine and Biology Society, (vol. 2009, pp. 3921–4). Jan 2009.
9. Belenky, G., Wesensten, N. J., Thorne, D. R., Thomas, M. L., Sing, H. C., Redmond, D. P., et al. (2003). Patterns of performance degradation and restoration during sleep restriction and subsequent recovery: A sleep dose-response study. *Journal of sleep research, 12*(1), 1–12.
10. Bergstrom, N., Braden, B. J., Laguzza, A., & Holman, V. (1987). The braden scale for predicting pressure sore risk. *Nursing Research, 36*(4), 205–10.
11. Bluestein, D., & Javaheri, A. (2008). Pressure ulcers: Prevention, evaluation, and management. *American Family Physician, 78*(10), 1186–94.
12. Brink, M., Müller, C. H., & Schierz, C. (2006). Contact-free measurement of heart rate, respiration rate, and body movements during sleep. *Behavior Research Methods, 38*(3), 511–1.
13. Brink, M., Lercher, P., Eisenmann, A., & Schierz, C. H. (2008). Influence of slope of rise and event order of aircraft noise events on high resolution actimetry parameters. *Somnologie-Schlafforschung und Schlafmedizin., 12*(2), 118–8.
14. Brüser, C., Stadlthanner, K., de Waele, S., & Leonhardt, S. (2011). Adaptive beat-to-beat heart rate estimation in ballistocardiograms. *IEEE Transactions on Information Technology in Biomedicine, 15*(5), 778–86.
15. Chen, W., Zhu, X., Nemoto, T., Kitamura, K.-I., Sugitani, K., & Wei, D. (2008). Unconstrained monitoring of long-term heart and breath rates during sleep. *Physiological Measurement, 29*(2), N1–10.
16. Collop, N. A., Mc, W., Anderson, B., Boehlecke, D., Claman, R., Goldberg, D. J., et al. (2007). Clinical guidelines for the use of unattended portable monitors in the diagnosis of obstructive sleep apnea in adult patients. *Journal of Clinical Sleep Medicine, 3*(7), 737–7.
17. David, C., Mack, D., Patrie, J. P., Suratt, P. M., Felder, R. A., & Alwan, M. A. (2009). Development and preliminary validation of heart rate and breathing rate detection using a passive, ballistocardiography-based sleep monitoring system. *IEEE Transactions on Information Technology in Biomedicine, 13*(1), 111–20.
18. Van Dongen, H. P., Maislin, G., Mullington, J. M., & Dinges, D. F. (2003). The cumulative cost of additional wakefulness: Dose-response effects on neurobehavioral functions and sleep physiology from chronic sleep restriction and total sleep deprivation. *Sleep, 26*(2), 117–26.
19. Eyers, I., Young, E., Luff, R., & Arber, S. (2012). Striking the balance: Night care versus the facilitation of good sleep. *British Journal of Nursing, 21*(5), 303–7.
20. Giovangrandi, L., Inan, O. T., Wiard, R. M., Etemadi, M., & Kovacs, G. T. (2011). Ballistocardiography: A method worth revisiting. *Annual International Conference of the IEEE Engineering in Medicine and Biology Society, 2011*, 4279–82.
21. Iber, C., Ancoli-Israel, S., Chesson, A., & Quan, S. (2007). *The AASM manual for the scoring of sleep and associated events: Rules, terminology and technical specifications*. Darien: American Academy of Sleep Medicine.
22. Joon Chee, J., Jeong, D.-U., & Suk Park, K. (2010). Nonconstrained sleep monitoring system and algorithms using air-mattress with balancing tube method. *IEEE Transactions on Information Technology in Biomedicine, 14*(1), 147–56.
23. Kärki, S. (2009) Film-type sensor materials in measurement of physiological force and pressure variables. Ph.D thesis, Tampere University of Technology, Finland.
24. De Koninck, J., Lorrain, D., & Gagnon, P. (1992). Sleep positions and position shifts in five age groups: An ontogenetic picture. *Sleep, 15*(2), 143–9.
25. Kortelainen, J. M., Mendez, M. O., Bianchi, A. M., Matteucci, M., & Cerutti, S. (2010). Sleep staging based on signals acquired through bed sensor. *IEEE Transactions on Information Technology in Biomedicine, 14*(3), 776–85.

26. Kurihara, Y., Watanabe, K., & Tanaka, H. (2010). Sleep-states-transition model by body movement and estimation of sleep-stage-appearance probabilities by Kalman filter. *IEEE Transactions on Information Technology in Biomedicine*, *14*(6), 1428–35.
27. Kurihara, Y., & Watanabe, K. (2012). Sleep-stage decision algorithm by using heartbeat and body-movement signals. *IEEE Transactions on Systems, Man and Cybernetics, Part A: Systems and Humans*, *42*(6), 1450–9.
28. Kushida, C. A., Littner, M. R., Morgenthaler, T., Alessi, C. A., Bailey, D., Coleman, J., et al. (2005). Practice parameters for the indications for polysomnography and related procedures: An update for 2005. *Sleep*, *28*(4), 499–521.
29. Martin, A., Julia, V. R., Khatami, R., & Landolt, H. P. (2006). Age-related changes in the time course of vigilant attention during 40 hours without sleep in men. *Sleep*, *29*(1), 55–7.
30. Morgenthaler, T., Alessi, C., Friedman, L., Owens, J., Kapur, V., Boehlecke, B., et al. (2007). Practice parameters for the use of actigraphy in the assessment of sleep and sleep disorders: An update for 2007. *Sleep*, *30*(4), 519–9.
31. Niizeki, K., Nishidate, I., Uchida, K., & Kuwahara, M. (2005). Unconstrained cardiorespiratory and body movement monitoring system for home care. *Medical and Biological Engineering and Computing*, *43*(6), 716–24.
32. Nukaya, S., Shino, T., Kurihara, Y., Watanabe, K., & Tanaka, H. (2012). Noninvasive bed sensing of human biosignals via piezoceramic devices sandwiched between the floor and bed. *IEEE Sensors Journal*, *12*(3), 431–8.
33. Paalasmaa, J., Waris, M., Toivonen, H., Leppäkorpi, L., & Partinen, M. (2012). Unobtrusive online monitoring of sleep at home. *Annual International Conference of the IEEE Engineering in Medicine and Biology Society*, *2012*, 3784–8.
34. Pancorbo-Hidalgo, P. L., Garcia-Fernandez, F. P., Lopez-Medina, I. M., & Alvarez-Nieto, C. (2006). Risk assessment scales for pressure ulcer prevention: A systematic review. *Journal of Advanced Nursing*, *54*(1), 94–110.
35. Panfil, E.-M., Gattinger, H., Flnkiger, R., & Manger, S. (2013). Bewegungen objektiver messen: Dekubitusgefährdung und -therapie. *Krankenpflege SBK*, *106*, 22–3.
36. Pilcher, J. J., & Huffcutt, A. J. (1996). Effects of sleep deprivation on performance: A meta-analysis. *Sleep*, *19*(4), 318–26.
37. Rajala, S., & Lekkala, J. (2012). Film-type sensor materials PVDF and EMFi in measurement of cardiorespiratory signals–a review. *IEEE Sensors Journal*, *12*(3), 439–46.
38. Roehrs, T., Burduvali, E., Bonahoom, A., Drake, C., & Roth, T. (2003). Ethanol and sleep loss: A "dose" comparison of impairing effects. *Sleep*, *26*(8), 981–5.
39. Shin, J. H., Chee, Y., & Suk Park, K. (2006). Long-term sleep monitoring system and long-term sleep parameters using unconstrained method. In International Special Topic Conference on Information Technology in BME 2006.
40. Shin, J. H., Choi, B. H., Lim, Y. G., Jeong, D. U., & Park, K. S. (2008) Automatic ballistocardiogram (BCG) beat detection using a template matching approach. In Annual International Conference of the IEEE Engineering in Medicine and Biology Society, (vol. 2008, pp. 1144–6), Jan 2008.
41. Shino, T., & Watanabe, K. (2010). Noninvasive biosignal measurement of a subject in bed using ceramic sensors. In SICE Annual Conference, (pp. 1559–1562).
42. Stone, K. L., & Ancoli-israel, S. (2008) Chapter 147: Actigraphy. In Principles and practice of sleep medicine (5th ed.). (pp. 1668–1675) Elsevier Inc.
43. Sung Chung, G., Hoon Choi, B., Jeong, D-N., & Park, K. S. (2007) Noninvasive heart rate variability analysis using loadcell-installed bed during sleep. In Annual International Conference of the IEEE Engineering in Medicine and Biology Society, (pp. 2357–2360).
44. Sung Chung, G., Lee, J.-S., Jeong, D.-N., & Suk Park, K. (2009). Slow-wave sleep estimation on a load-cell-installed bed: A non-constrained method. *Physiological Measurement*, *30*(11), 1163–70.
45. Watanabe, T., & Watanabe, K. (2004). Noncontact method for sleep stage estimation. *IEEE Transactions on Biomedical Engineering*, *51*(10), 1735–48.

46. Watanabe, K., Watanabe, T., Watanabe, H., Ando, H., Ishikawa, T., & Kobayashi, K. (2005). Noninvasive measurement of heartbeat, respiration, snoring and body movements of a subject in bed via a pneumatic method. *IEEE Transactions on Biomedical Engineering*, *52*(12), 2100–7.
47. Williamson, A. M., & Feyer, A.-M. (2000). Moderate sleep deprivation produces impairments in cognitive and motor performance equivalent to legally prescribed levels of alcohol intoxication. *Occupational and Environmental Medicine*, *57*(10), 649–55.
48. Woo Seo, J., Min Choi, J., Bum Shin, H., Lee, J. Y., Jeong, D. U., & Suk Park, K. (2007). Non-constraining sleep/wake monitoring system using bed actigraphy. *Medical Biological Engineering Computing*, *45*(1), 107–14.
49. Zhu, X., Chen, W., Nemoto, T., Kanemitsu, Y., Kitamura, K.-I., Yamakoshi, K.-I., et al. (2006). Real-time monitoring of respiration rhythm and pulse rate during sleep. *IEEE Transactions on Biomedical Engineering*, *53*(12), 2553–3.
50. Zhu, X., Chen, W., Nemoto, T., Kitamura, K.-I., & Wei, D. (2010). Long-term monitoring of heart rate, respiration rhythm, and body movement during sleep based upon a network. *Telemedicine Journal and E-health: The Official Journal of the American Telemedicine Association*, *16*(2), 244–53.
51. Ziefle, M., Röcker, C., & Holzinger, A. (2014). Current trends and challenges for pervasive health technologies: From technical innovation to user integration. In *Pervasive health: State-of-the-art & beyond* (pp. 1–18). London: Springer.

Further Readings

52. Kelly, J., Strecker, R., & Bianchi, M. (2012). Recent developments in home sleep-monitoring devices. *ISRN Neurology*. 768794, 10 (This paper provides a review of portable monitoring devices which are developed for sleep quality and quantity estimation in the home environment).
53. Kryger, M., Roth, T., & Dement, W. (2011). *Principles and practive of sleep medicine* (5th ed.). Elsevier, ISBN:978-1-4160-6645-3. (This book gives an excellent overview on many different aspects of sleep medicine).
54. Paalasmaa, J., Waris, M., Toivonen, H., Leppakorpi, L., & Partinen, M. (2012). Unobtrusive online monitoring of sleep at home. In *Annual International Conference of the IEEE Engineering in Medicine and Biology Society*, (Vol. 2012, pp. 3784–3788) (This paper describes an online sleep monitoring service, based on unobtrusive ballistocardiography (BCG) measurement in an ordinary bed. In combination with environmental information and user-logged tags, this approach is well suited for long-term monitoring at home).

Chapter 10
Interactive Infrastructures: Physical Rehabilitation Modules for Pervasive Healthcare Technology

A. J. Bongers, Stuart Smith, Victor Donker, Michelle Pickrell, Rebecca Hall and Stefan Lie

10.1 Introduction

Traditional physical rehabilitation exercise techniques can be enhanced through the application of interactive technologies. After studying rehabilitation practices for several years, we have identified three key areas where improvement can be achieved. These key issues are *motivation* (offering informative and rewarding feedback to the patients to support them to participate fully in the therapies), *customisation* (the ability to adapt and personalise the systems to the wide range of needs of different patients and therapies), and *independence* (enabling the patients to follow therapies away from the hospital, when and where it suits them, under remote expert guidance of the therapists and practitioners, including the highly desirable feature of automatically logging patient exercise data).

These key issues will be discussed in detail in the next section, as well as our approach for addressing the key issues by developing and applying interactive strategies. Our studies focused on staff practices in the hospital ward, and consisted of unobtrusive observations, appropriate interventions, unstructured interviews, and explicit requests for participation. In effect, our aim was to have the practitioners drive our research and developments, as is common practice in design research. Our proposals proceed from existing practices and our approach is inspired by actual

A. J. Bongers (✉) · V. Donker · M. Pickrell · R. Hall · S. Lie
Faculty of Design, Architecture and Building, Interactivation Studio,
University of Technology, Sydney, Australia
e-mail: bertbon@xs4all.nl

S. Smith
Healthy Eating, Active Living Technology (HEALTHY) Research Centre,
University of Tasmania, Launceston, Australia
e-mail: Stuart.Smith@utas.edu.au

V. Donker
Department of Industrial Design, Eindhoven University of Technology,
Eindhoven, The Netherlands
e-mail: victor@victordonker.nl

A. Holzinger et al. (eds.), *Pervasive Health*, Human–Computer Interaction Series,
DOI: 10.1007/978-1-4471-6413-5_10,

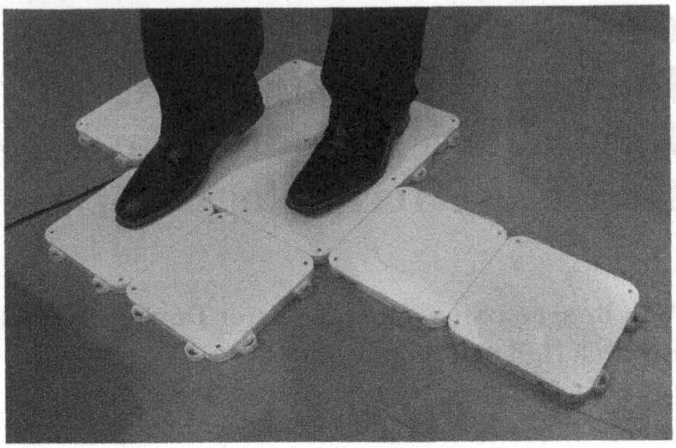

Fig. 10.1 The interactive rehabilitation tiles 3D printed modules

therapies. The work is based on the current mechanical and often very creative solutions of physiotherapists and other practitioners. Rather than replacing their practices, we are *extending* the way physiotherapists work by applying the digital technologies (Fig. 10.1).

10.2 Glossary

CAD Computer Aided Design; using computer software tools to design 3D models of a shape, which can then be produced using CAM technologies (see below).

CAM Computer Aided Manufacturing; computer controller fabrication techniques, including existing techniques under computer control (such as CNC Milling, a milling machine that is under 'computer numerical control') or new techniques such as laser cutting of flat materials and 3D printing (additive manufacturing).

DoF Degree of Freedom; a way of describing movement in 3D space, both for the lateral locations on the three axis and the rotational orientations around those three axis.

HCI Human-Computer Interaction; the field of study into the relationships between human(s) and computer systems, applied in the field of interaction and interface design.

Interactivation A design and research approach that encourages making things (objects, instruments and spaces) interactive. It is a means of enabling computer systems to interact with the users. through elaborate, engaging, sensitive, rich and spatial interfaces.

10.3 State-of-the-Art

The first phase of the project (in 2009 and 2010) explored the rehabilitation practices of various hospitals, through observations and conversations with practitioners, and collaborations with medical researchers reported in a previous publication [8]. We included an overview of the rich variety of rather effective mechanical and material solutions that the therapists worked with. The focus of the earlier work was around Spinal Cord Injury (SCI) patients. They are often young adults and we therefore explored the use of video games as structured interactive environments for them to carry out their exercises. This included the modification and appropriation of existing game controllers such as the Wii-mote (extending the switches to be more easily operated by the patient) and Wii balance board (which was adapted for wheelchair use). However we found this approach was limited due to the fixed mappings between player's movements as picked up by the controllers, and the game parameters. We therefore developed our own interfaces, using 3D printing techniques and wireless sensor modules. All this work has been reported in a book chapter [8] which also included an overview of the rehabilitation and medical practices.

10.3.1 Three Key Issues

Our studies since 2009 have identified key areas (motivation, customisation, and independence) which we will discuss in this section. Each of these have specific issues and challenges, and we have identified possible improvements and solutions by using techniques of interaction with computer generated guidance and feedback, and new product design techniques.

10.3.1.1 Motivation

The first key challenge for patients and therapists is boredom or lack of motivation to continue with rehabilitation because of the repetitive nature of the tasks. We propose that the (inherent and necessary) repetitive tasks can be made more acceptable by making the tasks more entertaining and engaging by applying multimodal and multi-levelled feedback. Motivating patients is crucial in rehabilitation exercises, and often relies on the skills and enthusiasm of the therapist. From literature on motivation and social psychology [14], we know that the best results come from intrinsic motivation [12]. While a patient usually will have a strong intrinsic motivation to get better, this is a long-term goal and only achieved through slow (and often barely noticeable) progress. The skill of the therapist is to transfer, as it were, the extrinsic motivation (the patient doing the exercise for the therapist) to an intrinsic one. Appropriate feedback, as presented by our systems, can play a crucial role in this process. It can also help to present rewards in the form of feedback, to motivate their development by achieving short-term goals in pursuit of the longer term goal [36]. Another function of the enhanced feedback and information presentation of an interactive system is to educate and inform the patient about the need and reasons to perform an exercise, explaining more of the process. This can be a problem in traditional practices, and has been found to be detrimental to the patient's motivation [25]. In interactive systems it is possible to add feedback and present information using various interaction modalities, for instance using video, graphics, lights, movement, sound and music. It can possibly be part of a trophy tangible object [2]. This motivation support can also be more entertaining. Video games have been found to be successful in this context as a motivating environment, and are suitable when the levels of achievement and reward are matched with the therapeutic goals, which will be discussed in a section below. Although we have investigated using standard game controllers and games (such as the Nintendo Wii), we remain focused on creating flexible, custom made interfaces and environments in which we can control the link between game play and therapy. We have also found that even very plain feedback from LEDs and sound can enhance therapy and motivate patients.

10.3.1.2 Customisation

From our research we conclude that an important factor in rehabilitation is to create personalised interfaces, experiences and therapies. Each patient's needs are different, and the therapeutic approach ideally covers the physical and the mental, matching their idiosyncratic characteristics which also change over time. We found that it is difficult to sufficiently customise the standard game controllers and other interfaces. Focusing on the physical interface, we have identified a number of parameters to be varied in the individualised solutions. These are weight, size (or form factor in general), reach (in a line, a plane or 3D space), orientation, compliance (or springiness—the response of a material), friction (related to texture) and force (lateral or torque, depending on the task). While in traditional rehabilitation techniques these parameters are fixed in any situation, the aim of our research is to have as many of these parameters under real-time control. This is possible using elaborate feedback mechanisms and actuator technologies for active haptic feedback, as explored in earlier projects [4]. Similar to traditional rehabilitation therapies, the aim is to develop extensive individual responses to the patient's particular needs.

In our current and near future projects we approach the customisability of the modules firstly by working in a modular way (such as the sensor tiles), further exploring the possibilities of mechanical adjustments, and utilise the flexibility offered by software and hardware. To extend the range of possible individualisation, we have explored the use of 3D printing and other CAM (Computer Aided Manufacturing) techniques which will be presented below.

10.3.1.3 Independence

It is often noticed that patients perform well when under full guidance in the rehabilitation ward, which is difficult to sustain outside the ward and even more difficult after discharge from the rehabilitation centre. This breach can be restored with novel ways of interaction between therapist and patient (and other carers/stakeholders). Many opportunities exist to address this by developing remote therapies, addressing the dichotomy of the current situation (intense therapy in the ward, left to one's own situation when discharged), and extending to a continuous therapy space covered by an ongoing but intermittent involvement of the therapist or other health professionals. It also means that the parts of the system have to be cheap, portable, and possibly based on technologies already present in the home (PC's, TV screens, loudspeakers) rather than relying on specialised and cumbersome set ups (projectors, screen mounting, overhead camera fixing for tracking purposes). Sophisticated analyses of an individual's movements will be possible and remotely located rehabilitation clinicians will be able simultaneously to provide meaningful and engaging feedback to their patients. This is particularly important for people living in regional, rural and remote areas where access to therapy is often restricted or non-existent.

10.3.2 Design Responses to the Key Issues

In response to the three main issues as identified and presented in the previous section, this section discusses possibilities we have explored to improve interactive rehabilitation. They are based on enabling technologies, and tangible interaction design approaches [22, 34].

Our design approach aims to blend in, is inspired by, and follows on from existing rehabilitation therapy techniques. We are using gentle, appropriate yet radical interventions, extending from established practices with a design approach that develops through proposing and testing.

10.3.2.1 Video Games and Multimodal Feedback

Patients can be *motivated* to carry out their rehabilitation exercises using enhanced and informative feedback. We used video games with alterations, and newly developed multimodal interaction styles.

Much of the recent work in home-based rehabilitation has been driven by the adoption of Wii-style video games by rehabilitation therapists. For example, Gil-Gomez et al [18] have recently shown that a modified balance training system based on the Nintendo Wii Balance Board improved standing balance in a sample of 17 patients with acquired brain injury. Furthermore McNulty and colleagues have shown that an intensive two-week intervention using off-the-shelf Nintendo Wii video games resulted in significant and clinically relevant improvements in functional upper limb motor ability in people recovering from stroke [26]. However off-the-shelf products like the Wii are not suitable for a wide range of patients.

The first phase of the project looked into using video games as a way of motivating patients, however it was found that with this approach it was difficult to obtain sufficient levels of customisation. We made several successful adaptations of Wii controllers, such as extending a Wii-mote with an external switch for a wheelchair user to operate with their elbow, and an extended platform for a Wii balance board to support wheelchair use. We found that these adaptations were still quite limited due to the fixed mapping between controller movements and game parameters, and we needed more freedom to design appropriate tangible interfaces. Others have designed new games for rehabilitation purposes, from quite straightforward feedback [23], colourful patterns [13], to programming 3D environments [17], however we focused on multimodal feedback to enhance the therapies which enabled us to find the optimal mappings between the patient's actions and the system's responses.

See also the work by Korean researchers elswehere in this book [33], who particularly look at how the gamefication can be used to support the transition from the hospital to the home.

10.3.2.2 Individual Products

In addition to the ability *customise* through the creation of individual interfaces through software, recent developments in 3D printing have made it much easier also to individualise the shape of a product. The recent trend in the field of industrial design is known as 'mass customisation' [20], as a response to the twentieth century mass-production. Individualisation through customisation was identified as a key need in medical rehabilitation processes, as discussed above.

The notion of individual products is a significant shift in the field of industrial design, a shift towards the rather unexplored territory between *craft* (highly skilled individual labour, production of single pieces) and *industrial production* (mass made by machines). Since the transition from craft to industrialisation as the main means of manufacturing during the industrial revolution, and the reorientation (as one could call it) of the role of craft through the Arts and Craft movement, Bauhaus and subsequent developments, each found its own part of the field of production. In the last decades there have been significant developments in CAD/CAM (Computer Aided Design and Manufacturing) which are now becoming mainstream and increasingly available to smaller studios and even individuals [19]. This has led to many new practices, techniques and approaches, and the opportunity to design individualised physical interfaces.

The possibilities of design (CAD) were always ahead of what was possible in manufacturing (CAM). The field of architectural design seemed to have been much further in developing parametric modelling, and "file-to-factory" approaches enabled architectural designs to rely on individually specified components rather than being limited to the use of standardised elements. This has led to the notion of non-standard architecture [27–29]. Product Design is now increasingly engaging with the possibilities.

Indicative of the limited notion of its potential CAM is often called rapid prototyping, which implies the (although useful) practice of using CAM to try out forms for user testing, and improving manufacturing, it is seen as a stage in the development towards mass production. There are many possibilities to explore when using CAM to create the final product. What we have been exploring in our projects is the possibility of creating *individual products* and particularly *interfaces*. We have known for a long time that, because each person is different, customisability is a crucial factor in each user interface. Until recently this was mainly applied on the software side of the computer, and to some extent through its sensors (input) and displays (output)—ideally through a mix of multiple modalities and modes (the iPhone is a good example). However the *shape*, and its physical appearance in general, is very fixed. This is in fact extremely limited, the iPhone can have text engraved, and until recently only came in the colours white and black (as in the original T-Ford marketing, ironically).

This approach of *mass-customisation* resonates well with our desire to make individual products to suit the needs of individual patients and practices. It could be described as meta-craft. It is very different from mass production, and it influences the whole design process. It offers new possibilities for including the user, client, or patient in the design process, delivering not a final product with fixed parameters but an open design with specified ranges of parameters to be determined by the user. This leads to the design approach that such a meta-craft designer needs in order to develop these 'product envelopes'. Moving away from traditional industrial design, there is a need for a different design approach when dealing with individual products and manufacturing than when designing for mass production. It influences all stages of a design process, not just the final ones. When designing for individual products, we design not just one product (or not even multiple products) but a *range* of products, through an envelope set by the encompassed parameters and their ranges. Part of our research aims to establish the heuristics, approaches and guidelines that drive and guide these design processes.

10.3.2.3 Networking and Logging

To support the need for *independence*, networks can be used for tele-rehabilitation in a pervasive computing environment. This would allow a therapist to oversee the development of remote patients, and guide their exercises. In the most recent phase of our project we implemented a logging system in our devices, in response to strong requests from the practitioners, to be able to directly track and store the patient's movement and other data which is now collected on paper and often doesn't get used. This was relatively easy as the data was already in the computer, as read from the sensors in the various products, and we extended our software to write this data to a file in real time. The file is in a spreadsheet format, so that the practitioner can import the data into their patient file (which for obvious ethical reasons we cannot access directly).

10.3.3 Interactive Infrastructure

Inspired by the rehabilitation practices and further informed by our earlier work, it became clear that a modular approach was very suitable. The modular approach was developed in other projects in audiovisual instruments [7] and architectural design and the development of the idea of an Interactive Infrastructure [10].

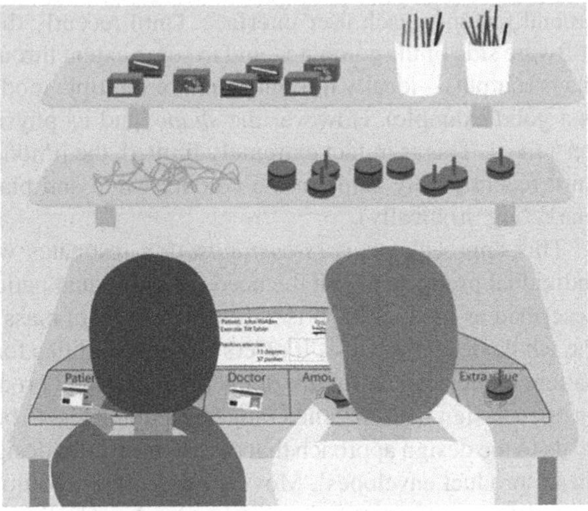

Fig. 10.2 Tangible programming table: impression of the usage scenario

The development of interactive infrastructures has become a common approach in HCI (Human-Computer Interaction) in the last decade. The approach can be seen in the fields of Ubiquitous Computing (or Ubicomp), Pervasive Computing (as IBM calls it), the Internet of Things (MIT's Gershenfeld [15, 16]), Sentient Computing (AT&T's term) or Ambient Intelligence (an approach supported by Philips) [1]. It is a kind of electronic ecology or *e*cology, inspired by the importance of natural ecosystems to emphasise interaction as the central area of design efforts [6]. The greatest possibilities of the *e*-cology or Ubicomp lie in the potential for de-centralised systems, such as the Internet. At the scale of products, MIT's proposal for the Internet of Things is the most relevant for our project. The idea is that all modules in the system can talk to each other, for instance, when carrying out a stepping task the number of repetitions can appear on the computer screen but also on the handheld digital counter module.

The development of an interactive infrastructure fits well with the notion of embedded interaction and pervasive computing. Modules can be input (through sensors that pick up the patients actions), output (displaying feedback to the patient visually, auditory, tactually), or both. Furthermore, there are active objects which are used to indicate modes and preferences. Modules we have developed so far are an interactive hand counter [11], a number of wearable modules for intimate tracking of arm and finger movements (bend, pressure, orientation) [30], and a wireless handheld reaching task module (with an RFID reader, and motion sensor and visual feedback, using RFID tagged targets) [9]. All these modules are interacting in real time. We are including off the shelf products in this infrastructure, such as Bluetooth speakers, tablets, keyboards, motion sensors, iPads and iPods (which we have used as wireless displays for instance).

The mapping between modules and the settings are established through placing the modules and other objects involved (representing the patient for instance) on a programming table as depicted in Fig. 10.2, using RFID tags and multiple RFID

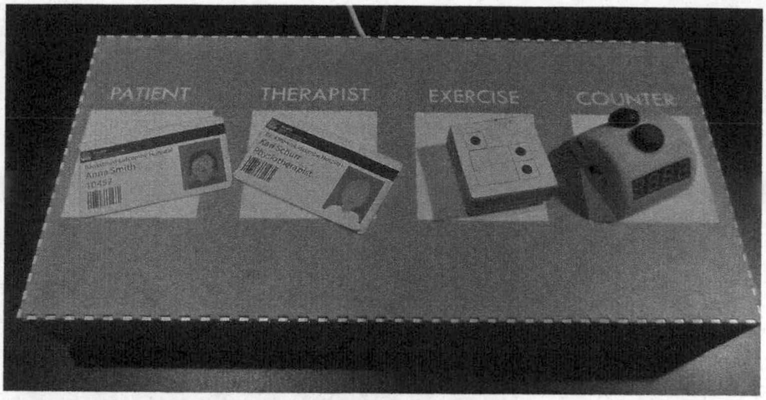

Fig. 10.3 Tangible programming table prototype

readers (we are using a sequential polling technique we've developed to avoid interference between readers and between tags). We are also developing 'programming modules', physical objects which are part of the modular system, and which enable the therapist (or care giver) to set the parameters and variables of the task through manipulating physical objects rather than screen based programming interfaces. This idea has been presented in a working prototype (shown in Fig. 10.3) to the practitioners on several occasions, from whom we have received positive feedback. The importance of supporting the therapists and practitioners to be able to control the parameters of the exercises has been identified by others as well [21].

10.3.3.1 Interactivated Reaching Task

One of the tasks frequently employed in rehabilitation is for the patient to practice picking up an object from a table surface, then to reach to a distant point to deposit the object.

The purpose of this task is that the patient can improve their ability to interact with everyday objects in the home. An initial experiment was put together to carry out such a reaching task with enhanced multimodal feedback. Here we used an object for the user to hold and move around with an RFID tag enclosed and readers on the table, as shown in Fig. 10.4. The task can be modified in range, and the trajectory and completion of the task is fed back with sonic and haptic signals. The trajectory can be further guided by an accelerometer attached to the upper arm, providing a means of further sonic articulatory feedback. The sonic feedback is generated in real-time using an FM-synthesis patch in Max/MSP.

Fig. 10.4 Reaching task tracked with RFID and motion sensor

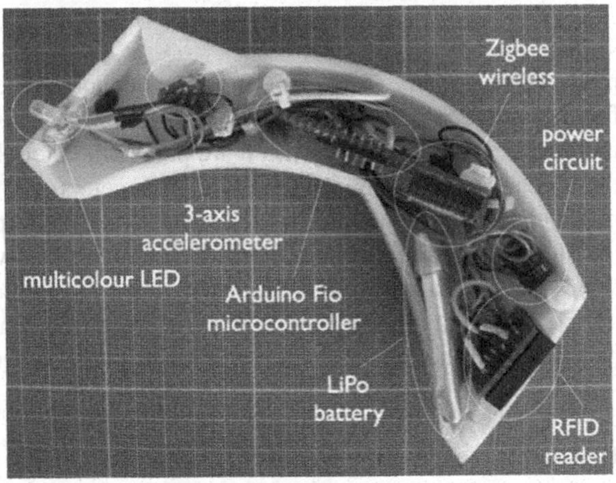

Fig. 10.5 The wireless reaching task device inside

Reaching Task Device Design

In 2010 a group of industrial design students and two research assistants developed a functional prototype. In this demonstrator, the reaching task targets are passive RFID tags which are colour coded, and the patient holds an interactive device which has an LED displaying the colour of the target to reach, which then reads the tag and motion data and wirelessly communicates with a host computer. The primary task is to follow a pattern of coloured lights by matching (reaching) the colour coded targets, further rewarded with musical feedback. The device contains an RFID reader, microcontroller, wireless transceiver, motion sensor for tracking 2 rotational DoF (degrees of freedom), rechargeable battery and multicolour LED as can be seen in Fig. 10.5.

The therapist can set the task by placing the tags in 3D space, and thus set the goals to be reached for a particular part of the session. The main task for the patient

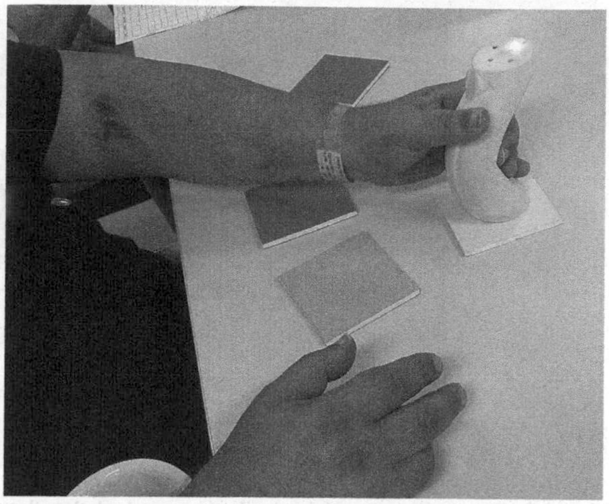

Fig. 10.6 Testing of the reaching task device

is to follow the colour coded targets (red, blue, green and yellow tiles) prompted by the colour of the LED on the device. The tiles are made of foamcore, a lightweight yet rigid material that supports the coloured paper. Further refinement of the therapy is possible through the motion sensor, for instance if the patient tilts the device in the wrong angle at any time, the guiding feedback can indicate this. Although the set-up is computer based, the computer screen is not the main focus of attention. The primary feedback is programmed in the microcontroller of the device, following the lights, and the music which is generated from the computer. The shape and weight of the basic device is kept to a minimum, leaving an appropriate range of customisation of physical parameters such as weight and shape by extending the device with passive elements. The basic shape is 3D printed, resulting in a rigid and light device. By adding material to the basic shape, different forms and weights can be made for individual patients.

Reaching Task Device Evaluation

We took the device to the rehabilitation ward and tried it with one of the patients as shown in Fig. 10.6. The device and the ideas behind it were positively received, and some problems and suggestions for improvement were made by the patients and staff. It was quickly found that due to the low weight of the coloured target objects (with the RFID tags), they tended to slide away. Sticking them to the table resolved the issue, however it decreases the flexibility. The patient also had troubles with the difference in height, as he tended to slide the device towards the objects. For a case like this it would be better to have the targets flush with the work surface, by making them thinner (which is possible) or by raising the work surface around them. These findings were interesting as the device had been tested on numerous occasions with visitors to the Interactivation Studio at UTS, many students, and a class of primary school children (3rd grade), and they never had these problems. It proved again how

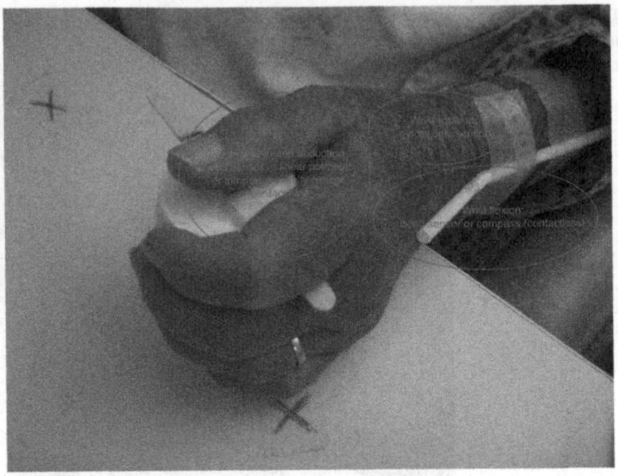

Fig. 10.7 Translation of a mechanically supported rehab task to potential sensor applications

important it is to test with the actual target audience. One patient in particular tried really hard to convey his feedback, and was highly critical and gave very useful feedback. Further requirements followed from our discussions with therapists and patients, as well as our own observations are: robustness, easy to set up and modify, avoiding wires, no dependence on mains supply during trials (few wall outlets in hospital wards and poorly placed), and no dependence on the local network.

10.3.3.2 Re-Ability Sleeve: A Modular and Wearable Interface

Figure 10.7 shows an example of the outcome of an analysis of a typical rehabilitation practice, where the therapist used low cost materials to create a compound of movement and orientation requirements for the patient. While the basic task for the patient is to move from one position on the table to another one, the practitioner has set further refinements of the task: the straw guides the patient to keep the wrist at a certain angle, the styrofoam cup puts the hand in a certain posture (and has to keep it in that posture without squashing the cup), the paddle pop stick guides the thumb in the right position, etc. We took this as input for a potential design of an interactivated system, where we would use specific sensors such as a gyroscope, accelerometer, pressure sensor, bend sensor, and proximity sensor.

A fourth year industrial design student Michelle Pickrell dedicated her major project in 2011 to this subject, after having worked with us on earlier projects. She made several visits to the ward, first for observations and later to bring prototypes and systems to the practice. The prototype developed was based on a number of iterations, and is shown in Fig. 10.8.

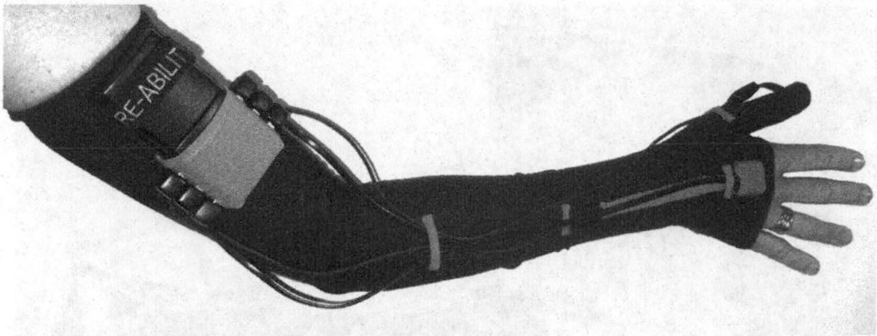

Fig. 10.8 The re-ability sleeve

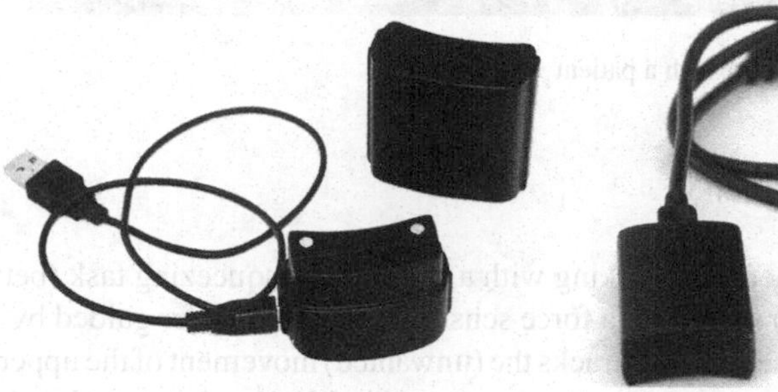

Fig. 10.9 The battery, charger, and receiver modules

Re-ability Sleeve Design

The system designed reflects the key issues identified in our earlier research of *motivation*, *customisability*, and *independence*. In early stages a number of interviews and brainstorming sessions were conducted with both patients, their carers and the physiotherapists at the rehabilitation clinics. At a later point of development, the design was tested by patients, modified and tested again. The final design consists of a (custom designed) sleeve, with pockets which hold the sensor modules in place. The main module sits on the upper arm, and contains a microcontroller board (Arduino Fio) and the digital radio (Zigbee), and a detachable battery pack (connected through magnetic contacts) as shown in Fig. 10.9. The individual sensor modules fit in pockets in the appropriate places, and are plugged in to the main module. The current version consists of sensor modules for bending (flex sensor on the elbow, and a two way flex sensor on the wrist), a 2-axis accelerometer on the upper arm, a distance sensor (measuring the gap between the upper arm and the body), and a pressure (force) sensor on the thumb. The appropriate form of the modules was found through a number of prototypes. By making a first 3D printed prototype we were able to recognise some structural problems or weaknesses, and ergonomic considerations leading to the curved shapes with rounded edges.

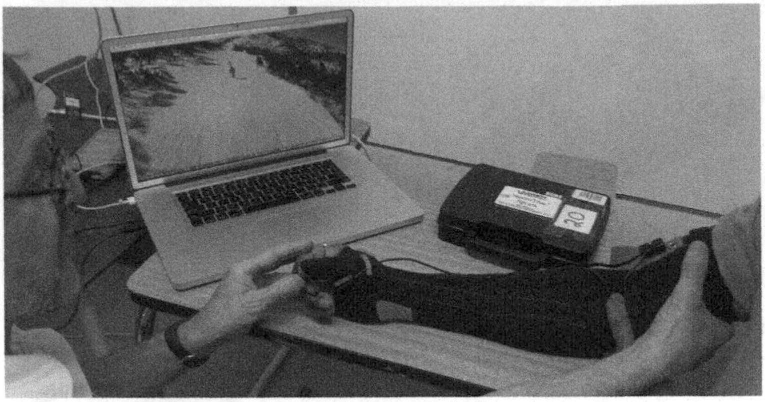

Fig. 10.10 A therapist working with a patient with the sleeve

Re-ability Sleeve Evaluation

Figure 10.10 shows a therapist working with a patient on a squeezing task (between thumb and index finger) sensed by a force sensor (FSR) and further guided by feedback from the accelerometer which tracks the (unwanted) movement of the upper arm.

Feedback is given from a computer programmed in Max,[1] using visual and auditory modalities. Various forms of feedback were tested, including videos that played according to the patient's performance. The videos would progress in response to successful moves by the patient. However we found that a simple counter or a scale display was already satisfying and therefore engaging for the patient. This principle was reinforced on several occasions by therapists and patients, confirming our approach to offer feedback in multiple modes and modalities, from which the patient and therapist can choose. This phase of the project resulted in many insights in interactivated rehabilitation practices, and was presented in demos and workshops at HCI conferences from which we received valuable feedback [30]. It was clear that the modular approach was very suitable to meet the variable demands of the rehabilitation practices, which we worked out as a key issue in our current work presented in the next section.

10.3.3.3 Interactivated Hand Counter

After having observed that a mechanical hand counter was an omnipresent tool in the rehab ward, we decided to redesign this as an interactive electronic counter. This work was carried out by student intern Victor Donker. Again we followed an

[1] Max/MSP/Jitter is an object based visual programming language for multimedia applications. In addition to the data manipulation part, it has a range of sound processing objects (MSP) and video processing capabilities (Jitter). See www.cyling74.com.

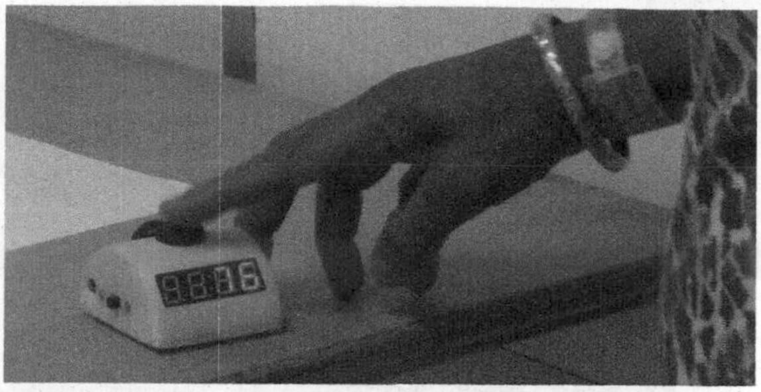

Fig. 10.11 A hand counter module in use in the rehab ward

iterative and inclusive design process, starting with a range of ten foam models as form studies, then offering a selection of eight different switches (mounted on blocks of foam) to choose from, and discussing the needs and design requirements with staff and patients in the ward. As always, one important requirement of the module was the connectivity, enabling the results of a rehab exercise to be uploaded directly to a computer file. We are using an Arduino-based 4-digit 7-segment LED display from Sparkfun, connected to a Zigbee radio, and powered by a rechargeable LiPo battery (using induction charging). The version in Fig. 10.11 shows the stage in the development where we had taken into account the stand-alone shape, which we further refined in a more ergonomic shape which is easier to hold and can be placed on a surface.

10.3.3.4 Modular Interactive Stepping Tiles

In response to the needs of the therapies we developed balancing and stepping task tiles. The current version is shown in Fig. 10.1. The first version was developed in 2012 with an industrial design major project student Rebecca Hall, which resulted in a prototype that was tested in the rehabilitation ward of a public hospital in Sydney, as shown in Fig. 10.12. This work was inspired by the exercise mat developed by Stuart Smith and colleagues at Neuroscience Research Australia [31, 32, 37], a design adapted from the DDR (Dance Dance Revolution) game paradigm. With this sensor mat (shown in the background of Fig. 10.12), elderly or less mobile people can practice balancing and stepping tasks in their own home.

The modular sensor floor consists of a main tile of 40 × 40 cm, on which the user can place both their feet, measuring the pressure at four points under the feet, for balancing exercises. Smaller tiles (20 × 20 cm) can be attached to the main tile on all four sides, so that stepping tasks can be carried out. The tiles are fabricated using CAM techniques. They are 20 mm high making them easy to step on, which is an important design requirement for the ease of use of the tiles. Other products such as the entertainment robotics tiles [24] are thicker and the Wii balance board is over 50 mm high. Our design process was very much driven by the medical practitioners, who also suggested not to have visual feedback in the tiles as the patients need to

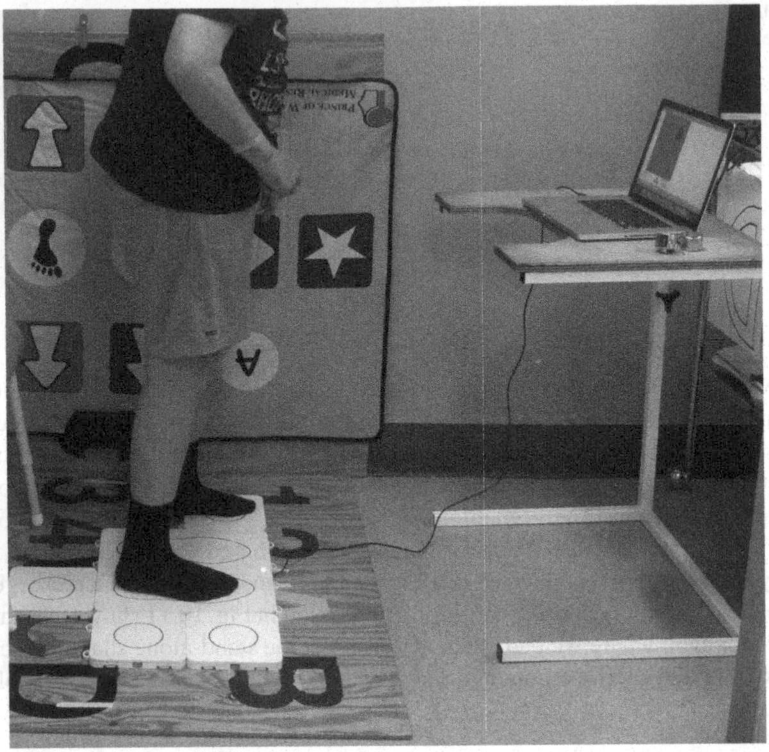

Fig. 10.12 The first prototype in use in the ward

not look at their feet during exercises. They asked for a surface with pressure points rather than a balance surface (such as the Wii).

Between the layers of the structure an FSR (Force Sensing Resistor) is placed under a layer of foam (3 mm EVA closed cell foam) to disperse the force of the feet. This sensing technique was initially developed by the first author in an architectural project of an interactive building The Water Pavilion in The Netherlands in 1997 [5]. This construction gives a continuous electrical signal proportional to the weight applied, converted by a microcontroller circuit into digital signals. The signals travel between the tiles using slightly modified littleBit[2] magnetic and spring loaded contacts [3].The tiles are connected via USB to a computer, which then provides visual feedback. The tiles are covered in a thin layer of neoprene rubber at the bottom to prevent sliding.

Early in 2013 a medical research group who are studying balancing exercises and falls prevention [35] in Sydney commissioned the development of two more sets of the tiles, enabling us to further develop the design. Improvements were made to the

[2] Littlebits are sensor and actuator modules that snap together with magnetic connections. The user can make various 'circuits' with these building blocks, a bit like Lego. See www.littlebits.cc.

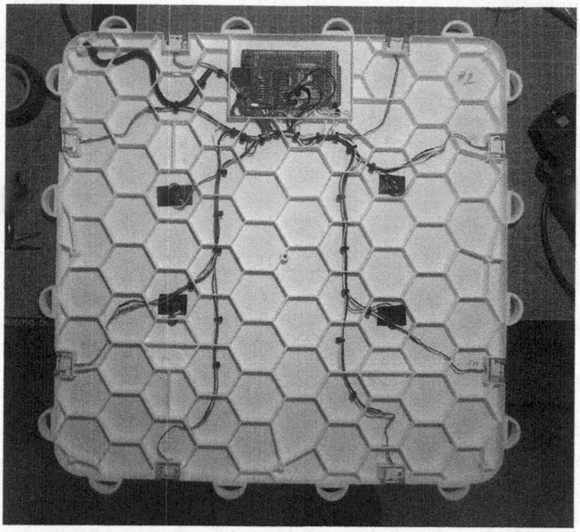

Fig. 10.13 The 3D printed structure of the main tile with the sensor interface

electrical connections and the mechanical linking of the tiles, and we made all the tiles pressure sensitive (some were switches in the earlier model). The main improvement however was to address the reproducibility by applying 3D printing techniques (the first version was made using a computer controlled milling machine, which is cheap but not suitable for larger numbers). The structure is shown in Fig. 10.13, and was designed in Solidworks by Rebecca Hall as research assistant.

A 'bridging' tile was developed, not containing any sensors but acting as a bridge to extend the range of the stepping task. We developed a way of sensing where the tiles are attached and what type of tile they are, (sensing or bridging) so that the on-screen layout changes dynamically in response to the actual placements of the tiles. The main tile contains a Sparkfun Arduino MegaPro which links to the host computer via USB, and is shown in Fig. 10.13.

Graphical Interface

A graphical interface for visual feedback, information presentation and control was developed by Victor Donker, a student intern from the TU Eindhoven, the Netherlands. The interface, shown in Fig. 10.14, was created in Max/MSP/Jitter which was already being used to read and process the signals from the tiles. This system allows the therapist to control a number of parameters and settings to configure different types of exercises, using a touch screen or a mouse. The screen shows which tiles are connected, and displays their pressure values represented by changing the size of a circle. For the main tile the pressure can also be displayed in percentages (for balancing exercises). The subtiles show a numerical value representing the number of steps taken by the patient. On the right hand side the overall stepping count is

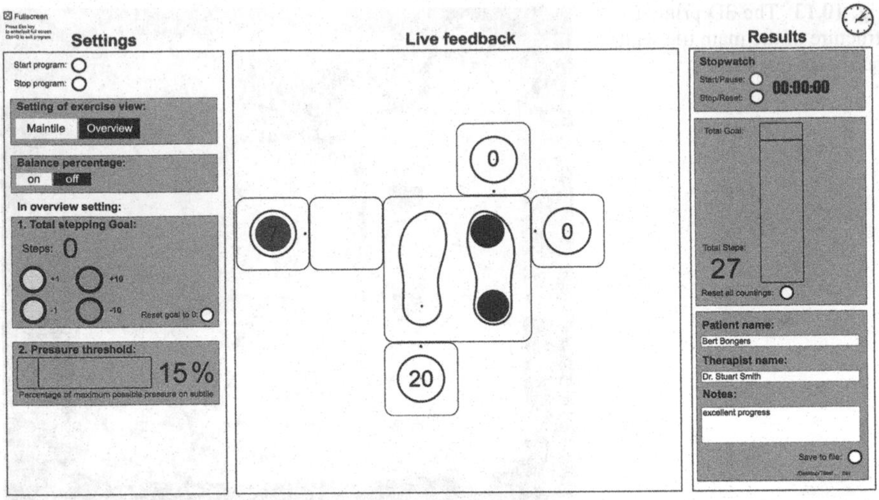

Fig. 10.14 A screen shot of the visual interface and feedback

displayed, as well as the goal to be reached. The patient's and therapist's ID are put in a field, for logging purposes. A stopwatch section of the screen allows the therapist to time activities. The left hand side of the screen is for setting the task parameters, such as number of steps and thresholds.

The modular sensor floor system is currently in frequent use in a Sydney hospital, and in the Adelaide repatriation hospital where a comparative test is being carried out (across various similar systems). Preliminary results and experiences are presented in below.

Design Process

One of the key elements of our ideas for a range of products is the customisability through individual manufacturing (this is increasingly possible using 3D printing on demand schemes). While 3D printing is relatively expensive, we needed to use this technique in order to explore the flexibility and freedom of form, so that we could create customised products for the patients. There is a strong trend of 3D printing gradually becoming more affordable. The costs of such manufacturing are largely dependent on the amount of material used, so we designed the 3D printed part to be as light as possible yet strong enough to bear the load of a person standing on it. This was achieved by designing a honeycomb structure, with 1 mm wall thickness. The material used to print is ABS or polyamide, and depending on the quality of the printing machine the density of the material can be over 90 %. Torsional stiffness is obtained by layers of acrylic, which are laser cut. The amount of this acrylic material is not an issue in this process, as it is cheap and the price of the process depends mainly on the length and complexity of the path that is cut. All this was done using the machines of the design faculty at UTS, with the final 3D print structures provided by the higher quality machines of the Shapeways Company (the major printing on demand supplier of 3D prints).

The tiles were developed iteratively, we made four different versions of the structure before we had the right balance between weight and strength. A finite elements analysis was performed on the computer model which confirmed the strength of the design. The torsional stiffness was important as it influenced the working of the sensor, finding the right balance. Every new version or part of the system was taken to the hospital for feedback and adjustments were made if necessary. The design took into account the situations of and knowledge from a wide range of stakeholders, such as therapists, patients, carers, medical researchers, people responsible for technical support and IT support, physiotherapists, and occupational therapists.

Preliminary Results

After several preliminary tests with the first set of the current version of the modular sensor floor system in the Sydney hospital (see Fig. 10.15), two further versions have been in use in the hospitals in Adelaide and Sydney since April and May 2013 respectively. In this section we present some of the findings as reported by the practitioners. Some of this data is acquired using our automatic data logging system.

Sydney Hospital

One of the physiotherapists, Daniel Treacy, has been working with a set of tiles at the Sydney hospital for five months, using the system for exercising with patients for two hours every day.

He has reported three experiences of patients who all benefitted from the enhanced feedback of the interactive system in balancing and stepping exercises.

The first patient was a 60 year old, admitted for rehabilitation following a left above knee amputation. After two weeks of slow progress and low motivation he started working with the tiles. His repetition of practice figures more than doubled in the following week, and after that week he was able to move independently with the aid of a rollator frame, whereas previously he needed the assistance of two people. The patient reported to have great benefit of the feedback, where previously he felt unclear about the purpose and progress with regards to the exercises.

The second reported patient experience was that of an 87 year old male with a background of left below knee amputation (similar to the person in Fig. 10.15), who had developed bad knee flexion contracture, and needed to do exercises to extend his hip in standing and walking. The sensor tile with the feedback was applied as a rehabilitation aid, after the patient's 5th day of therapy his results changed from a success rate in exercise task completing from below 10 % to a range between 60–86 % in the following four days.

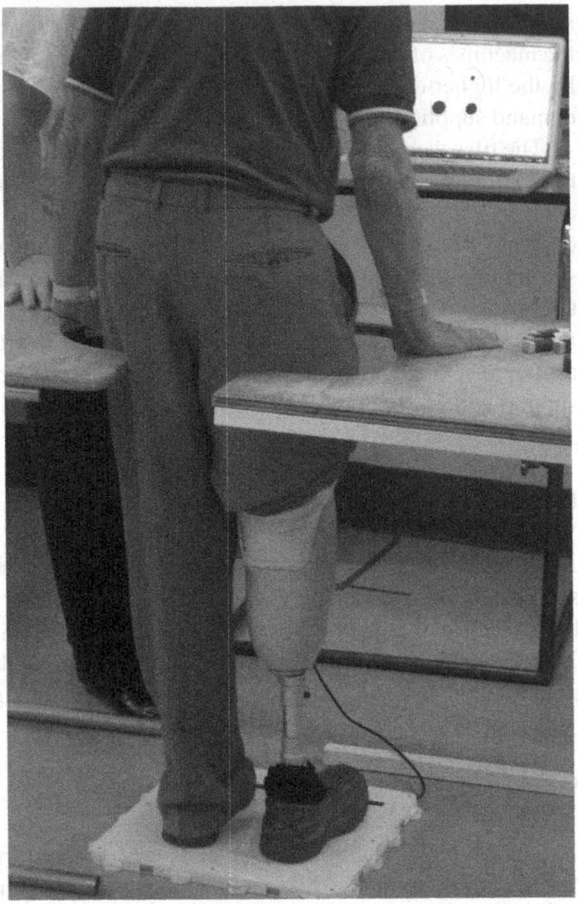

Fig. 10.15 The interactive rehabilitation main tile in use

The third patient experience reported by the physiotherapist involved an 86 year old female who was transferred to rehabilitation after a fractured right hip due to a fall. She previously had a left sided stroke with right-sided weakness. Before the fall and fracture she was able to mobilise independently with no aids. The sit to stand (STS) exercise she was prescribed to do had the aim of getting her to balance evenly between the two feet which was difficult due to the previous stroke and pain, improved from day 18 when the tiles were introduced. While the number of repetitions performed remained constant, she was able to receive more feedback on how effective each one of the repetitions was and resulted in an improved outcome measure in terms of how much weight she was putting through both legs while standing up (The aim is to have 5 % of weight through both limbs). Prior to using the stepping tiles the patient was only putting 20 % of her weight through the effected leg, while after implementing the stepping tiles she was able to more than double this amount to

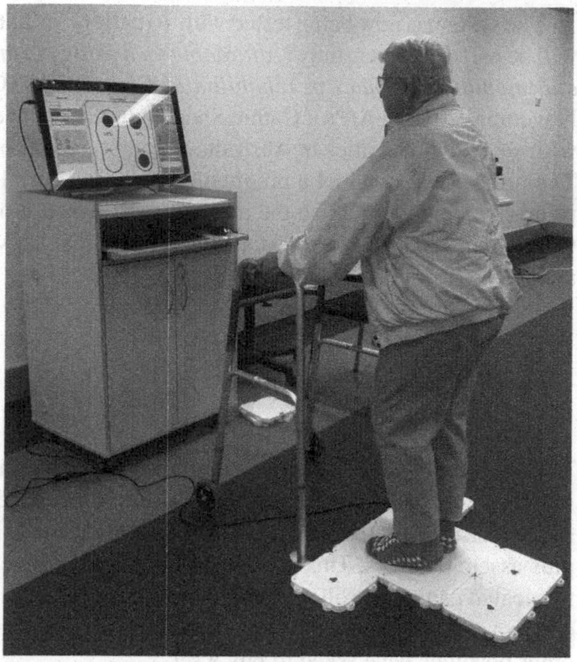

Fig. 10.16 The interactive floor tiles in use in Adelaide

over 40 %. The patient reported that only with this feedback she realised what her balance was, which helped her to reach the more positive results.

These results are informal, but it does reveal the possible application of the system in a clinical setting.

Adelaide Hospital

We are currently working with clinical researcher Dr. Maayken van den Berg who is undertaking a pilot study comparing several rehab exercise setups. The tiles are being used as part of the intervention program in an ongoing research study "*The effect of immediate feedback through video and computer-based interactive exercises on mobility outcome in geriatric and neurological rehabilitation*[3]" at the hospital in Adelaide. This is a space for comparative studies and therapies using several different interactive systems, such as Nintendo Wii based and Microsoft Kinect based systems, dedicated systems, and the interactive floor tiles as shown in Fig. 10.16. Of those patients that have used the tiles (6 out of 7) the average time they were active (not resting or moving in between exercise stations) during the therapy session was 30 min (based on 28 intervention sessions, intervention period still ongoing), of which on average 9 min were spent doing exercises on the tiles.

3 More information about the trial can be found at the Australian and New Zealand Clinical Trials Registry: https://www.anzctr.org.au/Trial/Registration/TrialReview.aspx?ACTRN=12613000610730

The system is now being tested with 40 patient volunteers. In 2014 the floor system will be part of a larger study "*Affordable technology to improve physical activity levels and mobility outcomes in rehabilitation*", an NHMRC[4] Project Grant awarded in November 2013 to A/Prof Cathie Sherrington form The George Institute, partnering with several universities in Australia (the first and second authors are investigators). The project will conduct a pragmatic randomised trial with 300 participants which primarily aims to establish the impact of tailored use of affordable physical activity technologies in addition to usual care on physical activity and mobility at 6 months after randomisation.

10.4 Future Outlook

The sensor tiles have been in continuous use in both hospitals, and a third set is in our lab for development and demonstration purposes. The material costs of each set (consisting of 1 main tile, 4 subtiles, and two bridging tiles) is about $1100, plus assembly costs. This puts the system competitively between the low end mass fabricated game controllers applied for this application domain (a couple of hundred dollars) and the purpose developed solutions which commonly cost $10–20k. Several other hospitals have asked to buy a set.

The aim has been to design the tiles in such a way that they can be assembled with minimal manual labour. The current version still requires quite a bit of skilled work to assemble, soldering all the connections, and some mechanical bits. The easiest way to resolve this is to make the tiles entirely stand-alone, and have them connect wirelessly to each other and/or the computer. Wireless technology however also requires a battery (the current version is powered from the host computer via the USB connection), and a charging system. We have developed all this in one system, assembled from off-the-shelf components, including induction charging which means the tiles can be charged without wires. It is then possible to seal the tiles, for easier cleaning. The increase in costs of the parts is justified by the potential decrease in costs of assembly, with the added benefit of a wider range of possible configurations of the tiles. Currently this is limited to eight sub-tiles, which is enough for a wide range of therapies and exercises but further possibilities include creating a path to walk along to perform gait analysis, which is often required in the wards.

It was interesting and rewarding to see that the tiles are used so intensively, and for many unforeseen purposes such as a sensor surface for pushing against for patients who exercise on a tilting bed, patients with prostheses, exercises which involved balancing on a thick piece of foam on top of the tiles, and stepping up. Some of these applications call for further extensions and modules (Fig. 10.17).

Several further extensions of the sensor tiles are under development, mostly prompted by experiences in the rehabilitation ward. For instance, due to the modular nature of the tiles, it is possible to put a sub-tile on a raised surface to create a more

[4] NHMRC is the National Health and Medical Research Council in Australia.

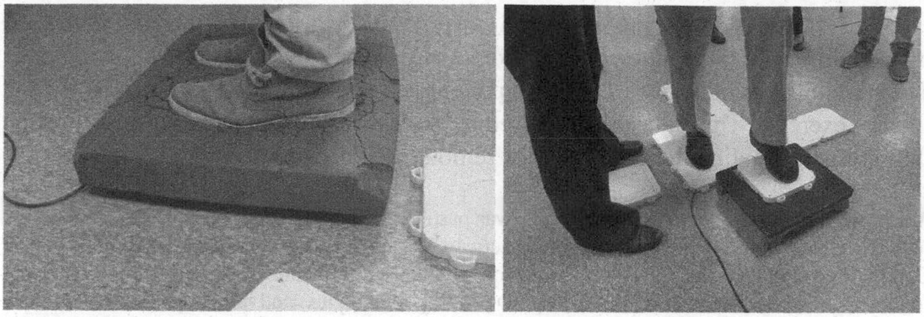

Fig. 10.17 Extended use and modifications of the interactive floor tiles

difficult stepping task. For this and similar activities it is useful to have an extension lead. The edges of the surfaces are a bit sharp, so we are experimenting with ways to create ramps out of acrylic or foam or 3D printed material.

There are further developments in the software too that we have not yet tested in practice, such as a method of visually cueing the patient's desired movements through highlighting the tiles on the screen.

We have shown in this chapter that the tiles fulfil the need for increasing patient's *motivation*. Furthermore, we have a lot of anecdotal evidence that it is really successful with patients, for instance a very problematic patient did not seem to be able to move by himself (in a pushing up exercise on the tilting bed), until he received the graphical feedback of the system. Furthermore we are working on sonic feedback to further support the exercises.

The interactive infrastructure approach can leverage the possibilities of the individual modules. This infrastructure consists of a number of modules and objects, each with a specific purpose such as sensing (weight, movement etc.), displaying (presenting information to the patient and therapist/trainer), or acting as tokens. The modules can communicate with each other (mostly wirelessly), so that there is a continuous flow of movement information and relevant feedback across the modules of the system. Together with the practitioners, and based on our own observations, we have identified a number of other possible modules for performing several measuring and feedback tasks as part of the exercises. There is also an ongoing need for simple and stand-alone modules (the hand counter can operate stand-alone) for patients to use in their own environment. This can possibly be based on smart phones and tablets, as many patients have these, for which we need to develop Apps that can present the patient's exercise data and give feedback in a similar way as applied by products such as the Fitbit, Jawbone and Nike+.

Through this approach of modularity a large part of the demand for *customisability* can be addressed, and it can be further extended by fully applying the printing on demand model where the practitioners can order the right size of the tile (within limits). Although several designs were developed for graphics to put on the tiles, in the end we decided to leave them blank which allows the use of stickers and whiteboard markers by the therapists supporting a wide range of uses.

The system is very easy to set up and can potentially be used by the patient in their own room in the hospital or even at home, supporting the need for *independence*. The logging system keeps track of the patients exercise results, linked to his ID and time of exercise. This data can be shared in real time with a physiotherapist through the Internet, enabling the possibility or remote rehabilitation.

Acknowledgments This phase of the work was partially funded by two grants of the UTS design faculty's Centre for Contemporary Design Practices. We are very grateful for the support of A/Prof Cathie Sherrington of the George Institute for Global Health at the University of Sydney, who funded the redesign of the floor tiles (using 3D printing techniques) and has adopted the two sets in clinical trials. We thank the staff of the hospitals involved for all their invaluable input and feedback on our developments. Particularly physiotherapist Karl Schurr has played a crucial role in all this work, with his deep understanding of all the issues related to patients exercises and motivation, and has driven many of the design processes presented in this chapter. The project has ethics approval nationally, site specific, and from the university.

References

1. Aarts, E., & Marzano, S. (Eds.). (2003). *The new everyday, views on ambient intelligence*. Rotterdam: 010 Publishers.
2. Bagalkot, N. L., Sokoler, T., & Shaikh, R. (2012). Integrating physiotherapy with everyday life: Exploring the space of possibilities through rehandles. *Proceedings of the International Conference Tangible, Embedded, and Embodied Interaction (TEI'12)*, pp. 91–98.
3. Bdeir, A., & Ullrich, T. (2011). Electronics as material: LittleBits. (2011). *Proceedings of the International Conference on Tangible Embedded and Embodied Interaction (TEI'11)*, pp. 341–344.
4. Bongers, A. J. (2004a). Palpable pixels, a method for the development of virtual textures. In S. Ballesteros & M. A. Heller (Eds.), *Touch blindness and neuroscience*, Madrid: UNED Ediciones.
5. Bongers, A. J. (2004b). Sensing systems for interactive architecture. *Proceedings of the Symposium on Gesture Interfaces for Multimedia Systems*, Leeds, March 2004.
6. Bongers, A. J. (2004c). *Interaction with our Electronic Environment - an e-cological approach to physical interface design, Cahier Book series no 34*. Hogeschool van Utrecht: Department of Journalism and Communication.
7. Bongers, A. J., & Harris, Y. C. (2002). A structured instrument design approach: The video-organ. *Proceedings of the Conference on New Instruments for Musical Expression (NIME)*, Media Lab Europe, Dublin, May 2002.
8. Bongers, A. J. & Smith, S. T. (2011). Interactivating rehabilitation through active multimodal feedback and guidance. In: *Smart Healthcare Applications and Services*, Ziefle & Röcker (Eds.), Chapter 11, IGI Global, pp. 236–260.
9. Bongers, A. J., & Smith, S. T. (2010). Interactivated rehabilitation device demo and short paper, *Proceedings of the OzCHI Conference*, Brisbane.
10. Bongers, A. J., & Van der Veer, G. C. (2007). Towards a multimodal interaction space—categorisation and applications, special issue on movement-based interaction. *Journal of Personal and Ubiquitous Computing*, *11*(8), 609–619.
11. Bongers, A. J., Smith S. T., Pickrell, M., Hall, R., & Donker, V. (2013). Interactivated physical rehabilitation modules. *Proceedings of the International ACM Creativity and Cognition Conference*.
12. Calder, B., & Staw, B. (1975). Self-perception of Intrinsic and extrinsic motivation. *Journal of Personality and Social Psychology*, *31*(4), 599–605.

13. Duckworth, J., & Wilson, P. (2010) Embodiment and play in designing an interactive art system for movement rehabilitation. *Second Nature: International Journal of Creative Media, 2*(1), 120–137.
14. Furnham, A. (1997). *The Psychology of behaviour at work—the individual and the organization*. Psychology Press.
15. Gershenfeld, N. (1999). *When Things start to think*. New York: Henry Holt and Co.
16. Gershenfeld, N., Krikorian, R., & Cohen, D. (2004). The internet of things. In. *Scientific American*, pp. 75–81, October 2004.
17. Geurts, L., Vanden Abeele, V., Husson, J., Windey, F., Overveldt, M., Van Annema, J. H. et al. (2011). Digital games for physical therapy: Fulfilling the need for calibration and adaptation. *Proceedings of the Tangible Embedded and Embodied Interaction TEI'11 Conference* , pp. 117–124.
18. Gil-Gomez, J.A., Llorens, R., Alcaniz, M., & Colomer, C. (2011). Effectiveness of a Wii balance board-based system (eBaViR) for balance rehabilitation: A pilot randomized clinical trial in patients with acquired brain injury. *Journal of Neuroengineering and Rehabilitation, 8*(30). http://www.jneuroengrehab.com/about.
19. Hague, R., Campbell, I., & Dickens, P. (2003). Implications on design of rapid prototyping, *Proceedings of the Institution of Mechanical Engineers, 217*, (Part C), 25–30.
20. Heskett, J. (2002). *Toothpicks and Logos: Design in everyday life*. Oxford : Oxford University Press.
21. Hochstenbach-Waelen, A., Timmermans, A. A. A., Seelen, H. A. M., Tetteroo, D., & Markopoulos, P. (2012). Tag-exercise creator: Towards end-user development for tangible interaction in rehabilitation training. *Proceedings of the Engineering Interactive Computing Systems Conference (EICS'12)*, pp. 293–298.
22. Ishii, H., & Ullmer, B. (1997)Tangible bits: Towards seamless interfaces between people, bits and atoms. *Proceedings of the CHI'97 Conference*, pp. 234–241.
23. Jacobs, A., Timmermans, A. A. A., Michielsen, M., Vander Plaetse, M., & Markopoulos, M. (2013). CONTRAST: Gamification of arm-hand training for stroke survivors. *Proceedings of the CHI'13 Conference*.
24. Lund, H. H. (2009). Modular robotics for playful physiotherapy. *Proceedings of the IEEE-ICORR*.
25. Maclean, N., Pound, P., Wolfe, C., & Rudd, A. (2000). Qualitative analysis of stroke patients in rehabilitation. *British Medical Journal, 321*, 1051–1054.
26. Mouawad, M. R., Doust, C. G., Max, M. D., & McNulty, P. A. (2011). Wii-based movement therapy to promote improved upper extremity function post-stroke: A pilot study. *Journal of Rehabilitation Medicine, 43*(6), 527–533.
27. Oosterhuis, K. (2002). *Architecture goes wild*. Rotterdam: 010 Publishers 2002.
28. Oosterhuis, K. (2003). *Hyperbodies—towards an e-motive architecture*. Basel: Birkhäuser.
29. Oosterhuis, K. (2011). *Towards a new kind of building- a designers guide for nonstandard architecture*. Rotterdam: NAI Publishers.
30. Pickrell, M., & Bongers, A. J. (2011). Re-Ability Sleeve—A Modular Wearable Rehabilitation Interface System. Workshop paper SmartHealth, OzCHI 2001.
31. Schoene D., Lord S. R., Delbaere K., Severino C., Davies T. A., & Smith S. T. A. (2013). Randomized controlled pilot study of home-based step training in older people using videogame technology. *PLoS ONE, 8*(3), e57734.
32. Schoene, D., Lord, S. R., Verhoef, P., & Smith, S. T. A. (2011). Novel *Video Game-Based Device for Measuring Stepping Performance and Fall Risk in Older People. Archives of Physical Medicine and Rehabilitation, 92*(6), 947–953.
33. Seo, K., & Ryu, H. (2014). RehabMaster^{TM}': A pervasive rehabilitation platform for stroke patients and their caregivers. In: *Pervasive Health: State-of-the-Art & Beyond*.
34. Shaer, O., & Hornecker, E. (2010). Tangible User Interfaces: Past, Present and Future Directions. *FnT in HCI, 3*(1–2), 1–138.
35. Sherrington, C., Whitney, J.C., Lord, S.R., Herbert, R, D., Cumming. R.G., & Close. J.C. (2008). Effective exercise for the prevention of falls: A systematic review and meta-analysis. *The American Geriatrics Society, 56*(12), 2234–2243.

36. Siegert, R. J., & William, J. T. (2004). Theoretical aspects of goal-setting and motivation in rehabilitation. *Disability and Rehabilitation*, *26*, 1–8.
37. Smith, S. T., Sherrington, C., Schoene, D., Studenski, S., & Lord, S. R. (2011). A novel dance dance revolution system for in-home training of stepping ability in older adults. *British Journal of Sports Medicine*, *45*(5), 441–445.

Further Readings

38. Anderson, C. (2006). *The long tail: Why the future of business is selling less of more*. New York: Hyperion.
39. Igoe, T., & D. O'Sullivan. (2004). Physical computing—sensing and controlling the physical world with computers. Thomson Course Technology PTR.
40. Maloney, A. E. et al. (2008). A pilot of a video game (DDR) to promote physical activity and decrease sedentary screen time. *Obesity (Silver Spring, Md.)*, *16*(9), 2074–2080.
41. Markillie, P. (2012). Special report: Manufacturing and innovation. *The Economist*, *403*(8781).

Chapter 11
The Ongoing Development of a Multimedia Gaming Module to Aid Speech, Language and Communication

Elizabeth Stokes

11.1 Introduction

This chapter establishes that learners with disabilities, such as those on the autistic spectrum have diverse therapeutic (speech, language and communication) needs. It suggests that intervention should be developed in collaboration with therapists specifically taking each learner's therapeutic needs into consideration, in order to help each learner's speech, language and communication difficulties. This chapter sets out to explain how a module was developed in order to solve this problematical issue. The aim is to demonstrate how a gaming module was successfully implemented over many years [1]. The objectives were for a lecturer to work in collaboration with practitioners on the completion of profiles (case studies) [2]. The chapter demonstrates how university students studying a multimedia module developed individualised therapeutic/educational games to aid each learner's speech, language and communication based on their profiles.

The collaboration of practitioners and the lecturer resulted in merging society and academia. The realism of this coursework motivated the students. This was through the knowledge that their efforts, not only resulted in them gaining theoretical and practical technological skills and passing the module [1], but that their attempts could potentially be a useful and supportive therapeutic aid for the practitioners. The chapter begins with a discussion of a case study using the 5–14 Elaborated Curriculum for monitoring [3] the use of non-computerised therapy for speech, language and communication. This was achieved with a representative group of five anonymous (verbal and non-verbal) primary school aged learners, on the autistic spectrum, in a representative special school.

E. Stokes (✉)
Department of Computer Science, Middlesex University, School of Science and Technology, Hendon, London, UK
e-mail: estokes12000@yahoo.co.uk

A. Holzinger et al. (eds.), *Pervasive Health*, Human–Computer Interaction Series,
DOI: 10.1007/978-1-4471-6413-5_11,

11.2 Glossary

AAC Alternative Augmentative Communication system is used in this chapter to mean high and low tech communication methods used for learners on the autistic spectrum. These are additional aids to the traditional speech, language and communication methods used by speech and language therapists and practitioners in the classroom.

AS The chapter uses the term Autistic Spectrum to mean learners with an Autistic Spectrum Disorder (ASD).

Elaborated Curriculum an alternative to the National Curriculum used by some schools.

GLAD Games for Learners with Autism and/or other Disabilities. The author's own software development company developing individualised, personalised educational software for these learners.

HCI Human Computer Interaction stated in this chapter refers to the study, planning and designing of computerised interventions and how people (users) interact with them.

HTA Hierarchical Task Analysis referred to in the chapter as a sub-division of tasks, which needs to be implemented.

ICT Information Communication Technology stated in the chapter in relation to computers and software being used in schools for learners on the autistic spectrum.

NAPC National Autism Plan for Children referred to in this chapter are the guidelines for identifying, assessing and diagnosing for interventions for learners on the autistic spectrum.

PEC Picture Exchange Communication. This is a low tech AAC system that enables learners with speech, language and communication difficulties to initiate interaction through an exchange of pictures.

SEN Special Educational Needs is referred to as learners who have learning disabilities and/or difficulties.

TEACCH Treatment and Education of Autistic and related Communication-handicapped Children. This is a low tech AAC system that helps learners with speech, language and communication difficulties through visual support.

11.3 Non-computerised Conventional Therapy

The investigation set out to establish how a representative group of learners' (on the autistic spectrum) therapeutic needs, had been taken into consideration with their achievements monitored using non-computerised conventional methods.

Table 11.1 No of learners who had completed each step in each strand in the attainment outcome: interaction section

Strands	Step 1	Step 2	Step 3	Step 4	Step 5	Step 6	Step 7
Strand 1 accepting and sharing feelings	5	5	2	2	1	0	0
Strand 2 attending and responding (receptive)	4	4	3	2	1	0	0
Strand 3 vocal/gestural production (expressive)	5	5	3	2	0	0	0
Strand 4 turn taking	5	5	4	3	2	0	0
Strand 5 interactive play	5	4	1	0	0	0	0

To monitor each learner's speech, language and communication achievements, practitioners from a representative school highlighted five learners' (E1–E5) therapeutic accomplishments. This was in relation to their attainment outcomes, Strands and seven steps identified in the Language and Communication section of the 5–14 Elaborated Curriculum (an alternative to the National Curriculum) [3], over 2 years, using conventional non-computerised therapeutic methods.

11.4 Results in Relation to Attainment Outcome: Interaction

The section Attainment Outcome: Interaction consisted of five Strands each with seven steps. The Strands monitored the use on non-computerised therapy to demonstrate each learner's therapeutic (speech, language and communication) achievements. Strand 1: Accepting and sharing feelings; Strand 2: Attending and responding (receptive skills); Strand 3: Vocal and Gestural production (expressive skills); Strand 4: Turn taking skills and Strand 5: Interactive Play.

Table 11.1 demonstrates that with the exception to Strand 2: Attending and responding (receptive skills), four of the Strands (Strand 1: Accepting and sharing feelings, Strand 3: Vocal/Gestural production (expressive skills), Strand 4: Turn taking, and Strand 5: Interactive play) had one or two steps, which had not even been partially completed by the learners. This shows that some of the steps had been partially or totally not completed by some of the learners in this study using non-computerised conventional therapeutic interventions demonstrating that over 2 years these learners were still not achieving the Attainment Outcome: Interaction.

11.4.1 Strand 1: Accepting and Sharing Feelings

The results (Table 11.1) shows how two of the steps (Steps 1 and 2), in relation to this Strand, were completed by all the learners, however, Steps 6 and 7 were not completed by any of the learners. Three of the steps (Steps 3–5) were partially completed by the learners. Figure 11.1 shows how only one learner (E1) had either partially or completed all the steps with one learner (E4) in the group, having a greater number of completed steps in Strand 1. Four of the learners (E1–E3 and E5) had partially completed more steps. Although this demonstrates that whatever non-computerised

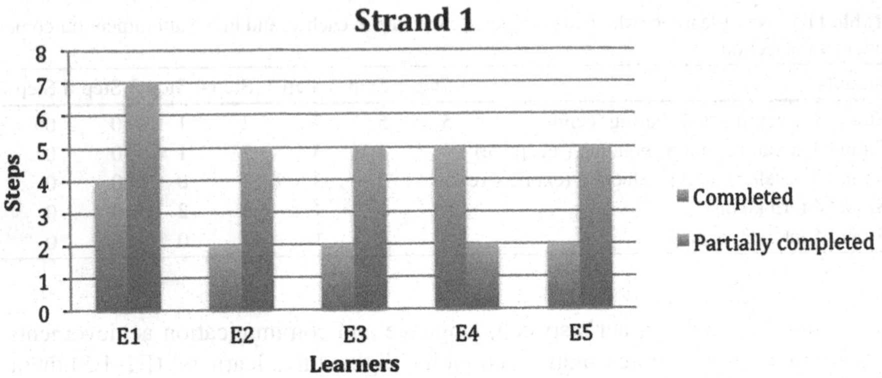

Fig. 11.1 Steps completed or partially completed by the learners—attainment outcome: interaction, strand 1—accepting and sharing feelings section

therapeutic intervention had been used has had some therapeutic effect, it did not totally help these learners to fully achieve the Attainment Outcome: Interaction and Strand 1: Accepting and sharing feelings section.

11.4.2 Strand 2: Attending and Responding (Receptive Skills)

The results (Table 11.1) show that four learners completed Steps 1 and 2. However, Steps 6 and 7 were not completed by any of the learners. Figure 11.1 shows that one learner (E1) did not complete any of the steps. It did not show whether their variance of therapeutic and spectrum of needs, strength, likes and interests had been taken into consideration. Equally, it did not, demonstrate what non-computerised intervention had been effectively used for the learners (E3 and E5) who managed to complete more steps in the Attainment Outcome: Interaction Strand 2: Accepting and responding (receptive skills) section (Fig. 11.2).

11.4.3 Strand 3: Vocal/Gestural Production (Expressive Skills)

The results (Table 11.1) show how all the learners completed Steps 1 and 2. However, Steps 6 and 7 were not completed by any of the learners. Figure 11.3 shows that three of the learners (E2, E3 and E5) had a greater number of partially completed steps. There were no indications as to what non-computerised conventional therapeutic method had been used effectively for helping the learners achieve this Attainment Outcome: Interaction, Strand 3: Vocal/Gestural production (expressive skills). Once again this did not show whether their variance in speech, language and communication needs had been taken into consideration.

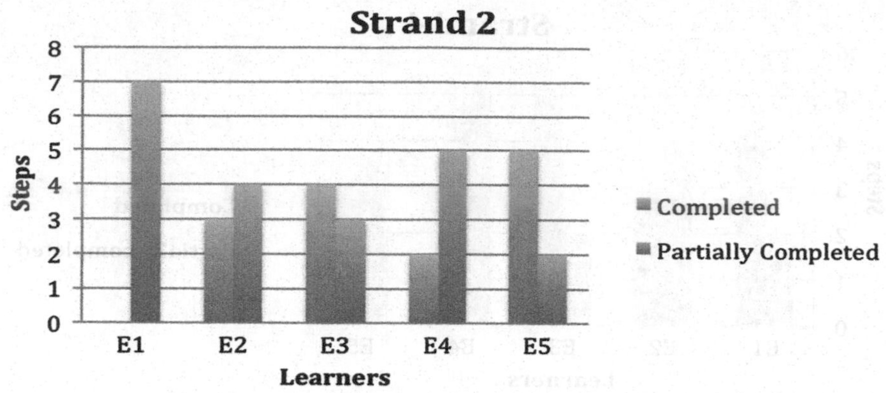

Fig. 11.2 Steps completed or partially completed by learners—attainment outcome: interaction, strand 2—attending and responding (receptive) section

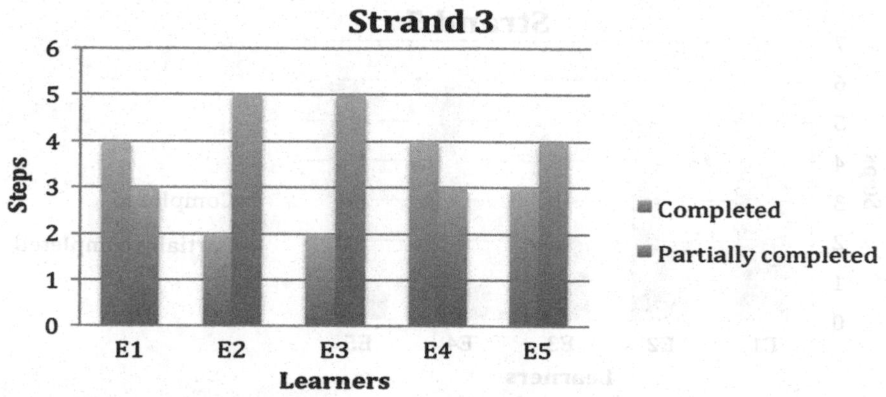

Fig. 11.3 Steps completed or partially completed by learners—attainment outcome: interaction, strand 3—vocal/gestural production (expressive skills) section

11.4.4 Strand 4: Turn Taking

The results (Table 11.1) show how all the learners completed Steps 1 and 2, whereas, Steps 6 and 7 were not completed by any of the learners. Figure 11.4, however, shows how two of the five learners (E1 and E3) had more partially completed steps, whereas, three out of the five learners (E2, E4 and E5) had a greater number of completed steps in Strand 4. However, there was no indication as to what effective non-computerised conventional therapeutic intervention had been used to help them achieve this Attainment Outcome: Interaction and Strand 4: Turn-taking section.

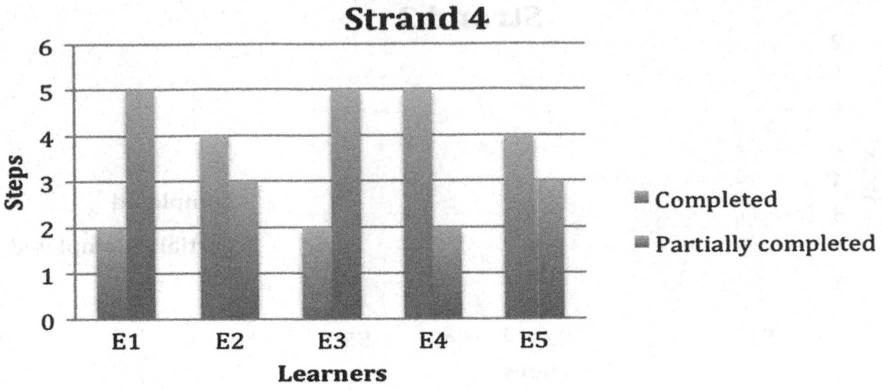

Fig. 11.4 Steps completed or partially completed by learners—attainment outcome: interaction, strand 4—turn taking section

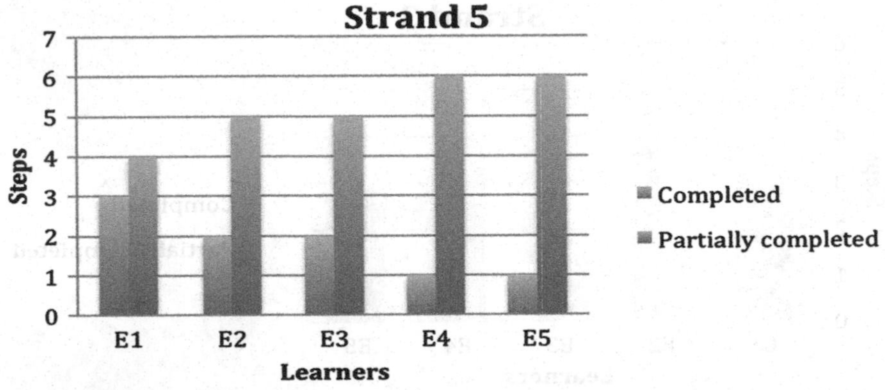

Fig. 11.5 Steps completed or partially completed by learners—attainment outcome: interaction, strand 5—interactive play section

11.4.5 Strand 5: Interactive Play

The results (Table 11.1) show that all the learners completed Step 1, however, none of the learners completed Steps 4–7. Figure 11.5 shows that two learners (E4 and E5) either completed or partially completed six of the steps. All the learners had a greater number of partially completed steps. However, there were no indications as to what effective non-computerised conventional therapeutic interventions had been used by each of the learners to assist them achieve the Attainment Outcome: Interaction and Strand 5 Interactive play section.

Table 11.2 No of learners who had completed the steps in each strand in the attainment outcome: listening and understanding section

Strands	Step 1	Step 2	Step 3	Step 4	Step 5	Step 6	Step 7
Strand 6 understanding first words and actions	4	4	3	2	1	1	0
Strand 7 listening for information and directions	5	4	1	1	1	0	0
Strand 8 listening in groups	5	2	1	1	0	0	0
Strand 9 listening in order to respond to texts	5	4	2	1	0	0	0

11.5 Results in Relation to Attainment Outcome: Listening and Understanding

Table 11.2 demonstrates that this Attainment Outcome Listening and Understanding contains four Strands (Strand 6: Understanding First Words and Actions; Strand 7 Listening for information and direction; Strand 8: Listening in Groups and Strand 9: Listening in order to respond to text). Step 1 (Strands 7–9) had been completed by all the learners over 2 years, whereas, Step 7 (Strands 6–9) had not be completed by any of the learners.

11.5.1 Strand 6: Understanding First Words and Actions

The results (Table 11.2, Fig. 11.6) show that Steps 1 and 2 were completed by four of the learners (E1, E2, E4 and E5). Step 7 was not even partially completed by any of the learners. One learner (E3) did not complete any of the step, however partially completed all seven steps. One learner (E4) had more completed steps. However, there were no indications if any effective non-computerised conventional therapeutic methods were used to help each learner achieve this Attainment outcome: Listening and Understanding Strand 6: Understanding First Words and Actions section.

11.5.2 Strand 7: Listening for Information and Directions

The results (Table 11.2, Fig. 11.7) show that Step 1 was completed by all the learners, however, Steps 6 and 7 were not completed by any of the learners. Four of the learners (E1–E3 and E5) had more partially completed steps. One learner (E4) had more completed steps. Although, all the learners had showed that the non-computerised conventional therapeutic aid had helped them achieve this Attainment Outcome: Listening and Understanding, Strand 7: Listening for information and direction skills had been effective, however, there was no indication as to what therapeutic aid had been used and whether the learners needs were taken into consideration.

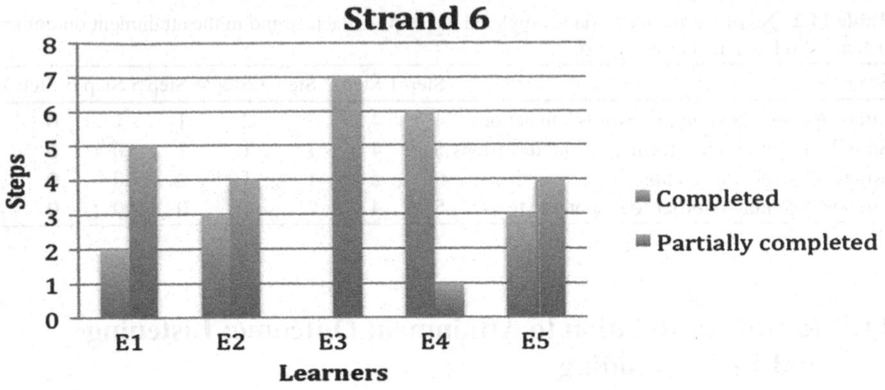

Fig. 11.6 Steps completed or partially completed by learners—attainment outcome: listening and understanding, strand 6—understanding first words and actions section

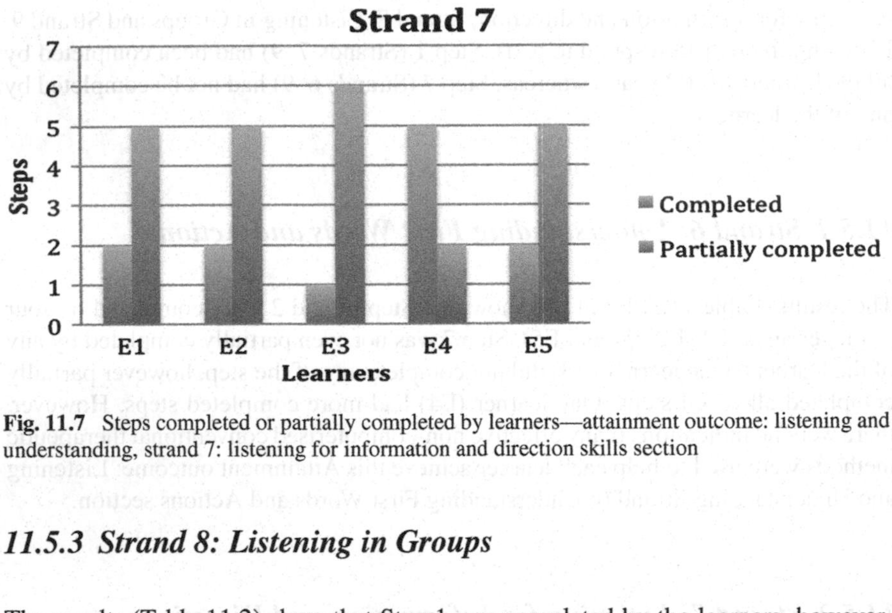

Fig. 11.7 Steps completed or partially completed by learners—attainment outcome: listening and understanding, strand 7: listening for information and direction skills section

11.5.3 Strand 8: Listening in Groups

The results (Table 11.2) show that Step 1 was completed by the learners, however, Steps 5–7 were not completed by any of the learners with Fig. 11.7 showing that Step 7 was not even partially completed by any of the learners. With the exception to one of the learners (E4), four of the learners (E1–E3 and E5) had more partially completed steps than completed steps.

However, there was no indication as to what non-computerised conventional therapeutic interventions were used to help each of these learners achieve this Attainment Outcome: Listening and Understanding and Strand 8: Listening in groups skills section (Fig. 11.8).

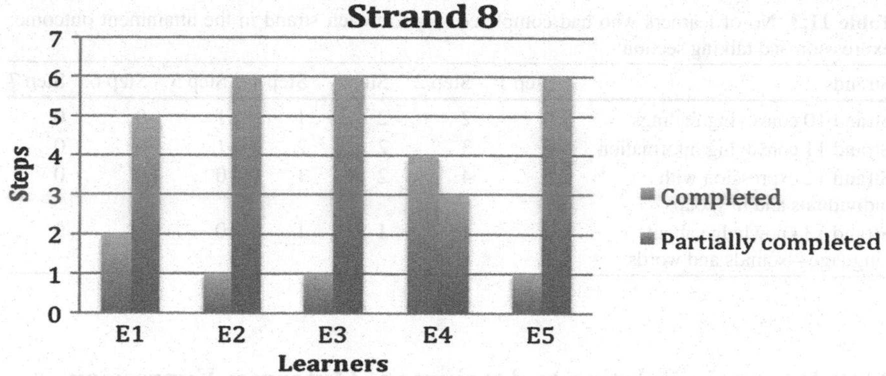

Fig. 11.8 Steps completed or partially completed by learners—attainment outcome: listening and understanding, strand 8—listening in groups section

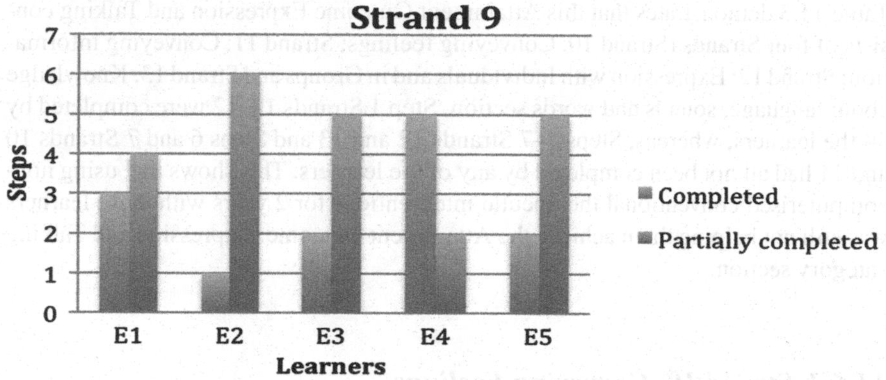

Fig. 11.9 Steps completed or partially completed by learners—attainment outcome: listening and understanding, strand 9: listening in order to respond to text section

11.5.4 Strand 9: Listening in Order to Respond to Texts

The results (Table 11.2) show that Step 1 was completed by all the learners, whereas, Steps 5–7 had not been completed by any of the learners. Figure 11.9 shows how Step 7 had not even been partially completed by any of the learners. Figure 11.9 also shows that with the exception to one learner (E4) who achieved more completed steps, the other learners (E1–E3 and E5) had more partially completed steps. However, there was no indication as to what non-computerised conventional therapeutic interventions were stated as being used in order to help these learners achieve this Attainment Outcome: Listening and Understanding and Strand 9: Listening section in order for them to respond to text skills.

Table 11.3 No of learners who had completed steps in each strand in the attainment outcome: expression and talking section

Strands	Step 1	Step 2	Step 3	Step 4	Step 5	Step 6	Step 7
Strand 10 conveying feelings	5	2	2	1	1	0	0
Strand 11 conveying information	5	3	2	2	1	0	0
Strand 12 expression with individuals and in groups	5	4	2	1	0	0	0
Strand 13 knowledge about language—sounds and words	3	1	1	1	0	0	0

11.6 Results in Relation to Attainment Outcome: Expression and Talking

Table 11.3 demonstrates that this Attainment Outcome Expression and Talking consists of four Strands (Strand 10: Conveying feelings; Strand 11: Conveying information; Strand 12: Expression with Individuals and in Groups and Strand 13: Knowledge about language, sounds and words section. Step 1 Strands 10–12 were completed by all the learners, whereas, Steps 5–7 Strands 12 and 13 and Steps 6 and 7 Strands 10 and 11 had all not been completed by any of the learners. This shows that using non-computerised conventional therapeutic interventions for 2 years with these learners was still not helping them achieve the Attainment Outcome: Expression and Talking category section.

11.6.1 Strand 10: Conveying Feelings

The results (Table 11.3) show that Step 1 was completed by all the learners, whereas, Steps 6 and 7 were not completed by any of the learners.

Figure 11.10 shows that four of the learners E1–E3 and E5 had more partially completed steps whereas; one learner (E4) had more completed steps. However, there was no indication as to what non-computerised conventional therapeutic interventions had been used to help this learner and the other learners to achieve this Attainment Outcome: Expression and Talking and this Strand 10 Conveying feelings section.

11.6.2 Strand 11: Conveying Information

The results (Table 11.3) show that all the learners completed Step 1, whereas Steps 6–7 were not completed by any of the learners. Figure 11.11 show that three of the learners (E2, E3, E5) had more partially completed steps. Two of the learners (E1 and

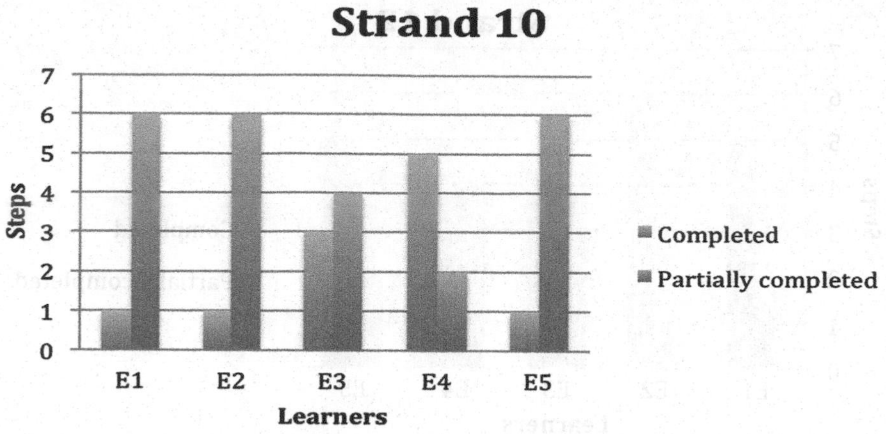

Fig. 11.10 Steps completed or partially completed by learners—attainment outcome: expression and talking, strand 10: conveying feelings section

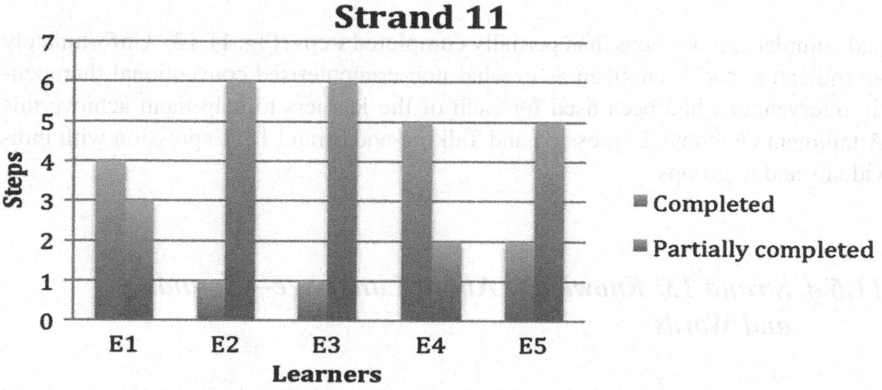

Fig. 11.11 Steps completed or partially completed by learners—attainment outcome: expression and talking, strand 11: conveying information section

E4) completed more steps than the other learners. However, there were no indication as to what non-computerised conventional therapeutic interventions were used with each of these learners to help them achieve this Attainment Outcome: Expression and Talking and Strand 11: Conveying information section.

11.6.3 Strand 12: Expression with Individuals and in Groups

The results (Table 11.3) show that all the learners completed Step 1 and Steps 5–7 were not completed by any of the learners. Figure 11.12 shows that three of the learners (E1–E3 and E5) had partially completed steps, whereas, one learner (E4)

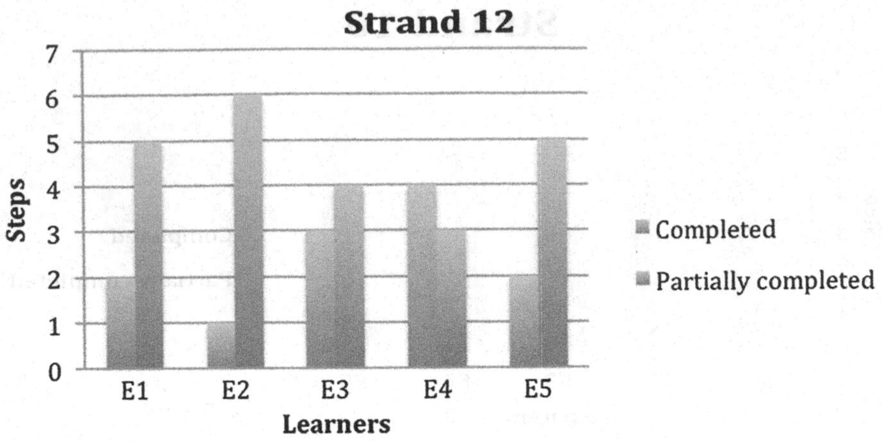

Fig. 11.12 Steps completed or partially completed by learners—attainment outcome: expression and talking, strand 12: expression with individuals and in groups section

had completed more steps than partially completed steps (Fig. 11.12). Unfortunately no indication had been given as to what non-computerised conventional therapeutic interventions had been used for each of the learners to help them achieve this Attainment Outcome: Expression and Talking and Strand 12: Expression with individuals and in groups.

11.6.4 Strand 13: Knowledge About Language—Sounds and Words

The results (Table 11.3) show that five steps (Steps 1–5) were partially completed by the learners, however, Steps 6 and 7 were not completed by any of the learners. Figure 11.13 demonstrates that two of the learners (E2 and E5) had not completed any of the steps, whereas, one learner (E4) had completed more steps. However, there was no indication as to what non-computerised conventional therapeutic intervention had been used to help the learners achieve this Attainment Outcome: Expression and Talking and Strand 13 Knowledge about language—sounds and words section.

11.7 Results in Relation to Attainment Outcome: Reading and Writing

Table 11.4 demonstrates that this Attainment Outcome; Reading and Writing contain three Strands (Strand 14: Reading for information; Strand 15: Reading for enjoyment; Strand 16: Matching and Sequencing). Steps 1–5 (Strands 14–16) were partially

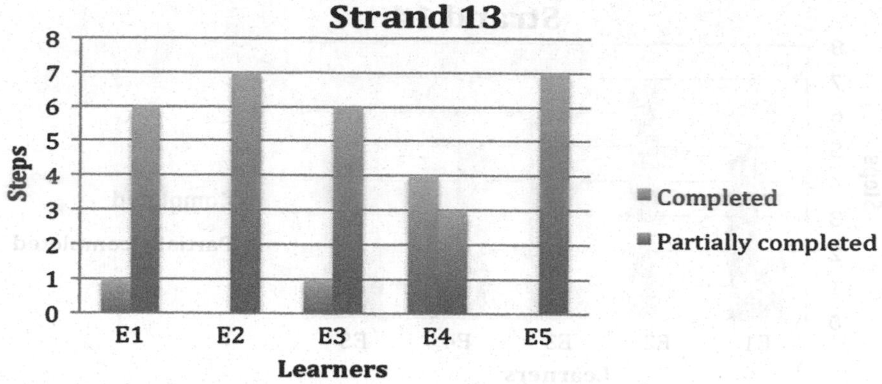

Fig. 11.13 Steps completed or partially completed by learners—attainment outcome: expression and talking, strand 13 knowledge about language—sounds and words section

Table 11.4 No of learners who had completed steps in each strand in the attainment outcome: reading and writing section

Strands	Step 1	Step 2	Step 3	Step 4	Step 5	Step 6	Step 7
Strand 14 reading for information	4	3	1	1	1	0	0
Strand 15 reading for enjoyment	4	4	3	3	1	0	0
Strand 16 matching and sequencing	4	3	2	1	1	1	0

completed by the learners. However, Strands 14 and 15 (Steps 6 and 7) and Strand 16 (Step 7) had not been completed by any of the learners. This shows that using non-computerised conventional therapeutic interventions for 2 years for these learners was still not helping them achieve the Attainment Outcome: Reading and Writing section.

11.7.1 Strand 14: Reading for Information

The results (Table 11.4) show that Steps 1–5 were partially completed by all the learners, however, none of the learners completed Steps 6 and 7. Figure 11.14 show that one learner (E2) had not completed any of the steps. However, one learner (E4) had more completed steps, whereas, three of learners (E1, E3 and E5) had more partially completed steps. However, there were no indications as to what non-computerised conventional therapeutic interventions had been used to aid these learners in achieving this Attainment Outcome: Reading and Writing and this Strand: Reading for information section.

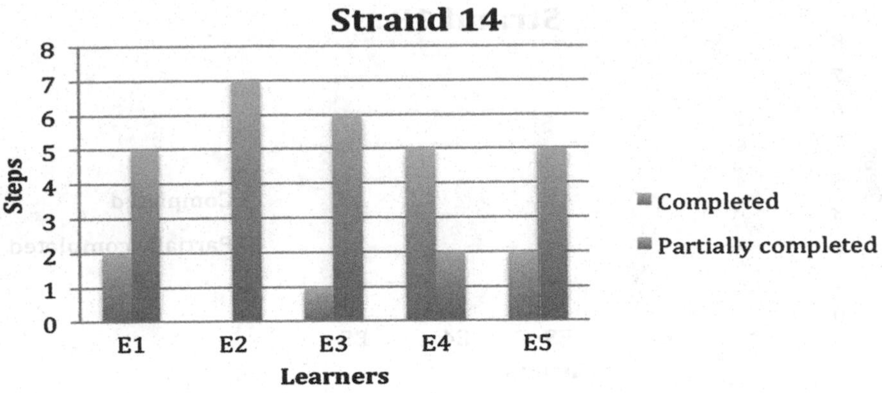

Fig. 11.14 Steps completed or partially completed by learners—attainment outcome: reading and writing, strand 14: reading for information section

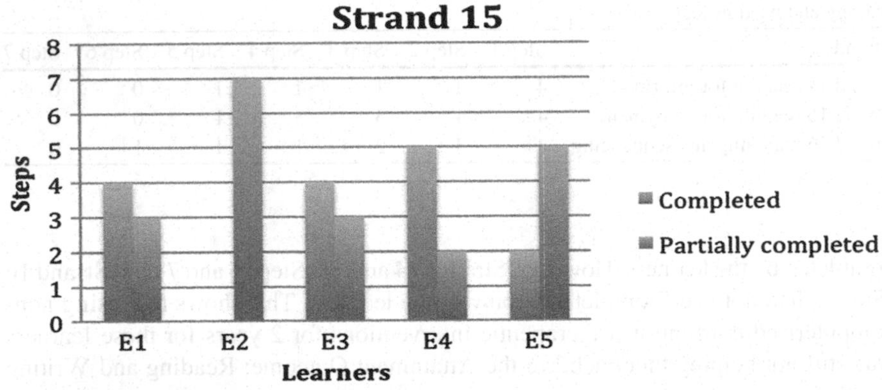

Fig. 11.15 Steps completed or partially completed by learners—attainment outcome: reading and writing, strand 15 reading for enjoyment section

11.7.2 Strand 15: Reading for Enjoyment

The results (Table 11.4) showed that Steps 1–5 were partially completed by all the learners, however, none of the learners completed Steps 6 and 7. Figure 11.15 show that one learner (E5) had more partially completed steps with one learner E2 not completing any of the steps. However, there were three of the learners (E1, E3 and E4) who had more completed steps than the other learners (Fig. 11.15).

However, there was no indication as to what non-computerised conventional therapeutic interventions had been used to help them achieve this Attainment Outcome: Reading and Writing for this Strand: Reading for enjoyment.

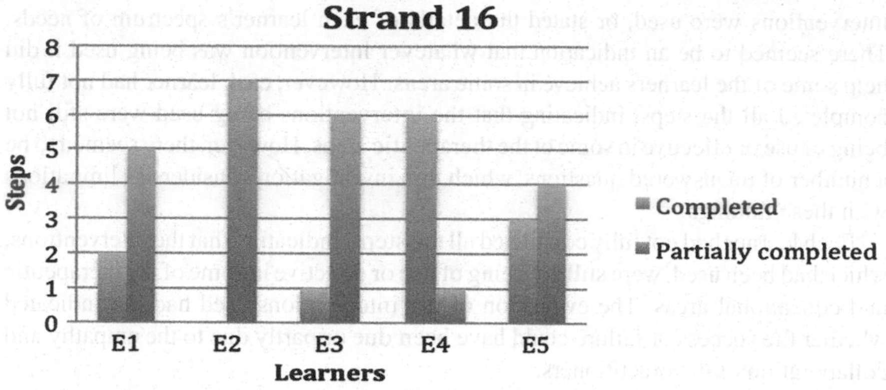

Fig. 11.16 Steps fully completed and partially completed for attainment outcome: reading and writing, strand 16: matching and sequencing section

11.7.3 Strand 16: Matching and Sequencing

The results (Table 11.4) showed that Steps 1–6 were partially completed by all the learners, however, none of the learners completed Step 7. Figure 11.16 shows that three learners (E1, E3 and E5) had partially completed steps and one learner (E2) did not complete any of the steps. However, one learner (E4) completed more steps than the other learners. However, there was no indication what non-computerised conventional therapeutic interventions had been used to aid the learners achieve this Attainment Outcome: Reading and Writing and Strand 16: Matching and Sequencing section.

11.8 An Evaluation of Non-computerised Interventions

The investigation questioned the very unsystematic inconsistent manner of monitoring, using non-computerised interventions, for speech, language and communication development. The analysis of the qualitative data, from the Language and Communication section of the 5–14 Elaborated Curriculum [3], which the practitioners had colour-coded, had demonstrated some therapeutic effectiveness of the non-computerised therapeutic conventional methods used for each learner's speech, language and communication over 2 years.

The results demonstrated that monitoring had been carried out, without indicating whether quantitative and/or qualitative data had been used and how the areas covered influenced the success of the achievement for each step. This made the analysis difficult to justify, although, the evaluation of the group highlighted various steps reached by each learner relating to their speech, language and communication. It did not show how these highlighted areas were achieved, what, when and how often the interventions were used, or stated the details of each learner's spectrum of needs. There seemed to be an indication that whatever intervention was being used it did help some of the learners achieve in some areas. However, each learner had not fully completed all the steps, indicating that the interventions being used were still not being of use or effective in some of the therapeutic areas. However, there seemed to be a number of unanswered questions, which this investigation considers as limitations with these findings.

Each learner had not fully completed all the steps, indicating that the interventions, which had been used, were still not being of use or effective in some of the therapeutic and educational areas. The evaluation of the interventions used had not indicated whether the success or failure could have been due or partly due to the empathy and collaboration of the practitioners.

Although, the conventional therapeutic non-computerised interventions used in the classroom were of some use and effective for the learners in the group with 15 % steps completed, 44 % steps partially completed and 41 % steps not completed by the learners over 2 years. There seemed to be an indication that whatever intervention was being used it did help some of the learners achieve in some areas. This demonstrates that conventional therapeutic methods were of use for some of the learners.

Therefore, the results from this case study have shown that some of these learners managed to complete some of the steps over the 2-year period. This was an indication that whatever non-computerised conventional interventions had been used, it appears that they were of some therapeutic use, for these AS learners, on the 5–14 Elaborated Curriculum [3].

11.9 Open Problems

In order to continue and discuss State-of the Art interventions, the investigation needs to indicate how it was not apparent whether some areas in the non-computerised study were taken into consideration. It was not evident whether a holistic individualised design-for-one approach [4, 5] had been adopted.

It was also not apparent whether each learner's diverse variance [2] in their speech, language and communication abilities, difficulties, medical conditions, comprehension, strengths, likes and interests had been taken into consideration.

This, as well as, each learner's preferential modality (tactile, visual and auditory) and favoured multimedia elements (text, sound, graphics, animation and video) [6, 7] were also not apparently taken into consideration.

It was not shown that these areas, through the collaboration of a multidisciplinary team, were used as a baseline, for the implementation in the non-computerised interventions, which has demonstrated to be of some potential therapeutic use for some of the learners.

11.10 Difficulties Addressed by State-of-the-Art Interventions

The investigation questions whether these difficulties were addressed by generic software being developed. Putnam and Chong's [8] study on software and technologies designed for people with autism used results from online qualitative and quantitative data from parents, family members, special education practitioners and other practitioners who worked with learners diagnosed on the autistic spectrum. They claimed that there has been minimal research into the development of useful technologies with its aim being for users' goals. However, Parsons et al. [9] have claimed that there is insufficient evidence of the effectiveness of multimedia therapeutic and educational interventions compared with others.

However, the researchers ontological and epistemological concepts and the case study already outlined, demonstrated many limitations. These were taken into consideration in the development of an assignment for a module which would give the students a real and meaningful coursework and which would be of therapeutic use for practitioners and ultimately for real end users.

11.11 The Development of the Module

The lecturer's ontological viewpoint was shaped from anecdotal and personal first hand evidence from her own experiences of having a 25-year-old daughter on the autistic spectrum and with complex difficulties. Her epistemological concepts were strengthened by the knowledge she gained from her professional work, her critical literature review findings, the data gathered for the investigation and her own publications.

The lecturer's daughter had difficulties with her speech, language and communication. This resulted in severe behavioural problems. Over the years her daughter received limited speech and language therapy, due to the lack of therapists and the little speech and language therapy she received had little effect.

11.12 How the Problems and Limitation Were Resolved

Section 11.9 highlighted the potential issues, limitations and problems, which developers, researchers, therapists, practitioners and others need to take into consideration when considering the development of therapeutic interventions.

The investigation discusses how a therapeutic and educational computerised multimedia module was used to develop individualised therapeutic software. This began with the development and production of a blank template of the profile (case study), which had been used as a baseline, in order to resolve the problems already highlighted.

First hand knowledge of the lack and limitations of speech and language therapy and as an academic, knowledgeable about the capabilities of multimedia authoring software resulted in the origination, development and implementation of an embedded unique assignment within a multimedia module. This was achieved through collaboration and participation of practitioners from one school using six of their learners on the autistic spectrum.

11.13 The Module

The aims and objectives of the multimedia module was to introduce students to the theory of multimedia, to develop research and academic writing skills, to teach scripting, digital and audio technology, image and sound editing skills, storyboarding and to develop a multimedia product using authoring software.

Assignments are used in academia to assess students, knowledge and academic skills learnt whilst studying the module. Students are often given completely hypothetical scenarios not relating to real-world situations by academics. They are sometimes allowed to choose an area as part of their coursework, which may also end up being based on imaginary situations.

The development and production of the coursework takes up a lot of the student's time and energy. This results in a stressful self-profiting venture of striving to make every effort to produce their best work possible, in order to achieve the best grade. However, after achieving the grade, all this sadly soon becomes forgotten with their efforts ending up being of pointless use to them or others, resulting in abandonment on a shelf to gather dust, stored away out of sight by the student or academic, probably never to be looked at again and ending up with the coursework being condemned to the bin.

Therefore, it was important to provide students with a real assignment, to achieve useful results outliving the life expectancy of the coursework. Furthermore, a real-life situation needs to be used, with students playing a participant role and focusing on the reality of the investigation. This, in turn, motivates them by making the student and the coursework part of a real situation, ultimately being of use in the real world long after its completion.

11.14 The Unique Assignment in the Module

The assignment was produced in order to assess the students' knowledge, understanding and academic attainment in relation to the learning outcomes of the module [1]. Students gained theoretical knowledge of planning, research and design methodologies, data gathering, design principles, the user interface, the nature of functionality, usability, accessibility and evaluation for quality control, for the development of games for real users in society. Students gained an understanding of the basic principles of multimedia and associated technologies, experiences of different software tools and an understanding of the appropriateness of multimedia elements (text, sound, animation, graphics) [4, 5] in relation to their End User's (learner's) preference to a tactile, visual, auditory modality and in relation to each of the learner's speech, language, communication areas completed by the therapists on the profiles [2].

Therefore, in order to produce a coursework, which could continue and be of use to others, a real-life problem in society was used, with students playing a participant role and focusing on producing therapeutic games [10] for real learners with disabilities in schools, using case studies (profiles) [2]. Roberts and Allen [11, 12] and Kimmel [13] have claimed that some students regarded their participation in research as being therapeutically beneficial to them by stating that...

> ...a good number of surveys broadly demonstrate that students believe they have benefited educationally from participation and that they do find it a positive and useful experience...[13, pp. 803-804].

11.15 Case Studies (Profiles)

The importance of case studies (profiles) [2], as pointed out by Shneiderman and Plaisant [14], is that it enabled some developers to produce effective products by not just considering the user friendliness or work from their own personal guidelines. Instead, developers using case studies (profiles) are able to acquire an in depth knowledge of diverse variation of each users needs together with a thorough appreciation of aims, objectives and problems which needs to be met in order to produce an effective product. This investigation was in agreement with Shneiderman and Plaisant [14] and Elrod [15] as to the importance that diversity brings, when using case studies (profiles) [2] in students coursework. The investigation is also in agreement with others [15] that the use of real case studies (profiles) [2], in student's coursework, resulted in being an effective learning and teaching aid with students gaining transferable skills through applying their learning to ...*real world projects*.

11.16 The Development and Production

The researcher/lecturer developed a blank template of a profile (case study), which was given to the practitioner to complete [2]. The profile [2] focused on numerous sections including speech, language and communication areas giving the practitioner the opportunity to rate 1–5, Severe/Excellent, Mild/Poor, n/a (not applicable), yes/no and blank areas in order to give comments. Permission letters were distributed by the school to parents and on return of the signed permission slips, profiles [2] were completed and returned to the lecturer.

Several hundred students were given a full explanation of their participatory role in this research and each student was randomly given a completed and anonymous profile [2], as a clear set of requirements, for producing an individualised therapeutic multimedia game, spanning over 12 weeks, for each particular autistic learner. Therefore, students got to understand a specific learner, by undergoing in-depth research, resulting in the production of a report based on a learner's profile [2]. Students began with their research findings based on the profiles [2]. This resulted in the production of storyboards and the development of customised games [10] with the focus on Speech, Language and Communication and the inclusion of the likes and interests.

Quinn [16] stated that…

> … software engineers must understand the needs of the users, access the strengths and weakness of the current system and design modifications to the software [16].

whereas, Donegan [17] further highlighted that…

> …because of their individual needs and difficulties, whichever technology they use to communicate requires a high level of personalization and customization if they are to be able to use it effectively [17, pp. 259–275].

11.17 Design-for-One Approach

The students would also be achieving from their studies: research, computing, scripting, Human Computer Interaction (HCI) and multimedia practical skills. The researcher developed a design-for-one approach [4, 5], which would be used adopting a holistic approach by taking into consideration all their diverse therapeutic needs concerning their speech, language and communication. These would be extracted from the completion of the profiles [2] and would help in developing personalised, individualised therapeutic games [10] for practitioners and real learners on the Autistic Spectrum in the society.

Therefore, in order to ascertain the diversity of the end users' needs, practitioners needed to complete the following categories on the profiles [2] to help identify and understand the end-users' entire spectrum of needs and their goals.

Categories on the profiles
First name
Gender
Age
Ethnic origin
Learning difficulties
Medical conditions
Behavior
Social communication
Low tech alternative augmentative communication (AAC) systems used
Social interaction difficulties
Rigidity of thought and imagination difficulties
Independent/self help difficulties
Play

(continued)

(continued)

High tech alternative augmentative communication (AAC) systems used
Software used
Modalities (senses) preferred
Elements of multimedia [4, 5] preferred
(Text, sound, graphics, animation, video)
Educational difficulties
Computer abilities
Strengths and weaknesses
Likes and dislikes
Personal skills/interests
Suggested software to be developed
Additional information
Social communication used?
Verbal language (vocabulary), articulation, non-functional communication (vocal sounds), sings /says rhymes, echolalia, responds to name, imitates, able to converse, responds to questions)
Verbalise more if he/she is not getting their way?
Suggestions to include in the software
Low-tech AAC systems used?
Communication book used?
Sign language used?
Use of symbols (TEACCH/PECS?)
Uses gestures?
Points?
Facial/body language used?
Uses more if excited?
Receptive + comprehension skills?
Suggestions to include in the software
Social interaction difficulties with adults/peers/family
Eye contact?
Turn taking?
Joining in with peer/group activities?
Able to take/follow/lead/copy?
Enjoys compliments and success?
Negotiating skills?
Suggestions to include in the software
Rigidity of thought and imagination difficulties
Through own interest/symbolic play?
Understanding of thoughts/feelings/emotion/facial expression?
Shows empathy?
Role play
Suggestions to include in the software
Preferred modalities
Tactile learner (prefers to touch, needs interactivity)
Auditory learner (prefers to listen, needs sound cues)
Visual learner (prefers to look, needs visual cues)
Suggestions to include in the software
Text
Size (large/small)?
No of words to be used?
Lower case/upper case?
Length of words

(continued)

(continued)

Sound
Pitch/tone preferred?
Loud/soft?
Type of music preferred?
Sound effects preferred?
Graphics and animation
Prefers photographs?
Prefers drawings/figures/maps/diagrams?
Prefers thomas the tank engine/disney characters?
Videos
Enjoys watching videos?
Videos to be included?
Suggestions to include in the software
Education
Curriculum (Elaborated 5–14 curriculum, Pscales, National curriculum)
Literacy level
English abilities and difficulties
Mathematics level
Numeracy abilities and difficulties
Comprehension levels
ICT Level
ICT (keyboard, mouse skills) abilities and difficulties
Suggestions to include in the software

Jones [18] has claimed that…

> … key variables usually include the age of the child; their intellectual level; interest; language level; social understanding and whether parental involvement is required or desirable. If these are not known, staff may introduce an intervention to a whole class group, some of who may not benefit from this [18, pp. 543–552].

The investigation acknowledges the claims Shneiderman and Plaisant [14] and Jones and Hack [19] have made as to the importance of not just considering the product's user friendliness or produce subjective guidelines or checklists, but to give professionals and practitioners…

> … across all sectors …further guidance on how best to ascertain the needs of the child or young person with ASD and then to provide appropriate support…[19, pp. 167–182]

and an opportunity to give developers a deeper and thorough understanding of the diversity of each learner's spectrum of needs.

Therefore, if the therapeutic information (e.g. the Attainment Outcome and Strands) (Tables 11.1, 11.2, 11.3 and 11.4 and Figs. 11.1, 11.6, 11.2, 11.3, 11.4, 11.5, 11.7, 11.8, 11.9, 11.10, 11.11, 11.12, 11.13, 11.14, 11.15 and 11.16) which has already been stated in this chapter, could have been incorporated into each learners profile [2], this would have given the development team further useful information for developing more precise individualised tailored software.

11.17.1 Early Intervention

This investigation is, therefore, in agreement with findings such as…

> … The SEN Code of Practice for Wales (Welsh Assembly Government 2008) advised the adoption of a range of strategies that recognise the various complexities of need and the National Autism Plan for Children (NAPC) (National Initiative for Autism: Screening and Assessment [NIASA] 2003) reported evidence that targeted interventions should begin as early as possible [9, pp. 1–278].

The Early Learning Site [20] and Kemp [21] have regarded the importance for early intervention for encouraging, developing and teaching learners on the AS with communication and language difficulties. This would help ease some of the learner's frustration and challenging behaviour. Therefore, this chapter suggests that this module and the development of personalised, individualised therapeutic computerised aid could be incorporated into each learner's early intervention when practitioners are assessing each learner's therapeutic needs. The module has provided practitioners with an on-going iterative [22, 23] therapeutic tool which allowed their complete involvement throughout the process (Fig. 11.8).

11.17.2 Feedback and the Next Cohort of Students

The practitioners involved carried out on-going assessment, monitoring and evaluation of the games [10]. This quality control validated the on-going exhaustive testing process resulting in making it easier to isolate and fix errors. This resulted in the academic gaining formative feedback from receiving on-going evaluation and the updating of profiles or new profiles [2] from the practitioners. Students took into consideration the updated profiles of the learners changing needs and the evaluated feedback from the practitioners, highlighting the strengths and weaknesses of the games developed [10] by the previous cohort of students to enable the appropriate modifications to be carried out [2]. Niès and Pelayo's [24] study showed how collaboration helped to…

> … resolve the limits of direct users involvement and usual problems pertaining to users' needs description and understanding [24, pp. 76–82].

Therefore, the module underwent an iterative approach [22, 23], with each new cohort of students receiving updated and modified profiles and feedback from the practitioners involved in order for ongoing amendments, modification and improvements to be made [1, 2].

The students would be able to learn from the mistakes made by their previous peers in order to perfect the games [10] for the practitioners and ultimately for the learners.

The module [1] used an iterative process [22, 23] through an ongoing continuous use of Human Computer Interaction (HCI) and Hierarchical Task Analysis

(HTA) approach [25] and a user-centred design with an ongoing validation or testing obtained for adapted and adaptive (tailored) systems. This gave the students an understanding of the end-users needs prior to the production and development of the personalised and individualised software [1, 2, 7].

11.17.3 The Responsibility of the Academic

The development and effective on going working of the module made the academic wholly responsible for working in collaboration with practitioners and acquiring the completed profiles and the new profiles and making sure these were randomly distributed to the students [1, 2]. The lecturer was also responsible for teaching the students research, theoretical and practical multimedia skills and to understand and interpret the profiles accurately. This resulted in the development of the most appropriate individualised therapeutic games [10], based on the practitioner's specifications and these would be met in the outcome of each student's contribution.

11.18 Students Useful Contribution and the Assets they Bring

Students had a great deal to contribute with a deep and caring optimistic approach to developing a game which would be of therapeutic use to their own learner with a disability. There have been several hundred students who have carried out this coursework over 13 years (2000–2013). The students came from different backgrounds, there is a variance in age, experience, intellectual ability, ethnicity and social class. Some of the mature students bring their personal lifelong experiences into the research, e.g. a retired headmaster of a school, studying the module [1]. The multicultural students had great empathy, knowledge and understanding with the equally multi-cultural learners' profiles issued to the students [2]. This enabled the students to transfer their personal knowledge and understanding, already acquired and brought into academia [26], with this coursework e.g. student saying "…great I have got a child from my part of the world". Therefore, students gained a great deal whilst accomplishing their studies.

11.18.1 Students' Motivation and Gains From the Module

The incentive for the students was more than just submitting the coursework in order to be assessed and graded for their knowledge and skills attained from undertaking the module. They acquired an understanding of what they were learning at university in their 'academic-world' with the ability to relate this to real-life situations in today's society in the 'real-world'. Many students continued their studies choosing to carry out projects relating to disabilities. Some students chose to continue their studies with the focus on disabilities for their placement year and their final year projects and dissertations, with some going on to postgraduate (Master and PhD) levels of research. Other students chose to obtain voluntary work in the disability community. One graduate was offered employment at her interview, from two large international computing companies due to her impressive demonstration and presentation of her therapeutic game she had developed whilst studying the module. The researcher is in agreement with Schuler [27] who stated that due to the fact that students were participants in the research this reduced their stress and anxiety.

Students were also in-directly collaborating with professionals in society whilst pursuing their studies. Therefore, this coursework resulted in students acquiring self-satisfaction and a sense of achievement that their work could be therapeutically beneficial to less able learners with special needs, thereby, making a real contribution to society.

Elective students, who have made the original decision to do the module, resulted in giving positive written and verbal feedback and praise for the Coursework and the module [1].

11.18.2 Theoretical Knowledge, Practical Skills and Design Techniques

Students learn the importance of research in order to implement a user-centred design. The theoretical knowledge and the practical skills learnt from doing the module resulted in the incentive of putting more effort into the coursework.

The students, therefore, were more aware that their hard work would result in not only producing good pieces of coursework to pass the module and be awarded a grade but they had an incentive that they were making a real contribution to a real member of society who would gain from their efforts [1].

11.18.3 Relating Academia With Society and Humanity

Students were able to relate what they were learning in the academic environment to what was actually happening in society. This gave them the opportunity to play a big part in humanity by helping someone less able by providing them with a game, which could potentially help their therapeutic needs, as well as providing the practitioners with a therapeutic aid for the classroom. Students were active participants in their own coursework and as well as their own personal achievement, which has shown to be far more rewarding for them.

11.18.4 Credits Towards Their Degree Programme

The students' participation in this coursework, gave them a real learner to research, in order to produce customised therapeutic games [10], by coercing them to carry out a very worthwhile venture, whilst enabling them to earn their credits towards their degree course from the completion of the game. Conversely, the researcher disagrees with past findings [28] questioning whether students gain from the experience, but agrees with them that students have a better understanding of research and the process by being a participant in the research.

11.18.5 A Real Coursework

Students are often assessed through reports, presentations, posters, essays and class tests individually, in pairs or group work. Students put a lot of effort into passing the coursework with some students finding the assignment a chore, leaving their work to the last minute and even some ending up not submitting. However, for several years it has become apparent that the majority of students carrying out this coursework have enjoyed it as it assessed their knowledge, understanding, abilities and skills achieved. This was demonstrated through the students producing far more work than requested of them, with some students donating cards and presents, as well as, the games [10] they have developed for the learners they have been researching.

Some students take the coursework so personally as to refer to their anonymous case study (profile) [2] as "my child". The majority of student's own written feedback indicate that they find the coursework "very rewarding".

11.19 What the Practitioners Gained

The practitioners gained the benefits of receiving ongoing individualised therapeutic games [10], developed to their specifications and for their learners with disabilities. It enabled them to specify exactly the therapeutic content of the games they required to be developed which would complement the areas being covered by the curriculum in the classroom and which would be of therapeutic use for each individual learner, through the ongoing updated profiles, evaluation and feedback process [1, 2].

11.20 What the Schools Gained

As well as the free games [10] made specifically for each learner in the school, the academic negotiated a financial deal with the student union shop and the university bookshop. As the students needed to buy a package (e.g. consisting of headphones with mic, CD, logbook etc.) from the student union shop in order to carry out the coursework and the recommended reading books from the bookshop, both shops agreed to donate a £1 on each package and book bought and this was in turn donated to the school used in the module.

11.21 What the Learners Gained

The learners gained by receiving personalised games [10]. If their first names were included on the profile, this was incorporated by the students it their first screen 'splash screen' e.g. 'Welcome Katie' and then throughout the game e.g. 'Well done Katie' or 'Try Again Katie'. No negative feedback was given. They would also have therapeutic computerised software produced for them taking all their therapeutic needs into consideration, as stated on their profile. The practitioners, prior to the learners playing with the games, would evaluate the software.

Therefore, this ongoing coursework has now been carried out by hundreds of students over 13 years (2000–2013), in collaboration with 44 practitioners of 148 disabled learners, from nine schools across the United Kingdom. The participants in this investigation have acknowledged the benefits of the whole collaborative iterative ongoing process [22, 23]. This real coursework is now achieving real effective, efficient, and enjoyable therapeutic results for the academic, the students, the practitioners and their learners and has resulted in the development of the GLAD software development company.

11.22 Future and State-of-the Art Research in Pervasive Health Technologies Outlook

This chapter would like to outline present and future research avenues, hot topics and research challenges.

11.22.1 Games for Learners with Autism and/or Other Disabilities (GLAD) Personalised, Individualised Software Development Company

Therefore, due to the on-going success of the module, the GLAD software development company was formed [11]. The company continues using the profiles [2] in order to develop personalised and individualised educational and therapeutic multimedia software [10] for learners on the autistic spectrum and for learners with other disabilities such as dyslexia. The process continues using an ongoing iterative design-for-one holistic approach [4, 5, 19, 22, 23] in collaboration with practitioners (teachers, speech and language therapists and parents).

11.22.2 Interesting State-of-the-Art Research into Pervasive Health Technological Innovations in this Book

This investigation, together with other interesting state-of-the-art research into pervasive health technological innovations, aids and devices have explored valuable, useful and informative concepts [29, 30]. This research and findings from studies in this book have demonstrated the importance of collaboration with multidisciplinary practitioners, designers and HCI practitioners. This study and many other researchers have discussed the importance of adopting a holistic approach when using methodologies for designing innovation for users such as those on the autistic spectrum (as in this investigation), care workers and patient support [31], the elderly [32] rehabilitating stroke patients [33] and sleep monitoring patients [34]. This is carried out in hospitals, laboratories, healthcare, homes (and home care systems) [35], nursing homes and schools as in this study. This was in order to establish current availability, suitability of technologies, hardware, software, mobile technologies [36] and support for interaction, speech, language and communication. It also has established innovative limitations and barriers in relation to niche markets, for various disabilities, impairments, individual and multiple users and end users with suggestions of patient-centric approach [37], low-cost solutions, roadmaps [38] a Brain Computer Interface (BCI) [39] and the creation of desired pervasive health systems [40].

11.23 Conclusion

To conclude this chapter met its aim by giving an explanation of the development of an ongoing multimedia gaming module developed with the collaboration, input and evaluation of practitioners (teachers and speech and language therapists).

The chapter began with a case study explaining the use and monitoring of a non-computerised conventional therapy (speech, language and communication) with a representative group of five anonymous primary school-aged learners, on the autistic spectrum, in a representative special school. The practitioners highlighted sections of the 5–14 Elaborated Curriculum, which they used to monitor these learners therapeutic achievements over 2 years. It showed that the learners had not achieved all the Strands and steps, however, some of the steps had been completed. It did not demonstrate what non-computerised conventional therapeutic methods had been used for each learner and when a design-for-one approach was used taking into consideration each users holistic needs [4, 5].

The chapter suggested that learners with autism and/or with other disabilities have a diverse variance in their speech, language and communication abilities and other needs and interests. It questioned whether commercialised computer games are using a collaborative holistic approach with practitioners, taking into consideration each learners spectrum of needs. This emerged from a multimedia university module, which has been carried out over many years adopting an ongoing iterative design-for-one approach [4, 5, 19, 22, 23]. This resulted in the production of a profile, which took specific learner's requirements, in relation to their therapeutic needs, into consideration. The importance has been focused on the on going updating of each learner's case studies, (profiles), the evaluation feedback together with a partnership with all parties concerned. This ethically [41] justifies the validity of this very real coursework. It demonstrates that by bringing a real-life situation into academia increases the student's stimulation, motivation and interest in a positive and beneficial way for them and others in society [26].

Therefore, the coursework brought together academia and society [26], resulting in all parties (especially the students) reaping many of the advantages from this coursework and module. The fact that the coursework was based on real users with the focus on therapy resulted in students doing more and better work as their efforts would be of help to others with therapeutic difficulties. A multi-disciplinary partnership of practitioners, the academic, and students all stood to benefit effectively, fairly, ethically [41] and therapeutically from the results of the on-going coursework. The module brought together a collaborative, multidisciplinary, customized, development approach. The amalgamation of academia and society [26] does not just make a contribution to the computing, science and technology discipline, but for therapeutic benefits to other disciplines. Therefore, this shows that giving the students a realistic situation for the development and production of the coursework, motivates them by giving them a major role to play in a real situation, with their contribution ultimately being of real use and benefit in the real world long after its completion. This has ultimately resulted in the development of the Games for Learners with Autism and/or other Disabilities (GLAD) personalised, individualised software development company.

References

1. Stokes, E. (2014a). The Ongoing Development of a Multimedia Educational Gaming Module. Serious Gaming Book Springer Series in Computational Intelligence Entitled Tentatively Serious Games, Alternative Realities, and Play Therapy due to be published 2014.
2. Stokes, E. (2014b). Profiles used in teaching research for developing multimedia games for pupils on the autism spectrum (AS) 2008. *International Journal Disabilities Human Development, 7*, 37–49.
3. Language and Communication section of the 5–14 Elaborated Curriculum (2011): 1–206.
4. Stokes, E., & Whitney, G. (2008). The utilisation of best practice in design theory to aid accessibility of ICT goods and services. In *Recent Advances in Assistive Technology and Engineering RASatE 2008, Coventry University, December 2008*

5. Stokes. E. (2008d). Design-for-All Research Group Workshop: ‘ *Utilising best practice in ICT An Autistic Design-For-One Multimedia Centred Learning Intervention Approach*’. Middlesex University, Trent Park, (June)—“Hidden gems: autism 2- An Autistic Design-For-One Multimedia Centered Learning Intervention Approach”—the European Design for All e-Accessibility Network (EdeAn) Workshop: Utilising best practice in ICT Design for All Teaching at the Trent Park campus June.
6. Elsom-Cook, M. (2001). *Principles of interactive multimedia*. London: McGraw Hill.
7. Dix, A., Finlay, J., Abowd, G., & Beale, R. (2004). *Human-Computer Interaction* (3rd ed.). Harlow: Pearson Education.
8. Putnam, C. & Chong, L. (2008). Software and Technologies Designed for People with Autism: What do users want? *ASSET'08 ACM* 978-1-59593-976: 3–10
9. Parsons, S., Guldberg, K., MacLeod, A., Jones, G., Prunty, A., & Balfe, T. (2011). International review of the evidence on best practice in educational provision for children on the autism spectrum. *European Journal Of Special Needs Education*, *26*(1), 1–278.
10. Stokes. E. (2013). Games for Learners with Autism and other Disabilities (GLAD) Personalised individualised educational software. In *Technology for Inclusion Conference Central Enfield City Learning Centre July*. NULL
11. Roberts, L. D. & Allen, P. J. (2013a). A brief measure of student perceptions of the educational value of research participation. *Australian Journal of Psychology*, *65*(1), 22–29.
12. Roberts, L. D. & Allen, P.J. (2013b). Student perspectives on the value of research participation 2012. In S. McCarthy, K. L. Dickson, J. Cranney, A. Trapp and V. Karandashev (Eds.), *Teaching Psychology Around the World, Newcastle Upon Tyne*, (Vol. 3, pp. 198–212). UK: Cambridge Scholars Publishing.
13. Kimmel, A. J. (2004). In defence of deception. American Psychologist, 53: 803–804 cited. In Foot, H. & Sanford, A. (2004). The use abuse of student participant. *The Psychologist*, *17*(5), 256–259.
14. Shneiderman, B. & Plaisant, C. (2004). *Designing the User Interface* (4th Edn). Boston: Pearson Addison Wesley.
15. Elrod, C., Murray, S., Flachsbart, B., Burgher, K. E. & Foth, D. M. (2010). Utilizing multimedia case studies to teach the professional side of project management. *Journal of STEM Education: Innovations & Research* Special Edition: 7–17.
16. Quinn, M. J. (2004). *Ethics for the Information Age*. Reading: Pearson Addison Wesley.
17. Donegan, M, Morris, J.D., Corno, F., Signorile, I., Chió, A., Pasian, V., Vignola, A., Buchholz, M. & Holmqvist, E. (2009). Understanding users and their needs. *International Journal of Universal Access in the Information Society*. *8*(4), 259–275.
18. Jones, G. (2006). Department for Education and Skills/Department of Health Good Practice Guidance on the education of children with autistic spectrum disorder, Child: Care. *Health & Development*, *32*(5), 543–52.
19. Jones, G. & Hack, E. (2008). Chapter 3. Parent/carer involvement in the commissioning of services for children and young people with autism spectrum disorder in the East Midlands. *Journal of Research in Special Educational Needs, Wiley Online Library*, *8*, 167–182.
20. Early Learning Site: Autism. Autism and PDD are Treatable http://aba.insightcommerce.net/contentbuilder/layout.php3?contentPath=content/o0/00p. Retrieved March 11, 2011.
21. Kemp, M. (2010). What is dyspraxia. In *Communication Summer: 29*.
22. Stokes, E. (2008a). Breaking down barriers for end users on the autistic spectrum, through an on-going iterative measurement off accessibility. In *Workshop 12 Innovations in Measuring Accessibility: Theoretical a Practical Perspective HCI2008 Conference Liverpool September*.
23. Stokes, E. (2008c). Future autistic centred therapeutic and/or educational interventions: A collaborative and iterative approach, using individualised variant in spectrum of needs. In *Autisms Neuroscience Conference (The National Autistic Society) The Royal Society, London. September*.
24. Niès, J. & Pelayo, S. (2010). From users involvement to users' needs understanding: A case study. *International Journal of Medical Informatics Human Factors Engineering for Healthcare Applications*, *79*(4), 76–82.

25. Cox, D. (2007). Task analysis, usability and engagement. Human–computer interaction. *Interaction Design and Usability Lecture Notes in Computer Science, 4550*, 1072–81.
26. Stokes, E. (2008b). *University Learning and Teaching Talk ' Bringing the Community into Academia'*. St Albans College Smallford October: School of Engineering and Information Science Computer Multimedia Technology Department.
27. Schuler, H. (1982), Ethical problems in psychological research. New York: Academic Press cited in Foot, H., & Sanford. A. (2004). The use abuse of student participant. *The Psychologist, 17*(5), 256–259.
28. Foot, H., & Sanford. A. (2004). The use abuse of student participant. *The Psychologist, 17*(5), 256–259.
29. Ziefle, M., Röcker, C. & Holzinger, A. (2014). *Current trends and challenges for pervasive health technologies: From technical innovation to user integration. Pervasive health: State-of-the-art & beyond* (pp. 1–18). London: Springer
30. Jacobs, A., Duysburgh, P., Ongenae, F., Ackaert, A., Bleumers, L., & Verstichel, S. (2014). *Innovation Binder approach to guide towards a social technical balanced pervasive health system. Pervasive health: State-of- the-art & beyond* (pp. 69–100). London: Springer.
31. Grönvall, E., & Lundberg, S. (2014). *On challenges designing the home as a place for care. Pervasive health: State-of-the-art & beyond* (pp. 19–46). London: Springer.
32. D'Angelo, L. T., Kreutzer, F. K., Neuhaeuser, J., Reimer, S., & Lueth, T. C. (2014). *Executing activities of daily living despite natural ageing-related changes. Pervasive health: State-of-the-art & beyond* (181–210). London: Springer.
33. Seo, K., & Ryu, H. (2014). *RehabMaster™': A pervasive rehabilitation platform for stroke patients and their caregivers. Pervasive health: State-of-the-art & beyond* (pp. 131–156). London: Springer.
34. Waltisberg, D., Arnrich, B., & Tröster. G. (2014). *Sleep quality monitoring with the smart bed. Pervasive health: State-of-the-art & beyond* (pp. 211–228). London: Springer.
35. Turner, K. J. (2014). *Managing telehealth and telecare. Pervasive health: State-of-the-art & beyond* (pp. 157–180). London: Springer.
36. Alnanih, R., Ormandjieva, O., & Radhakrishnan, T. (2014). *A new methodology (CON-INFO) for Context-based development of a mobile user interface in healthcare applications. Pervasive health: State-of-the-art & beyond* (pp. 317–344). London: Springer.
37. Jiménez Garcia, J., Romero, N., & Keyson, Havinga P. (2014). *An integrated patient-centric approach for situated research on total hip replacement recovery: ESTHER. Pervasive health: State-of-the-art & beyond* (pp. 345–367). London: Springer.
38. Böcker, M., & Schneider, M. (2014). *EHealth applications for those in need: Making novel interaction technologies accessible. Pervasive health: State-of-the-art & beyond* (pp. 47–68). London: Springer.
39. Lightbody, G., Galway, L., & McCullagh P. (2014). *The brain computer interface: Barriers to becoming. Pervasive health: State-of-the-art & beyond* (pp. 101–130). London: Springer.
40. Caporusso, N., Trizio, M., & Perrone, G. (2014). *Pervasive assistive technology for the deaf-blind: Need, emergency and assistance through the sense of touch. Pervasive health: State-of-the-art & beyond* (pp. 289–316). London: Springer.
41. Stokes, E. (2008). *Ethical justification of collaboration with professionals on the development of individualised tailored software for children on the Autistic Spectrum (AS).* In *Hillingdon Borough Talk. Hillingdon Borough SENDCO Newsletter. April.*

Further Readings

42. Bogdashina, O. (2011). Different Sensory Experiences/Worlds, Autism Today. Retrieved Feberuary 02, 2011, from http://www.autismtoday.com/articles/Different_Sensory_Experiences.htm

43. Centre for Autism. (2011). A Picture is Worth a Thousand Words: A Visual Workshop:1. Retrieved March 12, 2011, from http://www.autism.net/services/services-for-parentscaregivers/parent-training/special-topic-seminars/402.html?task=view
44. Centre for Autism and Developmental Disabilities Epidemiology (CADDE). (2011). John Hopkins School Bloomberg School of Public Health. Retrieved April 1, 2011, from http://www.jhsph.edu/cadde./Facts/autism.html
45. Department for Education and Employment and Qualification and Curriculum Authority. (2011). *Information and Communication Technology*, 1–44. http://curriculum.qcda.gov.uk/uploads/ICT
46. Disability. Gov (2011) Connecting the Disability Community to Information and Opportunities. Retrieved March 23, 2011, from http://www.disability.gov/viewResource?id=2408811
47. Equals. (2010). Entitlement and Quality Education for Learners with Learning Difficulties. Retrieved September 10, 2010, from http://www.equals.co.uk/p-scales.aspx?page=690B9533
48. ESRC. (2010). Framework for Research Ethics (FRE) Economic and Social Research Council. Retrieved September 23, 2010, from http://www.esrc.ac.uk/_images/Framework_for_Research_Ethics_tcm8-4586.pdf, pp. 1–50.
49. Fullarton, A. (2010). *Drawing Autism. Communication. Summer 2010: 43*, Geneva.
50. Grandin, T. (2011). My Experiences with Autism. What is Visual Thinking? Scientific American Frontiers, 3. Retrieved March 18, 2011, from http://www.pbs.org/saf/1205/features/grandin3.htm
51. Heimann, M., & Tjus, T. (2011a). The Delta Messages project. Multimedia Facilitation of Communication Skills In Learners with Various Handicaps. Retrieved March 11, 2011, from http://www.svenska.gu/se/svesj/DELTA/delta.html
52. Heimann, M., & Tjus, T. (2011b). The Use of multimedia Computer procedures to facilitate language growth among learners with autism $5U^h$ Congress Autism Europe Articles/Proceeding Autism—Spain. Retrieved March 11, 2011, from http://www.autismo.com/scripts/articulo/smuestra.idc?n=kl
53. Inclusive Technology. (2011). Autism and Information Communication Technology (ICT). Retrieved March 10, 2011, from http://www.inclusive.co.uk/articles/autism-and-information-communicationtechnology-ict-a242
54. O'Connor, C., & Stagnitti, K. (2011). Play, behavior, language and social skills: The comparison of a play and a non-play intervention within a specialist school setting. *Research in Developmental Disabilities, 32*(3), 1205–11.
55. Rahman, M., Ferdous, S. M., & Ahmed, S.I. (2010). Increasing intelligibility in speech of the autistic learners by an interact computer game 2010. In: *IEEE International Symposium on Multimedia Taiwan*, pp. 383–387.
56. Stokes, E (2006a) Teaching and Research into multimedia games for learners on the Autism Spectrum. In *Technology and Autism Conference. AHRC and Coventry University. Proceedings published on CD. October*.
57. Stokes, E (2006b). Free individualised tailor-made therapeutic and/or educational multimedia games, developed by students, for pupils on the Autistic Spectrum. In *First Cambridge Autism. Research Conference Proceeding September 2006*.
58. Stokes, E. (2003a). The effectiveness of computers as an educational aid to speech and language development. In *AAATE 7th European (Dublin) Conference 2003 for the Advancement of Assistive Technology in Europe. Published proceedings*.
59. Stokes, E. (2003b). The therapeutic use of videos for Autistic Children's Verbal Language Development. In *Proceedings from Technology and Persons with Disabilities 2003 LA Conference The Centre on Disabilities at California State University, Northridge*.
60. Stokes, E. (2003c). The decision-making process adopted for a computerised Multimedia Theoretical/Educational Intervention (MT/EI) model. In *BCS HCI 2003:Designing for Society (Bath) Conference Workshop paper*.
61. Stokes, E. (2003d). Methodological Investigation into the use of Multimedia for Autistic Learners's Verbal Language Development. In *Workshop paper for HCI International Crete Conference*.

62. Stokes, E. (2003e). Human Computer Interaction (HCI) approaches adopted for a Computerised Multimedia Therapeutic/Educational Intervention (CMT/EI) model Workshop Paper. In *Bath Conference Workshop paper*.
63. Stokes, E. (2003f). The Effectiveness of Computers as an Educational Aid to Speech and Language Therapy Development in Assisted Technology, Shaping the Future. In G.M.Craddock, L. P. McCormack, R. B. Reilly& H. T. P Knops, *AAATe'03*. IOS Press: Amsterdam.
64. Stokes, E., Lawrence, D. & Corner, T. (2001). Conventional Speech and Language Therapy vs. Computerised Multimedia Therapy. In Kluev, (Ed), *Advances in automation, Multimedia and video systems, and Modern Computer Science WSESPress. Malta Conference*, pp. 185–194.
65. Walsh, L. & Barry, M. (2009). An investigation of computer animated re-inforcers as a motivational tool for learners with autism. Research, Reflections and Innovations in Integrating ICT in Education. In *Proceedings of V International Conference on Multimedia and ICT in Education. Lisbon, Portugal: m:ICTE*, pp. 1251–1254.

Chapter 12
Pervasive Assistive Technology for the Deaf-Blind Need, Emergency and Assistance Through the Sense of Touch

Nicholas Caporusso, Michelantonio Trizio and Giovanni Perrone

12.1 Introduction

According to demographic studies by the World Health Organization (WHO), the world's blind population is about 37 millions [1]. Other studies estimate that the numbers are between 40 and 45 millions. This figure adds to 123 million people suffering from ipovision or vision impairments (i.e., the ratio between the blind and individuals affected by ipovision is 1:3.4), and 314 million have some kind of major visual impairment. In industrialized countries, approximately 0.4 % of the population is blind, whereas 90 % of the blind live in developing countries (i.e., 27 % S.E. Asia, 26 % Western Pacific, 17 % Africa, 10 % East Mediterranean, 10 % Americas, and 10 % Europe), where limited access to resources and technology aggravate the problem [1].

Less is known about the deaf-blind: statistics are unavailable in many countries. This is because there is no common opinion about what deaf-blindness is, and to what extent people are considered deaf-blind. Moreover, due to their particular condition, many deaf-blind individuals are difficult to categorize in censuses. Therefore, numbers are estimated, only. According to recent statistics, there are roughly 50,000 deaf-blind people in the United States, which represent roughly 0.016 % of the population. It can be calculated that there are about 150 million deaf-blind individuals, by taking into consideration the demographics of industrialized countries. Although deaf-blind people represent a small significant minority of the world population, they are an important challenge in terms of public health and policies. School and working-age blind individuals have very high unemployment rates (about 75 %, in the

N. Caporusso (✉) · M. Trizio · G. Perrone
QIRIS, Via Dieta di Bari 36, Bari, Italy
e-mail: info@qiris.org; info@intactheathcare.com; n.caporusso@qiris.org

N. Caporusso · M. Trizio · G. Perrone
INTACT Healthcare, Via Dieta di Bari 36, Bari, Italy
e-mail: info@qiris.org; info@intactheathcare.com

A. Holzinger et al. (eds.), *Pervasive Health*, Human–Computer Interaction Series,
DOI: 10.1007/978-1-4471-6413-5_12, © Springer-Verlag London 2014

most accessible countries). Moreover, only 10 % of blind children receive education in Braille. Not only is this a matter of social security, it involves the ability of the deaf-blind population to achieve autonomous living, independent mobility, and social inclusion [2, 3].

Nowadays, assistive technology and specifically, pervasive health technology [4], has a substantial impact on people with sensory, cognitive, and developmental impairments. Also, it has significant benefits for the deaf-blind: it allows them to achieve communication and to overcome obstacles that seemed overwhelming 10 or 15 years ago. As a consequence of the introduction and the use of technology to close the digital divide with people with disabilities, the deaf-blind will benefit from more options for education, training, and future employment. Regardless of the complexity of nowadays technology and of the level of innovation advancement, still individuals will require better systems to be autonomous in communication, to and independently move and interact with the environment, and to get unrestricted access to information. Most importantly, proper technology and training can help them decrease the feeling of isolation, and it can support them in having a complete and fun social life.

As such individuals are deaf and blind at the same time, they are not able to rely on their sight or on their sense of hearing to communicate with others and to interact with the external world. As a result, they are forced to utilize an alternative channel for achieving communication, interaction and access to information. In this regard, tactile and haptic interfaces have great potential in rendering the environment accessible to the blind. Particularly, they address specific shortcomings of traditional sensory substitution approaches based on auditory output and, thus, they are especially suitable for the deaf-blind. However, they have particular requirements in terms of design. In this chapter, we review the main assistive technology currently available to blind and specifically deaf-blind people, and we focus on the several different aspects involved in the design, development and adoption of novel tactile interfaces for the deaf-blind.

12.2 Glossary

Sender and Receiver With respect to directionality of messages, we intend communication processes as based on the concept of messages being passed from sender(s) to receiver(s). In this work, we apply a user-centric approach.

Input System (Input) refers to a machine agent capable of receiving messages sent by the human agent, or to the situaton in which the human agent sends messages.

Output System (Output) refers to a machine agent capable of sending messages to the human agent, or to the situaton in which the human agent receives messages.

Input/Output System (Input/Output) intuitively refers to a machine agent capable of receiving messages from and sending messages to the human agent.

System, Device, Peripheral, and Solution Where not explictly stated, the words *system, device* and *peripheral* and *solution* are utilized to refer to the object per se, and they are employed as synonyms, as they do not refer to any specific architecure, operating mode, or communication protocols.

Touch-Based Communication In this work, we will use the terms "*touch-based communication*" in reference to the tactile component of messages, only, even if several communication systems simultaneously use two perceptual channels in order to exchange information. For instance, the sign language utilized by the deaf combines tactile and visual communication; also, blind people utilize tactile displays in combination with auditory output. However, as this work focuses on people with a combined degree of visual and auditory impairments, we will only take into consideration touch. Moreover, when we refer to touch-based communication, our approach is extremely strict: although tactile communication can be associated with spoken language (as in the case of blind people) or visually-perceivable gestures (e.g., in sign languages employed by the deaf), we only focus on the tactile component of interaction (or communication), and we take less into consideration the visual or auditory elements.

12.3 State-of-the-Art

Although the world is mainly perceived as structured into visual and auditory stimuli, the sense of touch plays a fundamental role in human perception, as it enables individuals to communicate with others and acquire a variety of heterogeneous pieces of information about both the environment and the external world. Indeed, touch is the first sense being formed in humans: sensitivity to tactile stimulation is already developed at the eighth week of gestation of an embryo [5]. Also, it is among the senses that still are available when sight and hearing start to fade due to ageing.

Despite its simplicity and its longevity, the sense of touch should not be conceived as *primitive* with respect to vision and audition. In addition to being a sophisticated informative and perceptual system of sensing, it includes features that enable bi-directional exchange of information and rich communication [6]. Nevertheless, vision and hearing are the major senses through which individuals generally perceive the world and communicate with others, because they utilize the most convenient perceptual channels in terms of information throughput. As the majority of humans mainly rely on the visual and on the auditory channels to perceive the world, also verbal and nonverbal communication methods usually utilize the sight or the sense of hearing as primary channels for exchanging messages [7]. As a consequence, despite its potential, touch is fundamentally utilized for simply acquiring information about the environment in close proximity, and for manipulating objects in everyday tasks. Eventually, touch-based communication systems receive less attention.

Although research produced advances in technology that supports blind and deaf users, in the last decades less attention has been dedicated to people that are not able to rely on both the visual and the auditory channels. Also, there are several publications that review the main technology advancements devoted to people suffering from physical, sensory or cognitive impairments. However, there is poor literature about assistive and communication devices especially designed for the blind and, particularly, for the deaf-blind. Nevertheless, research addressed multisensory impairments as a hot topic in the last years. For instance, a paper published in 1986 [8] introduced a system based on Braille displays that could help the deaf-blind to receive messages from a computer. More than 25 years later, and despite the evolution of technology, the deaf-blind still have poor alternatives. In this chapter, we review the most relevant devices for people with sensory impairments. We take into consideration research projects discussed in papers published in international journals or presented at conferences, technology under development, and commercial products that already are on the market. In particular, our interest will focus on innovative Human-Computer Interfaces based on touch, which are the only suitable for the deaf-blind. For convenience, we distinguish assistive technology into augmented functional communication tools, language-based devices, and systems for environment interaction.

12.3.1 Aids for Functional and Augmented Communication

Augmentative and Alternative Communication (AAC) devices include all forms of communication aids that can be utilized to express thoughts, needs, desires, and feelings. In general, all individuals use AAC in their facial expressions or gestures; also, symbols, pictures, or writings incorporate features and pieces of AAC. People with severe disability or physical impairments rely on AAC as a supplement or replacement of sophisticated communication, especially if their goal is to simply communicate their needs and reach the final objective of being understood by the receiver of their message. Special Augmentative and Alternative Communication, such as picture and symbol communication, use aids (e.g., boards and electronic devices, picture cards, and all available objects that are meaningful) to help people express themselves. Moreover, AAC helps people with poor literacy or limited communication increase the performance of their social interaction, and enable them to achieve basic education. The devices described in this section fall in the category of technology for functional and augmented communication due to their limited complexity that, simultaneously, grants them effectiveness and low entry barriers.

12.3.1.1 ComTouch

ComTouch [9] augments remote voice communication with the use of touch. In order to do so, it converts hand pressure into vibrational intensity, so that two users can feel each others' touch cues in real-time, despite being remotely located.

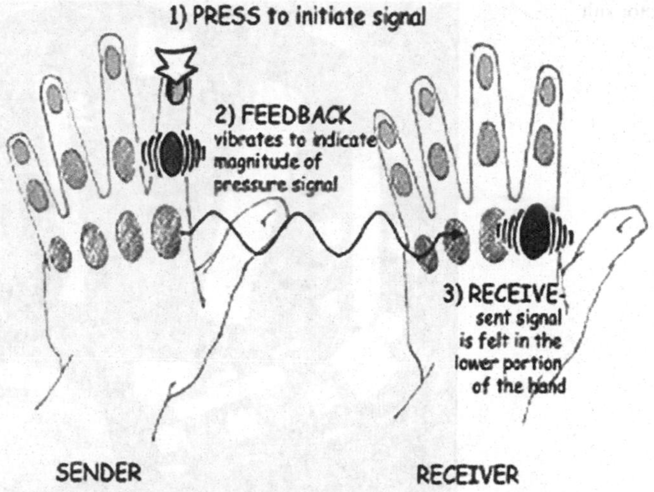

Fig. 12.1 Touch-to-vibration mapping in ComTouch

ComTouch consists in a handheld device that incorporates a vibrotactile-actuator-enabled sleeve that fits over the back of a mobile phone. The device supports bi-directional communication, so that users can simultaneously send and receive vibrotactile cues. ComTouch can be utilized to enable basic communication between the deaf-blind and their relatives. Figure 12.1 shows the touch-to-vibration mapping. Pressure sensorsare incorporated below the fingertips, and they convert pressure into vibrotactile actuation. Embossed areas in Fig. 12.1 help sighted users to understand the touch-to-vibration mapping. The device allows users to communicate by placing the left hand on the upper surface of the device so that the tip of the index finger corresponds to a colored pad. Pressing the button indicated by the arrow causes a vibration in the middle phalanx (i.e., using the actuator located on the pad). Simultaneously, vibration is generated on the other pad, where it is received in correspondence of the proximal phalanx (i.e., firing the blue pad). Unfortunately, this device is not on the market, to our knowledge [9].

12.3.1.2 Tactor Suit

Bloomfield et al. [10] employed smart textiles in the design of a method for providing blind and deaf-blind people with localized vibrotactile cues. The Tactor suit incorporates vibrotactile actuators (tactors) into a standard sweater. The location of tactors is associated to a human model so that the system can trigger real-time localized feedback on the torso. The objective is to train blind and deaf-blind people in moving into simulated environments, so that they can learn the position of obstacles by receiving vibrations when they collide with or when they approach objects. The authors hypothesize that vibrotactile feedback can effectively be employed in improving

Fig. 12.2 Tactor suit

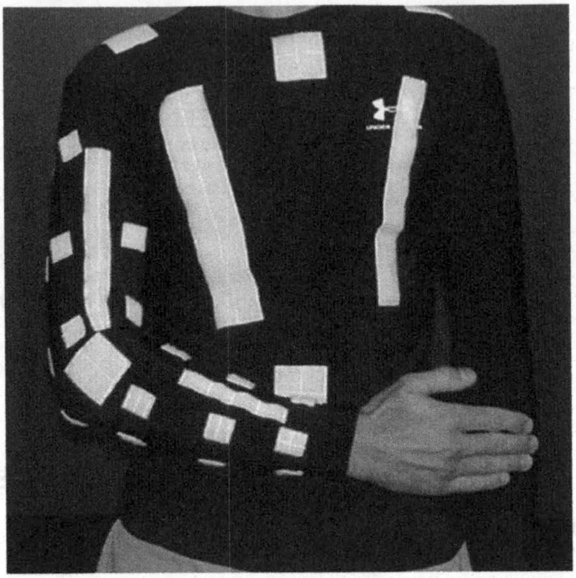

users' mobility in real-life scenarios. Thus, it is designed to provide physical realism in regard to interaction with objects and with the environment. Experimental results show that the vibrotactile suit is able to improve users' performance in navigating virtual environments. However, the system is not suitable for supporting users in their actual mobility. Currently, the device is under development and it is not ready for being utilized by final users yet, though smart textiles are supposed to be among the next trends for the market (Fig. 12.2).

12.3.1.3 Hey Yaa

Hey yaa [11] is a wearable system based on haptics that supports functional communication using vibrotactile cues. The purpose of the device is to deliver touch stimuli to signal events and to provide users with alarms. As shown by Fig. 12.3, Hey yaa is based on Arduino Lilypad, and it consists of two waist belts. Similarly to ComTouch, two devices communicate with one another. When one belt is pressed, the other one vibrates, drawing user's attention. In contrast to ComTouch, Hey yaa is wearable and thus, it can be utilized in everyday tasks to keep constant contact with an assistant. Currently, Hey yaa is a research project that has no ambition to go on the market.

12.3.1.4 The Hug Shirt and Hug Me

Similarly to the Tactor suit described previously, the Hug Shirt [12, 13] enables delivering touch cues on the torso. Specifically, the purpose of the device is to transmit

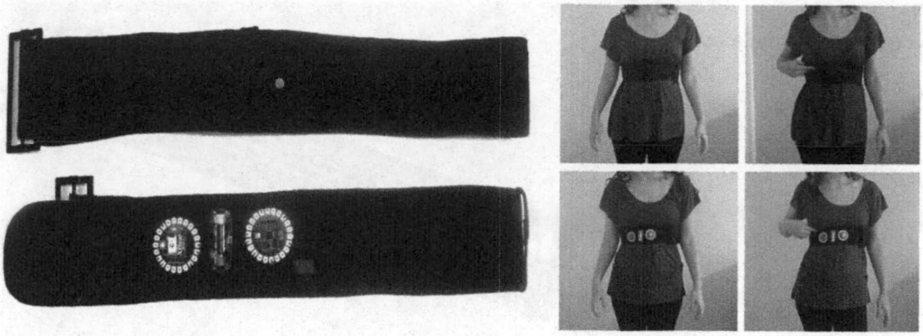

Fig. 12.3 The Hey yaa belt

hugs. Although it might seem trivial, it is crucial for the deaf-blind to receive comfort through physical contact. The device incorporates sensors capable of acquiring the strength of the touch, the warmth of the skin and the heartbeat rate of the sender. Also, the Hug Shirt includes actuators that reproduce the touch sensation of a hug, including warmth, so that the recipient can receive semi-realistic sensations. The system consists of a shirt equipped with sensors and actuators and a smartphone application that connects via Bluetooth to the shirt. The application enables the sender to design virtual hugs (i.e., without actually wearing the shirt) to be transmitted to the receiver, and vice versa. Several applications in the medical field (e.g., for children and the elderly) have been described in [14], but none of them has been implemented into viable products.

12.3.2 Language-Based Devices

Several touch-based systems are available for informative and communication purposes. Specifically, tactile languages allow exchanging messages between individuals, and they are particularly suitable for enriching or complementing verbal communication in situations of impaired sight or hearing. Furthermore, people who are affected by multiple sensory impairments to the visual and the auditory channels (i.e., the deaf-blind) have the only choice of using touch for accessing the external world both for communication and for information retrieval purposes. Thanks to novel sensors, actuators, and processing techniques, tactile interfaces can reproduce sophisticated interaction, including language-based communication. This is crucial to provide blind and deaf-blind people with means that go beyond basic communication. Technology for getting access to information and learning is the actual gateway to help them achieve social inclusion.

12.3.2.1 Braille Displays

The Braille code is the most famous and adopted system for encoding text in a tactile form. It utilizes series of raised dots to form letters: each symbol is represented

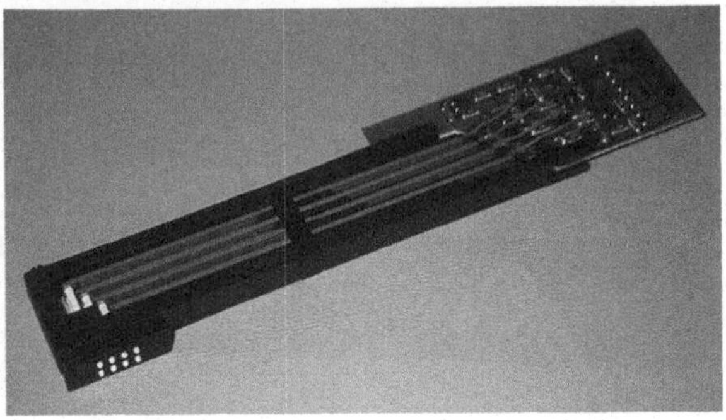

Fig. 12.4 Typical piezo-electric Braille cell

using a cell (see Fig. 12.4) consisting of six dots that can be set as raised or flat in order to obtain different configurations. As the Braille alphabet consists of 6 dots each assuming two values (i.e., raised or flat), each cell supports up to 64 configurations. Nevertheless, the Braille alphabet has a very powerful encoding: there are conventions for associating different meanings to the same configuration, and for switching between domains (e.g., music, or mathematics). Words are written as sequences of adjacent cells. These can be read by people who are blind (or whose sight is not sufficient for reading printed material) with their fingers, by simply passing the fingertip over the cells. Usually, teachers, parents, and others who are not visually impaired can read Braille dots with their eyes.

Indeed, as Braille is a code by which languages (e.g., English) can be written and read, individuals are required to learn the Braille alphabet, the grammar and the syntax, before they can communicate. Although studies in the literature demonstrate the efficiency of the Braille alphabet in encoding information, the Braille alphabet has important limitations from a learning perspective. Specifically, in order to understand Braille, individuals should be able to explore and recognize similarities and differences in objects and materials. This can be especially difficult in case of cognitive or sensory impairments, which usually occur in case of deaf-blindness. In general, discriminating the dots and associating configurations to letters has a long learning curve, and it requires extensive effort from both the learner and the assistant. Consequently, Braille displays (see Fig. 12.4) are not suitable for supporting education of children in their pre-school age and in K-12. Currently, all refreshable Braille displays [15] consist of Braille cells that incorporate 6–8 dots arranged in a 2×3 or 2×4 matrix. Braille cells use piezoelectric ceramic bimorph reeds to raise or lower Braille dots by approximately 0.5 mm above the reading surface.

12.3.2.2 Braille2Go

Braille to Go (B2G) [16] is a Braille-based mobile computing device. Basically, Braille to Go is a standard Android smartphone with a Braille display in place of visual display. It consists of an array of cells that works as an output system, Also,

Fig. 12.5 Braille keyboard and display consisting of 20 cells

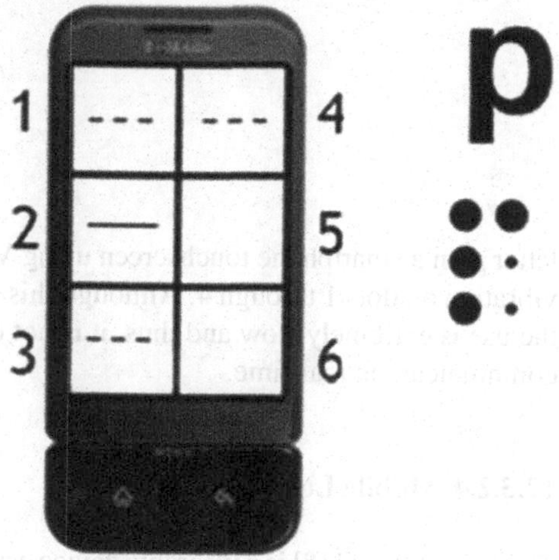

Fig. 12.6 V-Braille representation of the letter "p"

Braille2Go includes a Braille keyboard. The B2G is small and portable (its size is about half that of a sheet of paper) (Fig. 12.5).

12.3.2.3 VBraille

V-Braille [17] offers a way to represent Braille characters on a standard Android mobile phone, using the touch-screen and vibration. As shown in Fig. 12.6, the screen is divided into six parts each replicating one dot of the Braille cell. When the user touches an area of the screen containing a dot, the phone vibrates. Experiments showed that the average time required by participants to read a V-Braille character ranged between 4.2 and 26.6 s. Five out of nine users were able to read a character in less than 10 s, with 90 % accuracy. Figure 12.6 shows a representation of the lowercase

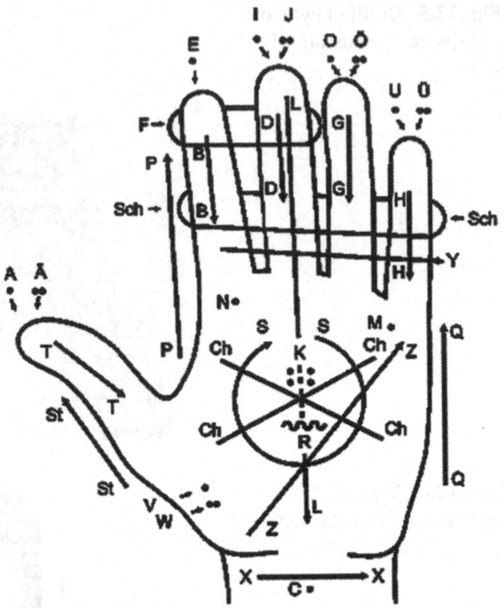

Fig. 12.7 The Lorm alphabet

letter *p* on a smartphone touchscreen using V-Braille. This is realized with localized vibration on dots 1 through 4. Although this system employs common smartphones, the use is extremely slow and thus, it is not convenient for many users who want to communicate in real-time.

12.3.2.4 Mobile Lorm Glove

The Lorm Glove [18] is a wearable device especially deisigned for the deaf-blind that enables exchanging messages using the Lorm alphabet (a touch-based communication language invented by a deaf-blind teacher), described in Fig. 12.7. It consists in a glove that incorporates electric fabric (utilized for sensing) and actuators. Letters are associated with different areas of the hand and with sets of touch patterns. The Lorm glove enables the deaf-blind to compose messages by pressing sensitive areas of the fabric placed on the palm of the glove, according to the touch cues defined by the Lorm alphabet. Acquired input is then transmitted to a mobile phone and translated into text. Moreover, small vibrating motors located on the back of the glove display messages to the deaf-blind user by simulating touch cues.

The device consists of a matrix of 35 fabric sensors [19] associated to the different characters of the Lorm alphabet. The rectangular sensor, located on the wrist of the glove, acts as a confirmation key, and enables indicating the end of the symbol. Sensors are located in pre-determined areas defined by the Lorm alphabet and consist in piezoresistive fabric. This, in turn, changes its electrical resistance under mechanical pressure. Output is realized with a matrix of 32 pager motors located

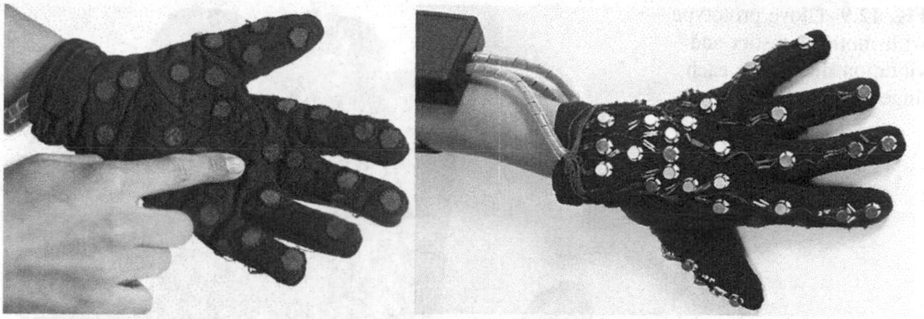

Fig. 12.8 Implementation of the Lorm glove

on the areas defined by the Lorm alphabet. They translate text messages into touch cues. Moreover, they provide direct feedback with respect to sensors. Both the sensor matrix of the input unit and the actuators of the output unit are connected to the control unit via flexible wires. The device operates in a half-duplex fashion: users are not able to simultaneously send and receive messages. The deaf-blind wear the glove on the left hand and they use their right hand to compose messages in the Lorm alphabet. The device has been tested in several research studies. However, it is not ready to be commercialized, yet (Fig. 12.8).

12.3.2.5 Touch Communication Glove With Tactile Feedback

The glove developed by Dinh et al. [20] allows users to send and receive messages by simply moving their fingers. This device is based on Finger Braille, a communication language in which the index, middle and ring finger of both hands function as the keys of a Braille typewriter. Each finger is associated with an accelerometer and with a vibration motor. Movements are decoded in Braille; input is sent from one glove another in the form of vibrations. In addition to co-located communication, the glove supports interaction with computers, smartphones, and appliances. The system requires two gloves in order to realize bi-directional communication (Fig. 12.9).

12.3.2.6 Sign Language Embedded in an Intelligent Space

The system described by Lisztes et al. [21] is designed to acquire and recognize signs from a video camera. These, in turn, are visualized using 3D rendering technique. This system consists of a standard personal computer, a video camera, and special software. The software is able to recognize letters from the sign language alphabet with the help of color markers. However, the device is only a piece of a larger system that can incorporate various sensors for physical contact and interaction, such as cameras, microphones, haptic devices (for physical contact), and a variety of

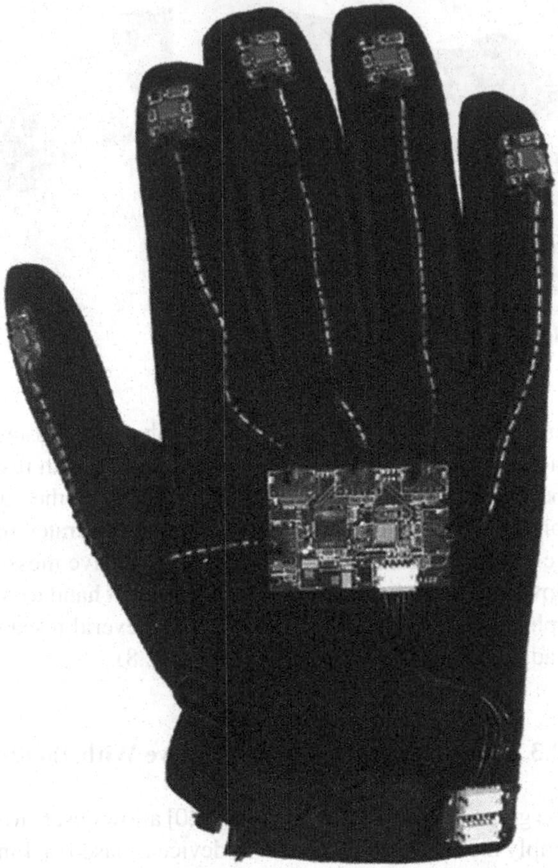

Fig. 12.9 Glove prototype with motion sensors and vibration motors on each finger

actuators. A sophisticated marking system is needed to capture the position of joints and fingers (Fig. 12.10).

12.3.2.7 Finger-Braille Interfaces

Finger-Braille [22] is a communication language employed by the deaf-blind community. Thanks to its simplicity, it can be utilized for enabling tangible interaction. Figure 12.11 demonstrates two examples of a Finger-Braille-based device consisting of vibration motors and solenoids. The system consists in two set of three rings each incorporating sensors and actuators. The former recognize movements of the fingers and convert them into Braille symbols, whereas actuators allow transmitting vibrotactile output in the form of six Braille dots; each dot, which is stimulated with vibration that represents a raised symbol, is associated with a finger.

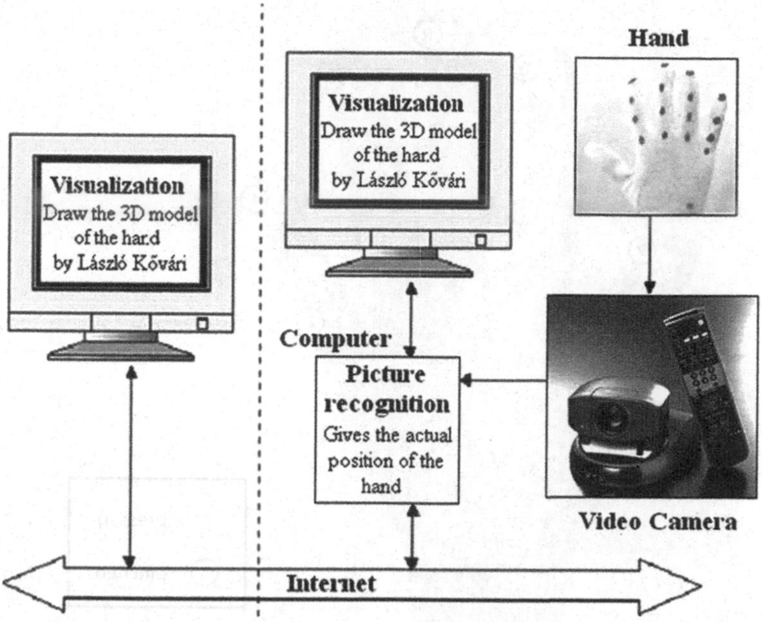

Fig. 12.10 Architecture described in [21]

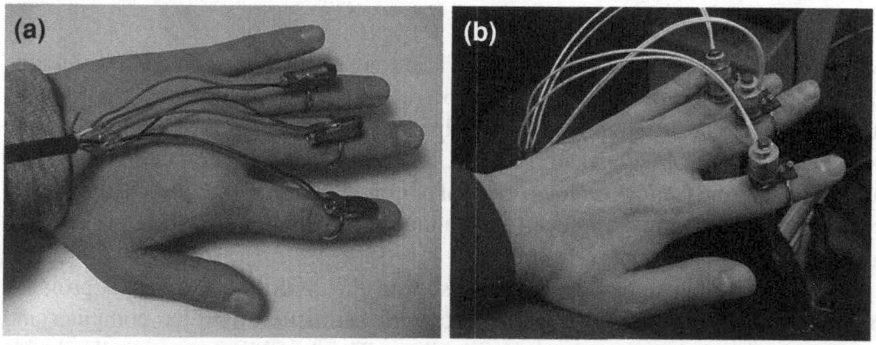

Fig. 12.11 Finger-Braille

12.3.2.8 dbGLOVE

The Malossi alphabet enables individuals to achieve touch-based communication thanks to a form of on-body signing based on a tactile code in which phalanxes represent letters. As each of the distal and the proximal phalanxes is associated with two letters, two pressure cues are employed to discriminate between touched letters and pinched letters. Individuals communicate in turns: the sender utilizes the left palm of the receiver as a typewriter, in order to transmit a message. By switching their roles, individuals can achieve full-duplex interaction. As the Malossi alphabet is

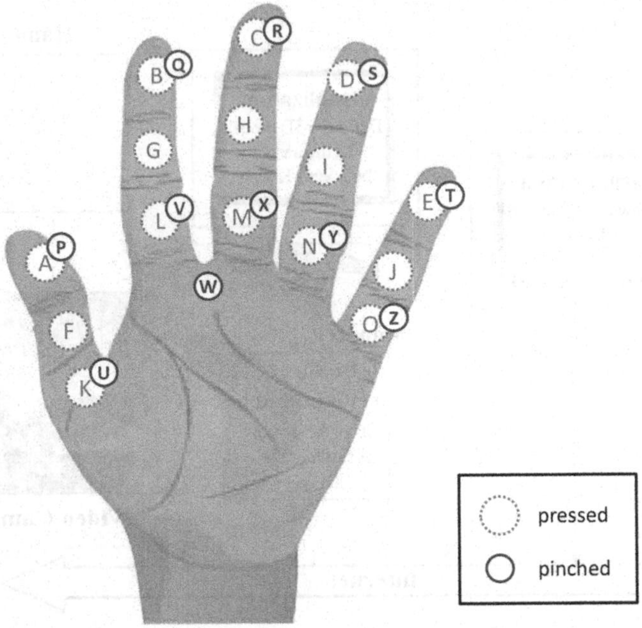

Fig. 12.12 Layout of the Malossi alphabet over the palm of the left hand

extremely easy to learn and understand, it is among the preferred education methods for the deaf-blind. Usually, children who are deaf-blind born receive the Malossi alphabet as one of the simplest form of alphabetization. Also, it is taught to people who become deaf-blind later in their life. Moreover, people who learn the Malossi alphabet continue using it for interpersonal communication, in addition to the Braille system, which is mainly employed for reading books and for accessing information available in digital formats (Fig. 12.12).

dbGLOVE is an interactive glove based on the Malossi alphabet. It provides blind and deaf-blind people with bi-directional interaction with the computer and computer-mediated communication with others. The deaf-blind can wear the device on the left hand, and they can type messages on their own palm, similarly to a keyboard with a different layout specifically designed for hand-based communication. The device incorporates an array of sensors and actuators into a pad that can be worn on the palm of left hand as if it was a glove. This can be connected to a computer, or to a smartphone. As a result, the deaf-blind can type on their own hand, instead of that of the receiver. Input is acquired and processed as a command to the PC (e.g., *open application*), or as a message to be displayed to another individual (e.g., *I want to eat*). Also, dbGLOVE includes a tactile monitor. So, the deaf-blind can receive messages in the form of tactile stimulations, as if someone was typing on their palm. Responses can be received by the user in the form of vibrotactile stimulation at different intensity and frequency that simulate touch and pinch cues, as if someone

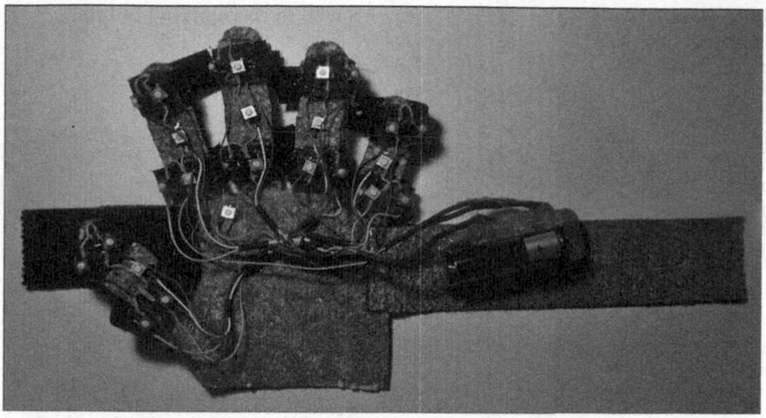

Fig. 12.13 A prototype of dbGLOVE: the *white dots* correspond to input/output areas

was typing on their hand. As a result, the device is able to provide the user with bi-directional communication without requiring the sender and the receiver to be in close contact or to utilize the same communication system. Figure 12.13 shows the device, whose architecture is extensively described in [23].

Although the Braille alphabet is the most widely adopted system for enabling blind and deaf-blind people to read text, it has limitations in terms of technological implementation and costs. Also, it requires cognitive abilities and sensory perception to be intact or well developed, and trained. Conversely, teaching AAC requires systems that can cope with developmental, physical, and sensory impairments [24]. In this regard, the Malossi alphabet is extremely intuitive, and it relies on basic touch cues. It is widely employed with people having cognitive impairments, who cannot learn more complex communication methods, such as alphabets involving shapes.

dbGLOVE was compared with Braille-based devices with the purpose of evaluating their learning curve. Results show that dbGLOVE is suitable for substituting Braille displays in everyday interaction, and particularly, during early life or in the first stage of deaf-blindness, that is, when individuals require an immediate system for basic communication. As shown by Fig. 12.12, the Malossi alphabet implemented in dbGLOVE outperforms the Braille alphabet both in speed and accuracy, in people with no previous training, as shown by Figs. 12.14 and 12.15. As a result, dbGLOVE can be utilized as a substitute of systems implementing the Braille alphabet, especially in circumstances in which a shorter learning curve is required. The device is market-ready and on sale. Moreover, its cost is extremely low (the price ratio is 1:12) with respect to the most employed technology for the deaf-blind (i.e., Braille Displays).

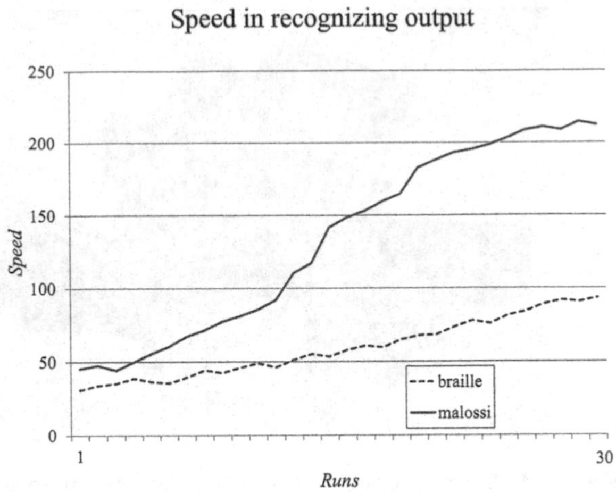

Fig. 12.14 Experimental results: speed of dbGLOVE compared to the Braille display

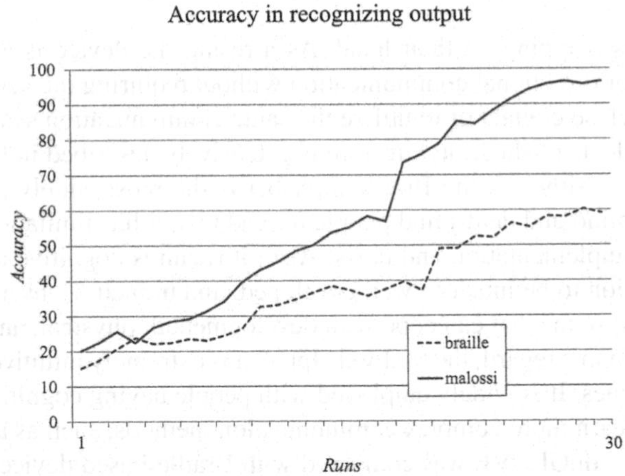

Fig. 12.15 Experimental results: accuracy of dbGLOVE compared to the Braille display

12.3.3 Systems for Environment Interaction

Assistive technology for blind and deaf-blind people include devices that allow individuals to interact with the environment and to realize to three main tasks, that is, mobility, interaction with everyday objects, and receiving alerts. In the next part, we will analyze different devices that serve such purposes.

12.3.3.1 Devices for Supporting Mobility

Electronic Travel Aids (ETAs) help people with disability achieve independent and autonomous mobility. Many systems for providing the blind with safe and independent mobility have been proposed over the last decades. Orientation devices have the purpose of informing the users of their current location and they assist them in tasks involving wayfinding. Regardless of the technology being utilized, they are based on systems for acquiring spatial information from the environment, for analyzing it, and for enabling its visualization through different sensory channels. As a result, they are employed to signal objects or to realize obstacle avoidance by means of algorithms. Such technology range from simple compasses to complex navigation systems. Several devices to support deaf-blind people in their mobility also require modifying the environment (e.g., embedding wires in pavements, or adding transmitters at salient points). As a consequence, their adoption requires complex decision-making processes at a municipality level. In the recent years, considerable resources have been devoted to developing navigation and wayfinding systems. There are low-tech tactile versions of compasses that use Braille. Langtao [25] introduced an electronic compass for the deaf-blind; it represents output in the form of electric pulses. Also, Nagel et al. [26] designed a compass that consists in a vibrotactile belt based on a set of vibrators.

Nonetheless, nowadays there is still no tactile equivalent to speech-based compasses in terms of granularity and promptness. Devices such as the Miniguide [27], the Ultra Cane [28] and the hand-held ultrasonic obstacle detector developed by Takes Corporation [29], indicate the distance to the closest object by vibrating when an obstacle is detected within a range from one to ten meters. The vibration frequency is an indicator of the distance of the obstacle: the faster the vibration rate, the closer the object. They are based on ultrasonic, laser or infrared technology, and they can be utilized by individuals to scan the environment and to obtain a spatial map of their surroundings. The Step-Hear [30] and the infrared remote signage developed by Talking Signs [31] are information and navigation reference point systems. In general, such systems consist of two units: Base and Activator. The Base is installed in key locations, with pre-recorded information. The Activator is held by the user, and vibrates to provide proximity and directionality to the location. For instance, Van Erp et al. [32] use a belt to indicate the direction towards the destination.

Also, landmark navigation systems have been implemented with low-cost technology for indoor localization [33]. Regardless of the underlying components for exchanging messages between the base and the activator, these systems require an infrastructure to be deployed in the environment. Although this can be a simple landmark transmitter, installing and maintaining permanent stations is extremely expensive; moreover, the system does not operate in areas that are not covered by any station. Portable orientation systems based on the Global Positioning System (GPS) are available to the deaf-blind population as extensions and add-ons to note-takers (e.g., the Braille Note, Braille Sense and the Pac Mate). Recently, they also come in the form of smartphone applications connected to Braille displays [34]. Studies about haptic forms of output for assisting GPS navigation are discussed in [35]. Unfortunately, nowadays there is no GPS system especially designed for the deaf-blind. Regardless of their output channel (i.e., Braille-based tactile output or speech-based auditory output), portable orientation systems allow the deaf-blind population to access basic information about current position, and to find routes toward

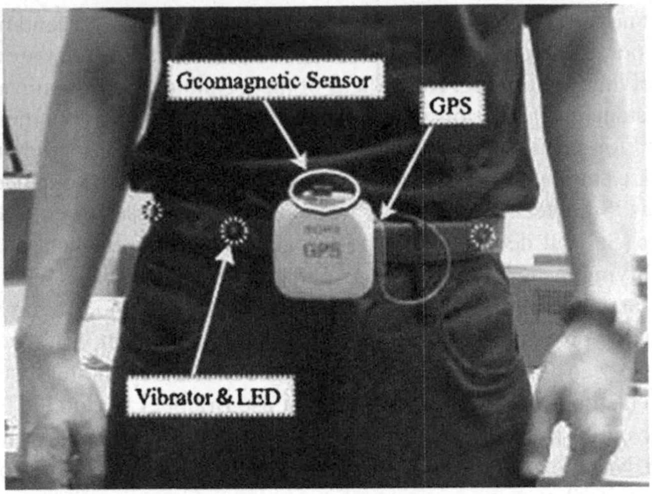

Fig. 12.16 Hardware overview of ActiveBelt

destinations. For instance, they can help understand the route of public trasportation and to identify where and when trains or busses stop. Although GPS provides the deaf-blind who are able to travel with useful information, navigation systems miss environmental information, such as whether there are sidewalks along the route. Indeed, GPS systems for the deaf-blind have the same accuracy of mainstream GPS, and therefore, they suffer from poor reliability: user's position can be represented within a few feet or meters with respect to their actual physical location. Therefore, GPS does not offer a true replacement for orientation or mobility skills though it offers crucial information that assists navigation tasks. Moreover, it does not substitute any of the tools deaf-blind travelers already use (e.g., cane or service dog). Nowadays, they do not offer (or support) any contextual information that can add to the experience of travelling, such as a description of the surrounding environment. Sylvain et al. [36] presented a device for obstacle detection based on a sophisticated multi-sonar system and on appropriate vibrotactile feedback. The system proved to be effective in conveying information about spatial proximity and in increasing the mobility of visually impaired people by offering new sensing abilities.

12.3.3.2 ActiveBelt

ActiveBelt [37] is a wearable interface that enables users to obtain directional information through touch cues. As information provided by the tactile sense is relatively unobtrusive, it is suited for embedding it into wearables to be utilized daily in the environment. It consists of a tactile display that can transmit directional information by means of a belt equipped with actuators (Fig. 12.16).

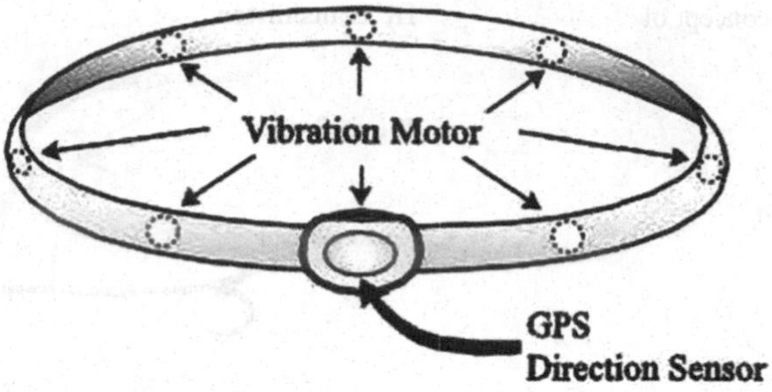

Fig. 12.17 Basic concept of ActiveBelt

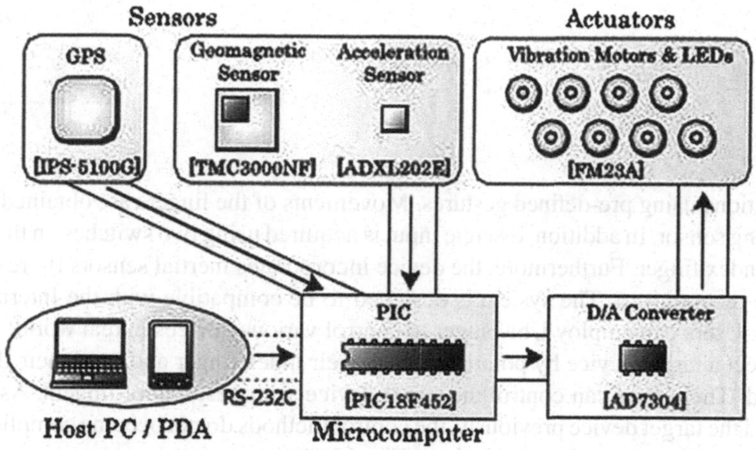

Fig. 12.18 System architecture of ActiveBelt

ActiveBelt can be used for a variety of applications and especially for localization services and applications, such as navigation or obstacle avoidance. It consists of two sensors (i.e., a direction sensor and a GPS) to detect user's location and orientation. Moreover, it incorporates multiple vibrators that transmit tactile information, and it relies on a small computer that controls the device (Fig. 12.17).

12.3.4 Devices for Interaction With Everyday Objects

In this section, we review assistive technology that provide people with support in interaction with everyday objects (Fig. 12.18).

12.3.4.1 Ubi-Finger

Ubi-Finger [38] is a compact device for gesture recognition. It is designed to be attached to the index finger, and it supports interaction with various devices and

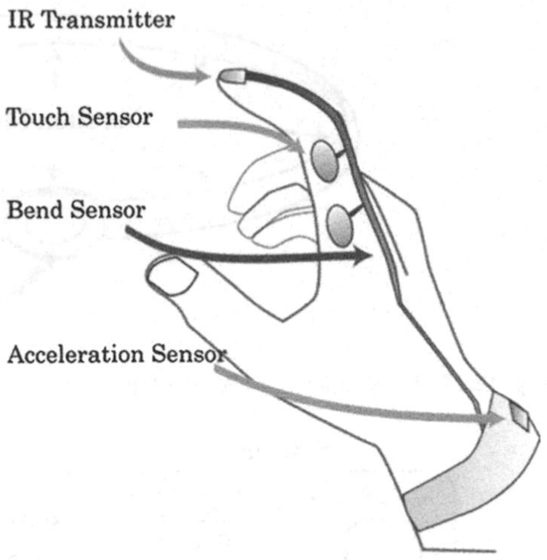

Fig. 12.19 Basic concept of Ubi-Finger

applications using pre-defined gestures. Movements of the fingers are obtained with a bending sensor. In addition, discrete input is acquired using two switches on the side of the index finger. Furthermore, the device incorporates inertial sensors (to realizes gesture recognition). The system is designed to be compatible with the Internet of Things. Users can employ Ubi-Finger to control various devices in real world: users can select a target device by pointing it with their index finger and send their ID via infrared. Then, they can control the target device with gestures of fingers. As they selected the target device previously, the control methods do not become complicated regardless of increase of target devices (Fig. 12.19).

The system is designed to work as follows. First, the user points at an appliance associated with Ubi-Finger. Then, gestures are transmitted via infrared to a server station. This recognizes both the gesture and the destination device. Consequently, the Ubi-Server transmits a signal to the appliance, so that it can change its state or actually realize the command (Fig. 12.20).

12.3.4.2 FieldMouse

FieldMouse [39] combines an ID detection system and motion detection. The former can consist in devices such as barcode or RFID tag readers; the latter can be a mouse, a gyroscope, or an accelerometer. The combination of inertial measurement and identification enables various types of applications. For instance, users can interact with the environment in a fashion similar to the Graphical User Interface of a computer. As an example, a barcode-reader enabled FieldMouse can act as a pointer and measure the relative movement of the device after having detected the barcode. This, in turn, can be utilized to control a menu or a slider. As barcode readers are extremely fast, the device operates with no interaction delay (Fig. 12.21).

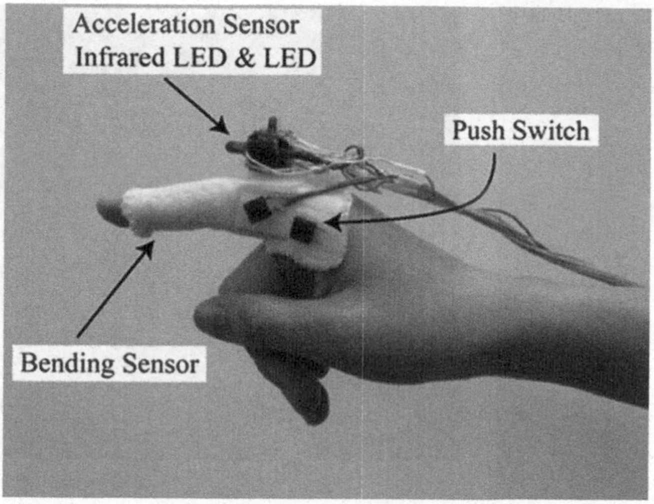

Fig. 12.20 Prototype of Ubi-Finger

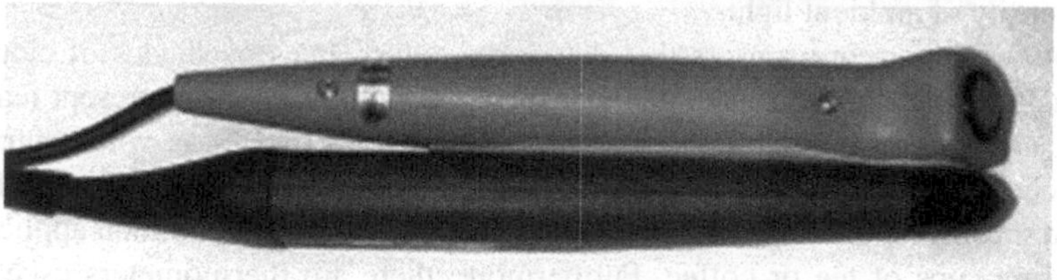

Fig. 12.21 FieldMouse incorporating a barcode reader and a mouse

12.3.4.3 5DT Data Glove

The 5DT Data Glove [40] is specifically dedicated to motion capture professionals. However, its technology could help the deaf-blind, as it translates finger flexure into messages, thanks to force resistors that generate voltage according to their bending (Fig. 12.22).

12.3.5 Indicators and Other Signaling/Alert Devices

Among indicators and signaling devices for the deaf-blind there are light probes, color sensors, and thermometers. The former indicate the presence of light using tactile output. In general, they use an optical sensor whose value modulates an output signal that can be auditory or tactile. For instance, passive light probes react to external light sources, whereas active light probes include a light source that measures the

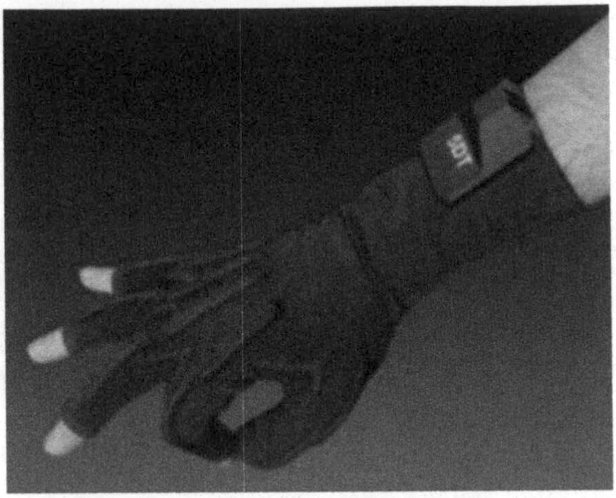

Fig. 12.22 The 5DT Data Glove

reflectivity of a surface; both emit a sound whose frequency or loudness represents the intensity of ambient light.

Moreover, there are sensors that determine colors, hues or shades of clothing, food ingredients, and objects in general; their main purpose is to represent features (such as shapes, colors, components and other characteristics) as voice output or touch cues. Liquid level indicators give audible or vibrotactile feedback when fluids reach a specific height (e.g., in a glass or container). Their most common application is pouring cups of tea or coffee. Furthermore, there are thermometers especially designed for the blind and the deaf-blind which provide audio or tactile output as well.

12.4 Open Problems

In addition to the problems mentioned in the previous sections regarding the availability and the readiness level of current assistive technology, PAT has to be socially pervasive, that is, people should be informed, aware, guided in the adoption, and trained in the use of innovative aids.

Nowadays, given the statistics of the deaf-blind and the costs of learning touch-based communication systems, only a minority of people with normal hearing and vision know tactile languages (see Sect. 12.5). This is because of personal factors (e.g., some of their relatives are deaf-blind) or because of their jobs (e.g., assistants). As a result, touch-based communication systems are basically known by primary users (i.e., blind, deaf, and deaf-blind), by their family (or their close milieu), and by their assistants, only.

In order to communicate with individuals that use tactile languages, people with normal hearing and sight who are not able to utilize any touch-based communication systems require the constant presence of an interpreter who has the purpose of translating from the tactile language of choice to verbal communication, and vice versa. However, the main issue with touch-based communication systems and, in general, with AACs is that, as they are not widespread in the community of non-impaired people, they require the deaf, blind and deaf-blind to need the constant presence of an assistant who plays the role of an interpreter in situations of interpersonal communication. This, in turn, poses strong limitations to their opportunities in terms of interaction with the external world. Moreover, as there are no official models to conceptualize touch-based communication systems, it is extremely difficult to learn such languages.

Two aspects have to be considered at the beginning of the process of introducing novel devices in the field of assistive technology, and specifically, structural (i.e., market) and functional (i.e., technological) barriers. The former are related to the scenario of technology for needs and, in particular, to highly customizable assistive technology, which has a different set of features with respect to other markets. Additionally, there are technological challenges related to the design and development of novel devices targeting individual needs, which have to be addressed with methods that are able to cope with the special requirements of end users.

The structural barriers to innovation in niche markets such as that of the deaf-blind include the following:

- **Limited support from public health** is an umbrella comprising a large set of issues. Despite research and development of assistive systems are highly encouraged by government, they receive limited financial support with respect to other sectors that are considered with much priority. This is the main cause of a major lack of coverage for equipment that could help develop products and services that could benefit people with impairments. Despite some research programs fund research at a national level, governments mainly apply a reactive approach and, thus, they are characterized as technology buyers. However, they apply restrictive funding policies for durable medical equipment. In addition to financial issues, both Medicare and MedicAid lack vision about assistive technology. Consequently, the market has no institutional guidance, and it is driven by companies, who are responsible for interpreting the needs of final users. The absence of a top–down approach increases fragmentation in the scenario of assistive technology, and it limits sharing best practices.
- As an additional challenge related to market fragmentation at the government level, each country has **different validation requirements** for approving the same technology.
- Companies usually receive and invest **limited funding in research and development**: although there is an increasing demand of custom and personal assistive technology, being a market extremely prone to risk, companies and investors prefer not to fund new technology, unless highly profitable, which is not the case of niche markets.
- *Ad hoc* technology suffers from **high vulnerability of patents**: custom-developed assistive technology having a few or no features in common lead to intellectual

property that has poor reusability and, therefore, low value for companies that invest in research and development. This prevents many stakeholders to focus on this market.

- There is large debate on the **budget for purchase**, which essentially defines which are the stakeholders responsible for buying assistive technology. As each case is different, new companies willing to enter the market invest large amounts of money to identify their revenue model and to determine whether final the National Health Service, insurance companies, or individuals are the buyers.
- **Assessment lacks of standards** that allow sharing results about the implications of the adoption assistive technology in terms of acceptability. In this regard, the Health Technology Assessment (HTA) is a step forward, though it is mainly applied to medical devices. Less attention is devoted to products, services, and best practice protocols that support individuals in their everyday tasks. Moreover, it is not possible to transfer knowledge about the application of a technology to different scenarios.
- **Experts are not available** and so are professionals and para-professionals working in the field of assistive technology services, such as physical and occupational therapists, speech pathologists, physicians, nurses, aids, and other health professionals.
- **Poor support** for family from the community of assistive technology experts.
- **Lack of awareness** about the potential of technology and its adoption process. In general, patients, people with disabilities and the elderly, including their families, and professionals assisting them have limited access to accurate and up-to-date information about assistive technology devices and services.

Furthermore, there are other deleterious factors that apply to specific circumstances. In order to deliver innovation in niche markets at a rate comparable with that of other types of markets, novel design and development methodologies are required to cope with the limitations posed by the inherent characteristics of any niche market itself. New approaches based on participation can change the way in which innovation is conceived, in order to save money and time, and to advance technology in a sustainable fashion.

In addition to structural barriers related to the way in which the market of assistive technology operates, there are technological issues related to the design and development of solutions that have to fit the diverse needs of different people having special requirements. Indeed, high levels of discontinuation are found in standard technology that does not adapt to users' needs. Therefore, one of the main challenges with respect to acceptability and adoption of human–computer interfaces (and, in general, technological devices) is the adaptability of the solution to the specific situation to which it will be applied. This is particularly true in assistive devices, because they have the role of supporting people living in diverse conditions, and affected by different impairments.

Usually, the majority of custom assistive technology are developed in laboratories and in small research centers. The largest market of assistive systems, that is, prostheses, makes no exception, as they need great adaptation to subjects' physical characteristics. Therefore, people have to visit development centers in order to get their prosthesis customized for their needs. Indeed, the cost of travel is worth the benefits of an effective and functioning aid. However, in other market verticals, and especially if products target more specific impairments, the process is less standard. The more devices are designed *ad hoc* to cope with specific requirements, the more different pieces of technology are utilized. As a consequence, in addition to market fragmentation, there is high diversity in the design of assistive devices. Also, being a niche market with limited number of users implies poor communication among laboratories and companies doing research on similar issues.

12.5 Future Outlook

One of the most frequent scenarios in centers devoted to sensory-impaired people involves assistants using several communication systems in order to exchange messages with different users who are deaf, blind, or deaf-blind. Moreover, caregivers use different methods for interacting with individuals depending on the specific condition and needs of the people they assist. For instance, the deaf use sign languages, whereas blind people speak and read Braille; on the contrary, others use the Malossi alphabet or print-on-palm, depending if they are deaf-blind born or have become deaf-blind in their later life, respectively. On the contrary, sensory-impaired children use objects for communicating, whereas adults with additional impairments at the cognitive level would exchange simple touch cues. It is impressive to see that, although different communication systems help people to interact with the external world, on the other hand, so many languages separate individuals living in an environment, sharing the same space, and experiencing similar conditions. Nevertheless, regardless of their specific situation, people with severe sensor and cognitive impairments are not able to interact with people other than assistants, family members, or close friends who do not know their language.

In this regard, a participative approach to the design and to the development of assistive devices may be a solution. Participatory design is a major research area in the scientific community and specifically in the field of human-computer interaction, especially in the domain of software development. Software benefits from being immaterial and thus, in the design of software systems, there are several solutions for achieving distance collaboration, parallel development, task management, and team synchronization based on Collaborative Work and Communication Systems (CSCW) tools. Conversely, dealing with hardware has several limitations due to the presence of physical objects that have to be manipulated, refined, and exchanged.

Indeed, remote collaboration in the design and development of hardware is known as being affected by poor scalability. Specifically, as assistive devices require particular attention to several crucial features, for hardware interfaces, meeting the requirements of software systems in terms of user participation is almost impossible. Consequently, the production of assistive solutions is either extremely customized, that is, *ad hoc* (and, therefore, very expensive), or completely standardized and less adaptable to the needs of final users. As a result, there is a number of effective *on-demand* solutions tailored for the needs of specific people, whose characteristics are difficult to implement in industrially-produced devices. Nevertheless, there is a missing link between systems realized with a participatory approach and standards in the industrial production of devices is among the major challenges in assistive technology. Overcoming current fragmentation in the scenario of solutions for people with disabilities, where it is necessary to aggregate development standards and customization techniques, will be crucial for fostering innovation in the field of assistive technology.

12.6 Reading

Further information about deaf-blindness and about dealing with the blind and the deaf-blind can be found in the following books and readings. In [41], the authors detail the population of children who are deaf-blind, including the classification of vision and hearing loss, the types of additional disabilities that may be present, and the causes of deaf-blindness. The book *Collective Wisdom: An Anthology of Stories and Best Practices for Educating Students with Severe Disabilities and Deaf-Blindness* [42] details how an enlightened democracy can grow and prosper by including blind and deaf-blind individuals in society thanks to education programs. The book by Lieberman et al. [43] introduces the topic of physical education and sports for people with visual impairments and, specifically, deaf-blindness: physical interaction with the environment is crucial to help blind and deaf-blind individual achieve self-confidence in moving automously. Hartmann [44] discusses the concept of collaboration in teaching to support children with deafblindness: education has a crucial role in helping deaf-blind indivudals to overcome the condition of isolation, which is directly connected with poor alphabetization. In addition to technology, low-tech modifications to the environment can help blind and deaf-blind individuals live better, as discussed in the book by Lolli et al. [45].

References

1. The World Health Organization. (2013). *Visual impairment and blindness. Fact sheet N282*. Retrieved October 22, 2013, from http://www.who.int/mediacentre/factsheets/fs282/en/
2. Freeman, P. (1975). *Understanding the deaf/blind child*. London: Heinemann Health Books.
3. Mc Innes, J., & Treffery, J. (1982). *Deafblind infants and children: A developmental guide*. Toronto: University of Toronto Press.
4. Ziefle, M., et al. (2014). Current trends and challenges for pervasive health technologies: From technical innovation to user integration. In *Pervasive health: State-of-the-art & beyond*.
5. Lewkowicz, D. J. (2000). The development of intersensory temporal perception: An epigenetic systems/limitations view. *Psychological Bulletin*, *126*(2), 281–308. doi:10.1037/0033-2909.126.2.281
6. Klatzky, R.-L., et al. (1985). Identifying objects by touch: An expert system. *Perception and Psychophysics*, *37*, 299–302.

7. Reed, C.-M., & Durlach, N.-I. (1998). Note on information transfer rates in human communication. *Presence: Teleoperators and Virtual Environments*, *7*(5), 509–518.
8. Ladner, R., et al. (1986). A user interface for deaf-blind people (preliminary report). *SIGCHI Bulletin*, *18*, 81–92. doi:10.1145/1165387.30864
9. Chang, A., et al. (2002). ComTouch: Design of a vibrotactile communication device. *Proceedings of the Conference on Designing Interactive Systems: Processes, Practices, Methods, and Techniques*, June 25–28, 2002, London, England.
10. Bloomfield, A., & Badler, N.-I. (2007). Collision awareness using vibrotactile array. *Proceedings of the Virtual Reality Conference* (pp. 163–170).
11. Saba, M.-P., et al. (2003). *Hey yaa: A haptic warning wearable to support deaf people communication*. Lapa, Rio de Janeiro, Brazil: Escola Superior de Desenho Industrial.
12. CuteCircuit. (2008). *HugShirt*. Retrieved March 14, 2008, from http://cutecircuit.com/portfolio/hug-shirt/
13. Eid, M., et al. (2008).*HugMe: A haptic videoconferencing system for interpersonal communication*. Canada: Multimedia Communications Research Laboratory University of Ottawa.
14. Teh, J., et al. (20101). *Huggy Pajama: A remote interactive touch and hugging system. Art and technology of entertainment computing and communication* (pp. 161–194).
15. Runyana, N., & Blazieb, D. (2010). EAP actuators aid the quest for the "Holy Braille" of tactile displays, electroactive polymer actuators and devices. *Proceedings of Electroactive Polymer Actuators and Devices (EAPAD)*, Vol. 7642.
16. The Boston-Based National Braille Press (NBP), Center for Braille Innovation. (2010). *b2g (Braille to Go)*. Retrieved October, 2012 from http://www.nbp.org/ic/nbp/technology/braillepda.html
17. Jayant, C., et al. (2010). VBraille: Haptic Braille perception using a touch-screen and vibration on mobile phones. *Proceedings of the 12th International ACM SIGACCESS Conference on Computers and Accessibility.*
18. Gollner, U., et al. (2012). Mobile Lorm glove introducing a communication device for deaf-blind people. *Proceedings of the sixth International Conference on Tangible, Embedded and Embodied Interaction.*
19. Kobakant DIY Wearable Technology Documentation. (2012). *Sensitive fingertips*. Retrieved October 6, 2013, from http://www.kobakant.at/DIY/?p=531
20. Dinh, V. V., et al. (2010). *Wireless haptic glove for language and information transference*. United States Patent Application, Publication No.: 2010/0134327 A1.
21. Lisztes, A., et al. (2005). Sign language in the intelligent sensory environment. *2*(1).
22. Hirose, M., & Amemiya, T. (2003). Wearable finger-Braille interface for navigation of deaf-blind in ubiquitous barrier-free space. *Proceedings of the HCI International.*
23. Caporusso, N. (2008). A wearable Malossi alphabet interface for deafblind people. *Proceedings of the Working Conference on Advanced Visual Interfaces, ACM* (pp. 445–448).
24. Sigafoos, J., et al. (2008). A review of intervention studies on teaching AAC to individuals who are deaf and blind. *Journal of Developmental and Physical Disabilities*, *20*, 71–99 (Springer, US).
25. Langtao, L., & Balachandran, W. (1993). Electronic compass for blind or deaf-blind pedestrians. *Electronics Letters*, *9*.
26. Nagel, S.-K., et al. (2005). Beyond sensory substitution—learning the sixth sense. *Journal of Neural Engineering*, *2*(4), 13–26.
27. GDP Research. (2010). *Miniguide*. Retrieved January 13, 2013, from http://www.gdp-research.com.au/
28. Sound Forsight. (2009). *Sound foresight*. Retrieved February 11, 2011, from http://www.soundforesight.co.uk/
29. Takes Corporation. (2009). *Palmsonar and palmtip*. Retrieved July 3, 2012, from http://www.palmsonar.com/
30. Step Hear. (2010). *Step hear and call hear*. Retrieved October 6, 2013, from http://www.step-hear.com/

31. Talking Signs. (2010). *Talking signs, infrared communication system*. Retrieved October 6, 2013, from http://www.talkingsigns.com/
32. Van Erp, J.-B.-F., et al. (2005). Waypoint navigation with a vibrotactile waist belt. *ACM Transactions on Applied Perception*, *2*(2), 106–117.
33. Altini, M., et al. (2011). A cost-effective indoor vibrotactile navigation system for the blind. *Proceedings of the International Conference on Health Informatics*.
34. Azenkot, S., & Fortuna, E. (2010). Improving public transit usability for blind and deaf-blind people by connecting a Braille display to a smartphone. *Proceedings of the 12th International ACM SIGACCESS Conference on Computers and Accessibility* (pp. 317–318).
35. Ertan, S., et al. (1998). A wearable haptic navigation guidance system. *Proceedings of the Second International Symposium on Wearable Computers* (pp. 164–165).
36. Sylvain, C., et al. (2007). A wearable system for mobility improvement of visually impaired people. *International Journal of Computer Graphics*, *23*(2), 109–118.
37. Tsukada, K., & Yasumura, M. (2005). ActiveBelt: Belt-type wearable tactile display for directional navigation. In *Lecture notes in computer science*. Springer-Verlag (Oct 2004).
38. Tsukada, K., & Yasumura, M. (2002). Ubi-finger: Gesture input device for mobile use. Retrieved November 12, 2012, from http://mobiquitous.com/pub/apchi2002-ubi-finger.pdf
39. Masui, T., & Siio, I. (2000). Real-world graphical user interfaces. *Lecture Notes in Computer Science*, *1927*, 72–84.
40. Fifth Dimension Technologies. (2012). *5DT Data Glove 14 Ultra*. Retrieved October 21, 2013, from http://www.5dt.com/products/pdataglove14.html
41. National Consortium on Deaf-Blindness. (2007). *Children who are deaf-blind*. OR: National Consortium on Deaf-Blindness.
42. United States Department of Education. (2011). *Collective wisdom: An anthology of stories and best practices for educating students with severe disabilities and deaf-blindness*.
43. Lieberman, L.-J., et al. (2012). *Physical education and sports for people with visual impairments and deafblindness: Foundations of instruction*. Sewickley, PA: AFB Press.
44. Hartmann, E.-S. (2011). Conceptualizing collaboration: How teachers work together to support children with deafblindness.
45. Perkins School for the Blind. (2013). *Suggestions for modifying the home and school environment: A handbook for parents*. Watertown: Perkins School for the Blind.

Chapter 13
A New Methodology (CON-INFO) for Context-Based Development of a Mobile User Interface in Healthcare Applications

Reem Alnanih, Olga Ormandjieva and T. Radhakrishnan

13.1 Introduction

Pervasive computing can combine current technologies with wireless computing, voice recognition, and Internet capability. Its goal is to create an environment where the connectivity of electronic devices is unobtrusive and always available.

'Going mobile' is the next logical step in the pervasive computing era. Currently, mobile computing is a supplemental service in hospitals, complementing existing clinical information systems by providing an alternative means to access medical information [1] and supporting interpersonal communication [2]. Given the increasing role of technology, the risk of errors caused by poor design, and the complexity of healthcare itself, MUI design for healthcare applications is subject to growing scrutiny, precisely because the stakes are so high and the potential gains from technology development in this area are so significant [3].

Interface designers face a challenge in the healthcare context, in terms of meeting future technology needs and the ever growing complexity of technology. In the medical field, the reality is that medical errors are seldom a result of carelessness or negligence. More commonly, they are caused by faulty system design, specifically

R. Alnanih (✉) · O. Ormandjieva · T. Radhakrishnan
Department of Computer Science and Software Engineering, Concordia University, Montreal, Canada
e-mail: r_aln@cse.concordia.ca; reem_n2@yahoo.com

O. Ormandjieva
e-mail: Ormandj@cse.concordia.ca

T. Radhakrishnan
e-mail: Krishnan@cse.concordia.ca

R. Alnanih
Department of Computer Science, King Abdulaziz University, Jeddah, Saudi Arabia

A. Holzinger et al. (eds.), *Pervasive Health*, Human–Computer Interaction Series,
DOI: 10.1007/978-1-4471-6413-5_13, © Springer-Verlag London 2014

faulty interface design. Both Human-Computer Interaction (HCI), which is the study of the interaction between users and computers that occurs through the user interface [4], and human factors have a significant role to play in increasing the quality of healthcare, and consequently in reducing the number of errors, especially those associated with the use of medical devices [5]. The traditional approaches of HCI to interface design are essential to the design of MUI, but they are unable to cope with the complexity of the typical interactive devices available today in the safety critical context of medical devices [6, 7]. This has led to the development of a broad range of user-centered design (UCD) methods [8–10]; however, traditional UCD practices are insufficiently powerful to solve problems at this level of complexity.

The research described in this chapter constitutes an attempt to address these and related problems by proposing a new context-based MUI design methodology, which we call CON-INFO, that bridges HCI and Pervasive Healthcare (PH). Together, HCI and PH provide the potential to assist the designer in solving the most important issues in the realm of healthcare. The research contribution of this chapter lies in the novelty of the approach, in which the adaptation of MUIs is systematized, allowing for objective and subjective analysis in an incremental fashion. The proposed CON-INFO approach is structured in five primary phases: (1) healthcare context model, (2) healthcare user stereotype model, (3) context descriptors, (4) adaptation design approach using decision tables, and (5) measurement model for quality assessment.

This five-phase structured framework is important for designing adaptable context-dependent MUIs from different perspectives. The context model allows for flexible characterization of user needs, which is a key issue in user modeling in the context of healthcare applications. Context descriptors formalize the domain expertise captured in the context model in a language that designers who are not experts in the domain can understand, as they can use these descriptors to adapt the MUI to the specified context. The quality-in-use of the MUI is monitored using a new measurement model inspired by the ISO 25010 international standard (ISO/IEC 25010, 2011) [11] and adapted to healthcare. This model is validated both theoretically and empirically [12].

Designing adaptable MUIs in the healthcare domain provides a solution that adapts essential patient information for doctors in an easily accessible, clear, and accurate way, and makes it available at any time. The benefits of the proposed CON-INFO methodology for healthcare professionals include improved productivity, performance, and level of satisfaction, as well as increased patient safety, as doctors can access patient information whenever and wherever it is needed.

The rest of this chapter is organized as follows. A glossary of terms is provided in Sect. 13.2. A survey of the state-of-the-art and open research problems is presented in Sect. 13.3. Section 13.4 describes our CON-INFO methodology, and illustrates its use in a case study in Sect. 13.5. In Section 13.6, we summarize the chapter and outline avenues for future research that we plan to follow.

13.2 Glossary

Adaptation Rules A set of rules that defines the conditions in which the adaptation has to take place, and what kind of adaptation will be achieved. These rules map the mode of data representation on the MUI to the context of healthcare professionals.

Decision Table (DT) A table consisting of columns and rows, to which we can add any number of rules (columns) and any number of conditions (rows) in an incremental way. The DT is used to model all the adaptation rules in a logical way, so that the consistency and completeness of this incremental table can be easily checked.

Healthcare Context Characterization of the healthcare environment by healthcare professionals in order to match the design of the mobile healthcare application to user preferences.

Mobile User Interface (MUI) A screen space or screen layout that consists of various UI objects, known as widgets (buttons, task bar, dialog boxes, pull-down menus, pop-up menus, etc.). Each UI object is associated with a set of one or more performable user actions, such as touch-based (swipe, pinch, etc.), voice based, etc. The MUI allows the user to interact with the underlying software application in order to complete the task at hand.

Pervasive Healthcare The application of pervasive computing technologies to healthcare. This is a new discipline that promotes the systematic exchange of healthcare information, making it available everywhere, to anyone, at any time.

13.3 State-of-the-Art and Open Problems

In this section, we present a review of the literature related to each of the five phases of the CON-INFO methodology: healthcare context model, healthcare user stereotype model, context descriptors, adaptation design approach using decision tables, and measurement model for quality evaluation.

13.3.1 Context Model

The commonly used English word ‘context’ is, in general, understood intuitively, but its formal or technical definition as used in context-aware computing or in the design of adaptive software systems can be quite elusive. A clear and unambiguous understanding of the technical meaning of the term is becoming important as pervasive computing is now in use ubiquitously and at all times, and to communicate with individuals and electronic devices in remote locations.

The authors in [13] have presented the definitions or interpretations of the term ‘context’ by various researchers: for example, Schilit and Theimer [14], Brown et al. [15], Ryan et al. [16], Dey [17], Franklin and Flaschbart [18], Ward et al. [19],

Rodden et al. [20], Hull et al. [21], and Pascoe [22]. Dey and Abowd [13] are particularly interested in context-aware systems, and so they focus on characterizing the term itself. Pascoe's view of context [2] is based on the sensed parameters of the environment, and in Pascoe et al. [23], the authors introduce the notion of a universal context model which can enable applications to sense the environment surrounding them, so that they can either react or adapt.

In Gwizdka [24], the author considers what is internal (to the user) in a context and what is external, in dealing with contextual information. In Flanagan et al. [25], the authors are interested in the recognition of context based on the features of multidimensional data from different sensors. Schmidt [26] suggests that an implicit HCI model based on a situational context needs to be created for both input and output information.

Korpipää et al. propose sensor-based context awareness (SBCA) [27], which focuses on modeling at the sensor level, but does not take into consideration adaptation of the input, such as user interactions involving voice or touch. In [28], the authors introduce MIContext, which is a context model for mobile interaction that stays at the conceptual level. Earlier, Dey and Abowd [13] had defined context as an entity. This idea of linking contextual information to an entity or subject is a key aspect of our approach.

Open research problems Mobility provides additional opportunities for leveraging context, but potentially rapidly changing context and the need to synthesize it, and act on it, place an extra burden on the mobile computing platform.

In this chapter, we address this problem by introducing a two-level characterization of the term 'healthcare context' (made up of a basic level and a domain level) as a requirement and guide for designing and developing a context-based MUI.

13.3.2 User Modeling

Several techniques have been proposed by the HCI community to help researchers understand users and model their needs. These techniques include concepts such as persona [29, 30] archetype [31], and user profile [32]. Our method focuses on a stereotype-based user model.

Stereotypes are generalized beliefs about a given category, in this instance, people. Stereotypes and stereotyping are found extensively in user representations [33]. The stereotype can be understood to be based on a cognitive, a social, or a narrative approach [34].

For this research, two aspects of stereotyping were necessary: categorization and accentuation. With categorization, differences between people are simplified and attributed to their group membership; and with accentuation, differences between groups are maximized and differences between individual members of the same group are minimized [35]. This symbiosis between categorization and accentuation is an important trait of this proposed model, and it is based on the acquisition and use of long-term models of individual users.

Open research problems MUIs are being used by more and more individuals in the healthcare domain in all walks of life, from different backgrounds and with varying levels of experience. Consequently, MUI designers are certain to face ever more challenges in designing customized MUIs in the context of healthcare. They will have to optimize user interactions with the devices and their operating environment, identifying their needs and understanding the activities that are being supported by the devices.

In this chapter, we elicit user stereotype categories in order to make the MUI strategically adaptable to the 'type' of user.

13.3.3 Design for Adaptation

In recent years, a number of adaptive MUIs in healthcare applications have been described. Frohlich et al. [36] presented their LoCa approach to context-aware monitoring applications in digital homes. The LoCa project differs from our research in that Frohlich et al.'s adaptation is based on external sensors that monitor physiological parameters.

The process of developing context-based UIs has been explored in a number of other projects. Clerckx et al. [37], for example, discuss various tools to support the model-based approach. Yuan and Herbert [38] present a fuzzy logic-based context model and related context aware reasoning middleware that provides a personalized, flexible, and extensible reasoning framework for a context aware real time assistant (CARA). However, other than running simulations, they were unable to devise and carry out field experiments that yielded results with enough diversity to justify scientific application. Unlike previous work, our paper indexes all the information gathered by sensors from the basic context level as conditions. We then combine these conditions in a user stereotype model and collect all the possible adaptation rules using a decision table.

Many studies have been conducted on adaptation using a decision table. In [39], an approach is proposed for modeling adaptive 3D navigation in a virtual environment. In Vogt and Merier [40], the authors use a model-based approach and the user interface markup language (UIML) to create mobile and adaptive UIs for healthcare applications Their approach differs from ours in three ways: (1) our MUI adaptation is based on a context model, a stereotype model, and a set of context descriptors that captures the essence of the dynamic context; (2) our adaptation technique is based on decision-making rules; and (3) our adaptation model consists of all the parameters of the UI that adapt either at the time of design or at runtime, and takes into account the features and sensors embedded in the smartphone to help the doctor effectively input his or her needs to the application and obtain meaningful output by selecting from various choices.

Open research problems MUI design should benefit from the idea of adaptation of the UI with respect to the context. Therefore, there is a need for a formal representation of what context means in the healthcare domain and for the corresponding context-based adaptation techniques.

Table 13.1 Comparison of selected ISO standards

Standard/criteria	SW/HW	Healthcare	UI design	UCD method	Mobile usage	Context of use
ISO/IEC 25010	SW	√	√	×	×	√
ISO/IEC 62366	HW	√	√	×	×	×
ISO 9241-210	SW	×	√	√	×	√
ISO 9241-11	SW	×	√	×	×	√
New quality-in-use model	SW	√	√	√	√	√

In our solution, there are two categories of adaptation built on the CON-INFO context model: (a) the designer adapts the design to the mobile device, and (b) the device recognizes the context at runtime and adapts interface widgets according to preprogramming requirements. Our adaptation technique is based on the CON-INFO context model: it extracts values from sensors in smartphones and maps them to the CON-INFO user stereotype model, and then to the MUI using a decision table. The context descriptor, a new term introduced by the CON-INFO methodology, is used to capture domain expertise as a foundation for designing and developing adaptable context-based MUIs.

13.3.4 Quality-in-Use Measurement

Quality-in-use is more comprehensive than usability, as it is defined as the capability of a software product to enable specified users to achieve specified goals effectively, productively, and safely in specified contexts of use, and to be satisfied with the outcomes [ISO/IEC 25010 2011] [11]. It is based on the user's view of the quality of the system containing the software, and is measured in terms of the results of using the software, rather than the properties of the software itself. To specify and measure quality-in-use requires not only measures of effectiveness, productivity, and satisfaction, but also details of the characteristics of the users, their goals, and the relevant context of use [41]. In the healthcare environment, quality-in-use is related to a well-defined set of tasks that enables a doctor to achieve his or her goals, while usability is more technical, and concentrates on the quality of the specific task and how easy it will be to perform. In short, the upper limit of usability is the lower limit of quality-in-use.

The existing standards in the literature do not satisfy the requirements for measuring the quality-in-use of MUIs in the healthcare domain. In Table 13.1, we compare various standards, such as ISO/IEC 25010 [11], ISO/IEC 62366 [42], ISO 9241-210 [43], and ISO 9241-11 [44], with respect to quality in terms of designing UIs for software (SW) and hardware (HW) in the healthcare domain, specifically for mobile devices in different contexts of use.

Fig. 13.1 CON-INFO methodology

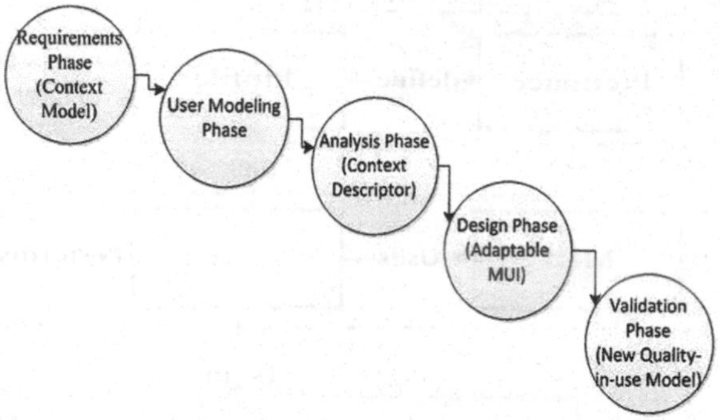

Open research problems The quality of MUIs is crucial in the healthcare domain, as the attention of healthcare professionals is usually on the patient and not on the system, and so low-quality UIs may lead to critical medical errors. Based on the existing standards referenced in our literature review, no method currently exists to measure the quality of MUI design in healthcare applications (see Table 13.1).

New guidelines for designing MUIs for quality-in-use models and quality evaluation/decision-making models have to be derived, as the current standards may not meet the specific needs of healthcare application users. To effectively evaluate the quality-in-use of mobile healthcare applications, new MUI quality-in-use measurements have been proposed in CON-INFO specifically designed for PH [45].

In this section, we have summarized related work and highlighted the most important challenges in designing and evaluating MUIs for healthcare applications. We have described and addressed the open problems in PH by introducing a new healthcare context-based methodology, CON-INFO, designed to unobtrusively combine mobile technologies with wireless computing, voice recognition, and Internet capability, and adaptable MUI features based on the user stereotype, the task, and the context of the work.

13.4 CON-INFO Methodology

Our CON-INFO methodology is a top-down modeling approach applicable in the beginning stages of analysis and development of an adaptable MUI. The major phases of this methodology are illustrated in Fig. 13.1.

13.4.1 Phase 1: Context Model for Pervasive Healthcare

In this section, we characterize the term ‘context’ from the MUI designer’s perspective, with a view to implementing an adaptable MUI. We define the vector <L, M, E> as the basic context (BC), where L indicates a location, M indicates the time when the task is performed, and E characterizes the physical environment. Zero or more

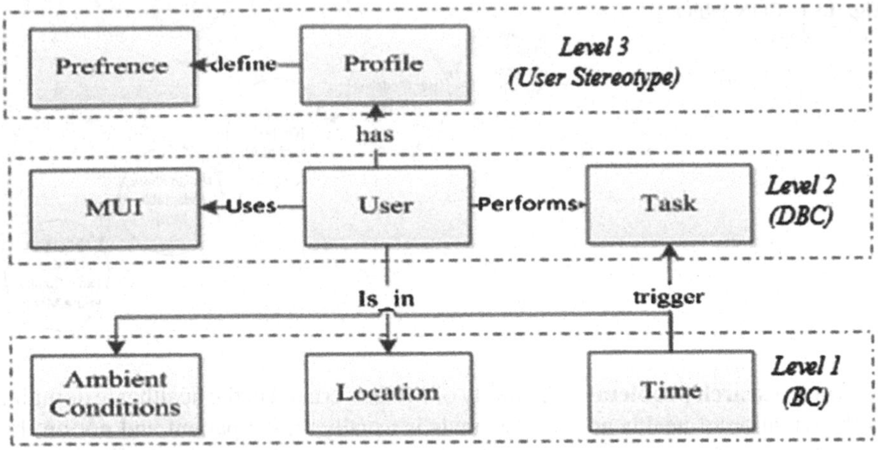

Fig. 13.2 Context model for pervasive healthcare applications

of the basic context parameters might be relevant to the set of tasks performed in the domain of application considered. Each of these parameters in the basic context can be characterized by one or more features at a varying level of granularity. For example, the location can be a patient's room, the patient's bed, the emergency room, a transplant ward, etc.

We define the vector <A, T, O> as the domain-based context (DBC), where A is an actor, T is the task performed, and O indicates the target object. Each of these parameters in the DBC can be characterized by one or more features. For example, the domain actor belongs to a user stereotype (a young doctor or a senior doctor, for example), and is characterized as such because we are interested in adapting the MUI to user stereotypes. The actor (a doctor) is playing a role (monitoring the patient), but that role may involve several tasks. Task T is obtained from the task model, where there may be different methods for performing the same task, but in a context with different context descriptors. The informational object set is made up of all the data objects on the MUI, e.g. recorded patient data. To narrow the domain in this chapter, we have taken one task performed by one actor, and considered that as the domain for discussion.

Separating the basic context parameters from the rest of the context-defining parameters creates the possibility of creating a Context Information Service CIS (Pascoe [22]) to facilitate the sharing of context recognition among multiple applications running in different places in a large hospital. With our definition of context, we can create many levels of application (Fig. 13.2). Level 1 is the BC, which is independent of the DBC, because it includes similar applications, whether or not they are mobile, that run in a particular location, at a particular time, and under particular ambient conditions, light and audio, for example. The BC is acquired from the sensors installed in the smart phone. Level 2 is the DBC, which is dependent on the BC, clearly referring to the adaptation of mobile-based data entry, rather than computer-based data entry, because the BC changes when the application is executed on the mobile device, while in a stationary case the BC does not. For example, when the user performs a task using a mobile device, the MUI will adapt the features based on the available BC, which is the handling context. Level 3 is the user stereotype, and represents the user preferences and profile. The MUI will also adapt the features to the user stereotype, as well as to the BC.

13.4.2 Phase 2: User Model for Pervasive Healthcare

In this section, we are interested in investigating the idea of creating a user stereotype model through an empirical study based on a questionnaire circulated among doctors and interviews conducted with them, with a view to implementing an adaptable MUI from the perspective of the designer.

Empirical research has been conducted in this work to lead to a better understanding of the nature of the stereotypes involved in healthcare, with a view to developing a practical MUI for these healthcare application users. Fifty Saudi doctors were recruited from various departments in Saudi Arabian hospitals, some of whom are currently working at the Children's Hospital in Montreal, Canada.

In order to understand the nature of the role that smartphone technology can play in a healthcare environment, and the relationship among the various user stereotype models proposed, a questionnaire was sent to these doctors, who perform different medical functions. The questionnaire was designed to collect:

- user characteristics, such as age group and gender;
- user experience in a domain or career;
- user behaviors in an environment, or with respect to an application, such as mobile technology adoption and use at work; and
- user preferences (likes and dislikes).

The interview was designed based on our context variables to enable us to derive context descriptors (see Sect. 13.4.1) related to the various physical environments in which the users and the mobile technology will be operating.

To generate the user model, we expressed the responses collected as percentages combining the individual responses given and the individual feedback provided by the doctors. In order to maintain a complete dataset for the users in the various age groups, 30 interviews were selected from the 50 conducted: 10 interviews per stereotype, and 5 male respondents and 5 female respondents per stereotype, were considered. We are not looking at an overall percentage, but rather at individual percentages related to each user group created among the 30 doctors selected. Table 13.1 illustrates how drilling down through the percentages yielded the three doctor stereotypes.

Our findings support three significant groups out of nine, taking into account their relative expertise based on the categorization rules. These are: Junior (novice: expert); Intermediate (intermediate: intermediate); and Experienced (expert: novice), as illustrated in Table 13.2.

Table 13.2 User stereotype model for pervasive healthcare applications

User stereotype	Junior	Intermediate	Experienced
Age group	25–34	35–44	45+
Domain experience[a]	Novice 100 %	Intermediate 90 %	Expert 60 %
Smartphone application experience[b]	Expert 80 %	Intermediate 60 %	Novice 70 %

[a] Domain experience is defined here as novice (less than 10 years), intermediate (more than 10 years, less than 15 years), or expert (more than 15 years)

[b] Smartphone application experience is defined here as expert (uses all the listed applications: medical, Facebook and Twitter, SMS and MMS, Email, WhatsApp), intermediate (uses all the listed applications, except medical), or novice (sends messages and makes calls only)

The interview and questionnaire results show that the choices made by doctors follow different patterns. We can clearly see that young doctors have had more exposure to the smartphone platform and are more familiar with its applications and their use, and the use of a smartphone in general. They also show little or no resistance to being introduced to new applications, especially if they will assist them with their daily work in the healthcare environment. These individuals easily fall into a single stereotype category. Intermediate doctors are very similar to junior doctors, in terms of their exposure to smartphones overall. They don't use them as much, but they also don't show resistance to using a new application that could assist them in their work. We can readily place these doctors in another stereotype category. Experienced doctors are likely to have had less exposure to the smartphone platform and show more resistance to using a new application that could support them in their daily work. We have no hesitation in placing them in a third stereotype category.

13.4.3 Phase 3: Context Descriptors

Based on the characterization of healthcare application contexts (phase 1) and the model of user stereotypes that we have developed (phase 2), we have conducted a thorough requirement analysis and drawn up a set of context descriptors through interviews with 30 doctors. A context descriptor (CD) is a sentence or sentence fragment that forms the basis for MUI adaptation [46]. From our interviews with 10 doctors for each of the 3 user stereotypes, we collected 7 different CDs for each stereotype. For the sake of brevity, we provide a sample of the CDs collected for each user stereotype in Table 13.3.

13.4.4 Phase 4: Design Approach for Adapting MUI

Our approach to adaptation is to change the MUI parameters based on context (phase 1) and user stereotype (phase 2). This allows users to easily handle information on the MUI, which shakes with the user's motion and is affected by various ambient

Table 13.3 Sample of context descriptors

User stereotype	Context descriptor
Junior	I want conversations taking place in meetings to be recorded automatically. When I am in a meeting, if someone calls twice, my phone should mark the call as urgent and vibrate. When I am calling another doctor, inform me if he or she is currently in a meeting
Intermediate	I want to be able to adjust the screen's brightness in daylight. I want to be able to adjust the volume when my phone is on the speaker setting. I want different access levels for patient profiles
Experienced	I have difficulty reading small fonts. My environment is noisy most of the time. I do not want to be disturbed during a meeting

Table 13.4 MUI Features

MUI features	Value (conditions)
Font size	Small, medium, large
Font color	An RGB color, black and white
Font format	Times new roman, Tahoma, etc.
Background color	Auto adjust, change manually
Data entry[a]	Typing, tapping, voice
Display information[a]	Text, sound
Message delivery	Text, voice, alert, silent, pre answer
Brightness level[a]	Increase/decrease
Ring volume	Low, medium, high, alert, vibration
Sound level	Mute, regular, loud

[a] These are the features that were implemented in the case study (see Sect. 13.4)

environmental conditions, and different combinations of conditions (i.e. light and noise levels). The UI features, which can be changed on a modern smartphone, are listed in Table 13.4.

Categorization of the contexts in which a doctor works in a hospital setting depends on the location in which the medical tasks are performed; for example, primary care, the emergency room, an operating room, inpatient care, an inpatient ward, an outpatient clinic, the intensive care unit, etc. [47].

The time constraints of this project made it impossible to consider the extent of the hospital services provided and their many context descriptors. To develop a prototype to validate the adaptable features of the MUI presented in Table 13.3, we focused on a particular area of the hospital, an inpatient ward, where physicians' services are provided. Our MUI is based on this area and on the junior healthcare providers working in this context, along with the context descriptors for these types of users. This step is performed from the MUI designer's perspective, and is a continuation of our previous work in this domain [46, 48]. Transformation rules are created by designers, who codify best practice patterns for predefined situations, as well as fall back rules, as suggested by de Melo et al. [49]. Rules at different stages can be developed independently of each other. At each stage, different contextual information is included—see the example below.

13.4.4.1 A 'Sub Domain' Scenario on a Hospital Ward

If a junior doctor wants to: (1) check the most recent CBC test result, and (2) order medication for a patient at night in the patient's room, which is quiet and dark, then the MUI can: display the result by sound, rather than by text; accept the order given by the doctor by voice, rather than typed on the keyboard of a smartphone; and increase the brightness level of the screen.

In this scenario, the UI features adapted or modified (temporarily) are: change to speech output while the doctor is in the room; change to speech input while the doctor is in the room; and increase the level of brightness of the display.

A Decision Table (DT) provides a schematic view of the inference process in decision making. The advantage of a DT is that it provides a more compact visual presentation, and so contributes to a better understanding of the selection problem. But probably the most important advantage of using a DT is that the completeness, correctness, and consistency of the information entered are easier to check.

All the condition attributes presented in our work are based on our basic context, which consists of the location (i.e. the inpatient ward), the time (morning and evening shifts), the ambient conditions (light level: bright or dark), and the noise level (low or high) (see Table 13.4) [46]. For the domain-based context, which consists of the user and the tasks, we defined three user stereotype models for healthcare applications based on experimental work: junior, intermediate, and expert [48]. Also, CDs for each type were collected. The tasks that doctors most frequently perform on a daily basis on the inpatient ward can be summarized in two categories, input tasks and output tasks, as follows:

- Output tasks: review laboratory, radiology, and pharmacology results.
- Input tasks: submit new pharmacology, laboratory, and radiology orders.

In the following subsections, all the possible rules for adapting MUI actions to the doctor's tasks are presented (Tables 13.5 and 13.6). For example, in Table 13.5, when conditions C2 and C3 are met (C2 and C3 = Yes) for an output task, then a set of features is adapted on the MUI (A1, A3, A5, A7, and A10). These rules can be specified by design experts and a healthcare provider. For the sake of brevity in this paper, and to be practical in terms of experimental work and the limited time available for conducting the research, we chose the junior stereotype, since this type performs most of the work on the inpatient ward, and they are the individuals most familiar with using a mobile device.

To verify the completeness of the rules, we simply calculate how many are represented in each column and compare the result with 2^{m}, where m is the number of conditions. Rule analysis also indicates that the proposed rules are consistent. In the next section, we validate our MUI adaptation approach.

Table 13.5 Decision table for output tasks (junior stereotype)

	Conditions	Rules			
		1	2	3	4
C1	The doctor is in the patient's room during the morning shift	–	–	–	–
C2	The level of light in the room is bright	Y	Y	N	N
C3	The level of noise in the room is low	Y	N	Y	N
Actions					
A1	Adjust the font size for displaying information to "user default"	X	X		
A2	Adjust the font size for displaying information to "large"			X	X
A3	Adjust the display brightness to "user default"	X	X		
A4	Adjust the display brightness to "high"			X	X
A5	Receive text message alerts by "ring tone"	X	X		
A6	Receive text message alerts by "vibration"			X	X
A7	Adjust the ring tone volume to "user default"	X			
A8	Adjust the ring tone volume to "high"		X		X
A9	Adjust the ring tone volume to "silent"			X	
A10	Receive information via a headset	X		X	
A11	Receive information via a "text"		X		X

Table 13.6 Decision table for input tasks (junior stereotype)

	Conditions	Rules			
		1	2	3	4
C1	The doctor is in the patient's room during the morning shift	–	–	–	–
C2	The level of light in the room is bright	Y	Y	N	N
C3	The level of noise in the room is low	Y	N	Y	N
Actions					
A1	Adjust the font size for displaying information to "user default"	X	X		
A2	Adjust the font size for the display information to "large"			X	X
A3	Adjust the brightness to "user default"	X	X		
A4	Adjust the brightness to "high"			X	X
A5	Receive text message alerts by "ring tone"	X	X		
A6	Receive text message alerts by "vibration"			X	X
A7	Adjust the ring tone volume to "user default"	X			
A8	Adjust the ring tone volume to "high"		X		X
A9	Adjust the ring tone volume to "silent"			X	
A10	Input the data using a microphone	X		X	
A11	Input the data by typing on a keyboard		X		X

13.4.5 Phase 5: Validation Using a New Quality-in-Use Model for MUIs

Our objective in this section is to present a new quality-in-use model tailored specifically to the MUI design process and adapted to the UI types used in the healthcare domain.

The proposed new quality-in-use model is aimed at helping the designer evaluate the mobile application to execute work-related tasks with: (i) increased effectiveness, productivity, efficiency, and satisfaction, through the ability to use the application anywhere and at any time; and (ii) increased safety, through error reduction by restricting the use of the UI to the options available, as well as making the UI more pleasant to use and easier to manipulate; and (iii) reduced cognitive load on the user, through a reduction in the number of navigation-related actions.

Table 13.7 presents the definitions of the objective and subjective factors of the proposed new quality-in-use model, as well as our interpretation of each factor.

Table 13.8 presents the base measures for each quality indicator that needs to be considered during data collection.

13.5 Case Study (PHIS)

An example of a healthcare application is the Phoenix Health Information System (PHIS), which is used at King Abdulaziz University Hospital (KAUH). After PHIS was designed, PHIS2, the desktop version, was introduced and redesigned to take into account the principles of the HCI in terms of mental model, metaphor, visibility, affordability, and feedback [50]. A new, mobile-based version of PHIS2 (PHIS2-M) has since been introduced in order to make PHIS accessible from a mobile-based platform. A quality-in-use measurement model was developed specifically for the MUI to evaluate the quality of the mobile-based version of PHIS2 (PHIS2-M) [12].

The proposed CON-INFO methodology for MUI feature adaptability was applied and then implemented on an iPhone 4.1 loaded with the PHIS2-M using Xcode 4 and SQLite, after a special framework for speech recognition (iSpeech iOS SDK) had been added. The result was a new version of PHIS2-M, which is PHIS3-MA for mobile adaptation (MA). The adaptable features of the MUI were evaluated on PHIS3-MA.

13.5.1 Experimental Design

Our participant sample was made up of 12 junior doctors at KAUH aged 25–35, 4 males and 8 females, who had had previous experience with PHIS for at least three months. The participants were interviewed and observed in a simulated environment

Table 13.7 New quality-in-use objective and subjective factors

Quality-in-use factors	Definition of quality-in-use objective measure factors	Interpretation
Effectiveness	Number of actions required to complete the subtasks of each task in a specified context of use. It is measured in actions per subtask	The closer to 1.0 the better
Productivity	Number of actions performed in a specified context of use relative to the time taken by the user to complete the task. It is measured in actions per second	The larger the better
Task efficiency	The efficiency of the user in completing the task in a specified context of use. It is measured in actions per second	The larger the better
Safety (error prevention and error recovery)	Safety of the user, in terms of the number of errors committed in each action of each task performed in a specified context of use. It is measured in errors per action	The closer to zero the better
Task navigation (cognitive load)	To perform a user task, the user may have to move from one screen to another, perhaps even back and forth. This will depend on three things: task complexity, screen size or form factor, and the way the designer has packed information on the various screens. Moving from screen to screen adds to the cognitive load. For a given user task, each screen view is weighted by the number of actions performed on that screen, which must be minimized to keep the user focused on the task at hand, but sufficient to increase the user's confidence in using the application and to reduce the possibility of the user losing interest during a task. It is measured in actions per view	The smaller the better
Definition of quality-in-use subjective measure factors		

(continued)

Table 13.7 (continued)

Satisfaction	The user's level of enjoyment as a result of interacting with the social networking application in a specified context of use in terms of learning the application, using the application, performing a particular task, finding the features, understanding navigation, recovering from error, and performing a task anywhere and at any time	Measured on a Likert scale

Table 13.8 Base measurement definition

Base measure	Definition
A	The minimum number of actions users need to complete a task is measured by the number of clicks recorded
C	The number of correct actions required by the user to complete a task, which is measured by the number of clicks recorded
X	The number of incorrect actions that a user performs when completing a task involving risk, which is recorded to help assess the level of safety of the MUI
T	The time required for the user to complete a task, which is recorded to help assess whether or not the MUI is sufficiently usable and simple
V	The number of screen views involved in performing a task

in which prerecorded background noise from the real hospital was played back one participant at a time. In order to determine the effect of MUI adaptable features, each participant was asked to perform the same set of tasks, once using PHIS2-M (no adaptable features and not considering the CON-INFO methodology), and once using PHIS3-MA (with adaptable features and considering the CON-INFO methodology). The two versions of the PHIS-based mobile application were loaded onto the same iPhone device. The test environment included the participants, the iPhone device loaded with two applications, a timer, and a tester. Prior to conducting the formal evaluation of the experiment, a list of materials to be used during testing was prepared, as suggested by Dumas and Redish [51], and included the following:

- Task list: A list of five tasks (Table 13.9) corresponding to the functionalities most frequently used by the doctors on a daily basis, and on the ways in which the doctors interact with the application: Search, Choose, Select, Read, and Write.

Based on the CON-INFO context model, the device recognizes the context at run time by extract values from sensors in smartphones (for instance, time, levels of brightness and noise) and maps them to the CON-INFO user stereotype model, and then to the MUI widgets using a decision table. For example, based on the stereotype

Table 13.9 List of tasks

Tasks	MUI feature
1.Search for the patient's name on the patient list	Text or speak
2.Choose laboratory result from the main menu	Tap or speak
3.Select the most recent complete blood count (CBC)	Tap or sound
4.Choose order radiology (chest X-ray) from the main menu	Tap or speak
5.Review the patient summary	Increase or decrease brightness

Table 13.10 New quality-in-use measurement formulas

Objective factors	Measurement formula
Effectiveness	$= A/(C + X)$
Productivity	$= C/T$
Task efficiency	$= \text{Effectiveness}/T$
Safety	$= 1 - X/(C + X)$
Task navigation	$= (C + X)/V$

of the user, time and level of brightness will increase or decrease and the font size will be adapted accordingly.

- Objective measurement (paper log): The base measurements (A, C, X, T, and V—see Table 13.10) for each participant for each UI type were recorded in a paper log: the time (T) taken to complete each task; the number of correct actions (C); and the minimum number of correct actions (A), incorrect actions (X), and screen views (V). The participants' comments were also noted.
- Subjective measurement (user satisfaction questionnaire): The participants were asked to complete a questionnaire containing two types of questions: general questions related to the user profile, and specific questions designed to capture their level of satisfaction using both applications.

13.5.2 Hypothesis

In order to empirically investigate the effect of MUIs with and without the CON-INFO methodology for the same healthcare application to be used by the same user in the same context, pairs of hypotheses related to PHIS2-M and PHIS3-MA were formulated for each quality-in-use objective and subjective factor (see Table 13.7), as follows:

HYP0: There is no significant difference in the corresponding factor between using PHIS2-M and PHIS3-MA.

HYPa: There is a significant difference in the corresponding factor between using PHIS2-M and PHIS3-MA.

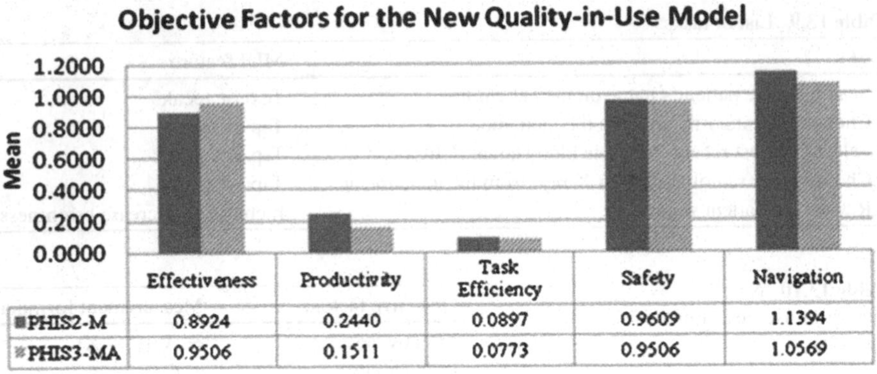

Fig. 13.3 Objective factors for all PHIS2-M and PHIS3-MA tasks

13.5.3 Objective Factor Analysis

The measurement data required to evaluate the objective factors effectiveness, productivity, task efficiency, safety, and task navigation were collected during usability testing performed with 12 doctors performing 5 tasks on PHIS2-M and PHIS3-MA. The raw data for the empirical study were tabulated in MS Excel for each of the 12 participants. We compared the means of all the quality-in-use measurement data collected for PHIS2-M and PHIS3-MA for all tasks and all participants in the test case. Figure 13.3 shows clear improvement for PHIS3-MA over PHIS2-M for the effectiveness and task navigation factors. The MUI for PHIS3-MA is more effective than that for PHIS2-M, indicating that the MUI is better in this respect for mobile adaptation. The task navigation for the MUI in PHIS3-MA is not as good as that for PHIS2-M, which also indicates a better MUI for mobile adaptation. The productivity and task efficiency features of the MUI in PHIS2-M score higher than they do in PHIS3-MA, indicating that the MUI is better in these respects for the mobile application without adaptability. The mean for safety in PHIS-MA is virtually the same as that in PHIS-M.

The hypotheses are verified for each factor, in order to investigate the statistical significance of the observed differences in the objective factors: effectiveness, productivity, task efficiency, safety, and task navigation, and, since we have two conditions (using PHIS2-M, and using PHIS3-MA) for the same participants, we can pair the data. Consequently, we used the paired t-Test for the data analysis. Based on the critical value approach of the t-Test at 11° of freedom, $\alpha = 0.025$ for the two-tailed test, the critical level of t being $\pm$ 1.79. Our decision rule is to reject the null hypothesis if the computed test statistic is less than -1.79 or more than 1.79. Table 13.11 shows the t-Test values and the P-value for all the factors for statistical validation.

Since the t-Test values obtained for effectiveness and safety fall into the positive critical region, we reject the null hypothesis for these factors. From the P-value

Table 13.11 Paired t-test and P-value for all the objective factors

	Effectiveness	Productivity	Task efficiency	Safety	Task navigation
T-Value	2.26	−4.86	−1.79	5.44	−1.32
P-Value	0.022	0.0002	0.05	0.0001	0.10

approach of the t-Test, the P-values for effectiveness and safety are less than α. Therefore, we reject the null hypothesis HYP0 and accept HYPa for these factors. Our conclusion is that there is a significant difference between PHIS2-M and PHIS3-MA for the effectiveness and safety factors. Since the t-values for effectiveness fall into the positive region, we can conclude that PHIS3-MA is better than PHIS2-M based on this factor.

Our t-Test values for productivity and task efficiency fall into the negative critical region, and so the null hypothesis is rejected. The P-values of the t-Test for productivity and task efficiency are less than α, and so the null hypothesis HYP0 is rejected. Since the t-values for productivity and task efficiency fall into the negative region, we can conclude that PHIS2-M is better than PHIS3-MA based on these factors.

Since the t-Test values obtained for task navigation do not fall into the critical region, we failed to reject the null hypothesis for this factor. From the P-value approach of the t-Test, the P-values for task navigation are greater than α. Therefore, we failed to reject the null hypothesis HYP0. Our conclusion is that there is no significant difference between PHIS2-M and PHIS3-MA for the task navigation factors.

13.5.4 Subjective Factor Analysis

For the subjective factors, the users were asked to complete our User Satisfaction Questionnaire to determine their impressions and opinions on the applications, and evaluate their interaction with PHIS2-M and PHIS3-MA. The subjective analysis was measured on a Likert scale. The results of the questionnaire reveal that all the users gave both PHIS-2M and PHIS3-MA ratings of 'easy' and 'very easy' to the features related to:

F1: learning the application,
F2: using the application,
F3: performing a particular task,
F4: finding the features,
F5: understanding navigation,
F6: recovering from error, and
F7: performing a task anywhere and at any time.

For the brightness features, more than sixty percent of the participants preferred to increase the brightness level at night. This indicates that PHIS3-MA is best suited to their needs. Thirty percent preferred to decrease the brightness level at night. This indicates that PHIS2-M is best suited to their needs. Ten percent preferred the default user preference level.

These results accept HYP0, which means that the level of satisfaction experienced by the participants when using the MUI is no different from that using the DUI.

In order to investigate the differences observed in the subjective factors, and since the measurement data are arranged on an ordinal scale and the factors are paired, we used the Wilcoxon Rank Sum Test, which looks at the size of the differences in rank orderings. The Wilcoxon Signed-Ranks Test is similar to the Rank Sum Test, except that it takes into account the magnitude as well as the direction of the differences. It gives more weight to a pair that shows a large difference than to a pair that shows a small difference.

HYP0: There is no difference between PHIS-MA and PHIS-M on the subjective feature 'learning the application'.

HYPa: There is a difference between the MUI and the DUI on the subjective feature 'learning the application'.

The hypotheses for each subjective feature listed are verified based on the Wilcoxon Test for the z-statistic value and the P-value (see Table 13.12) that shows the positive and negative ranks of each feature, F1...F7.

The data obtained were used to analyze the effect of the new mobile application in terms of each of the 7 features. The statistical significance was set at $P < 0.05$. All the statistical analyses were performed with SPSS 18 software (IBM, New York, USA).

The Wilcoxon Signed-Ranks Test verifies that two related medians are equal. It is based on the absolute value of the difference between two test variables.

For the first feature, 'learning the application', our null hypothesis HYP0 says that the median of feature 1 for mobile users is equal to a median of feature 1 for mobile adaptation users. The Wilcoxon Test gives no evidence against the null hypothesis of the difference between medians of feature 1 for mobile users and mobile adaptation users (we note that P-value = 0.059, which is larger than 0.05) (see Table 13.13). Consequently, we conclude that the new application does not change the level of user satisfaction. Moreover, the satisfaction of the user with both PHIS-MA and PHIS-M is the same.

Conclusion: From the above table, we cannot reject the null hypothesis HYP0 for all the features based on the z-statistic value and the P-value. We can conclude that the subjective quality-in-use of PHIS-MA is the same as that of PHIS-M.

13.6 Discussion of Research Findings

This controlled experiment, conducted with 12 doctors, showed that productivity and task efficiency favor PHIS2-M over PHIS3-MA. Since productivity and task efficiency depend on time and the other factors do not, entering input verbally using

Table 13.12 Ranks

		N	Mean rank	Sum of ranks
F1_MA–F1_M	Negative ranks	4a	2.50	10.00
	Positive ranks	0b	0.00	0.00
	Ties	8c		
	Total	12		
F2_MA–F2_M	Negative ranks	5d	4.00	20.00
	Positive ranks	2e	4.00	8.00
	Ties	5f		
	Total	12		
F3_MA–F3_M	Negative ranks	3g	2.00	6.00
	Positive ranks	0h	0.00	0.00
	Ties	9i		
	Total	12		
F4_MA–F4_M	Negative ranks	3j	2.67	8.00
	Positive ranks	1k	2.00	2.00
	Ties	8l		
	Total	12		
F5_MA–F5_M	Negative ranks	2m	3.00	6.00
	Positive ranks	2n	2.00	4.00
	Ties	8o		
	Total	12		
F6_MA–F6_M	Negative ranks	4p	3.00	12.00
	Positive ranks	1q	3.00	3.00
	Ties	7r		
	Total	12		
F7_MA–F7_M	Negative ranks	0s	0.00	0.00
	Positive ranks	2t	1.50	3.00
	Ties	10u		
	Total	12		

the voice recognition functionality on a mobile platform is slower than typing or tapping, and most of the tasks evaluated in the experiment for the adaptable version depend on the vocal features.

In terms of task effectiveness and safety, the results show a trend toward the superiority of the adaptable version based on the t-Test for these factors. This indicates fewer actions in each view in a specified context of use, and the incorrect actions are all in the best range. For task navigation, our results show that there is no significant difference between PHIS2-M and PHIS3-MA. It may be that the less sophisticated design is what is needed in the medical field. However, it is very early to come to this conclusion.

From the interviews conducted with the doctors, some inherent drawbacks were identified. One of these is the lack of privacy surrounding the use of the voice features. These features are the most useful when privacy is not an issue, or when the doctor is alone, his hands are not free to tap or type, and his eyes are busy looking elsewhere.

Table 13.13 Test statistic[c]

	F1_MA–F1_M	F2_MA–F2_M	F3_MA–F3_M	F4_MA–F4_M	F5_MA–F5_M	F6_MA–F6_M	F7_MA–F7_M
Z	−1.890[a]	−1.134[a]	−1.633[a]	−1.134[a]	−.378[a]	−1.342[a]	−1.414[b]
Asymp. Sig. (2-tailed)	0.059	0.257	0.102	0.257	0.705	0.180	0.157

[a] Based on positive ranks
[b] Based on negative ranks
[c] Wilcoxon signed-ranks test

For example, when the radiologist is in his office looking at a patient's image on his desktop or writing notes in a patient file, his hands and eyes are occupied, but he is free to talk. So, the ability to talk to the device when the other faculties are occupied is a useful option.

13.7 Summary

There are many research questions which have to be addressed in the relatively young and vibrant research field of pervasive computing [52]. In this chapter, we have introduced the new CON-INFO methodology for adapting the MUI to the context of the healthcare domain. This research led us to the firm conclusion that smartphones, which are currently being used in this environment, can benefit healthcare organizations. Adaptation of MUI features based on a decision table can introduce systematization into the design of adaptive systems, and enhance the acceptability of the technology in the healthcare domain, where diversity is an inherent characteristic. Finally, we have also introduced a new quality-in-use model for MUIs. This model was validated both theoretically and empirically.

We have analyzed the benefits of context-based MUI adaptation, and find that they are the following:

- Increased usability, e.g. if the MUI only supports one interaction model, such as typing or voice/sound output, the usability of the service would be drastically decreased.
- Increased awareness of social ethics, e.g. in a quiet, multi-bed unit after midnight, when the patients are asleep and the nurse needs to enter vital signs, sound-based interaction, such as voice/sound output for call notification, could be an obstacle, disturbing other patients. In this case, the sound could be turned off automatically.
- Improved productivity, by reducing redundancy and repetitive tasks in the workflow, like noting data on paper to be entered later onto a PC. Enabling nurses to enter vital signs immediately, preferably at the point of care, would allow them to be more efficient and productive.
- Improved level of attention, e.g. if the patient's result is outside the normal range, this would be recognized by the MUI adaptation, and the nurse notified based on his or her context.

13.8 Future Outlook

Our directions for future work include extensive testing of the remaining adaptable features with other categories of users in the hospital ward environment. We will also consider the effectiveness of the adaptable mobile healthcare application for use by doctors with a speech impediment. It is challenge to us to use and run different speech recognition modality which does not require a network connection in order to consider the best one that applicable in the hospital setting. We will then be able to examine the effect of using the new framework with different users such as intermediate and expert.

In order to improve the user's experience with using UIs in mobile applications in healthcare environments, we will investigate the incorporation of intelligent techniques into the mobile application through the user interface of mobile devices. A controlled experiment in a real environment with real users using an adaptable intelligent MUI will be carried out to test and evaluate the usability of the intelligent MUI from the end-user's point of view.

References

1. Bardram, J. E. (2004). Applications of context-aware computing in hospital work: Examples and design principles. In *Proceedings of the ACM Symposium on Applied, Computing* (pp. 1574–1579).
2. Bardram, J. E., & Hansen, T. R. (2004). *The AWARE architecture: Supporting context mediated social awareness in mobile cooperation* (pp. 192–201). Chicago: ACM Press.
3. Kinkade, S., & Verclas, K. (2008). Wireless technology for social change. Washington, DC, and Berkshire, UK. Retrieved April 27, 2012, from http://mobileactive.org/files/MobilizingSocialChange_full.pdf.
4. Dix, A., Finlay, J., Abowd, G., & Beale, R. (2004). *Human-computer interaction* (3rd ed.). England: British Library Cataloguing.
5. Alvarado, C., et al. (2004) Panel: The role of human factors in healthcare—2020. In *Proceedings of the Human Factors and Ergonomics Society 48th Annual Meeting, SAGE Publications* (Vol. 48, pp. 1764–1767).
6. Thimbleby, H. (2007). User-centered methods are insufficient for safety critical systems. In A. Holzinger (Eds.), *HCI and usability for medicine and health care: Third symposium of the workgroup human-computer interaction and usability engineering of the Austrian computer society* (Vol. 4799, pp. 1–20). Springer: Berlin, Heidelberg, New York.
7. Thimbleby, H., & Thimbleby, W. (2007). *Internalist and externalist HCI*. Lancaster: British Computer Society.
8. Holzinger, A., & Errath, M. (2007). Mobile computer Web-application design in medicine: Some research based guidelines. *Universal Access in the Information Society International Journal, 6*(1), 31–41.
9. Holzinger, A. (2005). Usability engineering for software developers. *Communications of the ACM, 48*(1), 71–74.
10. Holzinger, A. (2004). Application of rapid prototyping to the user interface development for a virtual medical campus. *IEEE Software, 21*(1), 92–99.
11. ISO/ IEC 25010. (2011(E)). *Systems and software engineering—systems and software quality requirements and evaluation (SQuaRE)—system and software quality models*. Geneva, Switzerland: International Organization for Standardization.
12. Alnanih, R., Ormandjieva, O., & Radhakrishnan, T. (2013). A new quality-in-use model for mobile user interfaces. In *Proceedings of the 23nd International Workshop on Software Measurement, IWSM-MENSURA* (To appear).
13. Dey, A. K., & Abowd, G. D. (2000). Towards a better understanding of context and context awareness. In *Proceedings of the CHI (2000) Workshop on the What, Who, Where, When and How of Context-Awareness*. New York: ACM Press.

14. Schilit, B., & Theimer, M. (1994). Disseminating active map information to mobile hosts. *IEEE Network, 8*(5), 22–32.
15. Brown, P. J., Bovey, J. D., & Chen, X. (1997). Context-aware applications: From the laboratory to the marketplace. *IEEE Personal Communications, 4*(5), 58–64.
16. Ryan, N., Pascoe, J., & Morse, D. (1997). Enhanced reality fieldwork: The context-aware archaeological assistant. In V. Gaffney, M. Van Leusen & S. Exxon (Eds.), *Computer applications in archaeology*. Oxford: British Archaeological Reports.
17. Dey, A. K. (1998). Context-aware computing: The cyberdesk project. In *Proceedings of the AAAI 1998 Spring Symposium on Intelligent, Environments* (pp. 51–54).
18. Franklin, D., & Flaschbart, J. (1998). All gadget and no representation makes jack a dull environment. In *Proceedings of AAAI 1998 Spring Symposium on Intelligent Environments. AAAI TR* (pp. 155–160).
19. Ward, A., Jones, A., & Hopper, A. (1997). A new location technique for the active office. *IEEE Personal Commun, 4*(5), 42–47.
20. Rodden, T., Cheverst, K., Davies, K., & Dix, A. (1998). Exploiting context in HCI design for mobile systems. In *Proceedings of the Workshop on Human Computer Interaction with Mobile Devices*.
21. Hull, R., Neaves, P., & Bedford-Roberts, J. (1997). Towards situated computing. In *Proceedings of the 1st International Symposium on Wearable Computers* (pp. 146–153).
22. Pascoe, J. (1998). Adding generic contextual capabilities to wearable computers. In *Proceedings of the 2nd International Symposium on Wearable Computers* (pp. 92–99).
23. Pascoe, J., Rodrigues, H., & Ariza, C. (2006). An investigation into a universal context model to support context-aware applications. *Springer, 4278*, 1884–1893.
24. Gwizdka, J. (2000). What's in the context? In *Proceedings of the Workshop on the What, Who, Where, When, and How of Context-Awareness*.
25. Flanagan, J. A., Mintyjarvi, J., & Himberg, J. (2002). Unsupervised clustering of symbol strings and context recognition. In *Proceedings of the IEEE Conference on Data Mining* (pp. 171–178).
26. Schmidt, A. (2000). Implicit human computer interaction through context. *Personal Ubiquitous Comput, 4*(2/3), 191–199.
27. Korpipää, P., & Mantyjarvi, J. (2003). *An ontology for mobile device sensor-based context awareness (CONTEXT-03)* (pp. 451–458). Stanford, CA, USA: Stanford University.
28. Savio, N., & Braiterman, J. (2007). *Design sketch: The context of mobile interaction* (pp. 5–7). Singapore: IJMM.
29. Floyd, I. R., Jones, M. C., & Twidale, M. B. (2004). Resolving incommensurable debates: a preliminary identification of persona kinds, attributes, and characteristics. *Artifact, 2*(1), 12–26.
30. Nielsen, L. (2013). Personas—user focused design. *Human—computer interaction series* (1–154). Springer: London. (ISBN 978-1-4471-4083-2).
31. Dantin, U. (2005). Application of personas in user interface design for educational software. In *Proceedings of the 7th Australasian conference on Computing, Education* (pp. 239–247).
32. Versloot, C. (2005). Information filtering: Personal profile usable as stereotype profile?
33. Turner, P., & Tuner, S. (2011). Is stereotyping inevitable when designing with personas. *Design Studies, 32*(1), 30–44.
34. Hamilton, D. L., & Sherman, J. W. (1994). Stereotypes. In J. R. S. Wyer & T. K. Srull (Eds.), *Handbook of social cognition* (2nd ed., pp. 1–68). Hillsdale, NJ: Macmillan.
35. Oaks, P. J., Haslam, S. A., & Turner, J. C. (1994). *Stereotyping and social reality*. Oxford, UK: Blackwell.
36. Fröhlich, N., et al. (2009). LoCa—Towards a context-aware infrastructure for eHealth applications. In *Proceedings of Fifteenth International Conference on Distributed, Multimedia Systems (DMS'09)* (pp. 52–57).
37. Clerckx, T., Winters, F., & Coninx, K. (2005). Tool support for designing context-sensitive user interfaces using a model-based approach. In: *Proceedings of the 4th International Workshop on Task Models and Diagrams, Gdansk, Poland* (pp.11–18).
38. Yuan, B., & Herbert, J. (2012). A fuzzy-based context modeling and reasoning framework for CARA pervasive healthcare. In *Proceedings of 3rd International Conference on (ANT 2012), Procardia Computer Science* (Vol. 10, pp. 357–365).

39. Shi-wei, C., & Shou-Qian, S. (2009). Adaptive 3D navigation user interface design based on rough sets. In *Proceedings of the IEEE 10th International Conference on Computer-Aided Industrial Design and Conceptual Design* (pp. 1935–1940).
40. Vogt, J., & Meier, A. (2010). An adaptive user interface framework for eHealth services based on UIML. In *Proceedings of the 23rd Bled eConference eTrust: Implications for the Individual, Enterprises and Society (Bled 2010)* (pp. 409–422).
41. Bevan, N. (1999). Quality in use: Meeting user needs for quality. *Journal of System and Software, 49*, 89–96.
42. IEC 62366. (2007). *Medical devices-application of usability engineering to medical devices*. Switzerland: International Organization for Standardization.
43. ISO 9241–210. (2010). Ergonomics of human-system interaction—part 210: Human-centered design for interactive systems. Switzerland: International Organization for Standardization.
44. ISO 9241–11. (1998). *Ergonomic requirements for office work with visual display terminals (VDTs)—part 11: Guidance on usability*. Switzerland: International Organization for Standardization.
45. Huang, K. (2009). Challenges in human-computer interaction design for mobile devices. In *Proceedings of the World Congress on Engineering and Computer Science, San Francisco, USA* (Vol. 1). Retrieved from http://www.iaeng.org/publication/WCECS2009/WCECS2009_pp236-241.pdf NULL
46. Alnanih, R., Radhakrishnan, T., & Ormandjieva, O. (2012). Characterising context for mobile user interfaces in health care applications. In *Proceedings of 2nd International Workshop on (PASTH 2012), Procardia Computer Science* (Vol. 10, pp. 1086–1093).
47. Battisto, D., Pak, R., Vander, M. A., & Pilcher, J. J. (2009). Using a task analysis to describe nursing work in acute care patient environments. *Journal of Nursing Administration, 39*(12), 537–547.
48. Alnanih, R., Ormandjieva, O., & Radhakrishnan, T. (2013). Context-based user stereotype model for mobile user interfaces in health care applications. In *Proceedings of the 3rd International Symposium on (FAMS, 2013), Procardia Computer Science* (Vol. 19, pp. 1020–1027).
49. De Melo, G., Honold, F., Weber, M., Poguntke, M., & Berton, A. (2009). Towards a flexible UI model for automotive human-machine interaction. In *Proceedings of the 1st International Conference on Automotive UI and Interactive Vehicular Applications* (pp. 47–50).
50. Alnanih, R., Al-Nuaim, H., & Ormandjieva, O. (2009). New health information systems (HIS) quality-in-use model based on the GQM approach and HCI principles. In *Proceedings of the 13th International Conference on HCI, Part IV. Berlin Heidelberg* (pp. 429–438).
51. Dumas, J. L., & Redish, J. C. (1999). *A practical guide to usability testing* (3rd ed.). Wiltshire: Intellect.
52. Ziefle, M., Röcker, C., & Holzinger, A. (2014). Current trends and challenges for pervasive health technologies: From technical innovation to user integration. In *Pervasive health: State-of-the-art and beyond.*
53. Fenton, N. E., & Bieman, J. (2014). Software metrics: A practical and rigorous approach (3rd ed.). UK: Taylor and Francis. (For publication 2014).
54. Peter, H. J. (2013). *Design for care: Innovating healthcare experience*.
55. Dumas, J. L., & Redish, J. C. (1999). *A practical guide to usability testing* (3rd ed.). Wiltshire: Intellect.
56. Klasnja, P., & Pratt, W. (2012). Healthcare in the pocket: Mapping the space of mobile-phone health interventions. *Journal of Biomedical Informatics, 45*(1), 184–198.
57. Cook, D. J., & Das, S. K. (2012). Pervasive computing at scale: Transforming the state of the art. *Pervasive and Mobile Computing, 8*(1), 22–35.
58. Curtis, B. (1980). Measurement and experimentation in software engineering. *Proceedings of the IEEE, 68*(9), 1144–1157.
59. Victor R. B., Richard W. S. & David H. H. (1986). Experimentation in software engineering. *IEEE Transactions on Software Engineering, 12*(7), 733–743.

Chapter 14
An Integrated Patient-Centric Approach for Situated Research on Total Hip Replacement: ESTHER

Juan Jiménez Garcia, Natalia Romero, David Keyson and Paul Havinga

14.1 Introduction

In the last decade, we have observed several technical innovations and societal transformation processes that have had direct impact in the design of pervasive healthcare systems [52]. In the context of hospital post-surgery care, the growing demand of hospital resources and the advances in surgery technology have led to a reduction of in-patient care and shorter hospitalization times [11]. In response the healthcare system is adopting e-health solutions leading to new approaches in care practices. These solutions embrace a variety of online communities and health services with the aim to facilitate connectivity between patient and medical staff. In addition, the rapid developing applications based on wearable sensor-monitoring devices and context-aware systems aim to improve the access of personal health data to the patients and health professionals. With the increasing amount of personal data offered by these solutions, patients are gradually changing from passive health consumers to pro-active choice-makers [42]. Health practices are therefore experiencing a paradigm shift from being solely delivered by professionals in hospitals to considering the home as a self-care environment and the patient as an active responsible receiver of care.

J. Jiménez Garcia (✉) · P. Havinga (✉)
Electrical, Mathematics and Computer Science, University of Twente,
PO Box 217 7500 AE, Enschede, The Netherlands
e-mail: j.c.jimenezgarcia@ewi.utwente.nl

P. Havinga
e-mail: p.j.m.havinga@ewi.utwente.nl

N. Romero (✉) · D. Keyson (✉)
Department of Industrial Design Engineering, Delft University of Technology,
Postbus 5 2600 AA, Delft, The Netherlands
e-mail: n.a.romero@tudelft.nl

D. Keyson
e-mail: d.v.keyson@tudelft.nl

A. Holzinger et al. (eds.), *Pervasive Health*, Human–Computer Interaction Series,
DOI: 10.1007/978-1-4471-6413-5_14, © Springer-Verlag London 2014

Total Hip Replacement (THR) is a highly demanded surgery, therefore subject to the aforementioned paradigm. THR is an effective and conventional solution for moderate or severe osteoarthritis, the prevalence of joint disorders that affect the older population [1]. This procedure improves the quality of life of people that suffer from this condition enabling them to return to their daily life [49]. Due to the high demand for this surgery and the scarcity of medical resources, Total Hip Replacement procedure has adopted an early discharge strategy resulting in a quick transition from surgery to post-operatory home recovery. Wong et al. [49] state that in early discharge, hospital staff limits their effort to support the functional recovery, with little attention to the psychological needs of patients living with a new hip. This situation creates an environment of fear and uncertainty for the patients by not getting adequate educational preparation to manage their recovery [10, 11]. The existing educational programs and the physiotherapist's verbal instructions that patients get before discharge are reported as insufficient in helping them and their families to make adequate decisions about recovery at home [48]. Patients might forget or misunderstand spoken information, or they might not get all their questions answered. As a consequence they do not know the rules they have to follow during rehabilitation [43] and make uninformed decisions [29]. Once at home, the recovery is monitored on the basis of sporadic weekly or biweekly check ups between the professional and the patient, which take place at home or in the hospital. In between these meetings the patient is left with a list of home assignments, which she should perform daily without supervision. This creates a communicational gap between health professional and patient, leading to insufficient information on the progress of recovery. A reduction in the frequency of monitoring and feedback during the recovery may severely aggravate the emotional state of the patient when emotional and psychological problems have a direct effect on the recovery process [21]. Homecare technologies may open an opportunity to provide more frequent guidance and to extend the support beyond the functional.

For surgeries like THR, current technology developments aim to primarily assist homecare practices with the possibility to automatically and even remotely monitor patients' functional performance. The focus on assistance implies a passive role of the patient since all the responsibility lies on the judgments and advises processed by the system. Relying entirely on the system, current developments are primarily focused on the technical challenges to capture functional aspects such as foot pressure, balance and movement in an accurate and efficient way. As pointed by Grönvall and Lundberg [14] the challenges of implementing pervasive healthcare solutions go beyond functional-related aspects. Despite its relevance, these innovations are not considering in their approach an understanding of the complexity of patients' home, their lifestyle, attitudes and preferences. Let's imagine the following scenario: Lia is in her second day at home after surgery and the homecare system detects that she has done too little physical activity today and sends her a reminder to perform the prescribed exercises for today. She does not understand why she gets a reminder as she considers that she has moved enough today and feels very tired and even with some pain. But the system only persists with reminders making Lia feel only more anxious and stressed. What should the system present to Lia so she can be better informed of what is best to do at that moment? How can the system incorporate Lia's feelings and emotional state to better support her? Supportive homecare technologies adopt a reflective approach by providing users with relevant information they can reflect upon to become self-managers of their own care [18] whereas assistive technologies assume a more persuasive approach, where the system takes a prominent role by nudging people towards a goal [32]. The shift from assistive to supportive technology is considered a relevant research direction to avoid scenarios like the one presented above.

Design research on Human Computer Interaction (HCI) provides methods and tools to investigate and design technologies driven by people's needs and desires [16]. In particular the field of User Experience considers people's feelings in relation to their daily practices as an important focus for the design of technologies that aim to have a positive impact on people's life [17]. The goal to support patient's reflective process of their physical and emotional state during the recovery requires a holistic understanding of people's momentary experiences. These experiences relate to individuals' moment-to-moment changes of feelings regarding a specific situation (Roto et al. 2010) therefore the use of traditional methods like interviews and questionnaires are considered insufficient to capture the rich and lively aspects that can be extracted from them. Relying primarily on participants' ability to recall past memories, shortcomings of these methods result in obtaining an inaccurate view of past experiences based on guesses and estimations.

This chapter reflects on the authors' experience in developing and implementing a research tool that aims to capture the recovery process from the perspective of the patient, contextualized to when and where this process takes place, with the goal to inform the design of technology innovations that will be accepted and adopted as part of the daily life practices of patients. The chapter bases on research and field studies done around the design and development of a novel research tool that considers User Experience as a key element in understanding acceptance and long-term adoption. The purpose of this chapter goes beyond describing and evaluating the tool and potential home care applications, which have been reported elsewhere, but aims to reflect on the challenges and opportunities this approach opens for HCI in the design of home care innovations. It ultimately aims to contribute to the existing research approaches, discussing why and how innovations should address patients' experience early in their design process to guarantee the acceptance and adoption of innovations that are designed to support home care.

First, the state of the art as related to HCI research on homecare technologies in the context of THR is presented. Next, Experience Sampling Method (ESM) and Stage-based model of Personal Informatics are briefly introduced to report on existing developments of in-situ tools as well as applications to support self-reflection. Third, ESTHER, an in-situ and ecological research tool in the context of THR is introduced describing the experiences in implementing the tool in different interventions. The chapter closes with a discussion on the opportunities and challenges that a patient-centric, in-situ and ecological tool creates when used in health related life settings.

14.2 Glossary

Total Hip Replacement (THR) Total Hip Replacement (THR) is an effective and common surgery for moderate or severe osteoarthritis. This medical intervention reduces considerably pain and returns patients to function [49].

Experience Sampling Method (ESM) An ecological, in-situ data collection method in which participants respond to repeated prompts that are triggered at random or specific moments over the course of a day. The reports are related to emotional aspects that people experience around living activities in their natural life settings [19].

Personal Informatics (PI) An emerging area in the field of Human Computer Interaction that facilitates people to collect personal relevant information for the main purpose to support self-reflection and gaining self-knowledge regarding their emotional and physical state as well as behavioral practices [26].

Outcome measurement methods in Total Hip Replacement Standardized tools and techniques to establish the baseline status of a patient at different stages of the THR intervention. It provides a means to quantify progress in the patient's functional recovery. They mainly used at the early stages of recovery (1–8 weeks) providing a common language with which to evaluate the success of physical therapy interventions [35]. Examples of these techniques are Western Ontario and McMaster Universities (WOMAC), Short-Form 36 (SF-36) and Oxford Hip Score.

Pictorial Mood Reporting Instrument (PMRI) PMRI is a cartoon-based pictorial instrument for self-reporting and expressing moods. The use of cartoon characters enables people to unambiguously and visually express or report their mood in a rich and easy-to-use way [47].

Experience Sampling for Total Hip Replacement (ESTHER) ESTHER is a research and design tool initially developed to study THR patients' experiences after surgery and to evaluate design interventions to support patients in the complexity of home recovery. This tool is based on Experience Sampling Methods to capture patients' self-report on their recovery process and to support self-reflection processes in relation to daily life practices.

14.3 State-of-the-Art

14.3.1 Research Developments of THR Post-operatory Home Recovery Technologies

Clinicians are constantly seeking better ways to coordinate care, and ensure that people undergoing THR receive a personal and tailored therapy [43]. Therefore, measuring both patients' health perceptions in surgical recovery and how their experiences change during recovery is becoming an important element in the evaluation of THR after surgery, to predict short-term outcomes [41, 49]. Currently, medical teams are using standardized techniques in stages of the recovery to measure functional progress. For example, the Western Ontario and McMaster Universities osteoarthritis index (WOMAC) and the multi-purpose health survey questionnaire (SF 36), in combination with several physical performance measurements (e.g. 6 Min Walk Test, Time Up and Go) are widely used prior and several months after surgery [9, 30, 44]. These standardized clinical methods have a strong cross-sectional ability that provides useful information from a wide population in a particular time. Although several studies suggest their high validity and reliability, physical performance measurements focus only on a single isolated functional status resulting in a low correlation in their results [44]. THR recovery is strongly related to the individual experiences of the patient, which are left unobserved by these methods. Woolhead et al. [50] reported that only after complementary in-depth interviews it was possible to get a more global reflection on the recovery process, where patients admitted that they still perceived limitations during their process. Additionally, [13] emphasize the importance to consider the evolution of patients' needs, however these methods capture snapshots situations overlooking meaningful changes overtime [4]. Finally, these questionnaires often fail to elicit more constructive critical responses from the patients' points of view overlooking their emotional responses [10].

Few studies have explored aspects of recovery beyond the functional rehabilitation. Fielden et al. [10] and Grant et al. [13] used in-depth interviews to investigate patient's perspectives about surgery service and their satisfaction after discharge. These studies opened new insights about the psychosocial determinants involved in THR though the information is based only on two pre-defined periods, one just after discharge and another several weeks later. Van den Akker-Scheek et al. [45] and Fortina et al. [11] identified the importance to educate patients and assist in their recovery process after discharge involving both physical and psychological aspects. One example was a tailored made guidebook to support patients' physical function and satisfaction after surgery [11]. The guidebook provides information to the patient and family about the physical implications of the surgical intervention. It also collects patients' satisfaction rates post-surgery. Stevens et al. [43] developed a strategy using a home-based program that aims at supporting the rehabilitation at home. The strategy consists of an exit-video (practice session of patients' home exercises, including instructions and explanations, which are video taped and given to the patient for later reference), newsletters and telephone follow-up appointments to support the transition from hospital to home recovery and the process of rehabilitation at home for a period of 6 months. Both examples provided valuable information about the use and effectiveness of the proposed material to support patient during recovery. Customized guides were well accepted, and perceived as satisfactory in providing valuable information, but a low effect of the intervention was observed possibly due to a lack of moment-to-moment feedback. Since these methods are designed to document experiences in a snapshot format with high demands on patients' recalling

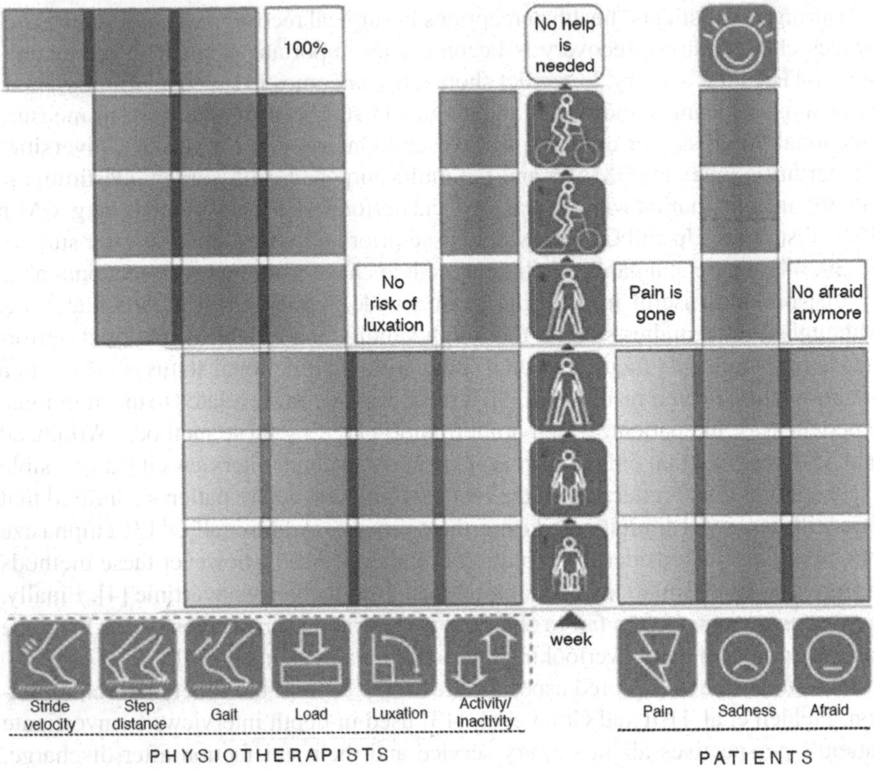

Fig. 14.1 THR recovery process. Physiotherapist and patient's main concerns during the 7 initial weeks of rehabilitation and their relevance through time. It was identified that during these weeks of recovery, physiotherapists are more concerned about the functional outcomes of the recovery while patients are more focused on their emotions and experiences

skills, it is argued that these questionnaires are limited to understand how patients experience their recovery process, and how changes affect their state of progress.

With a closer view on patients' individual psychosocial experiences, Hassling et al. [18] used cultural probes as a method for elicitation of requirements for the design of supportive technologies including emotional aspects. They implemented a self-documentary media kit for the collection of data to capture patients' experiences from living with a chronic disease. Although participants were able to capture interesting family and personal activities around the disease, it was still challenging to express emotions and to provide more reflective thoughts on what they reported. The authors suggest that explicit mechanisms need to be developed to motivate emotional reports.

A study based on user centered design methods was conducted to define the functional and non-functional aspects of a THR supportive system [22]. The study showed the value of using workshops, scenarios, and individual interviews with various stakeholders (elderly, physiotherapists, engineers, and researchers) to uncover different aspects of the recovery procedure. One of the main findings describes the recovery process as a journey in which both functional and emotional aspects are dynamic and inter-related. This journey is illustrated in Fig. 14.1 recognizing the several stages of the THR recovery process in which mobility, general health, independency, pain, family, friends, and emotions are involved.

These insights reveal the need for in-situ methods to capture patients' experience during their rehabilitation. The design of such methods requires the development of mechanisms to support people to self-report their experiences and to provide visualizations in ways that are relevant and appropriate to patients in the homecare context. These methods will help to identify the role of experiential aspects in the recovery and gradually investigate how these experiences can provide relevant information to support patients to self-manage their progress.

14.3.2 In-situ and Self-Reflection Methods

Designing for experiences in relation to care and in the context of home poses a major challenge to design technologies that become part of the current practices of patients in their home environment. As pointed out by Rogers [37], new pervasive technologies should address a wider understanding on how people experience daily life, moving from laboratory to more realistic design and testing settings. Intille et al. [20] state that developing meaningful ubiquitous computing applications first requires a global understanding of how people behave in context. Experience Sampling Method (ESM) [19] has been developed with the purpose to capture user experiences in-situ, i.e. in timed and situated, and for extended period of times to elicit people's feelings and emotional change of state. ESM takes advantage of the popularity of mobile devices to ask people for feedback at random times during the day. With ESM participants make a quick record close to the moment of interest, providing instant reports on momentary experiences instead of having to recall what they did in the past. The involvement of context-aware technologies in ESM opens the opportunity to automatize the capturing of context around participants' self-reports [2, 7, 20]. Furthermore, contextual information could help to adapt the timing and content of the prompts minimizing interruptions as well as tailoring the research questions according to what is been observed [46]. The downside of this method is that participants may perceive the prompts as too frequent and/or repetitive, which could result in undesired interruptions, burden and boredom negatively influencing participants' experience. One interesting way to overcome this drawback, is by providing participants visualizations of (part of) their reports which may result in a more positive experience, as they become aware of personal situations that other wise would be difficult to envisage [24, 38].

The Stage-based model of Personal Informatics [26] defines five stages to support behavioral change based on personal data. The first three relates to preparation, collection and integration of data while the last two refers to reflection and action. Whereas the tendency is on automating the first three stages, we question the late involvement of people at only the reflection stage. To support people's reflection and action, the integration stage plays a crucial role in selecting what is relevant. We instead envision the use of self-report methods to link the collection stage with the integration stage by inviting people to add personal insights to the automatic collected data. The opportunity that participants' reflections on the reported data could enrich the information gathered from the self-reports needs to be carefully studied as there is a fine line separating this from influencing participants' actions and their experiences in unexpected ways.

As defined by Li et al. [27] people iterate between two phases of reflection, discovery and maintenance. People in the discovery phase are seeking understanding of what affects their current situation, while in the maintenance phase they look for help to achieve a set goal. In the design of a tool that motivates patients of THR to report their experiences during the recovery weeks, the implementation of an in-situ self-report method should gradually introduce elements that support the integration stage to support discovery but prevent maintenance. In this way possible unwanted influences, such as making participants increasingly worried or overly confident, could be detected on time.

14.4 Open Problems

There is an existing lack of tools to remotely follow patients at home and to measure beyond the functional aspects of recovery. It gives to the medical team an incomplete assessment of patients' health status and current progress. There is an increasing body of research reporting that many diseases and physical complications are related to psychosocial factors in particular during the recovery phase [33, 41, 51]. However, most of the current methods that are available and commonly used to follow THR recovery focus on functional aspects with few studies exploring other aspects of recovery. There is limited knowledge into how patients experience the recovery process and how they would experience the use of technology that supports their current situation.

Several technical approaches co-exist in the development and implementation of a supportive system for healthcare that consider the home as the main care environment instead of just the clinic (context-aware systems, on-body sensor networks, telemedicine). Developing a tailored system that is able to understand patients' situation and communicate this information to health stakeholders poses several challenges. From the point of view of engineers, the design of systems architecture needs to specify clear requirements for the management of the collected data, reliability, algorithmic design, and interoperability of architectural components. From interaction designers' perspective, user related issues such as trust upon technology, acceptability of usable and attractive technology should be well understood in order to be translated into user requirements.

Existing research efforts focus on combining different information sources for better understanding user activity and context (physical state and situation) [5, 27].

However, few studies have been conducted to understand users' state and context in relation to situated support [15]. Recently, we can see this effort in commercial products such as Nike+ that has started to shift the responsibility on users to record certain activities. FuelBand and Nike+ app (2013), involves self-reporting as a powerful mechanism to engage users and it is read like a major departure from the original design intention of a carefully streamlined user experience [34]. This shows a potential for using different sources of information in a complementary way to provide better detection of user state and context and right motivational feedback.

Although further research is needed to understand self-reporting as a source of meaningful information for the user, these new developments are opening a new channel to investigate how this information can trigger in-situ motivational feedback in relation with the user state and context. It might become a powerful self-reflection tool with a positive impact to the wellbeing of patients, The potential of this can be investigated by means of an integrated patient-centric approach that combines User Centered Design (UCD), Experience Sampling Method (ESM) and Personal Informatics (PI), providing instruments to address the challenges in developing a supportive tool for healthcare.

14.5 ESTHER: Tool to Explore the Context of Total Hip Replacement

THR involves a personal and highly dynamic process where physical and emotional states are affected by unpredicted changes. Experience Sampling for Total Hip Replacement (ESTHER), is a toolkit based on Experience Sampling Method (ESM) [19] developed with the purpose to inform the design of a supportive system for homecare recovery [23]. It goes beyond the architectural components of sensing technologies as such, by aiming to provide a description of the situation of the patient, capturing the changes of determinant factors throughout the recovery period. Special attention is given to understand the influences of issues related to patients' emotional transition in this process.

Four iterations were designed and implemented as situated design interventions. Self-reporting mechanisms and the combination of sensing and subjective data analysis were considered as a patient-centric way to address patients' needs during recovery. ESTHER 1.0 was first introduced as a mean for researchers and developers to get a better understanding of meaningful experiences of THR recovery. ESTHER 1.0 was a step-by-step interactive questionnaire embedded in a touch-screen device (see Fig. 14.2, left). It triggered prompts to patients in a fixed interval asking about their individual physical and emotional daily experiences. An open question "How are you doing?", was followed by an open/close question that asked the patient to position themselves in a diagram of eight moods (see Fig. 14.2, right). The diagram was based on the Pictorial Mood Reporting Instrument (PMRI) the precedent version of Pick-A-Mood (PAM) tool [8]. The tool is specially designed to support in-situ

Fig. 14.2 ESTHER 1.0: *Left*, patient reacting to a prompt, self-reporting; *Right*, the PMRI tool applied in this design iteration

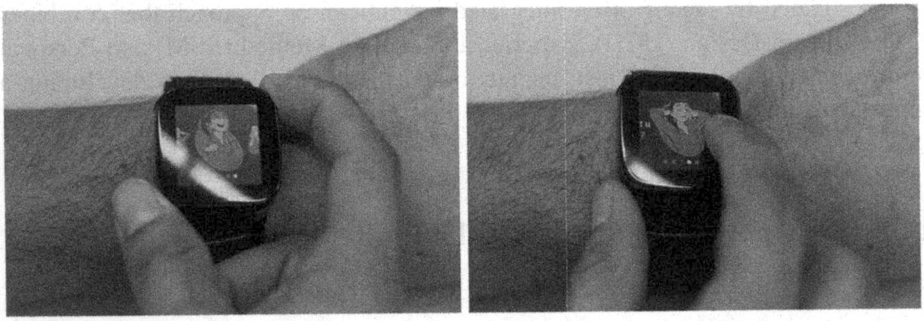

Fig. 14.3 ESTHER 1.1: Mood self-reporting actions; choosing and selecting a mood

reporting of moods. Based on the circumplex model of Russel [40], PAM identifies eight moods to represent arousal and valence dimensions in a circular space. PAM developed a female, male and robot avatars to adjust to different context and target groups. The eight moods are: excited, happy, calm, relaxed, angry, tense, bored and sad (in a clock-wise order). Reporting a mood involves to select one (or more) expressions that identify one's mood state at that moment. This is expected to be a lighter cognitive process than compared to the act of position one's mood in an open two-dimensional circle space or from a list of words. Though not recommended by the authors, we have deliberately added the text to each avatar for ESTHER. The patients must select at least one mood, and maximum two, that they feel represents them at the moment of the prompt, with the option to explain in words their choices. All of the patients' inputs with the system were logged and sent to a web server for later analysis. The server scheduled prompts and stored participants' inputs by a timestamp and type of question.

ESTHER 1.1 was a wearable version of the tool aimed to explore new input mechanisms (see Fig. 14.3). It focused on facilitating in-situ reporting by decreasing the burden of carrying along bulky devices, in particular when patients are dealing with crutches or walker during their recovery. ESTHER 1.1 also modified the prompt-

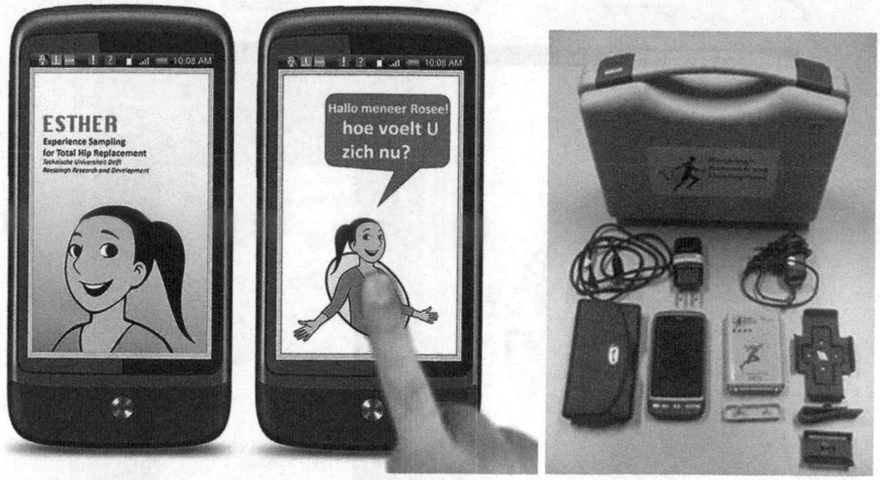

Fig. 14.4 ESTHER 1.2: *Left*, the application running on an Android phone; *Right*, the complete kit including the sensor node, the mobile phone, chargers and belt holders

ing protocol of the version 1.0 by moving the open question at the end of the day. This tool was built on the LiveView^{TM} watch connected wirelessly via Bluetooth to an Android smartphone. The small physical display of 1.3 inch OLED entailed a different interaction showing a small set of four moods from PMRI to select from.

ESTHER 1.2, an application implemented on a mobile phone along with wearable sensors (see Fig. 14.4), aimed to gain more in-depth information on 'critical moments' during recovery. Problems such as being too passive or being too physically active corresponded to 'critical moments' of a day, where, if captured and linked to mood reported could better describe a holistic recovery process of a particular patient. To achieve this, this iteration was designed to use data from on-body sensors to trigger the mood prompts to link changes in physical activity behavior with emotional aspects of recovery. With an inertial sensor placed on the patient's hip, ESTHER 1.2 captured values for physical activity (IMA). Pre-defined thresholds in physical activity were used to prompt patients about their mood when too low or too high physical activity was detected within an hour. This iteration was the first one exploring the technical challenges of monitoring and storing data in the integration of physiological and subjective/personal data.

ESTHER 1.3, an Android application, proposes a more reflective system to improve self-awareness in physical activity behavior (see Fig. 14.5). It is presented here as an in-between iteration to validate self-reflective mechanisms in a context that is less critical and sensitive than THR recovery patients. This prototype supports knowledge workers to reflect on their own physical behavior during working hours, allowing users to set targets of physical activity breaks over the day, monitor their progress and report on their mood states and current activities. By means of a

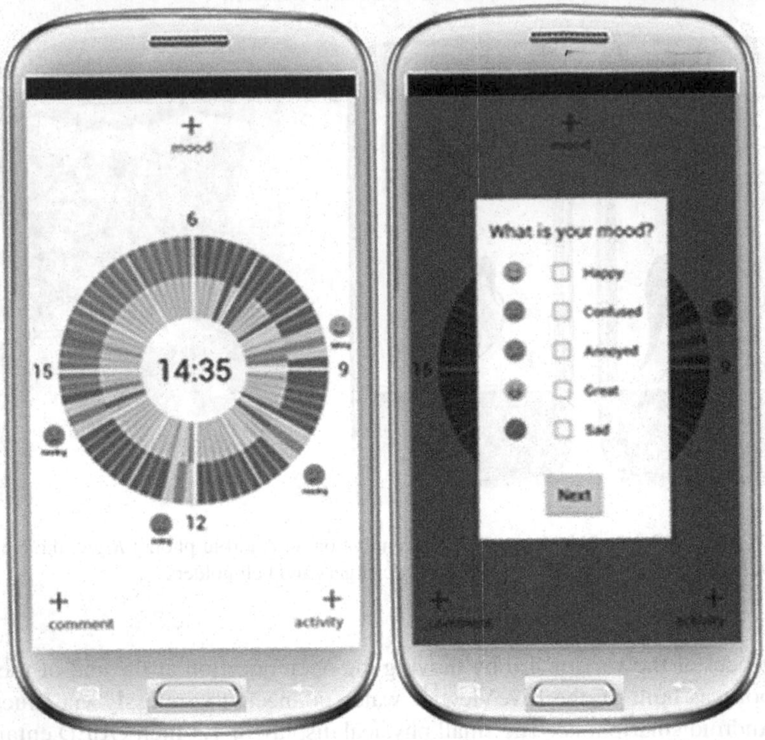

Fig. 14.5 ESTHER 1.3: *Left*; the application showing the state of 3/4 of a day gone, the planed activities (*outer green strips*), the actual physical activity progress (*inner red, yellow* and *green strips*) and the mood/activity reported (*outer emoticons*). *Right*; the mood self-reporting menu

pedometer, this application tracks the recommended healthy amount of steps during a regular working period, which for 8 h is calculated to 2000 steps [12].

ESTHER 1.3 builds on top of the Personal Informatics framework (PI) by implementing mini self-reflection cycles that empowers the user to have deeper reflection moments by means of in-situ self-reporting mechanisms. The rich information provided by ESTHER 1.3 aims to actively support people to reflect based on the integration of sensed data and people's own reports at several intervals. It is proposed that these mechanisms may subtly and even unconsciously influence knowledge workers' reflection and awareness during work hours. It is expected that the user will gain a personalized understanding of the data, which may trigger deeper and more critical reflection.

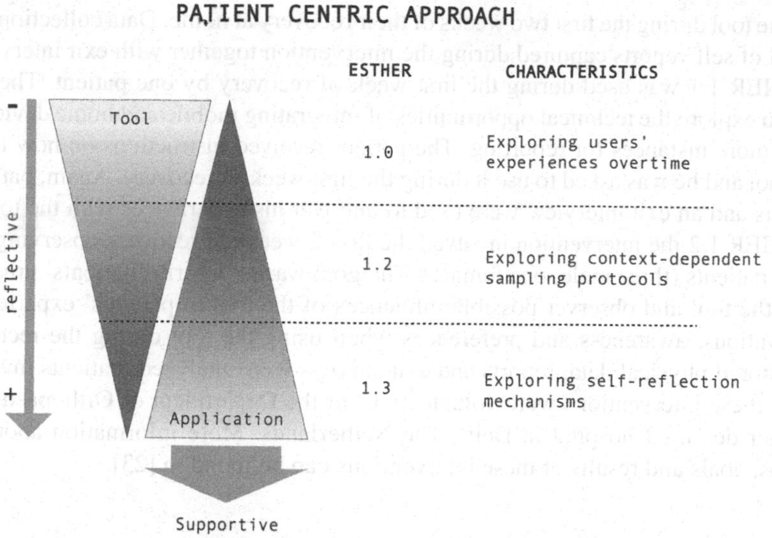

Fig. 14.6 Transformative method: from research tool to application by extending self-reporting techniques with self-reflection

14.6 Integrated Patient-Centric Approach: From Reporting to Reflecting

Total Hip Replacement served as a test bed scenario to demonstrate the implementation of ESTHER in the context of post-operatory recovery. Where the initial goal was to investigate the value of the tool to capture momentary experiences, a transition from acquiring insights into investigating the effects of a supportive tool were gradually revealed and iteratively explored along the interventions (see Fig. 14.6). Two points are identified that explain this transition. First, the transformation of an initially framed exploratory research to a more focused research opened the opportunity to support more complex participation. Gradually, the research tool evolved from an exploratory tool that offered open and technologically simple mechanisms, to a more focused tool that provided more specific and technological complex mechanisms. Second, as participants' needs changed along the recovery the tool was forced to adapt to such need to maintain a valuable experience.

The reflection presented in this section touches upon the aforementioned points by discussing the experience gained in each intervention and the role that the technological developments of the tool have in what could be framed as transformative research: from reporting to reflecting. The iterations of ESTHER were implemented in small interventions with THR patients with different goals in mind. In ESTHER 1.0, five THR patients (three males, two females) participated. The goal was to explore patients' experience during recovery and get insights on the usefulness and value of reporting techniques in their recovery process. Participants were asked to use the tool during the first two weeks of their recovery at home. Data collection consisted of self-reports captured during the intervention together with exit interviews. ESTHER 1.1 was used during the first week of recovery by one patient. The goal was to explore the technical opportunities of integrating mobile and home devices to offer more instances for reporting. The patient received instructions on how to use the tool and he was asked to use it during the first week of recovery. Again, patient's reports and an exit interview were used to uncover his experiences with the tool. In ESTHER 1.2 the intervention involved the first 2 weeks of recovery observing four THR patients (three male, one female). The goal was to describe patients' practices with the tool and observer possible influences of the tool in patients' experiences, motivations, awareness and preferences when using the tool during the recovery. Monitored physical data, reports and exit surveys were analyzed. Patients involved in all these interventions were volunteers from the Department of Orthopaedics of Reinier de Graaf hospital in Delft, The Netherlands. More information about the setups, goals and results of these interventions can be found in [23].

14.6.1 The Evolving Needs of Patients Along the Recovery Process

The intervention of ESTHER 1.0 showed a distinction between the first week and second week of recovery. The first week, described by participants as a physical and emotional rollercoaster, was characterized by continuous ups and downs that involved a health condition that was new to the patient. Therefore, participants during the first week considered reporting a valuable experience as they could freely express their feelings and worries without having to bother their relatives. However, as the recovery became more familiar and stable along the weeks, reporting on a frequent basis was considered to be less valuable; instead participants expressed the need to keep themselves aware of their progress on a regular basis. Aligned with the two reflective phases defined by Li et al. [27], the value on reports experienced by participants in the first week relate to the discovery stage whereas their need for more awareness in the following weeks relate to the maintenance stage. Therefore, a tool that gradually becomes part of the recovery process needs to adapt its support from discovery to maintenance stage. In this manner the patients are continuously stimulated to report as they obtained valuable experiences in the different stages of the recovery.

Following up on these remarks ESTHER 1.1 was developed with the purpose to minimize the load of moment-to-moment reports while requesting a somewhat extensive and more reflective report at the end of the day. By prompting for shorter reports along the day, patients would be triggered to make mini reflections, which may at the end of the day facilitate an assessment of the experiences of the day. This relates to what [39] define as episodic experiences that involve reflection and assessment of a specific situation [39]. The intervention of ESTHER 1.1 showed that the reports captured at the end of the day were generally informative, but because the momentary prompts were time based and not context dependent, they did not

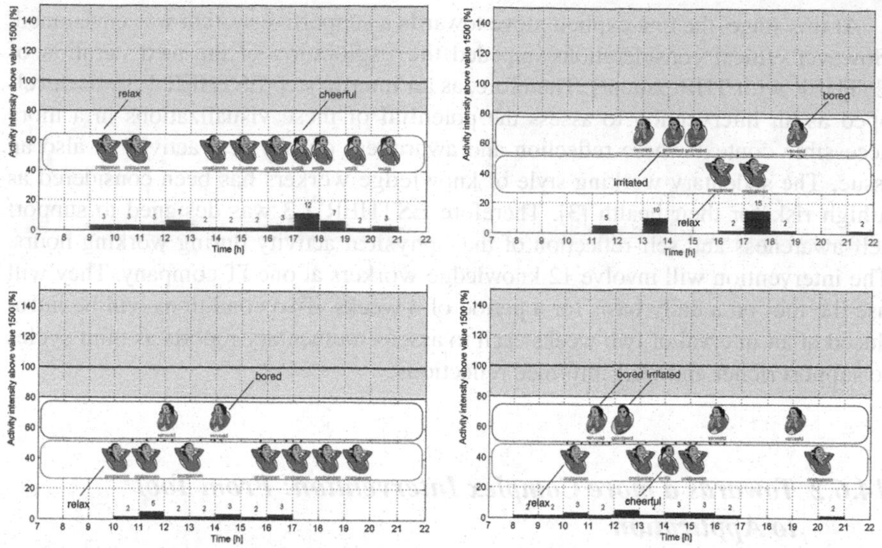

Fig. 14.7 The third day of physical recording and mood reports for each participant. The *blue bards* represent the level of physical activity per hour; positive mood reports are outlined in *green* (relaxed and cheerful) and the negative mood reports are outlined in *red* (bored and irritated)

support patients' reflection in relation to a critical moment. Critical moments such as underdoing and overdoing physical activity could provide richer reflections of that particular situation if the momentary reports (moods in this case) are explicitly linked to them.

The following iteration, ESTHER 1.2, explored more explicit links between sensing and subjective data by triggering questions only when special events were detected. In ESTHER 1.2 the benefits of providing an overview of momentary reports linked with physical performance were expected to explicitly support the report of episodic experiences by means of reflections based on richer visualization of momentary reports. The preliminary results were analyzed based on similar visualizations that the patients could see, integrating both the intensity of physical activity per hour and the reported mood when available. Figure 14.7 shows the third day of recovery of each patient to illustrate the value of integrated visualizations using physical and mood reports. Looking at patients 1 and 2, it can be observed that though their physical activity was comparable their mood changes were clearly different. Similarly, patients that showed hardly any physical activity, like patients 3 and 4, also varied in their reported moods. The reported moods were also in line with the insights gained from informal discussions and exit interviews, where patients' personalities and individual cases corresponded to their daily mood overview. Patients 1 and 3 were confident and felt easy with their operation and recovery. Patient 2 struggled with a difficult recovery, and patient 4 was the only female and was more expressive than the male participants.

At this stage, the first explicit move towards a supportive system was envisioned. However ethical considerations impeded the exploration of the next iteration of ESTHER with THR patients. Therefore, as an interim step ESTHER 1.3 was developed as an intervention to assess the potential of these visualizations in a more accessible context where reflection and awareness on physical activity is also an issue. The sedentary working style of knowledge workers has been considered as a high risk for their health [3]. Therefore ESTHER 1.3 was designed to support self-awareness and self-reflection of their physical activity during working hours. The intervention will involve 12 knowledge workers at one IT company. They will use the tool on a daily basis for a period of 4 weeks. Two conditions will be introduced at an interval of two weeks each to assess momentary reports as mini cycles to support richer and well-informed reflections.

14.6.2 Towards a more Complex Intervention: From Tool to Application

The prompting mechanisms in ESTHER, evolved from a simple fixed protocol to a context-dependent sampling protocol that combined sensing and subjective data. This complexity is the result of a gradual transformation of the design research from exploratory to analyzing the influence that different reporting mechanisms have on participants' experience.

The analysis of the three iterations of ESTHER localizes significant events and actions that describe the recovery process of a THR patient. Patients' emotional and social aspects vary over the day affecting their progress. For instance, the visit of a patient's granddaughter in the morning, or a notification to slow down walking during a visit to the physiotherapist, replicate in the physical and emotional state of the patient. The in-situ mechanisms explored in ESTHER opens opportunities to offer more personalized overviews of ones progress, bringing insights into the value of data integration to empower people in a particular situation.

The impact of an integrated and patient-centric approach in the development of ESTHER, results in further investigations on the value of supporting patients' active role of patients in the data integration process to personalize automatic captured data. Context dependent prompts opened the possibility to explore self-reports as personal tags of relevant moments in the day to support the reflection of momentary and episodic experiences. The current development of ESTHER 1.3 is a response to this transition. With the focus on supporting self-reflection by means of self-reporting, the new challenge is to understand how explicit visualizations of mini prompts would support self-reflection and eventually self-management of peoples' own actions.

Based on [26] stage-based model of Personal Informatics, ESTHER 1.3 aims to support patients' journey from integration to reflection by means of mini-prompts to ask for quick reports on their state. Integrated visualizations of automated health

Fig. 14.8 Micro-cycles of self-reflection: personalization of data via self-reports

information with patients' mini self-reports are expected to support richer reflections and empower the self-management of actions.

Figure 14.8 illustrates an adaptation of Li's model to represent the vision to support the collection of raw data with mini prompts, which resulted in visualizations of data that has been stamped with personal reports. This stamped data is expected to make the momentary reflections captured along the day visible supporting a richer assessment towards setting and eventually reaching ones goals.

14.7 Future Outlook

Acceptance of technology is a major threat in the design of innovations for daily use. Designing innovative technologies that aim to positively influence people and their lifestyles, require a holistic and realistic understanding of people's experience in relation to their everyday lives [37]. This realistic view request a shift from laboratory studies to research practices that are applied into real life settings. One common critic to this approach is the general low cardinality of subjects involved, considering the complexity of studying real settings and even more when the goal is to assess the effect of technology based interventions. As Rogers' argues for a shift in the way these works are assessed where the question should move away from how many participants to what the time span and the granularity of the data collection. ESTHER offers a way to enrich the monitoring of the functional aspects of the recovery process by capturing the full experience of being a THR patient. The approach discussed in this chapter proposes new research practices to capture people's experiences using interventions that gradually become part of the daily life practice of patients in their home environment.

Considering the four user experience stages described by Roto et al. [39] interactions with technology in daily life practices are anticipated, experienced, assessed, and reflected upon. The emergence and adoption of new practices will succeed if the assessment and reflection of experiences is positive. To support that assessment innovative technologies are expected to provide reflective mechanisms to facilitate peoples' ability to self-reflect and become aware of their situation. This opens the opportunity to design for supportive technologies that aim to empower people to try out and adopt new practices helping them through out the stages of anticipating, experiencing, assessing and reflecting upon new practices.

The holistic, subjective and dynamic aspects of experiences bring interesting challenges to the design of interactive technologies that aim to positively influence the experience around certain practice [17]. Yoshiuchi et al. [51] point out the importance of assessing the relationship between symptoms in physical conditions with psychosocial factors in natural settings. ESTHER addresses these challenges by obtaining an understanding of the patient's situation in context, based on self-reports and involving physical and emotional aspects around the recovery. The addition of self-reports to monitoring data is expected to support patients to assess and improve their overall health status by providing meaningful and personal feedback. Considering the two reflective stages of Li et al. [27], discovery and maintenance, an integrated and personalized visualization may empower self-management by providing a stage of understanding and a stage of awareness. The technology is there; the challenge lies in an understanding what reporting and reflective mechanisms are best suitable for each case.

Although ESTHER iterations gradually focus only on the patient, opportunities to extend it to involve other stakeholders are considered relevant for further investigation. As concluded in Jiménez Garcia et al. [22], the self-report data gathered in ESTHER 1.0 could help physiotherapist to build a more personalized judgment of the progress of patients' recovery. The patient's in-situ reports represented patients' background and attitudes, which eventually could help the physiotherapist to have a more sensitive judgment compare to only looking at the objective information of a patient. In addition, considering self-reports a less dense data collection in terms of data points (compare to sensor data) it was perceived as potential filters of the sensor data to be able to raise flags when attention is needed. This could address one of the important trade offs between physiotherapist's workload and their need for more personalized support to patients. In the same study, when consulting the needs of the medical community, the non-systematic nature of the self-report data (as patients were not obliged to provide constant feedback), defied the need of the community for quantified metrics on the subjective wellbeing of patients. Future work may look at existing measurements and investigate the value of deploy them as part of the-situ self-reports to personalized the objective data gathered.

ESTHER is an example of a tool that follows an integrated and patient-centric approach to understand patients' experiences regarding a care situation. Throughout the four versions this chapter presented the evolution of ESTHER from a research tool to a design intervention and to an application, with the shared goal of informing future iterations and introduce an application that supports patients to reflect on their own recovery. The shift in the role of ESTHER can be seen as part of a process to inform the design of supportive technologies while uncovering challenges in relation to technological (stability, complexity), research (validity, resources), user (engagement, acceptance) and design (interaction mechanisms, feedback). Furthermore, ESTHER was found to empower patients in ways that were not intended. The question of whether this unintended influence results in positive or negative experiences opens an ethical discussion on the implications that complex interventions may have on patients' care situation. One way to address such concerns is by adding interim interventions to validate new elements of the method in a similar but less sensitive context. This is the case of ESTHER 1.3, which due to its complexity will be first tested in a different context than THR. The associate cost would likely embrace some adaptation to fit the tool in the new context. The adaptation could affect design and technical components, but it seems necessary to take this interim step to validate the mechanisms proposed and minimize the risk of negatively influencing the patients' recovery experience. This requires a careful selection of the alternative context in which to apply the intervention.

Acknowledging that the digitalization of medical data provides substantial information to physicians and eventually to patients, it is argued that only exposing patients to data is far from providing them with meaningful information and ultimately meaningful experiences for the patient. The data remains static and patients are playing an inactive role towards their own information. The reflections discussed here, address opportunities to make patients active participants in the creation of information about their recovery, with the ultimate goal to empower them to become self-managers of decisions and actions regarding their own recovery.

A review of the last decade research developments in supportive technologies for physical activity shows the interest in the design of glanceable (non-literal) displays that provide feedback using abstract representations of physical activity. Fish'n'Steps [28] provides real-time information with glanceable visualizations about levels of physical activity with the purpose to serve as external motivation and provide awareness. Houston [6] is a mobile application that tracks step counts allowing users to set weekly goals and promote physical activity awareness, sharing their goals and meet targets within a group. Of particular relevance to this research, is the work of [5] UbiFit Garden, where the idea of manual journaling was explored by inviting users to tag the activities inferred by the system with corrections or personal comments. Although the mechanisms for journaling were perceived as light and simple, participants reported that the value of the journaling could be improved if better integrated with sensor data. Other commercial devices for fitness and sports such as Nike+ or Adidas miCoach automatically collect physical activity data and display it in the form of graphs and statistics. While they also support some kind of journaling this is done in a form of reconstruction of the activity after it was finished, therefore the focus is more on assessing the experience rather than collecting aspects of the experience itself. But as argued in this paper, episodic experiences are hard to assess if no view on the momentary experiences is presented. Just presenting overviews and statistics of one physical performance is not enough to help individuals to become self-management of their own goals and actions. As mentioned by Moore et al. [31], current personal information technology is being designed to optimize productivity rather than self-understanding. Li [25] similarly states that physical activity behavioral change is also related to identify opportunities for change; focusing only on the amount of physical activity, it is argued to be insufficient to help find opportunities. Optimizing performance relates to systems that have a stronger persuasive approach where the user gets little opportunities to learn, but just receive instructions. The value of reflection has been critically examined as a positive influence in providing empowerment to change behaviors [36]. To our understanding, there are no systems that support Total Hip Replacement patients in capturing deep reflections in physical recovery and activity. The approach here presented and ESTHER are first steps in helping THR patients to find opportunities to improve their condition and become active managers of their recovery process.

14.8 Conclusions

This chapter discusses an integrated patient-centric approach to design homecare technologies considering patients' personal experiences and context as crucial aspects when providing care support. It reflects on the authors' experience in developing and implementing a research tool that aims to capture the recovery process of Total Hip Replacement (THR) from the perspective of the patient and contextualized to when and where it takes place. The goal is to extend the design research from functional to experiential aspects of a recovery, which requires a closer intervention in the context of patients' home to capture the changes they go through in relation to their physical and emotional state during the recovery. In-situ methods and tools are therefore developed to investigate their power to provide a holistic view of patients care experience as well as support interventions in the context of use.

Given that THR is a dynamic process that involves important physical and emotional changes overtime, ESTHER is proposed as a means to support patients in self-reporting their experiences during their recovery at home. Based on Experience Sampling Method (ESM) the tool aims to provide a description from the patient's view of their states and the changes throughout the recovery period. Four iterations were designed and implemented as situated design interventions where self-reporting mechanisms and the combination of sensing and subjective data analysis were considered to better address patients' needs during recovery.

The implementation of ESTHER in the context of THR recovery gradually revealed the effects that reflective mechanisms could have to support the patient which were iteratively explored along the interventions. Two points are identified to explain this transition. First, as participants' needs changed along the recovery the tool was forced to adapt to such need, to maintain a valuable experience for participants. Second, this transition was also explained by the transformation of an initially framed exploratory research to a more focused research. The complexity of the prompting mechanisms in ESTHER is the result of a gradual transformation of the research goal from exploratory to explain the effect of different reporting mechanisms on participants' experience.

The integration and patient-centric approach of the development of ESTHER, led to investigating the value of data integration where the patient has an active role in personalizing automatic captured data. The shift to more context dependent prompts opened the possibility to explore self-reports as personal tags of relevant moments in the day to support the reflection of momentary and episodic experiences. ESTHER addresses a holistic approach where subjective and dynamic aspects of experiences are integrated by obtaining an understanding of the patient's situation in context, based on self-reports and involving physical and emotional aspects around the recovery.[53–56]

Acknowledgments This work has been partially financed by SENIOR project consortium. Special thanks to the Department of Orthopaedics of Reinier de Graaf hospital for their support in gathering participants which kindly volunteer to contribute to this research.

References

1. Arden, N., & Nevitt, M. C. (2006). Osteoarthritis: epidemiology. *Best Practice & Research Clinical Rheumatology, 20*(1), 3–25.
2. Barrett, L. F., & Barrett, D. J. (2001). An introduction to computerized experience sampling in psychology. *Social Science Computer Review, 19*(2), 175–185.
3. Brownson, R. C., Tegan, K. B., & Douglas, A. L. (2005). Declining rates of physical activity in the united states: what are the contributors? *Annual Review of Public Health, 26*, 421–443.
4. Busija, L., Osborne, R. H., Nilsdotter, A., Buchbinder, R., & Roos, E. M. (2008). Magnitude and meaningfulness of change in sf-36 scores in four types of orthopedic surgery. *Health and Quality of Life Outcomes, 6*, 55.
5. Consolvo, S., et al. (2008). Activity sensing in the wild: A field trial of ubifit garden. In *Proceedings of CHI '08*, (pp. 1797–1806). New York: ACM Press.
6. Consolvo, S., Klasnja, P., McDonald, D. W. & Landay, J. A. (2009). Goal-setting considerations for persuasive technologies that encourage physical activity. In *Proceedings of the 4th International Conference on Persuasive Technology* (p. 8). ACM Press.
7. Consolvo, S., Harrison, B., Smith, I., Chen, M., Everitt, K., Froehlich, J., et al. (2006). Conducting in situ evaluations for and with ubiquitous computing technologies. *Journal of Human Computer Interactions, 22*, 107–122.
8. Desmet, P. M. A., Vastenburg, M. H., Van Bel, D. & Romero, N. (2012). Pick-A-Mood; development and application of a pictorial mood-reporting instrument. In *Proceedings of the 8th International Design and Emotion Conference* (pp. 11–14).
9. Dohnke, B., Knäuper, B., & Müller-Fahrnow, W. (2005). Perceived self-efficacy gained from, and health effects of, a rehabilitation program after hip joint replacement. *Arthritis and Rheumatism, 53*(4), 585–592.
10. Fielden, J., Scott, S., & Horne, J. (2003). An investigation of patient satisfaction following discharge after total hip replacement surgery. *Orthopedic Nursing, 22*, 429–436.
11. Fortina, S., Gambera, D., Crainz, E., & Ferrata, P. (2005). Recovery of physical function and patient's satisfaction after total hip replacement (thr) surgery supported by a tailored guide book. *Acta bio-medica: Atenei Parmensis, 76*, 152–156.
12. Fortmann, J., Stratmann, T., Poppinga, B., Boll, S.,& Heuten, W. (2013). Make me move at work! An ambient light display to increase physical activity. *Pervasive Health*, 2013, Venice, Italy.
13. Grant, S., & St John, W. (2009). Recovery from total hip replacement surgery: "it's not just physical". *Qualitative Health Research, 19*, 1612–1620.
14. Grönvall, E. & Lundberg, S. (2014). On challenges designing the home as a place for care. In: *Pervasive Health: State-of-the-Art & Beyond.*
15. Groönvall, E. & Verdezoto, N. (2013). Beyond self-monitoring: understanding non-functional aspects of home-based healthcare technology. In: *Proceedings of UbiComp 2013*. ACM Press.
16. Harper, T., Rodden, T., Rogers, Y. & Sellen, A. (2008). Being human: Human computer interaction in the year 2020. http://research.microsoft.com/en-us/um/cambridge/projects/hci2020/download.html
17. Hassenzahl, M., & Tractinsky, N. (2006). User experience—a research agenda. *Behaviour and Information Technology, 25*, 91–97.

18. Hassling, L., Nordfeldt, S., Eriksson, H., & Timpka, T. (2005). Use of cultural probes for representation of chronic disease experience: Exploration of an innovative method for design of supportive technologies. *Journal of Technology and Health Care,13*, 87–95 (IOS Press).
19. Hektner, J. M., Schmidt, J. A. & Czikszentmihalyi, M. (2007). Experience sampling method: Measuring the quality of everyday life. Thousand Oaks:Sage Publications.
20. Intille, S. S., et al. (2003). Tools for studying behavior and technology in natural settings. In *Proceedings of Ubicomp'03* (pp. 738–739). ACM Press, New York.
21. Jiménez García, J., Boerema, S., Hermens, H., & Havinga, P. (2010). Fine-tuning a context-aware system application by using user-centred design methods. *In Proceedings IADIS 2010* (pp. 323–327).
22. Jiménez Garcia, J., Romero, N., & Keyson, D. (2011). Capturing patients' daily life experiences after total hip replacement. *In Proceedings of Pervasive Computing Technologies for Healthcare 2011* (pp. 226–229).
23. Jiménez Garcia, J., Romero, N., Boerema, S., Keyson, D., & Havinga, P. (2013). ESTHER: A portable sensor toolkit to collect and monitor total hip replacement patient data. In *Proceedings of the 3rd ACM MobiHoc' 13* (pp. 7–12). ACM Press.
24. Li, I. (2009a). Designing personal informatics applications and tools that facilitate monitoring of behaviors. In *Proceedings of UIST'09*.
25. Li, I. (2009b). Beyond counting steps: Using context to improve monitoring of physical activity. In *Proceedings of Ubicomp'09 Doctoral Colloquium*.
26. Li, I., Dey, A., & Forlizzi, J. (2010). A stage-based model of personal informatics systems. In *Proceedings of CHI'10* (pp. 557–566). ACM Press.
27. Li, I., Dey, A., & Forlizzi, J. (2011). Understanding my data, myself: supporting self-reflection with ubicomp technologies. In *Proceedings of UbiComp'11* (pp. 405–414). ACM Press.
28. Lin, J. J., Mamykina, L., Lindtner, S., Delajoux, G., & Strub, H. B. (2006). Fish'n'Steps: Encouraging physical activity with an interactive computer game. In *Proceedings of UbiComp'06* (pp. 261–278). Springer.
29. Macario, A., Schilling, P., Rubio, R., Bhalla, A., & Goodman, S. (2013). What questions do patients undergoing lower extremity joint replacement surgery have? *BMC Health Services Research,3*, 11.
30. Maly, M., Costigan, P., & Olney, S. (2006). Determinants of self-report outcome measures in people with knee osteoarthritis. *Archives of Physical Medicine and Rehabilitation*, *87*(1), 96–104.
31. Moore, B., Van Kleek, M., Karger, D. R., & Schraefel, M. (2010). Assisted self reflection: Combining lifetracking, sensemaking, and personal information management. In *Proceedings of CHI'10*, ACM Press.
32. Munson, S. (2012). Mindfulness, reflection, and persuasion in personal informatics. In *Proceedings of CHI'12*, ACM Press.
33. Myin-Germeys, I., Oorschot, M., Collip, D., Lataster, J., Deles-paul, P., & Van Os, J. (2009). Experience sampling research in psychopathology: opening the black box of daily life. *Psychological Medicine*, *39*, 1533–1547.
34. FuelBand and Nike+app: Nike's new fuel SE highlights. (2013). http://www.fastcodesign.com/3020080/nikes-new-fuelband-se-highlights-its-ux-flaws. Retrieved from 21 January 2014.
35. Outcome measures in patient care. (2013). http://www.apta.org/OutcomeMeasures/. Retrieved from 21 January 2014.
36. Pirzadeh, A., He, L., & Stolterman, E. (2013). Personal informatics and reflection: A critical examination of the nature of reflection. In *Proceedings of CHI'13 Extended Abstracts* (pp. 1979–1988). ACM Press.
37. Rogers, Y. (2011). Interaction design gone wild: striving for wild theory. *Interactions*, *18*, 58–62.
38. Romero, N., Rek, M., Jimenez Garcia, J., & van Boeijen, A. (2013). Motivation to self-report: Capturing user experiences in field studies. In *Proceedings of CLIHC'13*, Springer.
39. Roto, V., Law, E., Vermeeren, A., & Hoonhout, J. (Eds.). (2011). White paper: User experience white paper. in *Outcome of the Dagstuhl Seminar on Demarcating User Experience*, Vol. 39 (pp. 1161–117).

40. Russel, J. (1980). A circumplex model of affect. *Journal of Personality and Social Psychology*, *39*, 1161–1178.
41. Salmon, P., Hall, G., Peerbhoy, D., Shenkin, A., & Parker, C. (2001). Recovery from hip and knee arthro-plasty: patients' perspective on pain, function, quality of life, and well being up to 6 months postopera- tively. *Archives of Physical Medicine and Rehabilitation*, *82*, 36–56.
42. Sergio, F. (2013). Healthcare needs innovation now. *In Mobile Ecosystems Evolving, Frog Design*. http://www.frogdesign.com/pdf/mobile-ecosystems-evolving.pdf
43. Stevens, M., van den Akker-Scheek, I., Spriensma, A., Boss, N., Dierck, L., & van Horn, J. (2004). The groningen orthopedic exit strategy (goes): a home-based support program for total hip and knee arthroplasty patients after shortened hospital stay. *Patient Education and Counseling*, *54*, 95.
44. Stratford, P., Kennedy, D., Pagura, S., & Gollish, J. (2003). The relationship between self-report and performance-related measures: questioning the content validity of timed tests. *Arthritis and Rheumatology*, *49*, 535–550.
45. Van den Akker-Scheek, I. (2007). *Recovery after short-stay total hip and knee arthroplasty*. The Netherlands: Thesis University of Groningen. NULL
46. Vastenburg, M. H., & Romero, N. (2010). Adaptive experience sampling: addressing the dynamic nature of in-situ user studies. In: *ISAmI International Symposium on Ambient Intelligence*, Vol. 72 (pp. 197–200). Guimaraes. (Springer Advances in Soft Computing)
47. Vastenburg, M. H., Romero, N. A., van Bel, D. T., & Desmet P. M. A. (2011). PMRI: development of a pictorial mood reporting instrument. In: *Proceedings of CHI 2011*, Vancouver, BC, Canada.
48. Williams, M., Oberst, M., Bjorklund, B., & Hughes, S. (1996). Family care giving in cases of hip fracture. *Rehabilitation Nursing*, *21*, 124–131.
49. Wong, J., Wong, S., Brooks, E., & Yabsley, R. (1999). Home readiness and recovery pattern after total hip replacement. *Journal of Orthopaedic Nursing*, *3*, 210–219.
50. Woolhead, G., Donovan, J., & Dieppe, P. (2005). Outcomes of total knee replacement: a qualitative study. *Rheumatology*, *44*(8), 1032–1037.
51. Yoshiuchi, K., Yamamoto, Y., & Akabayashi, A. (2008). Application of ecological momentary assessment in stress-related diseases. *BioPsychoSocial Medicine*, *2*, 13.
52. Ziefle, M., Röcker, C., & Holzinger, A. (2014). Current trends and challenges for pervasive health technologies: From technical innovation to user integration. In *Pervasive Health: State-of-the-Art & Beyond*.

Further Readings

53. Bont de, C., Ouden den, P. H., Schifferstein, R., Smulders, F. & Voort van der, M. (Eds.). (2013). Advanced design methods for successful innovation. Den Haag: Design United.
54. Brubaker, J. R., Hirano, S. H., & Hayes, G. R. (2011). *Lost in translation: Three challenges for the collection and use of data in personal informatics*. Paper Presented at the CHI 2011 Workshop on Personal Informatics & HCI: Design, Theory, & Social Implications, Vancouver, BC, Canada.
55. Medynskiy, Y., & Mynatt E. (2010). Salud!: An open infrastructurefor developing and deploying health self-management applications. In *PervasiveHealth 2010* (pp. 1–8).
56. Visser, F. S. (2009). Bringing the everyday life of people into design (Doctoral thesis, Delft University of Technology, 2009). ISBN 978-90-9024244-6.